AMERICAN AIRCRAFT DEVELOPMENT OF THE SECOND WORLD WAR

AMERICAN AIRCRAFT DEVELOPMENT OF THE SECOND WORLD WAR

RESEARCH, EXPERIMENTATION AND MODIFICATION 1939-1945

BILL NORTON

FONTHILL

Fonthill Media Language Policy

Fonthill Media publishes in the international English language market. One language edition is published worldwide. As there are minor differences in spelling and presentation, especially with regard to American English and British English, a policy is necessary to define which form of English to use. The Fonthill Policy is to use the form of English native to the author. Bill Norton was born and educated in the United States; therefore, American English has been adopted in this publication.

Fonthill Media Limited
Fonthill Media LLC
www.fonthillmedia.com
office@fonthillmedia.com

First published in the United Kingdom and the United States of America 2019

British Library Cataloguing in Publication Data:
A catalogue record for this book is available from the British Library

ISBN 978-1-78155-725-9

Typeset in 10.5pt on 13pt Sabon
Printed and bound in England

Foreword

This is the last of a five-part series presenting America's aircraft development of World War II emphasizing experimental and non-production military variants. The first volume addressed fighters (*U.S. Experimental & Prototype Aircraft Projects, Fighters 1939–1945*, Specialty Press, 2008), the second bombers (*American Bomber Development in World War 2*, Midland Publishing, 2012), the third gliders (*American Military Gliders of World War II*, Schiffer Publishing, 2012), and the fourth special types (*American Aircraft Development in World War 2; Special Types 1939–1945*, Crécy Publishing, 2016). As the title indicates, this book encompasses unique aircraft or modifications to existing types for the purpose of research and experimentation in support of development, advancing aeronautical technology, or meeting some narrow needs of the evolving battlefield during the war. Some of these topics are enforced by examples in the earlier books.

These books discuss the technological maturation of American aviation weapons under the pressure of war with emphasis on advanced technology and experimental models. The war years were particularly noted for rapid changes in aircraft design, with many remarkable aircraft coming and going in quick succession, some missions and types arising or disappearing altogether, and much aeronautical experimentation with modified machines. The great value of these works, I hope, is their illumination of little-known projects that significantly advanced the science and technology of aeronautics, propulsion, aircraft systems, avionics, and ordnance, but did not go into full-rate production and deployment. They focus on changes in several classes of weapons throughout the war years, and so is not a general presentation of American airpower or the air war.

Unlike the Fighters, Bombers, and Gliders books, this volume is more "episodic" like Special Types, each chapter introducing another topic under the subject of the chapter title. These examine the state of the art at the beginning of the war and advantages pursued or adopted during the conflict. This is the vehicle to examine the modifications and projects that are minimally documented. Emphasis will be on those efforts that matured to the point of significant design development such as mock-ups, wind tunnel models, and especially those yielding flying testbeds

Other than the name Space Waif associated with the photographs, nothing is known of this project by the author. The aerodynamic shape is meant to be dropped from the PBY (suggesting a Navy project) for free-flight testing, the antenna suggesting data transmission as it is not the type associated at the time with remote radio control. The control surfaces suggest an effort to collect data on "tailless airplane" maneuverability. (*National Archives*)

and experiments. I trust this makes the volume an important singular source for a fascinating and diverse collection of wartime aircraft and projects seldom discussed and never before brought together under a single cover.

There is only minimal discussion of the conduct of the war and associated personalities. Instead, the "war stories" are those of military staffs, engineering teams, and test pilots struggling against short schedules and tight resource constraints to push the bounds of technology. These epic and sometimes life-threatening endeavors were as vital to the war effort as actual combat operations.

Although considerable research was performed in preparing this volume, it is not exhaustive. There were thousands of projects and tests performed with aircraft (modified or standard) during the war. Documentation has become scarce or non-existent for many or they remain classified or lost to history. This book could not contain all such information in any event. Hence, an overview of the aviation research, development, and experimentation during the war, with emphasis on the most illustrative examples, is the best that can be presented and is, for popular aviation reading, the optimal solution. It is also suitable insight into the difficulties of aircraft development today as then. As one professionally devoted to that pursuit, the author is endlessly struck by the similarities to present-day aviation development. The elements and their attendant difficulties remain the same: technology, people, money, and schedule.

The text presupposes the reader has a fundamental understanding of aircraft, how they fly, how aero engines work, and the basic course of World War II air war, permitting an appreciation of combat needs and leadership decisions. A glossary plus list of acronyms and abbreviations is found at the front of the book for ready reference.

The author welcomes comments and additional research material, especially photos. He can be contacted at williamnorton@earthlink.net.

Bill Norton
Lancaster, California, 2018

Acknowledgments

For their kind assistance, the author wishes to thank the following individuals and organizations, in alphabetical order: Gerald Balzer; Mal Holcomb; Lloyd Jones; Tony Landis; Dan Shumaker; the late Ray Wagner; Kase Decker, Hayden Hamilton, and Paul Minert of the American Aviation Historical Society; Jay Miller and the people of the Jay Miller Collection; Jessica Jones, John Little, and the archival team at the Museum of Flight; Connie Moore and Gwen Pitman of the National Aeronautics and Space Administration; the National Air and Space Museum archives team; personnel at the National Museum of Naval Aviation; Sandra Fye and the personnel of the National Museum of Nuclear Science and History; Brett Stolle and the National Museum of the United States Air Force; Curtiss Utz and the staff of the Naval Aviation Archives; Larry Feliu and the people of the Northrop Grumman History Center; Dennis Jenkins; the folks at the San Diego Air and Space Museum; and the United States National Archives.

Contents

Glossary

Afterburning: Also known as augmentation, reheat, and secondary combustion, this is the injection of fuel into the hot exhaust of the turbine, forward of the nozzle, to produce additional jet engine thrust.

Air-cooled engine: A piston engine employing the passing air to cool the cylinders and other components. This requires a properly formed cowling and baffling encircling the engine, and usually cowl flaps to regulate the flow of air while reducing cooling drag.

Airfoil: A wing cross-section shape determining flight lift characteristics.

Angle of attack: Angle between the wing's mean chord line and the incident airflow.

Anti-ice: The systems aboard an aircraft that works to prevent atmospheric ice from accumulating on the exterior in flight that can compromise safety. During World War II, these were heated surfaces like windscreens and aero surface leading edges, the latter usually from heated air passed locally within the structure, and alcohol or glycol fluid emitted to be spread across a surface by the passing airflow or, for the propeller, radial acceleration.

Arrestment: Means of capturing and decelerating an airplane landing on an aircraft carrier deck. This usually consists of a series of parallel cables stretched across the deck, one of which is engaged by a tailhook hanging below the aft fuselage of a landing aircraft. The cable is payed out and gradually restrained by an energy absorption system below deck.

Aspect ratio: The square of the wingspan divided by the area of the wing. A high aspect ratio wing is comparatively long and narrow.

Assisted take-off (ATO): In the context of World War II land-based aviation, this consisted of small rocket motors attached to the aircraft to provide additional thrust to get an aircraft off in a shorter distance or a heavy aircraft off in a standard distance.

Axial-flow jet engine: A turbine engine through which air flows along the longitudinal axis without being radially redirected as through a centrifugal compressor.

Bombsight: An optical device for estimating the impact point of bombs dropped from an aircraft at considerable altitude.

Boundary layer: The thin layer of air adjacent to a surface in an air stream in which the flow goes from zero velocity at the surface to freestream velocity. A thick or turbulent layer would possess greater skin friction drag than a thin or laminar boundary layer.

Boundary layer control (BLC): This involves forcing the boundary layer to a smooth laminar profile by either sucking off the air at the surface or blowing air out to energize the layer and keep it attached for much of the surface chord length rather than separate into a high-drag turbulent layer.

Camber: The upper curvature of an airfoil.

Catapult: A means of launching an airplane off an aircraft carrier deck, usually by a bridle between the aircraft and a shuttle in a slot along the deck. The shuttle is propelled by a hydraulic or gas piston below deck to accelerate the aircraft to take-off velocity.

Center of gravity (CG): The point at which the aircraft would balance if suspended from that point, or the center of gravitational attraction acting on the mass of the vehicle. A CG too far forward or too far aft could render the airplane uncontrollable.

Centrifugal-flow jet engine: A turbine engine through which air flows through a centrifugal compressor, redirecting the air radially outward to pass through combustors on the outer perimeter of the power plant.

Chord length: The width of a wing or the line between the leading and trailing edges, usually referred to as chord length or a mean chord for a tapered wing.

Constant-speed propeller: Possessing variable blade pitch, this mechanically changes the pitch to automatically maintain steady rotational speed (rpm).

Compressibility effects: Refers to the effects on aircraft performance, stability, and control resulting from air compressing into shock waves as the aircraft approaches the speed of sound. These include such hazards as Mach tuck and locked-in steep dives.

Contra-rotating propeller: Also known as a dual-rotation propeller or "contraprop," this employs two propellers, front to back, turning in opposite directions on coaxial power shafts.

Counter-rotating propeller: Propellers on opposite sides of the aircraft (as in a twin-engined installation) that rotate in opposite directions to eliminate asymmetrical thrust effects.

Critical Mach number: The flight velocity at which compressibility shocks first begin to appear on the aircraft (see also transonic flight).

De-ice: The systems aboard an aircraft that work to shed atmospheric ice from the exterior in flight. During World War II, these were usually pneumatically inflated leading-edge rudder boots or thermal heating.

Dive brakes: Flaps or other deployed surfaces intended to limit the dive speed of the aircraft thereby reducing the recover *g* or preventing exceedance of the critical Mach number.

Dive recovery flaps: Flaps beneath the wing restoring some lift lost via compressibility to allow recovery from a dive for which pull-out is rendered ineffectual by the compressibility effects.

Drag: The resistance of the air to the passage of an aircraft. It is made up of induced drag from the creation of lift and profile drag that includes skin-friction drag, the overall frontal area offered to the incident air, cooling drag from air passing through a cowling and engine baffling, and other elements.

Drooped ailerons: Ailerons that can be biased to a downward-deflected neutral angle (droop) about which normal differential up-down displacement is still performed for aircraft roll control. The droop enhances overall lift (as well as drag) and is usually performed for low-speed landing approach.

Dual-rotation propeller: (see contra-rotating propeller)

Feathering: Turning constant-speed (variable pitch) propeller blades edge-wise to the line of flight to stop rotation and reduce drag when an engine has stopped during flight.

Flaps: An articulated portion of a wing trailing edge that enhances lift at the expense of drag and is usually employed on landing approach to allow a reduced landing speed. The split flap is a lower portion of the trailing edge that rotates down. The Fowler flap slides aft and down, usually creating a slot between the wing main plane and flap surfaces through which air accelerates.

Flutter: An unstable oscillation of a portion of the aircraft or control surface that can grow to catastrophic amplitude. The instability is induced by unsteady air loads interacting with elastic deformation of the structure or control surface rotation at like frequencies (resonance).

Ground resonance: An on-gear instability at certain rotor speeds that could make the rotorcraft oscillate dangerously and risk an overturn.

Gunsight: A mechanism for aligning aircraft projectile weapons with a target. This is usually in front of the pilot or gunner, allowing a visual sighting through an optical device that may also compensate for firing errors.

Hardpoint: A strengthened structural portion within the bottom surface of a wing or fuselage with fittings for carriage of weapon or fuel tank mounts.

Inline engine: A reciprocating engine ("recip") in which the pistons are arranged in one or more longitudinal lines parallel to the power shaft. An upright or inverted V-arrangement was typical for engines for high-performance combat aircraft.

Intercooler: One or more heat exchangers cooling supercharged air passing to the carburetor to void engine knock or to further increase density. The intercooler drops the air temperature before addition of fuel while an aftercooler decreases the heat of the charged fuel–air mixture before reaching the engine.

Laminar flow: Boundary layer of air adjacent to a surface in an air stream with an even pressure distribution, as opposed to turbulent, and possessing less skin-friction drag. A laminar flow wing is one with an airfoil designed to maintain laminar flow for more of the chord length before becoming turbulent towards the trailing edge than typical airfoils.

Lend-Lease: U.S. Government policy by which weapons and other materiel assistance was purchased by the United States and provided as a form of a loan to nations fighting, or arming to fight, the Axis powers.

Lift coefficient: A quantity indicating the gross lift capability and so permits various lifting surfaces to be compared.

Liquid-cooled engine: A piston engine employing recirculated liquid to cool the cylinders and other components. The liquid is itself cooled via one or more radiators open to the passing air.

Load factor: A measure of acceleration in the vertical axis of an aircraft defined as units of gravitational pull on the surface of the Earth (1 *g*). This is a primary criterion for structural design to ensure the airframe can withstand maneuvering air loads and inertia, plus a factor of safety.

Mach number: The speed of sound at the aircraft's operating altitude.

Power loading: The ratio of aircraft gross weight to engine take-off power.

Pressurization: A system that pumps compressed air into the sealed cockpit to maintain pressure at a safe "cabin altitude" as the aircraft climbs into the rarefied air at high altitude.

Prop wash: The flow of air off a propeller passing back over aircraft elements aft (assuming a tractor propeller). The prop wash can create asymmetrical rates on the aircraft but also ensures control effectiveness at low aircraft velocities for those surfaces within the wash.

Propeller cuff: Fitting near the base of a propeller blade that expands the width (chord) to improve thrust or alter the flow off that portion of the blade for improved cooling air passing into an engine cowling immediately aft.

Propeller reversing: The ability to reverse the pitch on a constant-speed propeller (variable pitch) to reverse the thrust for slowing on landing or backing the aircraft on the surface.

Propeller synchronization: The process of ensuring similar rpm for each propeller on a multi-engined aircraft to prevent an annoying rhythmic noise.

Radial engine: A reciprocating engine in which the pistons are arranged radially about the center power shaft. One or two rows of these radially grouped cylinders are typical.

Radar or radio altimeter: A device measuring height above the ground or sea by reflected electromagnetic waves and permitting safer night flying at low altitude.

Radio control: The remote control of an aircraft or missile in flight via radio signal causing specific responses permitting desired behavior or actions.

Ramjet: An engine using an inlet accelerated to high speeds to compress the air for combustion and so eliminating rotating components like the compressor and turbine, though it lacks low-speed thrust.

Service ceiling: Altitude at which climb rate decays to 100 fpm (31 mpm).

Shocks: The compression front of air as it flows around a body near sonic speeds. These shocks increase drag and can have a profound effect on the stability and control of the aircraft.

Slats: A segment of a wing-leading edge that slides forward to increase wing camber (inflection) to add lift. This usually creates a slot between the surface and the wing main plane through which air is accelerated to energize flow downstream and delay stall.

Slot: A narrow spanwise opening between the lower and upper surface of a wing, allowing the high-pressure air below to accelerate up and over the top of the wing to energize the airflow and delay stall. Also a gap created when moving a control surface or flaps, the flow through the slot enhancing the effect of the surface deflection.

Specifications ("specs"): An agreement between a manufacturer and the military as to the characteristics of an aircraft or other product yet to be designed and built.

Spin: An out-of-control condition produced by the stall of one wing coupled with high yaw angle. The result is a descending flight path with the aircraft rotating about a vertical axis. Classical recovery is by arresting the yaw and then pushing the nose over to break the stall, then pulling out the resulting dive

Spin-recovery parachute: A packed parachute installed at the aft end of a test aircraft. Its deployment in the event of a locked-in spin, not responding to recovery control inputs, causes the nose of the aircraft to pitch down to break the wing stall and permit safe recovery of the aircraft after which the parachute is jettisoned.

Stall: The turbulence and separation of air on a wing or other surface due to a high angle of attack and adverse pressure gradients within the boundary layer that causes an enormous loss of lift.

Supercharger: A spinning compressor impeller, usually driven off the engine accessory gear case, through which the fuel–air mixture from the carburetor is ported and compressed to higher density before passing into the intake manifold. This "boosts" power output and especially helps maintain intake pressure nearer sea level even at the lower air density at altitude for sustained high performance.

Swept wing: A wing in which the mean chord line is less than 90 degrees to the aircraft centerline. An aft sweep is most common, meaning the mean chord line is farther forward at the root than at the tip.

Telemetry: The transmission by radio of sampled data from an aircraft to a ground station for safe observation of results during a flight event.

Transonic flight: Transonic airspeeds are, at the lower velocity, the critical Mach number at which shocks have begun to form on portions of the airframe and, at an upper end, the flow over the exterior surface is likely entirely immersed within shocks.

Tufts: Usually a length of yarn or string taped to the surface in rows. These align with the airflow to show direction of the streamlines to be photographed from an onboard camera or another aircraft.

Turbojet: A turbine (jet) engine for which the motive output is an accelerated mass of air for thrust.

Turboprop: A turbine (jet) engine for which the principal motive output is shaft torque to a propeller.

Turbosupercharger: A turbine spun by engine exhaust gases that, in turn, spins a compressor to 'charge' air taken in via a ram air duct. This air is then passed to the carburetor or supercharger.

Torque: The rate (lateral displacement tendency) created by a propeller, especially at high power on take-off and low speed on landing. This is a combination of mechanical effects from turning the heavy prop as well as the asymmetrical airflow effects on the aircraft elements aft of the propeller.

Water injection: The introduction of a metered flow of water (usually a water–alcohol mixture) into the carburetor fuel-air charge to cool hot-spots in the cylinder during combustion. It increases the density of the fuel-air charge to avoid detonation while increasing combustion pressure for higher power output.

Wind tunnel: A fabricated tunnel in which fans cause air motion through a test section in which a model of an aircraft or part thereof is mounted for data collection. In a full-scale wind tunnel, the test section is large enough to mount the entire aircraft and operate it remotely.

Wing loading: Aircraft gross weight divided by wing area. High wing loading via high aircraft weight or a small wing (reducing structural weight and aircraft drag) implies higher maneuverability than at lower wing loading. However, without devices like Fowler flaps, landing speed—and by association landing distance—can be uncomfortably high.

Acronyms and Abbreviations

AAA: anti-aircraft artillery
AAB: Army Air Base
AAC: Army Air Corps
AAF: Army Air Field
Adml: admiral
AGF: Army Ground Forces
AR: aerial refueling
ARU: Aircraft Repair Units
ASR: Air-Sea Rescue
ATI: Air Technical Intelligence
ATO: assisted take-off
ATSC: Air Technical Services Command
BLC: boundary layer control
Brig.-Gen.: brigadier-general
BuAer: Bureau of Aeronautics
BuNo: bureau number
C: centigrade
cal: caliber
Caltech: California Institute of Technology
CAP: combat air patrol
Capt.: captain
CBI: China-Burma-India
CCAAF: Clinton County AAF
CEAU: captured enemy aircraft unit
CG: center of gravity
Col.: colonel
c/n: construction number
CNO: Chief of Naval Operations
CO_2: carbon dioxide
Corp.: corporation

C. P.:	circular proposal
CVE:	escort carrier
CWS:	Chemical Warfare Service
D.C.:	District of Columbia
DDT:	dichloro-diphenyl-trichloro-ethane, insecticide
ERCO:	Engineering and Research Corp.
ETO:	European Theater of Operations
ETPS:	Empire Test Pilot School
F:	fahrenheit
Flt Off.:	Flight Officer
FM:	frequency modulation
FRL:	Flight Refueling Ltd.
fpm:	feet per minute
fps:	feet per second
g:	acceleration due to gravity
gal:	U.S. gallons
GALCIT:	Guggenheim Aeronautical Laboratory at the California Institute of Technology
GE:	General Electric
Gen.:	general
GI:	government issue (referring to American military personnel)
GW:	gross weight
hp:	horsepower
HQ:	headquarters
intel:	intelligence
JPL:	Jet Propulsion Laboratory
kN:	thousands of Newtons
ktons:	kilotons
lbf:	pounds force
LOX:	liquid oxygen
lpm:	liters per minute
LST:	Landing Ship, Tank
Lt:	lieutenant
Lt-Cdr:	lieutenant commander
Lt-Col.:	lieutenant colonel
Lt-Gen.:	lieutenant general
Ltd.:	limited
Maj.:	major
Maj.-Gen.:	major-general
mph:	statute miles per hour
mpm:	meters per minute
mps:	meters per second
N:	Newtons
NAA:	North American Aviation

NACA: National Advisory Committee for Aeronautics
NAF: Naval Aircraft Factory
NAMC: Naval Air Materiel Center
NAMU: Naval Aircraft Modification Unit
NAS: Naval Air Station, National Academy of Sciences
NDRC: National Defense Research Committee
NRC: National Research Council
OC: Officer Commanding
ops: operations
OSRD: Office of Scientific Research and Development
OSS: Office of Strategic Services
P&W: Pratt & Whitney
prop: propeller
psi: pounds per square inch
R&D: research and development
RAE: Royal Aircraft Establishment
RAF: Royal Air Force
recip: reciprocating engine
rep: representative
RN: Royal Navy
rpg: rounds per gun
rpm: revolutions per minute
Sgt: sergeant
S/Sgt: staff sergeant
STOL: short take-off and landing
SWPA: Southwest Pacific Area
TAIU: Technical Air Intelligence Units
TDL: Technical Data Laboratory
USAAC: United States Army Air Corps
USAAF, AAF: United States Army Air Forces
USAF: United States Air Force
USCG: United States Coast Guard
USMC: United States Marine Corps, United Machine Shoe Company
USN: United States Navy
USS: United States Ship
USSR: Union of Soviet Socialist Republics
VARICAM: variable camber
VE: Victory in Europe

1
Foundation

Aviation is an industry of endless innovation and advancement in seeking improved performance for commercial benefit or combat advantage. By World War II, the basic shape of combat aircraft had been determined by this pre-war evolution: semi-monocoque metal construction, cantilevered wings with trailing edge flaps, enclosed cockpit, retractable landing gear, cowled engine with supercharger, and constant-speed propellers. However, there remained much room for rapid enhancement under the pressure of war in reaching for greater performance while retaining desirable pilot handling qualities. The growth of power loading and wing loading with increasing gross weight, adoption of tricycle undercarriage, new airfoils augmented with high-lift flaps, balanced or boosted controls, and turbosuperchargers continuously challenged designers and researchers to ensure a suitable warplane emerged from the constantly shifting engineering milieu. The time and performance pressures of war made this all the more difficult.

Fortunately, the United States of America faced the new world war with a sound foundation of aviation research, development, experimentation, and human talent ready to grow under government funding and national leadership. It grew to mammoth proportions in a few years with tremendous abilities to modify aircraft for varied missions, produce new models of existing aircraft types, and develop entirely new types and even new classes, with all that these entailed. Given an enormous rearmament effort initiated in 1939, and then the entire country mobilized after 1941 with motivation to win a war against an existential threat to liberty, it brought to bear resources beyond anything other nations could muster. The country saw airpower as one of the most decisive elements of war-winning forces. Consequently, particular attention was directed to aviation with remarkable results. The U.S. learned from those already at war, coordinated with allies and studied captured equipment, and worked to dominate the field with weapons suited to its unique circumstances and role. Research and experimentation, with associated aircraft modifications, were critical to those goals, either supporting government-directed improvement programs or finding solutions to design problems of specific manufacturer projects. The modest pre-war forces expanded rapidly to the largest and most powerful military airpower team in the world with many unique capabilities.

Combat aircraft are weapons of extraordinary complexity, now and during World War II. They require great care in design, manufacturing, and operation while striving to remain superior to the opposition in a field undergoing rapid advance during the 1940s energized by research, development, and experimentation. This image suggests the complexity as an F4U-1 undergoes systems checks on a factory jig during 1942. (*Jay Miller collection*)

Research Basis

Aviation research and experimentation was vested in several entities within the U.S. during the war years. The military services had aircraft development organizations that included laboratories for research plus prototype equipment assembly, test, and evaluation. Also under government funding and oversight was the National Advisory Committee for Aeronautics (NACA) that conducted pure research for the benefit of military and civilian users of the resulting data. This extended from analytical studies to laboratory testing and to flight trials. Academia also conducted fundamental research, frequently financed by the government. Individual companies performed similar work for commercial purposes. All were bolstered during the run-up to war in the period of rearmament, then mobilized and greatly enlarged for the total war effort.

The U.S. Army Air Corps (USAAC or just AAC)—which after June 29, 1941, became the United States Army Air Forces (USAAF or just AAF)—based its primary aviation development activity, the Materiel Division, at Wright Field in Dayton, Ohio. It had nine laboratories for major disciplines like aircraft, materials, power plant, and propeller. At the beginning of the war, 1,984 personnel were employed at Materiel Division of which 89 percent were civilian, growing to 50,000 people by 1944.

On October 2, 1939, the Chief of Materiel Division moved to Washington, District of Columbia (D.C.), with the core of his staff to better advise Chief of the Air Corps Gen. Henry "Hap" Arnold. This reflected Arnold's appreciation for the importance of technology in growing and sustaining airpower, especially reacting in a wartime environment to enemy advances and emerging combat requirements. Remaining behind in Dayton was the assistant chief and the chief of the Experimental Engineering Section, who supervised all of the labs. On March 9, 1942, the D.C. activity was redesignated Materiel Command and the Wright Field element Materiel Center. It was renamed again on March 29, 1943, as Materiel Maintenance and Distribution with the Materiel Division and the Development Engineering Branch in D.C., and Materiel Command in Ohio with an Engineering Division. In July 1944, the D.C. elements became Materiel and Services. Air Services Command, at nearby Patterson Field, Dayton, oversaw routine procurements and the Air Depots. It was merged with Materiel Command in April 1943 to form Air Technical Services Command (ATSC), headquartered at Patterson. On August 31, 1944, the Wright Field elements came to include Engineering and Procurement Division and the labs were reorganized under five branches. Materiel and Services back east came to include a Research Liaison

General Arnold visits the NACA Aircraft Engine Research Laboratory in Cleveland, Ohio, on November 9, 1944. He is being shown ice accretion on a propeller in a propulsion icing tunnel, part of a years-long effort to increase safety flying in such conditions. Arnold was appreciative of the importance of science and technology in attaining superior weapons and so he championed research where an advantage appeared within reach during the expected duration of the war. (*NASA*)

Branch in November 1944. The Dayton and Washington organizations sometimes clashed over authority and duplicative if not conflicting direction to contractors.

Once passed along from manufacturers or modification shops, Army aircraft were tested at Wright Field. Aircraft armaments were tested at Eglin Field, Florida, also known as the corps' Proving Ground after May 1941, and the Proving Ground Command after April 1942 with authority over other AAF test and evaluation activities. In this guise, it performed more and more aircraft suitability trials. In fact, activities at Wright Field had grown to such proportions by 1942 that something had to give. Some work was moved to the nearby Dayton Army Air Field (AAF) in Vandalia, just 11 miles (18 km) from Wright Field. Glider activity was moved to Clinton County AAF (CCAAF) in Wilmington, 25 miles (40 km) away. Service trials were undertaken in many locations but especially Patterson Field, and by several operational organizations. Cold weather testing was performed by a cold weather test detachment at Ladd Field in Fairbanks, Alaska. Eglin also began building a climatic chamber where entire aircraft could be subjected to extremes of weather such that functions could be checked in ground tests. Tactics development via testing was conducted at Orlando, Florida.

More and more hazardous flight testing was performed at Muroc Army Air Field as the war progressed. This was a small training facility in southern California's high desert north of Los Angeles (LA) where manufacturers had long brought experimental aircraft for testing away from the congested LA basin. It lay on the edge of the vast Rogers Dry Lake, though wet or muddy in the brief rainy season. A naturally flat and smooth surface, the lakebed allowed much margin for error, or engine and brake failures, while the dry climate lent good flying weather during all but a few days of the year. In summer 1941, a permanent base was built at Muroc and a paved runway laid. In 1942, Wright Field identified Muroc AAF as the Materiel Center Flight Test Site. In 1944, the Muroc Flight Test Base was established at the north end of the lakebed while the training activities were to the south.

For the AAF, project officers usually handled one to four efforts with a civilian deputy and a clerk. By December 1941, the AAF alone had some 2,000 projects underway.[1] To get a notion of the scope of work during the war years, Eglin alone handled nearly 1,500 individual projects during those five and a half years. Wright Field almost certainly had many more.[2] Decisions on how to proceed with projects were made up the chain of command with Arnold the supreme authority. In the emergency, he was granted vast powers and could make procurement decisions worth millions of dollars with little more than a memorandum. It was only in summer 1945 that the Army Air Forces Center was established to formulate standards in materials and tactics. Within this was the AAF Board, existing previously, that set priorities of projects and made overarching decisions that included requirements and procurement choices based on test results reviews.

The United States Navy (USN) aircraft acquisition agency was the Bureau of Aeronautics (BuAer) in Washington, D.C., also handling Marine Corps (USMC) requirements. The Chief of BuAer was commonly among the most senior and respected naval aviators and had a great deal of influence in materiel decisions. During the war years, the chiefs were Rear-Admirals John H. Towers, John S. McCain, Dewitt C. Ramsey, and Harold B. Sallada. Artemus L. Gates was named assistant secretary of the Navy for Aeronautics on September 5, 1940, a post that had been vacant since 1932. On May 15, 1942, the Chief of Naval Operations (CNO) ordered the creation of the Assistant Chief of Naval Operations (Air) under the Vice CNO. The post was filled by the Chief of BuAer as an additional duty. This proved short-lived as the functions were assumed by the new Division of Aviation under the Vice CNO in June 1942, who became the director. As a further step recognizing the growing importance of naval airpower, this morphed again in August 1943 when Deputy Chief of Naval Operations (Air) was created. Many elements of BuAer were moved under this new office that Vice-Adml John McCain initially headed.

The Naval Aircraft Factory (NAF) in Philadelphia, Pennsylvania, built a limited number of aircraft to gain insight for assessing contractor proposals. It also undertook a large number of research, modification, and test activities for BuAer. Flying was from the adjoining Naval Auxiliary Air Station, Mustin Field. The service principally tested aircraft at Naval Air Station (NAS) Anacostia in Washington, D.C., some tests at the Washington Navy Yard, and more at NAS Norfolk, Virginia. In 1942, the Aircraft Experimental and Developmental Squadron was established at Anacostia to determine the practicality of new aircraft equipment. That year, it was concluded that the growing air congestion and press of local inhabitants were not conducive to this hazardous activity with more modern aircraft. There was also a desire to consolidate test activities. Consequently, in November 1942, the Navy established the Naval Air Test Center at Patuxent River in the town of the same name on the Chesapeake Bay in southern Maryland, about 60 miles (95 km) south of D.C. "Pax River" was formally commission in April 1943 and the Anacostia flight test activities transferred there that summer. In 1945, this became NAS Patuxent River.

The naval aviation developmental workload expanded massively with the war. By summer 1942, the NAF employed some 10,000 persons and the need for reorganization was evident. (Unlike the USAAC's Materiel Division, BuAer consisted largely of officers.) The USN formed the Naval Air Materiel Center (NAMC) on July 14, 1943, that encompassed the NAF, various aeronautical laboratories, and the new Naval Aircraft Modification Unit (NAMU). This last was initially in Philadelphia then in Johnsville, Pennsylvania (at the former Brewster Aeronautical plant). As part of this reorganization, the Naval Air Experimental Station assumed responsibility for laboratories plus research and development (R&D). Recognizing the likely enormous impact of turbine engines in the future, the Naval Air Turbine Test Station was established on November 6, 1944, in Trenton, New Jersey. Lakehurst, New Jersey, was the site of lighter-than-air aircraft development and testing. The Naval Ordnance Test Station was established in Inyokern, California, for the development and test of aircraft weapons. Trials of aircraft rocket motors were performed at Dahlgren, Virginia, from 1944. Rockets and other ordnance were flight tested in the California high desert at NAS China Lake, near Ridgecrest. The Naval Research Laboratory in D.C. contributed to aviation in the areas of radio and radar.

The United States, like the leading industrialized countries that had fought in World War I, greatly appreciated the potential for aviation in warfare and peaceful national endeavors. The government encouraged aviation's commercial advancement, as the economy permitted, and created a government-funded body for fundamental aeronautical research. The NACA had a vital asset in the Langley Memorial Aeronautical Laboratory at Langley Field, Virginia. The lab possessed numerous unique test cells, like wind tunnels of various types, while also conducting flight trials. Apart from publishing research results, the NACA also held annual aircraft engineering conferences, though interrupted after 1939 by the war.

The NACA's relationship with the War Department was always close. Apart from Langley residing on a military installation, most of its flight research aircraft came from the Navy and Army. The NACA executive committee had representatives of these services as members, as well as on various technical subcommittees. In 1936, the Special Committee on Relation of NACA to National Defense in Time of War was established, chaired by the Chief of the Air Corps. In June 1939, the President directed that NACA policies and priorities would be arbitrated by an Army-Navy Aeronautical Board. The Mobilization Plan of the Aeronautical Board was approved by President Roosevelt in June 1939. Under this, the NACA would become "a consulting and research agency of the armed services." It did this in a rather seamless fashion after the U.S. entered the war, with the Aeronautical Board approving NACA projects.

The NACA had been established during World War I in an effort to catch up with the European nations that had advanced aeronautical science, particularly military aviation, well ahead of America. As war dawned again, the NACA was facing a similar mandate. To meet these obligations, Langley had to change its attitude and some practices. Instead of pure research, the preponderance of its work became more aerodynamics consulting and services, even allowing contractors to bring their own wind tunnel models whereas previously only NACA-built models were permitted for safety reasons. More industrial representation was accepted on its directing committee and equipment from aviation companies were installed as necessary. The proportion and number of projects associated with military aviation grew to dominance during the war years. New security measures had to be adopted as a consequence. Test data and research results were released without complete reporting and review; much was classified.

Manpower was a concern within industry and government labs alike during the war as valuable personnel were inducted into the armed forces and departed. The Aeronautical Board sought to keep this drain to a manageable level. However, the granting of deferments and retaining skilled people remained a problem throughout the conflict. A joint Army-Navy plan implemented in February 1944 allowed for drafted individuals in critical R&D positions to remain on inactive reserve assigned to NACA or in uniform and so assigned until the end of hostilities. Others who had critical skills and had served overseas, or were beyond twenty-six years of age, were released to take up R&D duties. Additionally, some technically talented foreign individuals fleeing persecution and violence that made it the U.S. were employed in ways assisting the war effort.

Academia played an important role as well, with the contribution of their labs and intellectual prowess growing during the war as all the nation's resources were engaged. Among the most important was the Guggenheim Aeronautical Laboratory at the California Institute of Technology (GALCIT) in Pasadena, California. Apart from intellectual advice, the GALCIT wind tunnel, so close to southern California aviation firms, was quite busy. Education was not neglected. More officers were sent to graduate school to gain a deeper understanding of specialized subjects, at least until the U.S. joined hostilities.

Stepping Up

In the interwar years, the U.S. military helped sustain the aviation industry struggling through the Great Depression with orders for experimental and prototypes aircraft while also advancing the state of the art. This ensured a knowledgeable and capable, if small, industrial base. The late 1930s saw many voices, such as the respected Charles Lindbergh and Jimmy H. Doolittle, air *attachés*, and NACA's observer in Europe, warning that the U.S. was falling behind other nations in aeronautics and aircraft development. That many of these nations expressed expansionist and ultra-right tendencies was of great concern. Germany, especially, was providing almost unlimited resources to aeronautical research and development. The number and scope of R&D facilities were increasing dramatically, and staffed with large numbers of highly qualified engineers, scientists, and technicians. Britain was also making notable strides and building up resources in response to the German expansion. Yet funding shortfalls in America associated with the isolationist sentiments continued to work against rapid progress.

Moves were already afoot to correct this situation. Along with manpower and materiel growth of the armed forces focusing on military preparedness, much was done in the year or two before World War II broke out to position U.S. aeronautical establishments for rapid growth. A 1938 report of how NACA could contribute to national defense served additional justification for those arguing for investment in new research facilities. The August 1939 report of the Special Committee on the Relation of the NACA to National Defense in Time of War emphasized that the United States was slipping to second-tier status. It recommended the formation of another NACA laboratory for aeronautics and aircraft structures. Lindbergh urged closer attention to engines and emphasized that liquid-cooled engines were being neglected. The Air Corps expansion act of April 1939 was the first expression of the growing appreciation for the role and potential of air power, from the Administration to Congress.

When war dawned in September 1939, the U.S. was clearly a world-class aeronautical power, but her military aviation was inferior and growing more so with each passing year. A state of national emergency was declared when the war finally broke out with Germany's invasion of Poland. Efforts continued apace in the two years until America's dramatic entry into the conflict during December 1941. These began to assist in growing the Navy and Army air arms and their capabilities. Without involvement as a combatant, however, America remained half a step behind Germany and Britain. Although Arnold had decided by June 1940 to focus massive production efforts on existing types that could be upgraded over time, promising new types were developed with advanced technologies inserted that appeared achievable during the span of the war.[3] The Navy's combat aircraft development was more paced by integration into carrier air wings, but they also developed new types and funded research with the potential to increase mission effectiveness in the near term.

Fortunately, by 1939, the USAAC had a separate HQ and chief and so more control over its destiny among an Army staff that frequently emphasized more traditional branches. The new Chief of the Air Corps, "Hap" Arnold, was one of the original American military pilots and an advocate of growing its role via new capabilities for more decisive contributions, especially strategic bombing. On October 30, 1940, he became Deputy Chief of Staff of the Army for Air and, beginning in early 1942, a member of the President's military staff, then one of four members of the Joint Chiefs of Staff. He also had a background in aircraft development via a World War I project to produce an unmanned winged missile: the Kettering Bug. Later, he ran a depot at Wright Field while also serving as Materiel Division's executive officer. So, he understood the role of R&D on advancing the cause of a strengthened air arm. President Roosevelt came to rely more and more on Arnold's insight and recommendations. Army Chief of Staff, Gen. George C. Marshall, was also behind an expansion of air power, both in size and role. The post of Assistant Secretary of War for Air was created with Robert A. Lovett taking the job.

In summer 1939, the Air Corps' Kilner Board laid out a five-year plan for the acquisition of new military aircraft with proposed characteristics. These included ambitious goals such as a 5,333-mile (8,523-km) range bomber, a 3,000-hp (2,237-kW) engine, and day and night operations. All bespoke some measure of supporting research to facilitate the development of such equipment. Although the program was altered a bit in September and thereafter throughout the war in reaction to Allied requirements and the needs of an evolving battlefield, it remained a general guideline. The entire research program went under intense review.

In the late 1930s, Gen. Arnold established a Special Committee for Air Corps Research under the National Academy of Sciences (NAS) to advise the USAAC on advances that might benefit the service. To this, he invited Dr. Theodore von Kármán to participate, a brilliant aerodynamicist of Hungarian origins teaching at the California Institute of Technology (Caltech) and director of the GALCIT. This establishing a long and fruitful relationship. The Air Corps could also draw on the expertise of the National Research Council (NRC), under the NAS, for guidance on developments beyond the specialized skills of their own laboratories. All this would assist AAC officers and civilian personnel who worked in weapons R&D, but who largely lacked college degrees and, for the officers, were usually placed in such positions between operational assignments. The Navy had a similar problem but had a larger percentage of officers with degrees.[4]

By spring 1940, the assessment from observers overseas had become so grim that one senior officer concluded that if the AAC flew into combat over Germany none of the aircraft would return.[5] Focus shifted to an immediate modernization in air weapons rather than the ultimate improvement over several years as guided by the Kilner board recommendations. Such USAAC programs as bombing through overcast, additional armor protection, de-icing equipment, leak-proof fuel tanks, and external tanks plus auxiliary bomb racks for fighters were all fast-tracked.

Weeks later, after the German conquest of France, there was a temporary focus almost exclusively on the production of current types and moving rapidly

Dr. Theodore von Kármán was a tremendously productive scientist and engineer. His theoretical work in aerodynamics plus practical advice to aircraft manufacturers and the military services were invaluable in the years before and during the war. Here he performs calculations on the wing of the Ercoupe used for assisted take-off rocket flight tests, August 1941—*from left to right*: Dr. Clark Millikan, Dr. Martin Summerfield, von Kármán, Dr. Frank Malina, and Capt. Homer Boushey. (*NASA*)

to production for those in development, while R&D was deferred until spring 1941. Some of the more abstract projects, such as bombing through overcast, were transferred to such agencies as the National Defense Research Committee (NDRC) under the NAS. Only in 1941 did a normal balance with R&D resume.

The NDRC originated on June 27, 1940, to "to coordinate, supervise, and conduct scientific research on the problems underlying the development, production, and use of mechanisms and devices of warfare." This supplemented the work performed by the military labs and had representatives of the War Department and services as members. The Office of Scientific Research and Development (OSRD) was created on June 28, 1941, and superseded the NDRC in coordinating military R&D. Dr. Vannevar Bush (President of the Carnegie Institute) chaired both organizations, answered to the President, and had access to almost unlimited funds. The AAF had the NDRC working some 125 projects during the war years.[6] The development of radar, which touched all services, was principally directed by these national organizations.

The government also established the National Inventors Council in 1940 within the Department of Commerce's Office of Technical Services. Its role was to review ideas from the public with potential national security benefits and pass the most promising along to the War Department.

One benefit of all this organizational milieu was reenergized R&D as guided by military imperatives during the war—what was perceived as most beneficial in achieving victory and with willingness to change course as battlefield realities evolved. Priorities were under periodic review and reordering for the same reason. This was not the case in the principal Axis nations where the scientific and engineering bodies were given more freedom to pursue what they saw as promising and which led to many poor choices in resource expenditures.[7]

Before the U.S. entered the war, input from observers in long-fighting Britain was an important element in decisions affecting R&D. The British Purchasing Commission, overseeing United Kingdom (U.K.) acquisitions of American aircraft and associate materiel (eventually through the Lend-Lease program), naturally took an interest into the R&D underlying the products it was to receive.[8] This was codified by the formation in September 1940 of the Army-Navy-British Purchasing Commission Joint Aircraft Committee. This ensured an exchange such that the U.S. benefited from the U.K.'s combat experience employing arms, impose some measure of standardization, avoid duplication, leverage off unique capabilities or existing programs of each county, and take advantage of America's distance from the battle. There were other joint committees, one seeking to determine a standardized cockpit layout for a single-engined fighter airplane for the Navy and Army. While the recommendations may have influenced some decisions, each service continued along its own path.[9]

The allies came to permit unprecedented levels of ally access to nearly all R&D efforts within their countries. The U.K. made input to and followed associated American work while Great Britain, in time, shared nearly everything they had to offer. Observers from both sides of the Atlantic were placed in development centers, laboratories, factories, and anywhere else insight was to be gleaned. The Americans generally listened keenly to the British observations and advice, but they did not adhere to all they heard or advice offered.[10] The cooperation had limits in that the U.S. could not let U.K. priorities dictate American priorities.

Growing

As part of the general rearmament effort, the R&D and experimentation budget also increased. In 1940 alone, the Air Corps budget for such things increased three-fold—from $3.6 million to $10.0 million. It grew steadily to $121.7 million in 1944; during that period, expenditures summed to $418.8 million. Only 13 percent of this was spent within the organization while 81 percent went to industry, 1 percent to academia, and 6 percent to other entities. Similarly, NACA's expenditures during the same period summed to $85 million whereas only $12 million had been spent to 1939. The BuAer expended $171.3 million and OSRD $347.9 million. By 1944, the entire Federal government was devoting $600 million annually on war-related R&D, or nearly 250 percent more than the 1939 peacetime expenditures. Personnel assigned to such endeavors grew from 1,984 in July 1939 to 17,276 on July 1, 1943, of which 8 to 10 percent were military officers.[11]

The NACA's personnel numbers increased from about 550 (roughly 39 percent professionals) in July 1939 to around 6,500 (approximately 25 percent professionals) in February 1945, while its budget grew steadily from $4.4 million in 1940 to $38.4 million in 1945.[12] By July 1944, the NACA was providing support to seventy-eight individual aircraft projects.[13]

Just before the war, the NACA had sought to expand to meet the growing demands of fundamental aviation research to support cutting-edge aircraft advancement. Langley added new facilities, but they reached the capacity of available land and electrical power. Another aeronautics laboratory was conceived and funded (authorized by Congress in August 1939) for the west coast. This became Ames Aeronautical Laboratory built at NAS Moffett Field in Sunnyvale, California. Construction of the facilities was underway in the early war years, and it began contributing in 1941. Ames and Langley eventually found themselves running around-the-clock operations to keep pace with the wartime R&D demands. The better weather in California also saw some flight testing transferred to Ames.

Pre-war, aircraft engine manufacturers were too conservative in an era of few customers and narrow profits to risk major changes to their products. Arnold would point out in October 1942 that this left a poor selection of engines to power fighter aircraft. The Navy also lamented that most of their engines were commercial derivatives, built for economy, and none real combat power plants.[14] Yet, much development was underway in Europe with the promise of marked performance improvements. The NACA had previously steered clear of engine development, leaving this to the manufacturers. It had a power plant committee by 1939, offering advice and encouragement, but it was backed by little in the way of specialized test facilities. Engines were not considered to be within its scope while the National Bureau of Standards directed some efforts to engine research. Instead, NACA focused on propulsion aerodynamics—low-drag cowlings and efficient cooling.

The clear evidence that the U.S. was behind in engine development compelled a change in policy and the Aircraft Engine Research Laboratory was created. Both the USAAC and BuAer supported the legislation funding the new laboratory. Congress approved the $8.4 million appropriation in June 1940, and a site was selected adjacent to the airport in Cleveland, Ohio. Ground was broken on January 23, 1941, and the first tests were performed in May 1942. This new NACA lab would assume experimental risks supported by, hopefully, a supportive and cooperative relationship with the competing manufacturers. By then, it was even clearer this was late to need given the revelation of British turbine engine development and the extraordinary progress of the Germans. The NACA was still a half-step behind.

There were sometimes disputes between the military services and NACA when new or expanded aeronautical R&D resources were sought.[15] However, any redundancy was quickly rendered moot as all were overwhelmed with requests by design teams for test cell time to collect data.

There was also some competition between the USAAF and Navy for resources supporting their individual aviation projects. When it came to NACA resources, this was resolved by the subcommittees and the War Department prioritization processes. The two services did work jointly on several projects, had liaison officers in the other's materiel centers, and had periodic consultation sessions to share information and results, avoiding conflicting and duplicative efforts. There were a few instances of one service adopting the other's aircraft, but this was not a large-scale phenomenon. These always involved some measure of alteration in detailed equipment for compatibility. Examples are the Army taking up dive bombers (the Douglas SBD becoming the A-24), the Marines using medium bombers (the North American B-25s becoming the PBJ), and the Navy adopting the Consolidated B-24 as a patrol bomber (the PB4Y).

The U.S. worked quickly and, with great effort, re-established its leadership in aeronautical capabilities, expanding R&D and production resources in reaction to what was observed aboard before and in the early years of the war. For example, the U.S. initially had no powered turrets in service or production but quickly developed such equipment. While following examples from overseas, the Americans also took their own course in many areas. The Allies established areas for each country to focus on and avoid duplication of effort.

Manufacturers also grew by leaps and bounds to meet rapidly growing order backlogs with ever-shorter delivery schedules. Taking Lockheed as an example, the June 1938 British order for 250 Model 14 Super Electra, recast as the Hudson patrol bomber, was the largest single order any American aircraft manufacturer had ever received, and about equaled all the machines the company had produced

Test aircraft provide a ready means of exploring solutions to problems uncovered with a specific type or to conduct research of a more general nature—all provided it can be done safely. This P-40 was temporarily modified with a leading-edge extension of enhanced camber at the root of the wings. Its purpose is unclear, although reducing buffeting and drag may have been possible reasons. (*NASA*)

to that time. It then had 2,000 employees. By December 1941, the firm employed 53,000 people. This would peak at 90,000 and they pushed out 20,000 airplanes before the conflict's end. This included more than 10,000 P-38 and F-4 photo reconnaissance variants of the airplane.

Get It Done

The U.S. military expansion in the war years was extraordinary by any measure. At the peak, some 50 percent of industrial output (which had been at least doubled) was directed to the war effort, and of that, 20 percent was focused on aircraft. Looking at aircraft production only, the Americans manufactured 2,141 aircraft in 1939, 19,433 in 1941, and 47,714 in 1945. Navy production (including Marine aircraft) was only about 25 percent of the Army's. The preponderance of export types was from the Army. By the end of 1942, the U.S. was out-producing each of Britain, Germany, and Japan, and in 1945 more than all those combined.[16] The Army aircraft fleet was 2,546 in 1939, 12,297 in 1941, and 63,745 at the end of the war.[17] The Navy went from 2,098 airplanes in 1939 to 3,437 in 1941, and 40,912 in 1945.[18] All this meant tremendous resources applied, especially as aircraft technology was far from static during this period. The supporting research, experimentation, and modification grew proportionally large and more varied.

There was a veritable avalanche of aircraft development and improvement programs plus research efforts in the year before America entered the war, and a deluge after. This strained resources to the limit even as these were pushed tremendously with the mobilization of the economy. Industry had to adapt to large orders after decades as a virtual boutique industry. The largest order until 1939 was for 200 aircraft and most contracts were for a fraction of this. An aircraft required roughly five years from conception to flight, refinement, and production, followed by force build-up, training, logistics train establishment, then deployment as a combat force. Engines required several more years and mechanics approximately a year to train. Continuous improvement in production aircraft was required to fill the gap before new types could be introduced. Consequently, Americans generally fought with aircraft already in production or detailed development at the time of Pearl Harbor, but these, and those that followed, illustrated the growing capabilities of the nation's industry, laboratories, and armed services. The resources were generally wisely applied and in concert with allies for efficiency and mutual benefit, though there was still some duplication, inefficiency, and waste. The Air Forces predicted a high of 25 percent losses of equipment and personnel per month, and so production and training plans rested upon that premise.[19] This ultimately proved too pessimistic but for a few early months of American involvement, and so a surplus resulted. Yet, as all this was done in haste, from a tardy start, and under the pressure of total war, the results were all the more remarkable.

The nature of this work was paralleled in all countries with a substantial aviation industry. Due to the nearly identical level of aeronautical technology in all, the goals were also nearly the same and only a few major advances can be exclusively attributed to any one nation. Until the outbreak of war and the imposition of strict security measures, progress was more or less widely and openly shared via international visits and conferences. After the large clampdown on such information exchanges, progress was governed by means and will as dictated by the fortunes of war but limited by the few years of the conflict.

The American air arms repeatedly confronted and overcame obstacles and performed feats never before undertaken or previously judged practical. This included precision navigation by routinely trained men such that they could guide an aircraft to tiny islands in the sea over more than 1,000 miles of travel, such extended over-water flights in two-engined aircraft, delivery missions across the North Atlantic and the ice cap, flight into the stratosphere and into the jet stream, little-known islands or areas mapped and airfields built in a matter of weeks, and daylight bombing over heavily defended objectives. Comparable feats were performed by other nations, compelled by the urgency of war. They were all preceded by research and experimentation, sometimes with modified aircraft. Like many commanders, Gen. Arnold fostered a "get it done" attitude of pushing hard for increased safety and system performance regardless of regulations or other paperwork impediments. Material Division ran with this and had Arnold's backing whenever "red tape" slowed progress.[20] The "get it done" imperative pervaded civilian organizations as well given the appreciation that the work affected troops abroad (friends and family members), either immediately or at some future date, with the goal of winning the war. Consequently, contractors frequently began work on new efforts even before signing formal contracts.

The improvisation of people in extreme circumstances was particularly instrumental. Although proudly dubbed "Yankee Ingenuity," it was the same everywhere. An American example was the Flying Tigers in China devising belly tanks for their P-40s by working with Chinese craftsman and local materials; layers of varnished cloth laid up over a mold of bamboo and mud.[21] Belatedly, the U.S. began a program to adopt external tanks to all their fighter-type aircraft (see Chapter 7). The range extension of the P-51 to make it the premier bomber escort fighter, to include an added internal tank aft of the pilot station, was prompted by Maj.-Gen. Barney Giles, who proposed the configuration that North American Aviation (NAA) engineering made successful. The Americans also took three Spitfires IXs shipped over by the Royal Air Force (RAF) and increased tankage, including adding two drop tanks, to extend the range to 1,300 miles (2,092 km), showing how they could be made into effective long-range escort fighters. The aircraft were flown back to London but were assessed as having degraded flying qualities, as were the modified P-51s until the added tank's fuel was burned down.[22]

Manufacturers or other firms (such as airlines unable to operate due to the war) were contracted to set up air depots in distant lands. Some company technical representatives assisted maintenance and supply shops in learning the best means of supporting their assigned aircraft or supervised installation of modifications. They also provided product advisors in theaters, though usually not in the most forward areas. The military services arranged for select industry representatives to visit training bases, aircraft carriers at sea, and forward operating areas to gain insight into how their products were being used and to hear gripes and suggestions from maintainers and operators for improvements. This particularly helped in formulating specifications for the next aircraft model or type.

There were such gifted aviators as Jimmy Doolittle, who could offer cogent insight after flying any airplane.[23] He demonstrated such maligned airplanes as the Martin B-26 Marauder (nicknamed Murderer) as both safe and very effective by flying them through various emergency conditions and extreme maneuvers, helping to increase the confidence of aircrew. For gliders, it was Mike Murphy showing the safety and capabilities of the Waco CG-4A after it, too, gained the reputation as a killer. In the case of Charles Lindbergh's actions as an advisor, he also flew during operational sorties in the Pacific and engaged in combat.[24]

At Gen. Doolittle's request, Lockheed's test pilot Tony LeVier, among other representatives, were sent to the U.K. to show P-38 pilots the finer points of the aircraft and lecture on subjects like compressibility dives (Chapter 5). LeVier demonstrated the P-38 to AAF pilots on both continents to dispel suspicion of the type in the wake of compressibility mishaps, turbosupercharger fires, and other feared behaviors. He especially demonstrated the safety of the aircraft by

Lieutenant Colonel Jimmy Doolittle poses on the deck of the USS *Hornet* with her skipper Captain Marc Mitscher along with the team preparing to launch B-25B bombers against Japan. Doolittle was a gifted aviator and engineer, among the first individuals in the U.S. to earn a doctorate in aeronautical engineering. His skills, intellect, and leadership served America well in the trials of World War II. (*The Norm Taylor Collection/The Museum of Flight*)

performing such things as single engine maneuvering and landing, helping to dispel rumors and permit line pilots to regain confidence in the machine. LeVier and others also showed benefits of the dive recovery flap and how it permitted a safe split-S combat maneuver.

The urgency of war drove much more risk-taking than in peacetime, and this extended to R&D. The outcome were results obtained in short order but also with a high number of wrecked aircraft and dead or injured personnel. As an example, the Lockheed XP-80 jet fighter was designed, built, and flown in just 143 days at the end of 1943 by just 120 people. On the first high-power engine run, the intake ducts collapsed and ruined the team's one and only engine. Once flying, there were many changes to optimize the aircraft, but the excessive tailpipe temperatures remained unresolved. The follow-on larger XP-80A and YP-80A, each with a more powerful engine, was designed and built in 132 days. Once flying began in 1944, the team had to contend with inlet rumble, unstable compressibility shocks inducing aileron buzz (see later), a turbine disc disintegrating that destroyed one of the prototypes in flight, pressure differential with throttle transient collapsing a tailpipe leading to a crash and fatality, then a fuel pump shaft shearing and yet another wreck with a dead test pilot. Trials with the Lockheed jets to develop tactics for the American prop fighters to deal with the German Me 262 was most helpful. Yet just a mission to have a B-25 crew assess the tail glow of a P-80 jet fighter at night ended with the aircraft colliding in the dark and two pilots killed.[25] Once in service trial, the attrition rate was so high, owing to residual issues given the rapid development and pilots still learning how to operate the jet, that the aircraft was grounded for a time. However, the P-80 went on to an illustrious career and most could count the wartime risks as justified.

Sometimes, it was easier to modify and test an aircraft than go through a prolonged period of analysis and lab testing. For example, when the French insisted that a twin tail on the Douglas DB-7 (predecessor of the A-20 medium bomber) would provide the dorsal gunner a better field of fire than the single tail, they could not be dissuaded. An aircraft had to be modified and then flown with gun cameras to photographs air intercepts and the gunner tracking of the target, and then compared with the same from a standard DB-7. The results were visually convincing that the gunner had more obstructed field of fire with the twin tails than the single.[26]

In the fury of high-rate production with constant efforts at improvements to meet the changing combat conditions in a total war environment, there was a constant battle between quality and quantity. Maintaining a steady pace on production lines often meant turning out aircraft that went immediately to modification on-site or (after 1941) to a modification center operated by manufacturers, grounded airlines, or the military. During the war, nearly 100 percent of bombers and 50 percent of all other aircraft visited 'mod centers' before delivery to operational units.[27] Even then, when the aircraft were delivered to an operational unit it still required further work before entering combat.

Fearing a shortage of aluminum, many non-combat types were ordered to be built of wood and some designs reworked to meet this objective. Furniture makers were mobilized to manufacture aircraft components. The U.S. Forest Service, Forest Products Laboratory, worked to create standards for such products. Some of the predominately wooden machines had short airframe lives and were time-consuming to maintain in the field. Assault gliders, as an example, deteriorated rapidly in the dry desert and humid jungle, with repairs being difficult. This was tolerated given the production of replacements, the service lives of combat aircraft then commonly measured in months. Even combat types were approached in hopes that some non-structural elements could be replaced with wooden substitutes. In some cases, this reached unreasonable proportions, with little gained and manufacturers balking at the demands this placed on design and production staffs. In time, the aluminum supply was judged secure and the best wood products to be a critical material.[28] In general, the freedom from enemy attack on home industries and early successes in securing lines of raw materials supply made quality in American products more easily obtainable.

Other material substitutes were the choice of manufacturers. The use of magnesium for 10 percent of the Convair XB-36 airframe was a weight reduction

An early production P-80A flies over the San Gabriel mountains at the end of the war. The Lockheed jet fighter was developed in just months as an extraordinary example of American aeronautical prowess. However, it was not without risks that manifested themselves in deficiencies that resulted in numerous wrecked airplanes and dead or injured pilots. (*San Diego Air & Space Museum*)

The 131st Douglas DB-7 for France (seen in New York without its turret) has a twin tail in place of the normal single vertical to address customer conviction this would improve the dorsal gunner's field of fire. Although the one-off modification by the manufacturer was not trivial, they did it to enable tests showing conclusively the notion was erroneous. The aircraft was restored to the standard empennage after delivery to the British. (*Ray Wagner collection*)

measure. This aircraft also introduced adhesive bonding of the skin to the underlying structure to avoid the use of rivets and other mechanical fasteners. The Budd RB-1 employed spot-welded stainless steel as a featured construction method. Alternative alloys of aluminum were also introduced with lighter weight or greater strength. Chance Vought of Stratford, Connecticut, devised Metalite—a pre-curved sandwich of thin aluminum sheets with balsa wood between. Eliminating rivets, joints, and stiffeners, it was also more rigid and lighter than single-sheet skin and gave a particularly wrinkle-free and smooth surface. However, it proved considerably more difficult to maintain.

Testing Challenges

As with all other aspects of aviation undergoing enormous change and growth, aircraft flight testing had to move ahead apace. Apart from prototypes of new designs or models, unique or specially modified aircraft serving various specific flight test purposes had to be flown through sometimes hazardous trials. These platforms and aircrew permitted data to be collected supporting basic research, development, and experimentation. The machines were modified for required instrumentation to measure and record airframe and systems behavior. The addition of special safety devices was also common. The techniques and equipment for successful flight testing increased and were refined during the war, with more data collected at improved resolution. Telemetry for transmitting data to the ground was introduced.

The NACA Langley flight test team was the exemplary professionals and particularly helped establish flight test as a recognized and essential specialty aviation field. They insisted that their test pilots possess an engineering degree in addition to deep aviation experience, yet less than half of the military officers, pilots, or otherwise had degrees. By 1944, the NACA and the services had established qualitative standards for desirable aircraft stability and control and handling or flying qualities which then guided flight testing. The NACA went farther and devised associated wind tunnel test methodologies to be followed by flight test techniques to collect validating data. They designed and produced flight test instruments and pioneered self-recording installations with multiple parameters.

The rapid growth in the number of aircraft projects and associated flight testing, executed at a rapid pace, demanded many more test pilots, flight test engineers, and instrumentation technicians than the pre-war years had sustained. The commercial organizations had relied upon highly experienced pilots for hire. This was indicative of the immature flight test organizations within the firms and few highly experienced test personnel in that austere time. Most had no dedicated flight test organization and depended upon the freelancers when the need arose. Design engineers served as onboard test engineers when the need arose. Only the largest manufacturers had small teams and most of the personnel had no formal training. Specialized knowledge was conveyed in-house. The NACA reports provided much-needed "how-to" information.

Vought's Corsair spin test aircraft F4U-1 02155 is fitted with a spin recovery parachute packed into a canister at the aft end of the fuselage. This is deployed if the pilot enters a spin that defies conventional recovery techniques and ground impact appears likely. When deployed, it pulls the aircraft's tail up, the nose down, to break the stall and so permits recovery from the resulting dive. (*Vought Historical Archives*)

The company's dive test F4U-1 (02169) shows evidence of this purpose. The cockpit (photographed on December 15, 1942) shows many additional instruments including two within the panel and read via a mirror. A movie camera is affixed under the large teardrop fairing ahead of the starboard horizontal stabilizer to photograph the tufts taped to the starboard wing (many likely having blown off during the course of a flight as they appear sparse). (*Vought Historical Archives*)

The test pilot profession came firmly into being during the war with specialized courses, skills, and experience. Manufacturers and research agencies formed integral flight test organizations to plan, conduct, analyze, and report on these complex and sometimes hazardous undertakings with very costly assets. Shown are NACA Langley test pilots in front of a P-47 on February 14, 1945—from left to right: Mel Gough, Herb Hoover, Jack Reeder, Steve Cavallo, and Bill Gray. (*NASA*)

Along with the test pilot is the flight test engineer who performs the considerable test and mission planning, and occasionally collects data on board the aircraft in flight. Here a NACA Aircraft Engine Research Laboratory engineer performs his task aboard a Lockheed A-29 fitted with flight test instrumentation from which the engineer is recording readings. (*NASA*)

The war brought an unbelievable increase in the breadth and scope of flight test projects, and with an unrelenting pace. Formal flight test organizations had to be established. Yet, few even experienced pilots possessed the requisite specialized knowledge. This had to be conveyed via on-the-job training and one-on-one instruction. Handbooks and other written materials were drafted and passed along. Some courses were put on to which individuals could travel for instruction. Still, the workload was so great that important tests were passed up and significant deficiencies missed.[29] Marginal pilots (in uniform and out) were sometimes taken up, some of whom perished with valuable flight test aircraft. By 1945, the military services were assessing the capabilities of a firm's flight test capabilities before trials of new or highly modified aircraft were undertaken. In some cases, they sent their own personnel to perform the initial and most hazardous phase of testing.

The USAAC established an Engineering School at Wright Field to help train service and civilian personnel for these activities. This permitted them to make better-informed decisions and understand the subjects presented by laboratories, NACA, and contractors. Probably at the time of change over to ATSC, the Flight Test Division was established at Wright Field with a Bomber Flight Test Branch, Fighter Flight Test, plus Cargo and Misc. The discipline and functions of a test pilot were passed along informally within the Flight Section at the base.

The U.K. had established the Empire Test Pilot School (ETPS) in 1943 and two Americans were in the second class.[30] An AAF Flight Test Training Unit was finally formed on September 9, 1944, under Maj. Ralph C. Hoewing and Col. Ernest K. Warburton who had both visited ETPS to gain insight. In January 1945, this was moved to Vandalia and renamed the Flight Performance School with Maj. J. R. 'Dick' Muehlberg as commandant. They graduated forty-six students from the three-month course in the 1944 and 1945 classes.[31]

NACA Contributions

At the beginning of the war emergency, the NACA had to prioritize improving the performance of military aircraft and resolving issues above basic research. American warplanes of World War II greatly benefited from prior NACA research on drag reduction, effective engine cowlings, efficient airfoils, and wing high-lift devices. During the war, the NACA found itself working to ensure all these aspects were effectively integrated. All variables of aircraft construction and flight were explored in an effort to improve performance and safety, research and test capabilities increasing in all these aspects. Particularly, Langley's contributions during the war were momentous, aided by its expansion and new research facilities. Apart from permitting design teams to collect data in their test cells, especially the full-scale wind tunnels, they also help in suggesting design choices and had an ongoing program of offering drag reduction advice backed by wind tunnel results. Some universities possessed wind tunnels, but the first capable tunnel built by an aeronautical manufacturer—Lockheed—was only constructed in 1939. They improved wind tunnel test data collection and introduced powered propellers on the models to assess slipstream effects. These effects were playing larger roles in stability and control with the introduction of ever more powerful engines turning enormous propellers. Their fundamental airfoil research and data publications, especially with respect to laminar flow sections saved much time for designers. They made design contributions or tested 137 different aircraft types between 1941 and 1944 or more than half of all military aircraft development programs. In July 1944 alone, they had projects touching seventy-eight different aircraft types.[32]

The Langley drag reduction program involved mounting the full-size aircraft in the 30 × 60-foot (9.1 × 18.3-m) Full-Scale Wind Tunnel to measure the forces and rates at certain flight conditions. Where the actual aircraft was too big to fit the test section (such as a bomber or flying boat), an accurate large-scale model was mounted. The first test was with all protuberances removed, such as exhaust stacks, antennae, and guns, gaps sealed with tape, steps faired with putty, surface roughness removed, and sources of leaks through the structure sealed. The test was then repeated with individual components replaced or tape removed such that the changes in data represented the effects of that change. Various corrective measures like added fairings could also be tested and a complete 'drag clean-up' report provided the customer. This methodology was also validated through flight testing. Between April 1938 and October 1940, eleven aircraft went through this process with Langley reducing drag by as much as half and improving performance by as much as 10 percent. The confidential reports of these results helped design teams focus on details in making choices that could substantially impact performance.[33]

Throughout the remainder of the war, the 'drag clean-up' tunnel test became almost routine for every aircraft or significant new model, with over thirty aircraft tested. The Full-Scale Wind Tunnel worked around the clock, seven days a week. While not all recommendations could be affected on a production line, on the order of 20-mph (32-kph) speed increase was realized. Design teams learned from these results such that they adopted lower drag features as a matter of course and later models were already reasonably well optimized without a tunnel entry. When the P-51B and P-63 came to Langley, little room for improvement was found, yielding just a 3-mph (4.8-kph) increase for the Mustang and a 6-mph (10-kph) increase for the Bell P-63 Kingcobra.

Ames built a 40 × 80-foot (12 × 24-m) full-scale facility, the largest wind tunnel in the world, which began operating in June 1944 to augment the Langley capacity. Among its smaller work-horse tunnels, Ames possessed a 16-foot (4.9-m) high-speed tunnel (680 mph/1,094 kph), an innovative 12-foot (3.7-m) low turbulence tunnel, and a supersonic tunnel was under design. Langley possessed a unique vertical tunnel permitting data collection on the spin characteristics of an aircraft model. Results from the spin tests helped correct adverse behavior via design changes before the hazardous prototype flight tests by which point such changes were costlier to introduce. However, the tunnel was also used to understand bad characteristics and suggest cures, such as the ventral strake added to the P-59.

The service labs and NACA fostered continuing research and development of high-lift devices. Langley had long performed tests of such features. Wing-trailing edge flaps had continued to evolve to include segments that slid aft as well as rotating down to increase wing area (Fowler flaps). Also introduced were slots between these surfaces and the main plane of the wing for higher pressure air beneath the airfoil to flow up and through the slot to help reenergize the upper surface flow. Full-span flaps, the outer segments also serving as drooped ailerons or spoilers, were also pursued (see Chapter 2). Such features were already appearing on production aircraft as war dawned. The Lockheed Hudson and associated Model 14 aircraft possessed wing outboard leading edge "letterbox" slots to combat wingtip stall during the low-speed approach and landing enabled by the slotted Fowler flaps and prop wash over the inboard segments. Full-span fixed leading edge slots or articulated slats, sliding forward at low airspeed to open such slots, permitted high-pressure air from below to flow over to the top of the wing to enhance low-speed lift. Such devices were being flown and results reported by the time warplanes of World War II were being designed.

Maneuvering flaps were also introduced. These were either dedicated devices or low-angle settings of existing high-lift flaps (provided they were suitably robust) serving to permit tighter turns in combat with less concern with the stall of what were typically high wing load designs.

Aerodynamic research has always sought to increase lift and reduce drag. Having achieved cantilevered wings, flush riveting, retractable undercarriage,

A British Hudson V on landing approach shows off the Fowler flaps and leading-edge slots. Lockheed was incorporating such high lift devices on their commercial transports before the war. The "letterbox" slots allow high-pressure air from below the wing to pass through to the top of the wing and combat tip stall of the wings at high angles of attack that degrades low-speed aileron roll effectiveness. (*San Diego Air & Space Museum*)

enclosed cockpits, and cowled engines, the next hoped-for reduction in drag was expected to be found in the wing itself. Drag is endemic to the generation of lift, promoting the transition from a smooth laminar flow on the surface of a wing to a turbulent flow, followed by separation with a loss of lift and a great increase in drag. Promoting laminar flow across more of the wing chord (width) does much to reduce overall drag. This was achieved to some extent by the introduction of special airfoils that keep the flow laminar to as much as 60 percent of the cord length from the leading edge whereas more common airfoils trip to turbulent a mere 15 to 30 percent back.

Developed at NACA Langley, the research that produced the laminar foil section, enabled by a new low-turbulence tunnel, had begun in June 1938 with Eastman Jacobs as the principal engineer. The laminar flow wing ideally reduced profile drag by two-thirds, but practical applications yielded much less efficiency.[34] The section that emerged was unusual in having the greatest thickness near or behind the half-chord point. This was termed a natural laminar flow section as opposed to mechanical methods of achieving this, such as sucking off the boundary layer or blowing higher energy air into the layer. The NACA issued a classified preliminary report in June 1939 and details were not openly available until after the war. Work on the next generation of such airfoils continued throughout.

The laminar flow airfoil brought forth flight research efforts to assess its practical effectiveness and comparison with the theoretical and tunnel results. Very smooth scale models in a wind tunnel, or even with modeled surface roughness, was good for verifying theoretical results but not for estimating true performance in an airplane application. Building a full-scale wing introduce imperfections such as butt or lap joints and rivet lines (even flush). Operational use would generate insect residue and dirt plus scrapes, dents, and paint flaking. Although instrumented "gloves" were attached to wings of existing aircraft to collect laminar flow flight test data, the researchers sought to measure gross performance with full wings. Fortunately, Langley did not have to wait long before getting to opportunity to test a practical application.

The laminar flow airfoil was soon being applied to many of the new aircraft under development by the U.S. armed forces. The first to reach production was the North American Mustang, developed for Great Britain but also taken up by the USAAC as the P-51. Gaining insight into the practical application of the laminar flow airfoil was cause for NACA to seek examples of the P-51 for evaluation, and the two XP-51s were eventually acquired. Aircraft 41-38 was sent to Langley for evaluation in 1941 and 41-39 followed in March 1943.[35] Langley would also operate P-15B, D, and H airframes at various times.

It became evident that the laminar characteristics were greatly reduced by insufficiently high manufacturing tolerances and the introduction of surface roughness by wear, chipped paint, and dirty residue.[36] Surface ripple or waves during high lift production and maneuvering also detracted from maintaining laminar flow. Regardless, the Germans put the wing of a captured Mustang in a wind tunnel and concluded the drag was markedly less than any similar German airfoil, and overall performance of the aircraft was superior aerodynamically.[37] Although the Mustang was noted as possessing among the best lift-to-drag ratio of World War II fighters, the laminar flow characteristics of the wing was not a major player in that achievement.

Performance of the original laminar flow airfoil in actual application and service use was felt to be less than desirable. Later refinement of laminar flow sections helped improve these aspects. These superior laminar flow sections were applied to the A-26, P-51H, P-63, P-59, and P-80.

Allies were also assisted by aerodynamics work as foreign (essentially British) aircraft came to NACA for evaluation. One benefit was Langley advising against the practice of covering the Hawker Hurricane fighter with heavy canvas, as was the RAF practice. This disrupted wing leading edge airflow and contributed to adverse stall characteristics.[38]

The NACA assisted significantly in curing problems and guiding beneficial design changes to improve performance and handling qualities of most American military airplanes. A good example is the Bell P-63 Kingcobra. Langley was provided two P-63As (42-68861 and 42-68889), which were flight tested in the baseline configuration and placed in the wind tunnel to measure drag increments. Most of this work was performed during 1943. Several ready improvements included raising the dorsal carburetor scoop above the surface boundary layer for greater ram pressure and adding a ventral strake to improve spin recovery. These features were adopted for the P-63C and later models. Improving efficiency of the wing leading edge radiator inlets was achieved through a modest redesign. Addressing longitudinal stability saw enlarged tailplanes (adopted for production) plus closer spacing on the elevator ribs to combat fabric ballooning, in addition to a recommended change in tail-plane incidence. For directional stability, they added 2.49 feet^2 (0.23 m^2) to the vertical tail, making it taller. The tall tail was adopted for the P-63F, though with a dorsal extension.[39]

Extensive NACA flight testing and consultation with military and industry agencies led to many design changes. In one case, the roll performance of the P-51 was doubled through aileron deflection angle increases and aerodynamic rebalancing for lighter stick forces, markedly improving combat effectiveness. The whole of this work, with dozens of aircraft evaluated, provided data for the 1941 specification describing suitable airplane handling qualities and control harmony for the first time in the US.[40] The armed forces leveraged off the document to create their own, suitable for their missions. By being specific as to desirable handling characteristics in engineering terms, manufacturers had more potential for creating a satisfactory warplane with less extended development. Part of the motivation was the deterioration in handling qualities of most of the principal combat aircraft during their evolution as weight, power, and speed grew, and external protuberances multiplied. Artificial means of addressing the issue, such as aileron boost in the P-38J to keep control forces tolerable while ensuring suitable roll acceleration, demanded some quantitative measure of improvement.

The NACA probably "touched" every American military aircraft of the war through its technical publications or more directly through wind tunnel and flight testing. At Langley, performance and flying qualities were the specialties, and the staff were often given examples to test. Among many modifications of the Bell P-63 Kingcobra, they introduced the taller vertical tail on this P-63A (compare the "before" image to the "after" image at top) to address directional stability deficiencies, a feature adopted for the P-63F. (*NASA*)

Most advanced flight control technologies were largely experimental and immature before the war. These included autopilots, control system boost with an artificial feel for the pilot, and stability augmentation systems like yaw dampers. All these had to be rapidly brought to the stage of mass production and combat introduction within just a few short years, though not always with infinite success. The Americans excelled with such innovations among the earliest production examples. These were preferable to altering control surfaces and expanding tail areas that more profoundly impacted production.

Compressibility effects such as marked drag rise and stability changes were also investigated. Langley helped to perfect the dive recovery flaps that permitted pull-out from a locked-in steep dive near supersonic speed (Mach tuck) that saved lives (Chapter 5). The United States lacked a wind tunnel suitable for testing to supersonic speeds. However, the engineers made progress substituting flight test data (Chapter 5).

Other important flight trials were dives to measure tail air loads (distributed pressure forces) at high speeds after a rash of structural failures in high-speed rolling pull-outs. The P-39, P-40, P-47, SB2C, and other aircraft had suffered failures and fatal crashes, bring the Army to approach NACA in 1942 seeking better understanding and solutions. The loads were measured in the wind tunnel and flight, usually during stalls, high-speed dive recoveries, and in the presence of transonic buffet (Chapter 5). These were hazardous tests. During one P-39N flight, NACA test pilot Larry Clousing suffered partial failure of the tail but managed to bring the aircraft and his data back to base. One finding was alarming bulging of the fabric on the elevator, sometimes varying over time with buffet, and even bulging or wrinkling of metal skins, contributed to unpredicted high air loads. The same phenomena accounted for excessive air loads and failures of P-47 tails. The Mustang suffered the same malady, the bulging of elevator fabric promoting violent 6-*g* pitch oscillations in transonic dives. This led to metal covering in later models of the P-51.[41] The resulting reports from all the testing greatly assisted design teams who had, in some cases, underestimated the loads.

A NACA tail loads investigation was also conducted in the wake of B-24 empennage failures and fatal crashes that were undermining confidence in this vitally important bomber. With a fully instrumented tail on the test aircraft, the flight testing initially revealed only that the loads appeared to be within design limits. However, it was discovered that landings produced excessive loads via sympathetic vibrations with the wheels spinning-up on the main landing gear struts. Over multiple landings, these vibrations fatigued the metal of the tail until it failed under normal flight loads. While the appropriate measures were taken to correct the Liberator's problem, a broader examination of landing loads in other aircraft was undertaken.[42] The shock loads on landing impacts became another area of research. The structures team came up with other design considerations, practices, and materials that helped shave weight from designs—always a priority in aircraft development.

Similar research was undertaken to examine the effects of the excessive loaded weight of large aircraft—an all-to-common wartime practice. Encounters with atmospheric gusts were overloading structure and accelerating fatigue. Langley employed their new Gust Tunnel to investigate the effects and was able to determine how quickly the degradation occurred. These results likely prompted alteration of inspection regimen and informed factors to be applied in future designs.[43]

The area of aircraft structures was addressed further. The services, NACA, and each manufacturer devoted energies in determining the ways to build the strongest yet lightest structure that did not flutter and could be safely tested. Existing methods of ground static testing were improved while the use of instrumentation and flight test techniques became more methodical. The employment of telemetry to permit monitoring and recording of data in flight was expanded for greater test safety. The Navy also pioneered the use of remote control of aircraft for exceptionally hazardous tests such as maximum load factor pull-outs from limit airspeed dives for dive bombers.

Another hazardous test program undertaken by NACA for the benefit of reducing dangers for military pilots was the investigation of aileron buzz. This arises at high speed where unsteady shock waves pulsate across the hinge line of the control surface and produce high-frequency oscillation. Apart from the structural failure potential, to include exciting flutter, this also causes annoying if not violently hazardous motion of the control column. Tests with the P-63 and P-80 yielded a better understanding of the phenomenon and design of a hydraulic damper or boost system that prevented the feedback to the pilot control, or installation of vortex generators atop the wing ahead of the ailerons. Clousing again was a principal pilot in this effort and, again, came away with damage: a P-80 with a buckled aileron trailing edge after a dive to Mach 0.866.[44]

Langley was also called on to assess how to reduce impact dispersal during bombing and tests were performed with a B-17G (44-8460). Langley found poor tolerance on bomb casing and fin assembly manufacturing, or bent fins from rough handling, that contributed to poor aerodynamic uniformity between individual weapons.

Helicopters were an area in which the Americans focused while the U.K. expended little effort on rotorcraft. The NACA was drawn into the growing rotorcraft segment of aviation to ensure safety, address concerns, and generally acquire knowledge supporting future efforts. Among the earliest projects was assisting the USAAC in correcting issues with the YR-1 autogyro. Langley also acquired a Pitcairn PAA-1 for evaluation that included mounting a camera above the rotor to photograph blade motion throughout the rotation cycle. Tests were then performed in concert with the Air Corps to understand and resolve several rotorcraft problems, particularly ground resonance and promoting vibration suppression.

To evaluate the hydrodynamics of seaplanes and optimize hull design, a model of the airplane, or just the hull or float, was towed through water at various speeds and attitudes with the resulting forces and rates measured as in a wind tunnel. Langley had built such a tow tank during the interwar years. This was over half a mile long at 2,960 feet (902 m), with 24-foot (7.3-m) width and 12-foot (3.7-m) depth (4 million gallons). The overhead carriage for towing the precision model and measuring the data could exceed 80 mph (129 kph). The smaller Tank No. 2 complement No. 1 when it began operating in 1942. A mechanism could produce periodic waves to study behavior in various sea states. These facilities aided designs in making for successful take-off and landing without skipping or porpoising, or adverse spray. There was also an impact basin, 360 feet (110 m) long, 24 feet (7.3 m) wide, and 8 feet (2.4 m) deep, that could move a model at 70 mph (113 kph) and 16-fps (4.9-mps) vertical velocity. Full-size wingtip floats were tested in the basin at realistic worse-case impact velocities to collect data

Ensuring the aircraft structure was strong but also light required careful design and test. Manufacturers, the military services, and the NACA all worked to improve analytical and test techniques to advance the state-of-the-art. Here a P-51D fuselage undergoes loads testing at North American Aviation in Inglewood, California, on May 10, 1944, portions of the structure rigidly restrained and others acted upon by hydraulic actuators to model a flight condition that is buckling the skin. (*NASA*)

This F6F-5 is raised above the deck in preparation for a "drop test" at Grumman Aircraft, Bethpage, Long Island. This represents a high sink rate landing and ensures the structure is suitably designed to withstand the resulting impact loads. The airframe already shows evidence of this abuse. (*Northrop Grumman History Center*)

Frank Piasecki and a small team of engineers, P-V Engineering Forum, developed a small but remarkably successful PV-2 demonstration helicopter. The Navy took notice and gave the firm a contract to develop an advanced naval helicopter. As part of that, the PV-2 rotor was evaluated in the Langley full-scale tunnel at the end of the war. (*NASA*)

supporting suitable structural design. These NACA resources proved vital in ensuring suitable sea handling of the Navy's flying boats, especially as their weight grew over time.

Considerable work had been performed since NACA's formation and up to the war in providing suitable engine cowling design for reduced drag but suitable engine cooling. Tighter cowlings with smaller air intake and exit areas were sought to reduce cooling drag. All air-cooled engine installations benefited from NACA's reports on these efforts. Considerations working against the liquid-cooled engine was the added weight of the radiator, vulnerability to enemy fire, real or perceived lesser reliability, and the lower fuel efficiency compared with air-cooled engines. The vulnerability was the U.S. Navy's rationale for avoiding inlines, plus not desiring to store the inflammable glycol coolant aboard ship. However, power increases might be more easily attained with the liquid-cooled than the alternative, which usually meant additional banks of cylinders behind the front (for the common radial engine) that were more challenging to cool effectively. Unlike the inlines, which could be "buried" within the fuselage, adding rows of radial cylinders added weight to the nose while further blocking the pilot's view. Still, the NACA contributed to design and improvement of radiator air intakes for greater efficiency and solved problems on such aircraft as the P-51B (duct

The development of flying boats required careful design of the boat hulls to ensure suitable take-off and landing characteristics. The NACA helped to facilitate this process with long tow tanks at Langley in which models of the airplane were drawn along and pressed into the water at various attitudes while the forces and rates were measured. Here the Hughes-Kaiser HK-1 giant flying boat is undergoing tests in Tank No. 1 during 1943. (*NASA*)

"rumble"), P-63, and F7F, to include learning to stand the base of the duct away from the surrounding surface to bypass the boundary layer.

Although the Air Corps had helped fund some liquid-cooled development, especially the Allison V-1710, this was not the same thing as providing research resources. This engine represented the hopes of those promoting inline liquid-cooled aero engine with its attendant drag reduction. Yet, it continued to suffer so many developmental and production problems that Arnold sent Doolittle to help resolve them. In the P-38 application, it would occasionally suffer cylinder pre-ignition (detonation) so severe the engine would come apart. In the U.K., the problem appears to have been aggravated by the local aromatic fuels. The P-38s operated there as escort fighters were suffering so many engine changes that they were eventually transferred out of the theater.

NACA engine R&D focused attention on carburetors and fuel injection, ignition, averting spark plug fouling, avoiding knock and pre-ignition, oil foaming, raising peak rpm, improving heat dissipation, increasing the capacity and efficiency of superchargers, and other elements of aero-propulsion. Fuels and lubricants also needed to be addressed. The Allies adopted 100-octane fuel by 1942, and 100/130 in mid-1944, that allowed higher manifold pressures if care was taken to avoid 'knocking' or uneven combustion within the cylinders. This was an advantage over the Axis who continued to use 87-octane fuel. A development program was underway for grade 94/114 and the "super" fuel 110/150. Work was also done on synthetic fuels, additives to help avoid knock, and avoiding fuel loss to evaporation.

The NAF in Phily and the Power Plant Laboratory at Wright Field were devoted to testing engines to ensure they met spec, not necessarily for R&D. The new NACA Cleveland laboratory would step a bit beyond research and into development because the need was so urgent. Within a year of its establishment, the country would be at war and research took a backseat to assist manufacturers to hasten engine development and resolve problems to ensure rapid production of safe and effective power plants. Apart from a valuable propeller laboratory, the facility sought a propulsion altitude wind tunnel more capable than any other in the country or any known in the world. The goals were 490 mph (798 kph) at 30,000 feet (9,144 m) and 250 mph (402 kph) at 1,000 feet (305 m) with a 20-foot (6.1-m) test section.[45] This would be achieved with an enormous physical plant to pumped down the pressure and chilled the air (as low as -48 degrees F/-44

Prototype aircraft featuring the latest in propulsion technology could also serve as *de facto* testbeds of that equipment, even if the aircraft did not go into production. An example is the Bell XP-39E with the Allison V-1710-47, a supercharger driven by auxiliary hydraulic pressure, wing root radiators, and several options for propeller including a four-blade unit. Although production as the P-76 was canceled, testing continued to collect data on the propulsion system. (*Lloyd Jones collection*)

degrees C) simulating operation at high altitude. This would prove especially useful in testing the new turbine engines, to include placing the entire P-59A (save for the outer wing panels) into the test section, followed by the P-80A.

The introduction of jet engines was another fundamental change in aircraft that gave generous room for innovative thinking. It was found that the high-velocity jet efflux at the exhaust entrained surrounding air into the flow. This altered the expected flow around the empennage surfaces and affected aircraft stability and control. At NACA Ames, the engineers considered the best means of introducing the large volume of air into the fuselage and so to the face of the engine with high efficiency but without increasing drag. Of their solutions, the most innovative was the NACA flush inlet that induced flow into the ramped cavity. It saw some use as a jet engine intake but more in the decades to follow for any low-drag air inlet.

Working with fundamentally new technology like jet engines drove much innovation. The need for a low-drag inlet was the inspiration for the NACA flush inlet seen on this Ryan FR-4 with a mechanical door to close it off and used in innumerable applications ever since. The FR-4, follow-on to the FR-1 Fireball, was in development during the late war years but did not reach the hardware stage before cessation of hostilities. (*Jay Miller collection*)

2

Aeronautical Achievements

Aeronautics had always moved ahead quickly during the first decades of manned flight. Even without wars and government funding, research and experimentation flourished in the United States. Universities, manufacturers, government labs, and private citizens all dived in and results were reported at technical symposia, in journals, and in the popular press. The motive was unchanging—the thrill of making aircraft fly better for potential profit, notoriety, or combat advantage. Where the technical risk made it wise to test new ideas separate from a new airplane *en route* to production, modified test aircraft provided data to augment laboratory results.

The efforts took many forms. Flying new airfoils and improving airflow were common tasks, seeing unusual alterations to the subject test aircraft. Devising and trying new flight control techniques were also popular in seeking to reduce aircraft weight and improve maneuverability. High-lift devices were all the rage in the years between the wars in pursuit of low landing speeds, spot landings, enhanced lift for short take-off and landing (STOL—not an acronym then in use but adopted herein for simplicity), or just getting a heavy airplane off in a standard distance. Apart from NACA contributions to these technologies, there were manufacturer examples to assist in application to warplanes. Military contracts were the impetus for designers to adopt new technologies in meeting ambitious performance goals. Yet data were required to assist the designers.

Flying Wind Tunnels

Wind tunnels have their limits in terms of airspeeds, size of test articles, and errors associated with the methodology. Collecting data in flight is always beneficial in validating or augmenting the lab results. In its simplest form, the test article could be flown in near-freestream conditions affixed to an airplane. Test instrumentation was sampled from within the cabin or cockpit.

Langley employed a Douglas B-18A bomber as an aerodynamic test aircraft. Airfoils shapes were mounted above the cabin while equipment inside measured data including lift and drag forces, making the aircraft a "flying wind tunnel." In November 1941, the aircraft was used to test an airfoil mounted just forward of the vertical stabilizer to collect boundary-layer and drag force data in which flight condition and angle of attack were varied independently. Pressures in the wake were measured via a "rake" of pressure-sensing tubes. A similar approach was applied using a Martin A-30.

In validating the laminar flow theoretical and wind tunnel results, flight data was sought to answer the question about practical application. Could wings be built with fine enough manufacturing tolerance to capture the airfoil shape and realize the benefits? Would normally collected dirt and bug residue degrade the laminar characteristics to insignificance? The earliest NACA flight testing of a laminar flow airfoil employed an airfoil "glove" test panel affixed over a portion of their B-18A's port wing in spring 1941. This was essentially a new airfoil shape wrapped around the existing wing section for a small portion of the span. Such gloves typically had pressure taps to measure values across a chord line and rakes at the trailing edge to measure the boundary layer pressure profile.

In 1940, the NACA proposed an experimental airplane to observe the practicality of laminar flow airfoil technology as applied to an entire aircraft—what might have been the first "X-plane." The armed forces could not be aroused to pursue a unique research aircraft so the NACA engineers conceived a purpose-built Laminar Flow Airplane. The design had many interesting features including very small tail surfaces at just 5 percent of the wing area for reduced static stability and trim drag, and pusher propellers to eliminate prop wash over the wings. Design and construction of an entire airplane was not in the NACA charter, nor was there the budget for such an undertaking forthcoming as the looming war changed priorities. Nothing came of the proposal apart from preliminary wind tunnel testing.

The NACA acquisition of the XP-51s and a P-51B (43-12111) gave the earliest data from a purpose-built airplane application of the laminar flow airfoil. These were tested at Langley and Ames beginning no earlier than late 1942. These had the usual taps and rakes. It became clear that the actual lift-to-drag ratio produced by the Mustang wings were less than predicted by theory and tunnel data owing to manufacturing imperfections, service wear, and dirt accumulation. It was desired to collect the data in the absence of propeller slipstream, so the propeller was removed from one of the P-51s and propulsion ducts sealed. The aircraft was cleaned and waxed, and precision test instrumentation added. The Mustang was towed behind a P-61A (42-5572) and released at 25,000 to 30,000 feet (7,620 to 9,144 m) for dives and glide recovery. At the bottom of the dive, the aircraft was reaching 500 mph (885 kph) and approaching Mach 0.76. The brief and quiet missions ended with landings on the vast dry lakebed surface at Muroc. During the third test flight on September 5, 1944, the tow lines from the Black Widow prematurely released and whipped back to wrap around the fighter. Despite partially jammed controls and a mere 1,200 feet altitude (366 m), test pilot Jim Nissen managed a survivable crash landing 1 mile from the Muroc base hospital.

Above: This Douglas B-18 (photographed November 5, 1941) was employed as a testbed by NACA Langley. It is modified to carry airfoil shapes above the cabin to measure lift force and pressures in the wake via a "rake" of pressure lines. This installation appears to be investigating the effects of an upwind surface like a wing on a downstream control surface like an elevator with a tab. (*National Museum of the United States Air Force*)

Below: The same B-18A was modified to test a new low-drag airfoil as a glove in the port wing. Air pressure is sampled at multiple points on the surface of the glove via flush taps to determine where the boundary layer transitions to turbulent flow. The aircraft was photographed in the first months of 1941 at Langley with a Republic XP-41 in the background. (*NASA*)

This is the model tested in the 12-foot wind tunnel of the Laminar Flow Airplane conceived in 1940 by NACA Langley engineers. The proposed research aircraft would have provided data on the practical application of the new laminar flow airfoil. Although not pursued, it is a notable design in the small tail surfaces, pusher propeller layout, and lift-generating fuselage. (*NASA*)

To collect clean data on the laminar flow airfoil wings of the Mustang, NACA towed a P-51B with its propeller removed. Jim Nissen piloted the aircraft behind the P-61A over the Muroc range and was released for glide to a lakebed landing. The testing ended when the tow lines (probably enhanced in this NACA illustration) prematurely released and whipped back to wrap around Nissen's airplane, forcing a crash landing which he survived. (*Jay Miller collection*)

This permitted a quick trip to the clinic for an X-ray, but he had cut the power line to the building in his descent so this proved futile. Although the Mustang was wrecked, the data were saved.[1]

A short time later, the NACA was able to collect similar data on an instrumented AAF P-80 which could exceed 550 mph (885 kph) in a dive with the engine operating and its latest-generation laminar flow airfoil. Diving from 40,000 feet (1,292 m), pilot Larry Clousing was touching 600 mph (966 kph) and Mach 0.85. This was the jet's limit as aileron buzz reached prohibitive amplitude and aerodynamic changes during recovery became hazardous owing to compressibility. This experiment also came to an unfortunate end when the engine flamed out at 30,000 feet (9,144 m) and would not relight. Clousing was unable to pump the gear fully down and locked before settling onto the Muroc lakebed. The gear collapsed, but he walked away and the data recordings were safe.[2]

Despite NACA findings, the military began specifying laminar flow wings for new types under development. Even lacking a contract, manufacturers sought to understand the airfoil and began testing them as gloves on aircraft conveniently at hand. Beech modified one of their AT-10s (42-2272) with extended leading edges to the inboard wing sections to create the semblance of a laminar flow section. This Model 25 was a simple twin-engined trainer built mostly of wood. Comprehensive airflow data was collected and the aircraft dived from high altitude to check for an expected increase in the critical Mach number (Chapter 5).[3] Grumman explored the potential of using a laminar flow wing on their F6F Hellcat. Begun in February 1942, the G-54 study concluded the benefits did not outweigh the need for rapid production. No test article was flown. Another aircraft fitted with wing gloves to investigate natural laminar flow airfoils was a Northrop A-17 (35-122). Drawn from the 90th Aero Squadron at Barksdale Field, the machine was passed to Langley for propulsion tests. It was eventually fitted with a 5-foot-wide inboard laminar flow glove on the starboard wing with pressure probe rakes behind the trailing edge. The smooth wooden glove was altered several times and the left wing also eventually received a glove. The landing gear had to be fixed down.

Metal gloves representing the airfoil of the Douglas C-74 Globemaster transport under design was also fitted to both wings of the A-17. These had various skin joints and finishing smoothness as expected from production. Representing the full-scale wing surface, the gloves exceeded the chord length and covered more than half the span of the underlying wing (out to the ailerons), also passing under the center fuselage. Eventually, both wings had a two-blade propeller mounted ahead of the leading edge to study swirling prop wash effects. These were driven by a small auxiliary motor, possibly in the glove's root beneath the fuselage.[4] The tests helped to establish the required manufacturing tolerances for the C-74 wing to meet the desired aircraft performance. However, poor measurement techniques on this semi-laminar flow airfoil testbed produced unsatisfactory data. The aircraft was returned to its original configuration and passed back to the service where it was retired on August 1, 1943.

Another testbed for airfoils flown in free-flight, instead of collecting data strictly in wind tunnels, was this Northrop A-17 (35-122). A fine view of the "glove" fitted over the port wing shows how smooth it was via careful assembly and polishing. The fitting extending beyond the trailing edge were mounts for pressure sensing probes to assess how laminar the flow remained after passing the full length of the chord. (*Lloyd Jones collection*)

This NACA P-51B (43-12105) was used for aerodynamic tests associated with its laminar flow wing and for other data collection. Here, in July 1945 at Langley, it is fitted with a lengthened vertical tail plus leading-edge extension, and a "glove" on the wing with a rake of pressure probes to collect wake data of more uniform airflow. A camera is installed behind the seat to photograph the tuffs visible on the wing. (*NASA*)

The A-17 semi-laminar flow airfoil testbed ultimately had gloves that almost completely submerged the primary A-17 wing. It also had a motor driving propellers ahead of each glove leading edge as one configuration. The flight tests collected data supporting development for the Douglas C-74 transport. (*Lloyd Jones collection*)

Even Langley's P-51B 43-12105 was fitted with wing glove panels plus trailing-edge rake and boundary layer pressure probes for measuring profile drag of a different airfoil. Flight testing began in July 1945.

Forcing Matters

Instead of natural laminar flow, the aerodynamicists also explored forcing the boundary layer to a smooth laminar profile by either sucking off the air at the surface or blowing air out to energize the layer and keep it attached for more of the chord length rather than separate into a high-drag turbulent layer. This boundary layer control (BLC) was entirely new and fundamental data needed to be collected before any production application could be considered. Such BLC work was commonly done with gloves over the wings of a test aircraft that also accommodated an added air compressor to suck or blow via slots in the glove surface and data collected via the usual assortment of taps and rakes, or cameras capturing the behavior of tufts taped to the surface to visualize the point of separated flow.[5]

One of the principal proponents of BLC was Professor Edward A. Stalker, and his work had gained the attention of the AAF. Stalker's employer, Dow Chemical of Bay City, Michigan, was awarded a $50,000 contract in 1942 for a practical BLC test to validate wind tunnel results. This funded radical modifications to an L-1 (40-255) with a new plywood wing employing both suction of the turbulent boundary layer and blowing. The wing had a two-segment, full span Fowler flap encompassing 40 percent of the chord and of very high camber, the first segment deflecting up to 35 degrees and the trailing edge to 82 degrees. The "blower" was installed in a tall fairing above the cabin, driven by an 80-hp (60-kW) Franklin O-180-1 motor within the fuselage. This sucked boundary layer air in through the three span-wise slots created at the interfaces between the wing primary structure and flap segments. With flaps extended, the suction helping to keep the flow attached through the large upper surface turn. This air was expelled out the back of the fairing, the adjustable louvers controlling the blower flow, but also exhausted from a duct just ahead of the aileron with flaps extended (blowing). The aileron had an additional 22 degrees of deflection, or 33 degrees drooped with flaps extended.

The "humpback" L-1 was taken up for the first time by Maj. R. E. Horner on March 6, 1944, from Tri-City Airport, Michigan. A subsequent nineteen flights were performed by Dow's test pilot R. B. Gorrill. Principally seeking short take-off and landing distance, the lift coefficient was elevated to only 3.6 from 3.5. However, the added weight of the equipment made for a higher landing airspeed.[6] The machine was passed to Wright Field where the testbed was destroyed in a fatal accident while undergoing stall testing. It entered a spin from which Lt P. A. Hobe was unable to recover. It was clear much more could be done in the BLC field and such experimentation has continued to the present day where weight and complexity continued to work against any but a few production applications.

Instead of relying solely on slots to provide flow up and over-slotted flaps to keep the flow attached over the high camber, air could be artificially blown over the flaps as another manner of BLC. Blowing into the slot helped to entrain freestream air through the slot for enhanced effect. This was probably tested by several entities, with Beech introducing it with their AT-10 testbed. They placed a four-cylinder Continental engine in the aft fuselage to operate a pump pressurizing a volume inside the wing. The air was expelled out holes in the aft spar to flow over the top of the flaps.[7]

The ultimate gloved aircraft was a P-38E (41-2048) specially modified and first flown on June 2, 1943, by Tony LeVier. The center pod was extended 30 inches (0.8 m) forward of the wing and 76 inches (1.9 m) aft, accommodating special test equipment. A new canopy enclosure was fitted over the pilot and a second cockpit. Although the aft station had full controls, it was usually occupied by a flight test

Photographed on July 8, 1944, this Stinson L-1 Vigilant (40-255, originally an O-49) has been radically modified for boundary layer control (BLC) experimentation. The aluminum panel on the side of the fuselage, with an exhaust tube emerging, testifies to the motor installed within driving a blower inside the "hump" above with exhaust louvers at the rear. With flaps full down and ailerons drooped, the upper surface suction slots are evident. (*National Archives*)

This eye-catching, highly modified P-38E was nicknamed Swordfish by the Lockheed employees after seeing its rakish extended center fuselage and nose boom. It included a second cockpit and the aircraft was employed in aerodynamic flight experiments. In this image, 41-2048 is seen with laminar flow airfoil "gloves" over the standard wings, the port glove featuring boundary layer blowing and a "rake" of pressure sensing tubes behind. (*Jay Miller collection*)

engineer who operated the test equipment and recorded data. The long sensor boom protruding from the nose earned the aircraft the moniker "Swordfish," although most simply called it "Nosey." Lockheed claimed this was the fastest P-38, topping 525 mph (845 kph) in dives, earning it the name "Mad Meteor" from the pilots.

One project for the P-38E research aircraft was BLC applied to one of the laminar flow gloves installed over a portion of the wings just outboard of the nacelles. The port glove featured slots in the surface through which air could be expelled from within the glove seeking to reduce drag. The pressurized air came via engine exhaust bleed air with external ducting adjacent to the boom.

Enhancing Control

Improving flight control or simplifying same was an ongoing research effort conducted in wind tunnels and via flight test of modified aircraft. One such was exploring the advantages of an all-moving "flying" horizontal stabilizer. This was to reduce adverse effects of wing downwash impingement on the tail, maintain elevator effectiveness in the presence of compressibility effects, improve effectiveness at landing and take-off speeds for greater center of gravity (CG) range, or permitting the area of the tail to be reduced for no change in effectiveness. Although a trimming tail with elevators, possessing a few degrees of travel, was known to retain longitudinal control effectiveness, eliminating the elevator and using the entire 'stabilator' as a control surface in its own right, with large travel, was promising and worth exploring. The fear was stalling the surface and losing longitudinal control altogether.

An all-moving stabilizer with servo tabs was tested on the singular XP-42 in 1942 at Langley as the first such experiment in the U.S. The 'stabs' were essentially the same size as the original XP-42 horizontal surfaces although of higher aspect ratio. Pivoting at the 24 percent chord line, foam rudder filled the gap between the moving surface and aft fuselage. A careful arrangement of servo tab and bobweights gave such low stick forces throughout the stab travel that test pilots felt uneasy, fearing they would overstress the aircraft with excessively fast stick longitudinal inputs. Consequently, this was altered to geared unbalanced tabs and with a spring in the system to give more conventional stick force per maneuvering g.[8] A cockpit control could change the gearing ratio to pilot preference and mode of flight. On take-off, pushing the nose down to lift the tail, it was noticed that during the motion there was a period of excessive nose-down pitch rate. This was determined to be due to the tail stalling at 10-degree trailing edge down and 13-degree tail-down airplane attitude. Consequently, maximum trailing edge down deflection was reduced to 6 degrees to avoid the stalled condition.

The XP-42 performed dives to respectable Mach numbers (compressibility region) and recovered with the benefit of the stabilator. The aircraft survived beyond the war until scrapped in 1947. The stab it helped develop would prove vital for aircraft approaching the speed of sound and then for swept-wing designs.

Among the flight research work with XP-51 41-38 was investigating the notably poor roll performance, which was half that of the Spitfire and Fw 190. The Army asked for more roll rate with no increase in stick forces. Through flight and tunnel testing, Langley increased the deflection travel by 70 percent and avoided excessive stick forces with aerodynamic balancing via a revised aileron profile. The profile change entailed beveled ailerons or surfaces with a compressed diamond section instead of the common taper. "False" wooden ribs were attached to the surface on the original aileron to which aluminum skin was secured. The added weight of the modification raised fears of reduced flutter margin and so testing was initially confined to 300 mph (483 kph) until entirely new ailerons were fabricated with the beveled section. A gap around the aileron trim tab was also eliminated. Aileron effectiveness was improved 55 to 70 percent up to 200 mph (322 kph) and 20 to 40 percent at higher speeds, although control forces did go up marginally. The deflection increase was introduced operationally along with aerodynamic balancing. The beveled profile was only adopted for the trailing edge. It was, however, used in modified form for the B-29 elevators.[9]

The possibility of building aircraft with V-tails or "butterfly" tails was also investigated. This offered the opportunity of reducing construction material, assembly time, weight, and drag. This required that the two trailing edge control

The sole XP-42 was turned to flight controls trials after years as a propulsion testbed. Its most notable modification was with all-moving stabilators shown here in flight and with details of the surfaces. Note it still has tabs that aided in reduced stick forces. (*NASA and Jay Miller collection*)

surfaces work as both elevators and rudders with the proper mixing of control inputs. It was important to explore this control technique as well as effects on stability.

Bell Aircraft of Buffalo, New York, undertook this work with the instigation of their engineer and test pilot Bob Stanley who had successfully built a glider pre-war with the empennage configuration. The P-63 Kingcobra, which he tested extensively, had its share of control problems and any idea for remedy was welcome. Stanley won Wright Field personnel over to the idea of an experimental program.

The XP-63 model with a notional V-tail was tested in the Langley 12-foot Free Flight tunnel on August 21, 1943. The first P-63A, 42-68861, was modified for proof of the fabrication design and ground tests. The tails were then installed on P-63A 42-69606. The standard horizontal tails were separated at the centerline and reconstructed with a 36-degree dihedral. A port side elevator was used on each to allow both to possess a trim tab. The control mixing was performed by a mechanism at the tail. The vertical tail was set aside but a ventral fin was included for more vertical surface area and suitable directional stability.

In nine and a half flight hours across a dozen sorties during spring 1945, the aircraft was subjected to the full regimen of stability and control trials to include spins. All appeared acceptable but for some deficiency in longitudinal control. Although the V-tail was considered for the P-63E, the advantages were too few to justify interrupting production to incorporate the change as the end of the war was in sight.[10]

In seeking a solution to P-63 stability and control issues that had seen many changes to the empennage surfaces, a change to a V-tail was attempted. This also held general promise for weight and drag reduction, plus less construction materials and time. At Bell Aircraft urging, this P-63A was modified for the testing that proved successful but nothing came of the effort so late in the war. (*Jay Miller collection*)

Another effort to collect flight test data on the unusual "butterfly tail" configuration saw this Beech AT-10 so modified. The wooden twin was an inexpensive test platform easily modified. Note that the extended leading edge of inboard wing sections that also marks this as Beech's laminar flow test aircraft. (*Jay Miller collection*)

Another aircraft modified to collect data on the V-tail was a Beech Aircraft AT-10 (42-2272). Set at a 40-degree angle, the twin surfaces were just 83 percent of the standard empennage surfaces area.[11] The test aircraft was flown just months after the war, in December 1945, about the time Beech was building their Model 35 Bonanza with an identical tail configuration. While the timing is significant, the AT-10 still bore military markings and so the work is expected to have been performed under Army auspices. The results were favorable with no control degradation, but the weight and drag reduction was meager (3-mph gain).

There was so much concern with the effectiveness of the empennage in the presence of shocks on the AAF's XS-1 notional supersonic testbed (Chapter 5) that a V-tail was considered but ultimately rejected.

Surrogates

Another method employed for testing aspects of a new aircraft design was surrogate testbeds. An example is a PT-19 trainer (41-20531) given the scaled tail and high aspect ratio tapered wing (value of twelve with 10 degrees dihedral) of a B-29. The Superfortress's unusually high wing loading was a concern and so flight test data were sought under MX-220.[12] The quarter-scale surfaces could be

This Fairchild PT-19A trainer has been modified by Boeing with B-29 bomber wings and empennage scaled to the light-plane. This surrogate testbed was a step beyond the wind tunnel to collect flight data on the performance of the aero surfaces and reduce program risk prior to construction of the prototype Superfortress. The forward cockpit was faired over and contained test instrumentation. (*The Peter M. Bowers Collection/The Museum of Flight*)

quickly modified and tested on the small trainer. Other aspects of the B-29 were tested on a B-17. Another example of a surrogate testbed was Hughes Aircraft's use of a Douglas A-20G bomber modified with the XF-11 photoreconnaissance aircraft's vertical tail to collect data supporting detailed design.

Rotor design for autogyros and helicopters was made difficult by the limits of instrumentation, data recording, and telemetry technology of the period, especially passing signals across rotating interfaces. Cameras in wind tunnels and above rotors of flying helicopters were one source of data, apart from measuring the resulting performance of an aircraft with rotor system revisions. The earliest rotor flight research was performed using some of the Kellett YG-1B autogyros the USAAC possessed. This included changes to explore collective blade pitch for accelerated take-off and a "jump" take-off capability. These trials were to be performed with the XR-2 (YR-1B 37-378 previously modified as the YR-1C), but this airframe had a short life owing to ground resonance claiming the aircraft. Another YG-1B (37-380) was modified as the XR-3 in seeking to understand and eliminate ground resonance plus exploring other vibration-induced problems. Data gathered from these tests were valuable in the helicopter development already underway. Once Sikorsky began delivering the R-4 and later helicopters, there were plentiful airframes for rotorcraft trails.[13] Yet at least one subscale rotor system testbed was created as an unmanned flight rig, either remotely piloted (radio or umbilical) or by simple mechanical programming.

Above: The Kellett XR-3 autogyro is seen fitted with a camera above the rotor to photograph blade motion during revolutions. Derived from a YG-1B, this machine possessed "jump take-off" capability and so was an important stepping stone to the long-sought helicopter. This particular aircraft was tested by the Army and NACA in understanding and resolving ground resonance that was initially the bane of rotorcraft. (*National Archives*)

Below: With at first little and then substantial resources given to helicopter development, progress was rapid. Sikorsky was the winner of all production contracts beginning with their initial practical helicopter, the R-4, here seen as a YR-4B (43-28255) in flight test at Langley with a data probe at the end of a nose boom. The NACA contributed only marginally to rotorcraft technology during the war, but their aerodynamics and control insights were valuable. (*NASA*)

Little is known of this subscale dual-rotation rotor flying test rig. The presence of the Army sergeant suggests it is a Wright Field lab effort. It appears to be battery-powered and controlled remotely, though an umbilical for power and signals may simply have been removed for the photograph. (*National Archives*)

Another means of collecting data on flight characteristics of a new airplane design prior to first flight is the free flight of a scale model dropped from an aircraft with data transmitted to a ground station. These might be remote controlled, have a timer and battery moving control surfaces in a pre-set sequence, or the surfaces set before take-off and drop. One wartime project known to have employed this technique was the Grumman F8F Bearcat using a quarter-scale radio-controlled drop model. The "mother ship" was a B-17F (42-3521) transferred to the Navy in 1943 to serve land-based heavy lifting tasks. It was stripped of its weapons and later upgraded to "G" standard. Designated PB-1 only on July 31, 1945, it was operated by the NAMC, or more specifically the Naval Air Experimental Station (probably referring to Mustin Field). The Bearcat initial suffered direction stability deficiencies that ultimately required a taller tail the model appeared to possess. It was employed post-war in high-speed dive tests.

To address the towed fuel glider XFG-1's spin problem (see Chapter 7), Capt. Adam J. Stolzenberger constructed a quarter-scale free-flight model of the "tailless" forward-swept wing aircraft at Wright Field. During August 1945, the glider was dropped from an M-Type Navy blimp flying from NAS Lakehurst, New Jersey, and flown via radio control. This permitted the spin modes and recovery techniques to be safely investigated, and the model recovered with a parachute. Motion picture film of the model motion was compared with film from a fatal spin accident event, and additional NACA spin tunnel work, to arrive at a safe recovery technique.

The Grumman F8F initial suffered directional control deficiencies, especially with the centerline external fuel tank. Drop of this quarter-scale Bearcat shape (under this Navy PB-1, a B-17F) may have been part of the engineering investigation. Hazardous tests like initial spin trials were also sometimes performed with such means, data transmitted via a telemetry antenna that may be protruding from the aft end of the model that was usually parachute recovered. (*National Archives*)

Captain Adam Stolzenberger shows off the quarter-scale model of the XFG-1 employed in drop spin tests. This was one measure of efforts to resolve the unfortunate spin characteristics of the manned aerodynamic testbed for the towed fuel glider that had claimed the life of one test pilot. The model was dropped from an airship and controlled remotely using target drone systems. (*National Archives*)

High Lift

Getting a carrier-based fighter off the deck at heavier weight held benefits without a catapult, especially for the small "jeep" carriers. Keeping landing speed down was equally vital for a carrier-based plane as weights rose with combat equipment additions.[14] Enhancing lift held this promise and Grumman followed up with their G-53 project. This was a hybrid created by installing full-span flaps (duplex flaps) to an F4F-4 (5262) fitted with F4F-3 non-folding wings. The inboard flaps were slotted and retained the standard pneumatic actuation. The outboard Fowler flaps forward of the ailerons were electrically actuated, sliding aft and down under the ailerons. First flight was in May 1942. The program came to a halt when test pilot Jimmy Taylor suffered a split-flap condition (different deflection angles side-to-side). The subsequent departure from controlled flight was not recoverable and Taylor died in the ensuing crash. The need for the design change was judged non-essential and not pursued to production.

In pursuit of STOL performance, Langley modified a Fairchild Model 22 procured by the Navy for NACA research and designated XR2K-1 (9998). In one of several iterations, the parasol wing was replaced in October 1940 with one possessing full-span cambered flaps. Having sacrificed the ailerons for lift generation, spoilers were installed for roll control. These "Zap" flaps, named after designer Ed Zap, were split flaps in which the hinge line moved aft with extension to effectively increase wing area and so provide more lift in addition to that lent by the greater camber. This was a half measure towards the Fowler flaps that also had one or more slots. The wing was built by Cunningham-Hall Aircraft and based on their earlier Hall high-lift wing.

An OS2U-4 model of the Kingfisher observation-scout floatplane was envisioned with enhanced lift. The initial production OS2U-1 (1681) was bailed to Northrop Aircraft of Hawthorne, California, for testing Zap flaps. Northrop was considering the flaps for their P-61 design. These sought to increase wing area by 25 percent when extended while maintaining a 55 mph (89 kph) landing speed. Under a September 25, 1940, contract, Northrop designed and built new wings spanning 36.5 feet (11.1 m) and encompassing 218 feet^2 (20 m^2) area with the full-span flaps and spoiler roll control.

This work gave birth in 1942 to two OS2U-2s (2189 and 3975) modified as XOS2U-4s with similar Zap flaps but adding wing folding. Instead of the one spoiler panel ahead of the aileron common on Kingfishers, this wing had three panels extending well inboard. The horizontal tail was also modified with straight taper and square tips. These features were to enhance stability accompanying a model with a more powerful engine. Vought modified 2189 while Douglas Aircraft took on 3975 by subcontracting to Vultee Aircraft of Downey, California. All remained on wheeled landing gear with a spin-recovery parachute added in the aft fuselage cone. To enhance longitudinal control at the expected low approach airspeeds, at least 2189 also received a variable camber (VARICAM) horizontal tail and elevator. This increased the percentage of horizontal tail devoted to

Getting a Grumman Wildcat off a shorter deck or at heavier weight without a catapult would help squeeze the most from the Navy fighter, especially on small carriers. Grumman explored this with a modified F4F-4 given the non-folding wing from a -3 modified with full-span Duplex flaps. The project was not essential and the idea was dropped after a split-flap condition led to the loss of the aircraft and test pilot. (*Northrop Grumman History Center*)

Above: The NACA acquired a commercial Fairchild 22 via the U.S. Navy, which designated it XR2K-1 with BuNo 9998. Following modification, it was flown in 1940 at Langley with "Zap flaps" that gave full-span lift enhancement mandating the use of spoilers for roll. Numbered 82 by NACA, it was photographed here on November 30, 1940, after a session in Langley's full-scale wind tunnel. (*NASA*)

Below: Northrop Aircraft performed the modification to this OS2U-1 (1681, first production example) to test Zap flaps. Also intended for their P-61 night fighter, the flaps slid out to expand wing area, further enhancing low airspeed lift while spoilers provided roll authority. A new wing was built to accommodate the flaps designed by Ed Zap. (*Vought Aircraft Heritage Foundation and The Peter M. Bowers Collection/The Museum of Flight*)

control surface using two articulated segments as elevators, effectively increasing the camber when deflected.

The XOS2U-4s were tested over a two-year period at Moffett Field. The spoiler roll was unsatisfactory and flap effectiveness was poor at high deflection angles. The VARICAM tail did yield improved pitch control.[15] The OS2U-4 was canceled when the decision was made to focus on Curtiss SC-1 seaplane production.

There was room for private inventors to offer solutions as well. Although the War Department mobilized all the industrial capacity of the country, individual citizens were not prohibited from building in their workshops and using existing materials like used light aircraft engines and propellers. This is how Willard R. Custer of Warfordsburg, Pennsylvania, came to build his wooden CCW-1 Custer Channel Wing demonstrator. This light-plane (NX30090) had two 75-hp (60-kW) Lycoming O-145s in a counter-rotating pusher arrangement mounted on a strutted mid-wing outboard of a short fuselage. The lower half of the propeller arcs passed through the aft end of 6-foot (1.8-m) diameter half barrel channels (half segment of a venturi) to which were also attached the main landing gear wheels. The flow into the propellers entrained and accelerated airflow across the channels' inner airfoil surfaces to create lift even at zero forward velocity. Mr. Custer expected this to provide sufficient lift to allow flight with no take-off roll. Attitude control would be lacking so some forward velocity was necessary for safe flight. Hence, he also had wing segments outboard of the channels with ailerons, along with the conventional rudders and elevator on the tail. Consequently, excellent STOL performance was anticipated without the complexity of flaps.

Custer inadvertently performed the first flight of the CCW-1 on November 12, 1942, when he was taxiing the aircraft before prospective investors. As he was not a pilot, his landing was hard and damaged the aircraft. Further flight testing in Hagerstown, Maryland, was conducted and the outer wing panels progressively reduced in span until removed entirely, roll being affected by ailerons above the channels. Zero ground roll tethered take-off was demonstrated, though control was dicey.

Custer managed to attract the attention of the military and the NACA. Flight demonstrations in 1943 at the Beltsville, Maryland, airport by E. Kenneth Jaquieth were followed up with an AAF test program begun in summer 1944 augmented with model wind tunnel data from Wright Field's 5-foot facility. The aircraft did take off in a remarkably short distance but had to be rotated within a narrow speed range and then climbed out at a very steep angle that would challenge vision over the nose in most conventional fuselage designs. The configuration also generated more drag and the wing structural complexity added weight over a conventional design. Low-speed single-engined-out scenarios could be more hazardous than with conventional twins, suggesting the need for heavy and complex engine cross-shafting. The conclusion was that the benefits of the channel wing over conventional STOL solutions did not outweigh the negatives and there was no follow up during the war years.[16]

During the war, the weight of combat aircraft continually rose, increasing wing loading and so driving up landing speeds as stall speeds edged up to lengthen

Above: The Zap flaps showed promise so two additional aircraft were modified as XOS2U-4s, prototypes of a proposed new Kingfisher model. This OS2U-2 (2189) was modified by Vought. The flaps appear to show some alteration in design. Unfortunately, the angle of the shot does not reveal the three spoiler panels atop the wing and the VARICAM horizontal stabilizer may yet to have been installed. (*Vought Aircraft Heritage Foundation*)

Below: Another Kingfisher, OS2U-3 3975, was modified by Douglas as the second prototype XOS2U-4. The bottom side view angle shows the tapered horizontal stabilizers with squared tips as well as the lines of the wing fold while the left side view (from January 21, 1944) shows the roll spoilers. Part of the spin recovery parachute mechanism in the tail cone is visible. (*National Museum of Naval Aviation and National Archives*)

The Custer Chanel Wing CCW-1 was built largely of wood by inventor Willard Custer to demonstrate his concept. This had the pusher propellers turning at the rear of the wings to induce flow into the channels shown to create lift at zero forward velocity. The USAAF tested the aircraft and associated wind tunnel model for STOL benefits but concluded these did not outweigh the drawbacks. (*Smithsonian National Air & Space Museum, NASM 7A19684 and 7A19686*)

landing distances. Higher-performing airfoils and flaps were to prove important in keeping this creep manageable. So, all the work on high lift bore benefits.

Into Practice

The Army had a long history of operating observation aircraft to scout ahead of ground troops and spot artillery shot falls. This demanded extended very slow cruise flight. They were also to support infantry divisions, possibly far removed from roads, with aircraft capable of landing in suitably firm and clear, and likely short, unprepared fields near the advancing forces. However, by the dawn of World War II, these machines had grown heavy and complex, rendering their continued suitability questionable. Alternatives began to be considered.

In the late 1930s, the Army was performing field trials with the YG-1B autogyros. These had exceptional short-field performance and slow-flight capabilities but were tricky to fly and of limited utility. Field exercises (maneuvers) and other training had shown value in the evolving light-planes for spotting and liaison by reservists bringing their private sport-planes. Coupled with the lighter FM radios from which airborne communication could actually be understood through static, the AAC slowly came around to accepting this premise and a notional distribution of such machines suggested a need for hundreds of such light-planes.

Army ground arms (infantry, armor, artillery, and cavalry) continued refining their requirement for a light, two-place, short-range, unarmed "courier" and artillery spotting airplane for operation over friendly lines.[17] Materiel Division surveyed available light-planes and were not encouraged. Yet, they felt a suitable type could be developed in a year. Military characteristics were approved in March 1938 as Circular Proposal (C. P.) 39-2 for a machine satisfying liaison and observation roles. This mandated a two-place, single-engined, fixed-gear (conventional arrangement assumed), high-wing machine with 40–125 mph (64–201 kph) airspeed spread, and with take-off and landing over a 50-foot (15-m) obstacle encompassing just 500 feet (152 m) ground run. This suggested some application of the new high-lift devices and shaped up as a compromised between the observation and the liaison aircraft. Consequently, the proposed machines grew beyond the sport-planes the field organizations had envisioned.

If Materiel Division needed any additional evidence of the possible, they observed Germany's Fieseler Fi 156 *Storch* (Stork). This had outstanding short-field performance, outperforming even autogyros, plus high utility for its light weight. The *Storch* was flown in the September 1938 Cleveland air races where it took-off in very steep climbs, landed in less than 100 feet (31 m), and could "hover" in a 25-mph (40-kph) headwind. It was demonstrated at Wright Field that fall.[18]

Released on August 23, 1938, the C. P. 39-2 competition was to close on February 23, 1939. Ten proposals were offered from which three were selected for prototyping. Contracts were approved on September 20, 1939. The technological risk for these light aircraft was considered so low that experimental models were dispensed with. The service sought three each of the aircraft to serve both development and operational test purposes. The competitors all had high, externally strutted wings with high-lift equipment. All also featured the fixed undercarriage and tandem seating for two.

Bellanca Aircraft of New Castle, Delaware, was well known for its cabin-class light airplanes. It built three YO-50s (40-741/3), construction and test all completed in less than a year for $181,693. It featured fixed leading-edge slots and two-segment Fowler flaps. The airframe was built of synthetic resinous plastic-bonded plywood covering, likely over wood framing for the wing and welded steel tubing for the fuselage. The YO-50 was powered by a Ranger V-770-1 air-cooled inverted V-12 inline at 420 hp (313 kW) turning a 10.5-foot (3.2-m) diameter Curtiss-Reed fixed pitch propeller.

Bellanca Aircraft YO-50 characteristics (* over 50-foot obstacle):

span	55.5 feet (16.9 m)	weight, empty	3,085 lb (1,399 kg)
length	36.2 feet (11.0 m)	weight, gross	3,886 lb (1,763 kg)
height	12.5 feet (3.8 m)	speed, maximum (sea level)	126 mph (203 kph)
wing area	491 feet² (46 m²)	speed, cruise	105 mph (169 kph)
fuel	54 gal (204 l)	range, normal (114 mph)	230 miles (370 km)
climb rate	1,000 fpm (305 mpm)	landing distance (27 mph) *	300 feet (91 m)
service ceiling	19,420 feet (5,919 m)	take-off distance *	410 feet (125 m)

Ryan Aeronautical of San Diego, California, who had been manufacturing a family of light sport-planes, built their YO-51 Dragonfly for $132,020 with a metal fuselage. The wooden wing was in a parasol arrangement permitting a clean, circular fuselage with open cockpits. The wing possessed a full-span leading edge slot and full-span Fowler flaps. The wheel track was exceptionally wide for ground stability, though enabled by more struts. Ryan chose a round engine with the P&W 440-hp (328-kW) R-985-21 Wasp Junior and 8.8-foot (2.7-m) Hamilton Standard constant-speed propeller.

The upper portion of the YO-51 outboard flap segments was manipulated as ailerons. This flaps and slot arrangement were created, however, with numerous projecting supports and hinges. This may have been to permit adjustment while

Bellanca's YO-50 (40-741) poses for the obligatory photograph at Wright Field on December 2, 1940, during or soon after the competition for the Army's new short-field observation type. The inline engine and constant-speed propeller are evident. The full-span leading edge slot accompanies the Fowler flap and conventional aileron. (*National Archives*)

the design was optimized, and all appears to have been cleaned-up later. Ryan may too have found unsuitable roll performance and moved to separate ailerons fixed to the wing aft spar while a flap segment still lay beneath. The more complex roll method, metal fuselage, and powerful engine helped make the Dragonfly the heaviest of the competitors.

The first of three YO-51s (40-703/5) took to the air on January 31, 1940, under the control of Robert J. Kerlinger. It was subsequently delivered to Wright Field on March 5 where it demonstrated a 350-foot (107.0 m) landing over a 50-foot obstacle and take off in less than 100 feet (31 m) with 32 mph (52 kph) minimum airspeed. However, against the specification conditions, it came in somewhat worse off:[19]

Ryan Aeronautical YO-51 characteristics (* over 50-foot obstacle):

span	52.0 feet (15.8 m)	weight, empty	3,430 lb (1,556 kg)
length	34.4 feet (10.5 m)	weight, gross	4,200 lb (1,280 kg)
height	12.0 feet (3.7 m)	speed, maximum (sea level)	130 mph (209 kph)
wing area	400 feet^2 (37 m^2)	range, normal (119 mph)	266 miles (428 km)
fuel	52 gal (197 l)	landing distance (30 mph) *	475 feet (145 m)
climb rate	763 fpm (233 mpm)	take-off distance *	350 feet (107 m)
service ceiling	19,700 feet (6,005 m)		

Stinson Aircraft of Wayne, Michigan, had built a long line of cabin-class commercial airplanes of increasing complexity. For the Army competition, their Model 74 flew last, as the YO-49, with a 295-hp (220-kW) Lycoming R-680-9 operating an 8.5-foot (2.6-m) Ham Standard constant-speed prop. It possessed drooped ailerons, biased 20 degrees down with lowering of the slotted flaps, and adopted full-span leading edge slats that automatically slid open at slow airspeed. The cabin-side windows projected out and up to afford excellent observation capability, and with overhead transparency for threat detection. This machine was much more conventional with steel tube and fabric construction. The O-49 flew remarkably well, with take-offs in 300 feet (91 m) and landings the same. Like the *Storch*, it could "hover" in a stiff headwind but also fly backward in even stronger winds.

Stinson Aircraft O-49A and L-1A characteristics (* over 50-foot obstacle):

span	50.9 feet (15.5 m)	weight, empty	2,670 lb (1,211 kg)
length	34.3 feet (10.4 m)	weight, gross	3,400 lb (1,542 kg)
height	10.2 feet (3.1 m)	speed, maximum (sea level)	122 mph (196 kph)
wing area	329 feet^2 (31 m^2)	speed, cruise	108 mph (174 kph)
fuel	47 gal (178 l)	range, normal (112 mph)	280 miles (451 km)
climb rate	408 fpm (124 mpm)	landing distance (31 mph) *	425 feet (130 m)
service ceiling	12,800 feet (3,901 m)	take-off distance *	450 feet (137 m)

These series of photos appear to show two different approaches to roll control on the YO-51. As the tail number of the bottom aircraft is not applied, it is unknown whether this is a different airplane or 703 modified. One shows articulated trailing edge elements of the two outboard Fowler flap segments while another shows aileron-like surfaces above the most-outboard element (though the surface on the opposite wing is not correspondingly deflected). (*Jay Miller collection and National Archives*)

Also displaying large fixed leading-edge slats and slotted flaps, the Stinson O-49 (photographed on September 3, 1940, at Wright Field) had drooped ailerons to enhance the lift. Much more conventional in appearance with a roomy cabin, the Stinson found favor with the Army selection team. This machine, 40-192, appears to have been the prototype and the first production article, yet did not have the Y-prefix. (*National Archives*)

During the mock-up board for the YO-49 in September 1939, the members seemed so impressed with the Stinson that they recommended going immediately to series production. They appear to have judged it a more mature and less complex design, and the company more capable of quickly starting to turn out the airplanes. Given the clamor for such machines, the AAC was under pressure to acquire the capabilities in the shortest time. Consequently, there were no actual Y preproduction machines for service trials. The contract option for production was exercised on September 20, 1939, for 100 O-49s at $1,853,452. The first was flown on July 15 by Al Schramm and series production had been established in a Nashville, Tennessee, factory by the end of the year.

By late 1940, the ground arms were growing increasingly impatient. They wanted a simple aircraft easy to maintain and operate by men in rough conditions, at the first level by the pilot himself. They feared the AAC fliers would always seek the high-end of speed and technology. The acquisition process seemed to be complicating a straight-forward requirement by applying military specifications to commercial products that, in trials, had appeared entirely suitable as-is. The slow progress in meeting perhaps the simplest aircraft requirement during the defense build-up suggested neglect of this ground support mission. The troops then concluded they needed their own organic air capability with pilots that "lived" with them rather than rely on the Air Corps. Yet, the fliers feared a dilution of their roles and a diversion of aircraft funding. The General Staff opposed small air elements in separate arms of the service but recognized some solution was necessary.

The O-49 appeared a fine aircraft but was markedly heavier and more complex than the light-planes the non-fliers had expected. It was costly, production was slow in ramping up, and it did not appear capable of meeting the numbers required. The immediate authorization was for 250 observation airplanes to meet the new requirements, though even this was clearly a woefully inadequate number. The C. P. 39-2 aircraft left 144 to be procured. This was partially met by increasing the O-49s order by forty-two in April 1940. Although the first Stinson was not accepted until September 1, it was clear this airplane was not what the field units had in mind. However, even buying commercial types required some manner of proper service trials before committing to millions of dollars in production contracts. Even while these efforts were underway, the Air Corps showed its distrust for the light-plane approach by purchasing 203 Curtiss O-52 Owls reflecting the past characteristics of Observation types. It was almost immediately judged obsolete and relegated to Stateside training.

Materiel Division drafted C. P. 40-550 in November 1939 to evaluate commercial light-planes with hopes some could be procured for maneuvers the following spring. The sod surface field length requirement was extended to 1,000 feet (305 m), with 500 feet (152 m) desired. Manufacturers submitted minimally altered variants of existing production designs. Stinson sent a Model 10 with a plexiglass roof. Fairchild offered their Model 24W, Rearwin a modified Sportster, Bellanca their Cruiser Jr., ERCO the Ercoupe, North American the NA-35 trainer, and Ryan put forth the YO-50 again. The evaluation was conducted at Wright Field with operations from

The USAAC's pre-war idea of an observation aircraft was a slow, long-endurance aircraft with expansive transparencies accommodating the pilot, gunner, observer, and possibly photographer. This Curtiss O-52 Owl is seen at Hammer Field, California, on March 22, 1942. Of these, 203 were acquired in 1941, although by that time such aircraft were shown by the war experience of Allies to be too vulnerable and so they were never committed to combat. (*National Archives*)

a muddy field rutted by crisscrossing B-17 tracks that mired most of the airplanes. Disappointingly, it ended inconclusively. The evaluation board, meeting in March 1940, assessed the utility of all the aircraft as too limited.

By spring 1940, observing the war in Europe, it was concluded that liaison and observation would be separate from reconnaissance and photography, the latter requiring greater speed to avoid pursuit while the latter operated in a realm of air superiority. The British were employing light-planes as Air Observation Posts that closely reflected what American Ground Forces sought. However, no suitable liaison types were yet at hand in the U.S. In late summer 1940, the Stinson and Bellanca aircraft were still being completed. By early 1941, the cries of neglect from the ground arms teams were growing strident and they asked that commercial models be purchased immediately as at least a stopgap. The manufacturers contributed to the clamor by actively lobbying Congress and the War Department for their products to be given a fair opportunity to contribute to the defense build-up. For maneuvers that year, the units hired Aeronca, Piper, and Taylorcraft to demonstrate their "puddle jumpers" with civilian pilots.

All this, again, frustrated the Air Corps, although Gen. Arnold understood the eagerness for effective training. Yet, the aviators persisted with their 'not invented here' attitude. A second order for 182 Stinsons was placed on January 27, 1941, estimated at $3,735,890, for the O-49A that had a fuselage stretch of 13 inches (33 cm). That summer, the Chief ordered production accelerated to three-shift operations. This did not satisfy the critics.

Development testing of the three C. P. 39-2 designs was performed during 1940–1941 at Wright Field and then passed along for service trials and maneuvers. The Bellanca and Ryan aircraft were scrapped soon after, each of the YO-51s with about 300 hours logged.[20] The Stinson production continued, with the last O-49A delivered on December 31, 1941.

It had been three years and the Stinsons were only slowly entering service. Such a period to develop an alternative was intolerable. Hence, it was no surprise when Arnold received a directive on August 19, 1941, from Assistant Secretary for War for Air Robert Lovett to immediately purchase twelve service test examples of Taylorcraft, Piper, and Aeronca light-planes. These "off-the-shelf" aircraft sold for about $2,000–3,000 and required just 300 man-hours to manufacture *versus* the 6,000 for the O-49.[21] They could be delivered at a rate up to thirty per week or better, whereas Stinson was striving for thirty per month on the O-49A contract. All of the light-plane models were very similar and completely lacked high-lift features, their take-off and landing performance coming by virtue of being exceptionally light and with good low-speed airfoils. They were mostly fabric over welded steel tube structure with some aluminum and wood, had externally strutted high wings, their four-cylinder 65-hp (49-kW) engines (Lycomings or Continentals) burning automobile fuel and turning wooden, fixed-pitch Sensenich propellers.[22] They could be easily handled and maintained by deployed troops.

Although he complied, Arnold's view reflected those of many air officers that the light-planes were of too little utility and would last only briefly in actual combat owing to their vulnerability. Yet maneuvers into 1941 generated still further evidence of the high potential value the "ground-pounders" placed in such "flying jeeps."

The three light-plane manufacturers were put on contract for four-each of their most representative models, minimally modified. These were the Aeronca Aircraft, of Middletown, Ohio, Model 65TC Defender that became the O-58; Taylorcraft Aviation, of Alliance, Ohio, building the O-57 from their Model DC-65; and Piper Aircraft of Lock Haven, Pennsylvania, with the popular J3C Cub delivered as the O-59. Interstate, Rearwin, and Stinson also offered examples of their planes for evaluation at their own expense. All these "flivver" types were evaluated to include service tests during maneuvers. They were found to be wanting in many respects as military aircraft and were definitely inferior to the O-49. However, scorned they were by Air Forces pilots, the "grunts" enthusiastically embraced them and there were few alternatives to rapidly increasing the number of observation airplanes.

In November 1941, the General Staff recommended acquisition of the light-planes begin immediately. The USAAF placed orders for 342 of the O-57 through O-59. Minimal alterations included accommodating a radio and so some needed an electrical system added. Few if any would get an electric starter, making hand-propping necessary—something the airmen surely chaffed at but the soldiers accepted as just part of doing business.

A Washington conference on January 14, 1942, established the urgent need of 4,000 liaison aircraft by the ground arms. Arnold directed that the light-plane procurement be increased to 1,000, raised to 2,960 six months later. In April, the Observation designation was dropped and Liaison adopted. The O-49 became L-1 Vigilant, and the light-planes the Taylorcraft L-2, Aeronca L-3, and Piper L-4 (all three referred to as Grasshoppers). By this time, the country was at war and everything became possible. Most privately owned airplanes were mobilized and given military designations.

Piper Aircraft L-4 characteristics (* over 50-foot obstacle):

span	35.3 feet (10.7 m)	weight, empty	730 lb (311 kg)
length	22.4 feet (6.8 m)	weight, gross	1,160 lb (526 kg)
height	6.7 feet (2.0 m)	speed, maximum (sea level)	83 mph (134 kph)
wing area	179 feet^2 (16.6 m^2)	speed, cruise	75 mph (121 kph)
fuel	12 gal (45 l)	range, normal (75 mph)	190 miles (306 km)
climb rate	347 fpm (106 mpm)	ferry (70 mph)	200 miles (322 km)
service ceiling	9,300 feet (2,835 m)	landing distance (40 mph) *	805 feet (244 m)
		take-off distance (1,160 lb) *	1,285 feet (392 m)

The L-1 production was not continued, making for 324 completed. Heavy and complex, it guzzled fuel and could not operate on the soft ground the lighter airplanes managed. It tended to be used for personnel and light freight transport while the Grasshoppers did more of the frontline aviation roles which took a heavier toll on the inexpensive machines.

The trio of "Grasshoppers" light airplanes is seen in montage. On top, the Taylorcraft L-2A (O-57, photographed on May 20, 1942) has the trailing wire antenna atop the vertical tail, middle the Aeronca L-3 (O-58B 42-36079 from May 15, 1942) with a wind-driven generator, and bottom the Piper L-4 (O-59 in July 1942) performs a crosswind landing. The Army phased-out the L-2 and L-3 during 1943 to reduce the training and logistics burden. (*National Archives*)

On June 6, 1942, the argument over operation of the Liaison types was settled by order of the Secretary of War. Army Ground Forces (AGF, created on March 9, 1942) were authorized an organic air organization that they would maintain and operate. The USAAF was responsible for procuring the aircraft and training the pilots to fly the machines. Ground Forces would then train the men to perform the combat mission.

Although the AGF was initially content with their light-planes, especially as the AAF had no mission for them, Materiel Division sought a similar machine with the short-field capability it understood the mission to require. They looked to an offer from Stinson to evaluate a new type. They had reworked a Model 10 from the Nashville division in 1941 into a tandem two-seater powered by a 175-hp (131-kW) Lycoming and with slotted flaps plus full-span leading edge slots on a wooden wing. The Model 76's maiden flight was on June 28, 1941. In spin tests, it entered a flat spin from which test pilot Al Schramm barely recovered. The solution was half-span slots at the tips and enlarged tail surfaces.

Evaluation teams had reported positive results by October 1941 and 275 of the Model 76 were ordered as the O-62 Sentinel with a six-cylinder 185-hp (138-kW) Lycoming O-435-1 to turn a 7.1-foot (2.2-m) Sensenich fixed-pitch wooden propeller. Soon redesignated L-5, these cost $7,000–9,000 apiece. By this point, Stinson had become a division of Vultee Aircraft and the work was being done in Wayne, Michigan.

Stinson Aircraft L-5 characteristics (* over 50-foot obstacle):

span	34.0 feet (10.4 m)	weight, empty	1,515 lb (687 kg)
length	24.1 feet (7.3 m)	weight, gross	2,200 lb (998 kg)
height	7.9 feet (2.4 m)	speed, maximum (sea level)	130 mph (209 kph)
wing area	155 feet² (14.4 m²)	speed, cruise	115 mph (185 kph)
fuel	36 gal (136 l)	range, normal (112 mph)	420 miles (676 km)
climb rate	781 fpm (238 mpm)	range, ferry (104 mph)	460 miles (740 km)
service ceiling	15,800 feet (4,816 m)	landing distance (43 mph) *	1,000 feet (305 m)
		take-off distance (2,200 lb) *	800 feet (244 m)

Another contender was the Interstate S-1B Cadet that had been well-liked during the field exercises at the end of 1941. The AAF was pressured to add this to the initial contracts. After a brief evaluation by Materiel Division, production of the O-63 (later L-6) was ordered on July 1, 1942, from Interstate Aircraft and Engineering Corporation in El Segundo, California. It was still a maturing design and there was room for improvements to meet the Army mission. Flaps were added and the transparencies were sloped outboard at the top to assist in downward observation. It grossed 1,775 lb (805 kg) and required 735 feet (224 m) to take off and 1,000 feet (305 m) to land over the 50-foot obstacle. However, the 90-hp (67-kW) Franklin O-200-5 engine suffered overheating problems that defied resolution, among other deficiencies, and deliveries were late. The 250 L-6s, costing about $7,000 each, were employed principally for training.

Stinson reworked a commercial design into a product suitable for the liaison category the Army was seeking. Slotted flaps and outboard leading-edge slots, combined with a 185-hp (138-kW) engine, yielded a machine with performance approaching that of the L-1 but in a light machine. The Army went for the L-5 (42-14799 shown) and it became a standard along with the L-4. (*The Peter M. Bowers Collection/The Museum of Flight*)

The AAF worked with Interstate Engineering to revise their Cadet into a liaison airplane of marginally superior performance. The flaps and 90-hp (67-kW) engine gave it field length like the L-5 but kept down complexity and weight. Unfortunately, engine cooling problems plagued the airplane and the Ground Forces were seeking to reduce the number of types in service, so the L-6 (XL-6 42-15895 seen on October 6, 1942) fell to the contracting ax. (*National Archives*)

Thousands of L-2 through L-6 aircraft were produced in 1942 and 1943, also filling training needs, tactical requirements of the Office of Strategic Services (OSS), Civil Air Patrol, and some export under Lend-Lease. The USAAF also operated liaison squadrons and L-5s initially went to them. By December 1943, the Army was operating approximately 178 L-1s, 1,497 L-2s, 1,055 L-3, 2,079 L-4s, 900 L-5s, and 208 L-6s. Minor changes were introduced during production to simplify manufacturing or enhance mission effectiveness, the latter including expanding transparencies and installing a swiveling observer's seat. Some of the changes increased gross weight, such as radios requiring a trailing antenna and a wind-driven generator mounted beneath the fuselage or on a wing strut, or mounts for a camera. Consequently, field length increased, though it was accompanied by few complaints.

Only the L-1 reflected the short-field performance the ground troops had initially insisted was mandatory, though the L-5's capabilities were good. Some improvements were introduced to the L-birds to improve utility by making them more rugged and improve short-field performance. The L-2M introduced a fully enclosed engine cowling and wing spoilers to increase the approach angle to reduce landing distance. The L-4J was initially fitted with the Beech-Roby R002 controllable pitch propeller for a 15-percent improvement in take-off performance, but the R002 proved problematic and was replaced with the earlier wooden prop. The L-5D may have been intended to take leading edge slats, but this was eliminated before reaching the prototype stage.[23] Instead, the L-5E introduced fifteen degrees drooped ailerons and improved brakes for better stopping, while the L-5G got a controllable-pitch prop.

On July 19, 1943, the AGF sought to standardize on fewer types and eliminate production of the others, permitting a reduction in the training and logistics burden. They expressed a desire to press ahead with the L-4 that had superior low-speed handling qualities. The simplicity of the Piper was preferred over the L-5 that was a step too complicated and too "hot" for AGF pilots. There was concern the perception of the AGF operating the same type as the AAF, which tried to hold most L-5s for their own missions in any event, would suggest the air service should be performing the combat liaison mission. Yet the AAF felt the Stinson was the superior Liaison type since it most closely matched the L-1 in performance. Some Sentinels were "liberated" from the AAF by AGF crews and found to have many desirable qualities. During 1944, the Army took up an additional 1,904 L-4s and 1,361 L-5s. The L-2 and L-3 production tapered off with just 306 more delivered while the L-6 was dropped.

The Navy bought Piper J-3Cs with dual controls for training, designated NE, and another Piper for casualty evacuation (see Chapter 10). The USMC found they needed the Grasshoppers' capability and, after borrowing some Army examples, many NE-1s were transferred to the Marines for spotting and liaison. The Marines also took up 306 L-5Bs and Es as OY-1s.

With the strong desire to "shoot back" or strike targets of opportunity, the Grasshoppers would occasionally drop smoke grenades or flares to mark a target for fighter attack. The aircrew could reach out with their personal weapons to fire down at the enemy or drop hand grenades. The soldiers also attached three bazooka tubes on the struts of the L-4s, both sides, although the 2.36-inch rocket was not so stable in flight when launched in this manner. The L-5 was more suitable for such modifications given its greater payload weight and more stout structure. More improvisation saw additional field trials of air-launched rockets. The Army 4.5-inch rocket motor was too powerful, tending to blow a hole in the wing, but the slower-burning Navy 5-inch projectile was more suitable, the Marines adopting this weapon for their OY-1s. The Americans saw this as a possible answer to sending ordnance into the mouth of Japanese caves.[24] Yet, other than firing rockets to mark targets for attack by fighters, such missions were encroaching on Air Forces roles.

These airplanes could also drop light cargo and retrieve same (snatch, see Chapter 10), perform medivac, plus delivering vital personnel, small parts, and mail. Their ability to operate in short distances on unprepared (but suitably hard and flat) surfaces made them valuable beyond their "puddle jumper" appearance. Not previously envisioned, night flights were also executed with good lunar illumination (the aircraft not equipped for night flying or instrument conditions). When greater range or endurance was desired, the teams improvised reserve fuel tanks and fuel lines, mounted either internally or between the main landing gear struts. For the D-Day landings, this permitted the light-planes to fly from Britain to Normandy. Alternatively, some were flown off the decks of ships (see Chapter 11).

The Army and Marines employed Pipers and L-5s in ways not originally envisioned. Among those with field modifications was attaching small bomb shackles to struts to take light weapons like these bazooka shells being mounted during ops in the Philippines. This was only effective if dropped with the airplane diving almost straight down at the target in an attack one pilot characterized as a way to ensure you did not survive the war. (*National Archives*)

In early 1942, as several commercial light-planes were rushed into mass production, the Materiel Division looked at standardizing on a purpose-built design that a number of companies could manufacture. They developed specifications for an aircraft with a pusher engine to permit excellent forward visibility. Of six firms to be forwarded the specification, three were selected for advanced design studies.[25] The press of other work and the need to maintain high rate production of existing types meant this effort was shelved.

By 1944, the Ground Forces had to admit the L-4 was underpowered and would benefit from flaps. However, they feared seeking a more powerful plane would bring back the argument about USAAF control of the aircraft. Yet, the air arm had begun delivering L-5s, though this was criticized for less advantageous view below and less rugged undercarriage. Regardless, the effort to build purpose-designed L-types for standardization was resurrected. In the meantime, a transitional type based on existing airplanes was sought, all to be followed at a future date by helicopters.

In early 1944, the AGF prepared a requirement for an aircraft falling between the L-4 and L-5. To this end, Materiel Command tested the L-5, the Piper L-4X, and the Taylorcraft 9-X. The L-4X had been created as an ambulance airplane for the AAF (see Chapter 10). Several elements within the AGF preferred the L-5X, a modestly upgraded Sentinel. This was probably the XL-5F converted from an L-5B (44-17103) with a Lycoming O-425-2 and a 24-V electrical system for a revised radio installation.[26] Still, the AGF selected the Piper, then labeled the L-4K, principally because it was not an L-5 and the Taylorcraft came in last during the evaluation. However, this meant months delay before production aircraft could be delivered and so they took up L-5s anyway as a stop-gap.

The L-4K, redesignated L-14, grossed 1,800 lb (817 kg), half again as heavy as the basic L-4, but with larger tires and a sturdy tailwheel to help restore ground flotation. The bungee shock absorber arrangement between the main gear posts was eliminated in favor of long shock struts between the gear and the fuselage frame. A 130-hp (97-kW) Lycoming O-290-3 was coupled with flaps and full-span leading edge slots allowing it to take-off and landing in 600 feet (183 m) or less. The empennage area was also increased. Stall speed was reduced to 23 mph (37 kph). These features had provided development challenges for Piper and test pilot Clyde Smith, Sr.[27] A wooden Sensenich propeller was retained and an electric starter incorporated. Interior and exterior lights, along with a generator in the engine, supported night ops. However, the line abreast seating in front for the pilot and observer came in for criticism as it reduced the latter's field of view.

Five YL-14s (45-55525/9, s/n 5-3001/5) were ordered. The first of these, converted from a J-5C Cruiser, flew on September 9, 1944, and the second, built anew, on February 29, 1945. Along with the original prototype, service trials commenced in May 1945. Production was quickly ordered with 850 (45-55530/6374) on account. Only nine more of the aircraft (s/n 5-3006/14) were completed by the end of the war when the order was canceled. All were returned for Piper to do with as they wished.

Piper Aircraft L-14 characteristics (* over 50-foot obstacle):

span	35.8 feet (10.9 m)	weight, empty	1,100 lb (499 kg)
length	23.4 feet (7.1 m)	weight, gross	1,800 lb (817 kg)
height	9.0 feet (2.7 m)	speed, maximum (sea level)	102 mph (164 kph)
wing area	181 feet^2 (16.8 m^2)	speed, cruise	90 mph (145 kph)
fuel	30 gal (114 l)	range, normal (90 mph)	315 miles (507 km)
climb rate	500 fpm (152 mpm)	range, ferry (80 mph)	400 miles (644 km)
service ceiling	14,500 feet (4,420 m)	landing distance (23 mph) *	550 feet (168 m)
		take-off distance (1,800 lb) *	600 feet (183 m)

For the purpose-built airplane, Materiel Division intended that it would "do it all" as an optimal liaison/observation and photography platform, carry a litter patient, and land "anywhere" with short-field performance. They would be easily maintained in the field, of all-metal construction, and folding wings for ready storage or transport without cumbersome dismounting of wings as was occasionally done with the Grasshoppers. The World War II liaison aircraft were broken down and crated for overseas shipment. Damaged aircraft were sometimes partially disassembled to be placed in a 2.5-ton truck for movement to a more suitable location for repair. Such transport could be rolled off a landing craft during an amphibious assault. Sometimes the fuselage was towed on its wheels.

The first YL-14 (NX-41552) is seen in test on August 25, 1944, before delivery. The full-span leading edge slots are not very evident but the long-stroke shock struts (an aero fairing added to those that followed) are clear as are the trailing edge flaps. Not seen are hinges for the aft portion of the transparency behind the wing to be raised to admit a litter. (*The Peter M. Bowers Collection/The Museum of Flight*)

The tiny L-4 Cub was a very simple machine that even the pilots helped maintain. An unintended feature of this simplicity was the ability to break down into major components for crating or to move it from a forced-landing location to another where it could be more readily repaired. These images from July 1942 show how the fuselage is being towed by a jeep or the entire aircraft fit into a 2.5-ton truck. (*National Archives*)

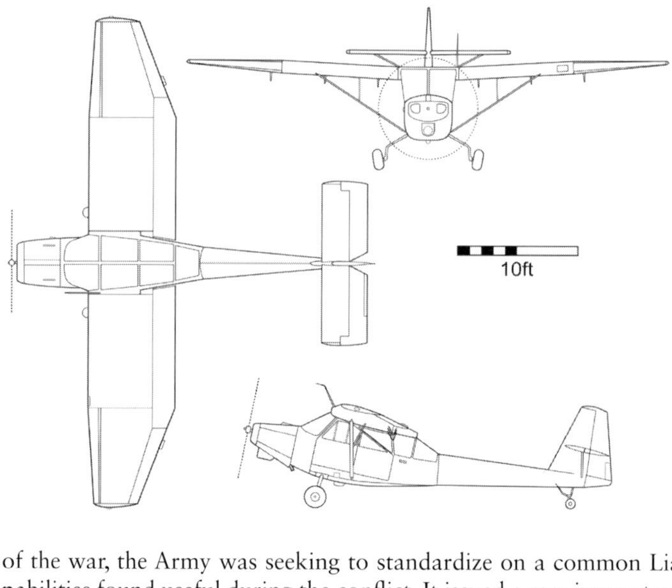

Near the end of the war, the Army was seeking to standardize on a common Liaison airframe with all the capabilities found useful during the conflict. It issued a requirement and firms began work, among these Stinson then under Consolidated-Vultee. Their all-metal XL-13 is shown here in basic concept three-view, which does not do justice to the unique features like folding wings and tail-plane, swiveling wheels, and ability to take a litter. (*Drawn by the author*)

A contract went to the Stinson Division of Consolidated-Vultee for the two Model 105s or XL-13s (45-58708/9). The then-common outboard leading-edge slot and wide-span slotted flaps were expected to give suitable short-field performance, eschewing the complexity and weight of slats, Fowler flaps, drooped ailerons, spoilers, and the like. A 245-hp (183-kW) Franklin O-245-5 would provide sufficient power via a two-blade controllable-pitch wooden propeller. The side transparencies sloped up for downward vision for the crew of two seated line-abreast (despite criticism of this arrangement in the L-14). A third person could be carried behind or two litters accommodated. There were provisions for bomb shackles under the wings. The wheels all swiveled for ease of ground movement in confined spaces. Floats or skis could be fitted and it was to be capable of being towed and release in flight at up to 150 mph (241 kph).[28] Along with the wing fold, the horizontal tail also folded up, probably to fit specified folded dimensions for truck, crate, or cargo aircraft transport. This L-13 was to span 40.6 feet (12.4 m) and gross 2,900 lb (1,315 kg) with a maximum 115 mph (165 kph) and minimum 44 mph (71 kph). Normal range would be 425 miles (684 km) and take-off and landing were expected to be under 500 feet (152 m).

Detailed design and initial assembly had begun in Wayne by the end of the war. The first YL-13 flew in March 1946 and the type was chosen for post-war production, although simplified as the L-13A.

3
Propulsion Challenges

The long maturation of engines, on the order five to ten years even before integration into a specific airframe, made it nearly impossible to develop entirely new models during the comparatively short span of the war. Consequently, many of the existing models were pushed to their limits through upgrades and add-ons while new types were refined as quickly as practical in hopes of production. Basic engine integration with each new aircraft type usually required some power plant alterations and a new model number. New engines or advanced models were first tested on ground rigs. Flight testing on some surrogate aircraft was also common to uncover issues and optimize performance. Some of this work could be done in a large wind tunnel simulating flight conditions. A number of projects incorporating alternative engines on existing aircraft were executed to explore benefits for potential production. As many were developmental power plants, the aircraft became *de facto* engine testbeds. The push to derive ever more power from the reciprocating power plants led to "monster engines" that strained the limits of practicality given their size and weight, while complexity grew beyond proportion to the additional power yielded. The end of this progression was in sight, but a war was still to be won. Modification and optimization of existing engines for greater power output was the more practical avenue followed. All this pointed to ongoing research, development, and testing. Of course, all nations did this, but American efforts were of greater scope.

Scope

Power plant manufacturers were under persistent pressure to increase engine performance (power-to-weight ratio), extend fuel efficiency, improve lubrication, lower operating temperatures, reduced vibration, increase performance (particularly at high altitude) via supercharging, simplify operation and maintenance, extend time between overhauls (reliability), employ better materials, and produce units more simply with less labor (higher output). On the airframe side, cowling improvements were aimed at reducing exposed area by more tightly enclosing the engine while maintaining cooling (for air-cooled power plants) with suitable cowl flaps, moderating exhaust flow effects on lifting and control surfaces aft, and increasing the critical Mach number for the cowl inlet. Supporting all the air intake needs of carburetion even at high altitude meant accommodating superchargers with their extensive ducting and intercoolers. Liquid-cooled engines demanded coolant lines to and from heat-exchangers that had to be provided suitable air intakes and exhaust. New model engines were frequently late in delivery in a program of headlong pace to production and fielding. The integration of the power plant and airplane was vital, but usually done with little time for refinement.

Of elements developed separately and then offered or forced on engine manufacturers was turbosuperchargers to improve the high-altitude performance of the carburetor, and fuel injection to aid in improving combustion by eliminating the carburetor altogether. The efficiency and practical control of these features became an effort unto themselves. Accessories like generators and pumps needed attention as well, especially in ensuring they did not sacrifice too much engine power.

Water injection is one case in point. This introduces a water–methanol mixture into the carburetor fuel-air charge to cool hot-spots in the cylinder during combustion. It increases the density of the fuel-air charge to avoid detonation while increasing combustion pressure for higher power output. It began when the AAF sought a quick means of boosting power from the R-2800 in their P-47s to counter the superior climb performance of the German Fw 190. The Army turned to Pratt & Whitney who assured the airmen that the engine would withstand delivery of more power if detonation could be prevented. Two P&W engineers had long held patents on water or anti-knock fluid injection. These men and others on the engineering staff performed a hurried assessment and felt certain this was the answer to drawing a few hundred more horsepower from the Double Wasp. It had to be carefully introduced to avoid immediate engine damage. With a go-ahead from Wright Field, they had the first system flying in less than three months. Two kits were then assembled and sent to Europe to be installed on combat aircraft for evaluation.[1] As much as a 10-percent hp boost or up to 40 mph (64 kph) was realized for a few minutes, though it stressed the engine mightily. By summer 1943, the war emergency power was a common feature on fighters.

Great efforts were expended in the decades since manned flight began to reduce the cooling demands of aero engines that added to aircraft drag and so subtracted performance. The NACA undertook a good deal of the theoretical and exploratory research effort along these lines. Their resulting reports were invaluable to design teams throughout the country. For NACA's work, the Air Corps passed one of its few Northrop A-17A (36-184) aircraft to Langley as one of the first propulsion testbeds. There, the aircraft's Pratt & Whitney R-1535 Twin Wasp Junior engine was cowled in various ways in an effort to provide adequate cooling while reducing overall drag. Flight test data were collected during 1939–1940. Thereafter, cowling work was largely conducted on prototype aircraft, dedicated testbeds generally not being necessary. Another A-17 (35-122) was employed by NACA to test exhaust pipe designs.

Development of advanced aero engines during the time of World War II was a long and complex affair. Engine test stands and test cells were not adequate for full optimization and so airborne operation on dedicated testbed aircraft was necessary. This April 3, 1940 images shows a Northrop A-17A 36-184 at NACA Langley, heavily modified to test a radial engine with unique cowling configuration greatly reducing cooling drag but adding wing root leading-edge ducts. (*NASA*)

Development of fuels to sustain high performance (higher manifold pressures) without knocking was another avenue of advance. The higher-octane fuels with tolerable potential for detonation was a marked advantage for the Allies. Operating at higher temperatures demanded metallurgical advances, especially for the turbosupercharger.

Basic component developmental may be performed in the lab, but the integrated engine operation and problem resolution is performed on ground run stands and perhaps in altitude chambers (wind tunnel). Flight testing is essential to optimize the entire power plant and demonstrate suitable service use. While prototypes of new aircraft models are dedicated to optimizing all aspects of the design, including engine installation, this is not ideal for power plant development. This brought in the engine testbeds. Platforms to test new engines, cowlings, and accessories yielded some unusual modifications to existing aircraft but also a few unique types.

As usual, airscrews sought to efficiently convert engine horsepower, via power shaft torque, into thrust. This took on greater complexity with the constant-speed propeller and its adjustable blade angles (always seeking to do this faster) and feathering to stop the propeller from spinning with the engine shut down to reduce drag. Exploring the advantages of propeller spinners in drag reduction and improved engine cooling was a common theme. Anti-ice devices (Chapter 9) added more complexity. Weight savings were sought with some work on alternative materials as well as hollow metal blades. Automatic synchronization of propeller settings on

Above: The nacelle of the Curtiss SC-1 has been built-up on a structure representative of the aircraft fore-body for trials (July 22, 1944 image). Although the Wright R-1820 was familiar, the -62 model coupled with a turbosupercharger and four-blade Curtiss Electric propeller demanded integration testing and optimization with the cowling and all accessories more efficiently performed on the ground. Such work was commonly done on less sophisticated rigs, but the war made many resources available. (*NASA*)

Below: Installed tests in a wind tunnel allowed more comprehensive data to be gathered uncovering detrimental aerodynamic interactions and correcting them prior to flight tests. This November 1941 picture is of a Douglas XA-26 engine nacelle and wing segment in NACA Langley's 16-foot transonic wind tunnel. Working out the integration of the R-2800 with single-stage/two-speed supercharger in a laboratory *versus* flight environment saved months in the program that ran frustratingly long. (*NASA*)

multi-engined airplanes was also developed to a practical level. Reversible pitch props (for landing deceleration and backing) were introduced during the war, though under development for years—an example of the war accelerating efforts already underway. A closer look at pusher propeller installations and stabilizing long drive shafts sought to reduce drag from prop wash.

Propeller manufacturers continually sought to improve efficiency or just sustain what they had as airspeeds were increased and sonic tip speeds were approached with its attendant drag rise. The propeller tips reach sonic speeds first owing to their rotational speed added to aircraft forward velocity. The breakdown in the flow, moving inboard from the tip as speed increases, produces a loss of thrust-generating efficiency. At pre-war airspeeds the airscrews were commonly achieving 80 to 85 percent efficiency at the design flight conditions—that is efficiency in converting engine power-shaft torque to thrust. This deteriorated to 70 percent or less at off-design conditions and as aircraft airspeeds were pushed up with new models. The greater speeds saw supersonic blade tip velocities that degraded performance via flow separation. The move to greater diameters to generate more thrust from greater power exacerbated tip speeds while also reducing ground clearance. "Paddle" blades were developed to move more of the thrust generation closer to the hub. These paddle blades commonly possessed just 1.5 times the width of the more common blade. The USAAF tested such blades at Wright Field on B-24D 41-11707. New blade airfoils, some pioneered by NACA, also assisted efficiency gains. Where introducing new blade profiles were impractical in the push for continual high production rates, propeller cuffs with high-speed airfoil shapes were installed near the hub (usually just a rounded shank) to move the center of the thrust towards the root. This also assisted in cooling the engine downstream. However, it was all an endless game of chasing efficiencies with the propeller designers barely keeping up.

Work was performed to develop engine exhausts with flame damping to reduce visual detection at night. There was already some knowledge and experience using jet exhaust to enhance thrust of conventional piston engine aircraft, and this was pressed forward. Engine exhausts and supercharger exits were shaped as nozzles for jet augmentation. The past practice had been to collect all exhaust into a ring or manifold for discharge overboard via a single pipe. Eliminating this saved weight and simplified engine access for maintenance. Several aircraft went to exhaust stacks, jet or simple, and realized some speed gain. A few aircraft attempted to augment cooling flow through the engine cowling by employing the exhaust to entrain low-pressure air from outside through slots as an "exhaust pump" and the mix passing out duct flaps. Such measures always struggled to show sufficient benefit for the added weight and could not be judged as providing any great performance advantage.

Research and experimentation into advanced propulsion technology were usually government-funded and aimed at some tactical gains. The integration of superchargers and turbosuperchargers was a continuing effort with an attendant increase in complexity. The eventual success with this equipment was a tremendous

The U.S. did work seeking to extract thrust from engine exhaust. This May 2, 1942 photo shows such a jet propulsive stack or optimized exhaust for each cylinder, noted as retractable, on the XP-40 that added an average 15 mph (24 kph) to the fight speed. Such changes had to be done carefully so as not to disturb the pressure balance within the engine. (*National Museum of the United States Air Force*)

The Kaiser-Fleetwings XBTK-1 sought added thrust from an "exhaust pump" directing exhaust gases into steel ducts within the forward fuselage sides where it mixed with air flowing out the rear of the cowling then exited out flaps aft of the cockpit. The BuAer innovation was abandoned because it ultimately mattered little to performance while exacerbating engine overheat and airframe vibration, and it also made cockpit ingress/egress tricky given the hot skin. (*Jim Hawkins collection via Dennis Jenkins*)

boon for American military aviation in the boost to high altitude performance. This took another turn with an investigation into the turbo-compound engine in which exhaust gases turned a turbine that fed that energy back into rotational power of the engine via a shaft to the crankshaft. This was an example of an investment that failed to yield military hardware during the war.

Arnold directed P&W and Wright to develop fuel injection systems, which the Germans were already using, within twelve months.[2] Elimination of the carburetor held promise of simplifying fuel–air mixture control and eliminating the hazard for carburetor icing. It was also hoped this would help prevent the induction fires in the R-3350 powering the all-important Boeing B-29. Production was moving ahead too rapidly for the immediate introduction of the system. Although it was eventually added to the R-3350, the fires persisted. It took many other measures to make the engine acceptable in a wartime scenario. The NACA Cleveland team assisted in small ways that could be introduced into the existing production, including changes to the valves, cylinder heads, and baffling.[3]

The next generation of reciprocating aero engine were monsters in size, weight, and complexity. They represented significant R&D investment with testing difficulties and were ultimately abandoned with the advent of turbine power plants. Attempting to drive a propeller-equipped airplane to higher speeds was only exacerbating compressibility problems (Chapter 5). Introducing greater power generally only contributed to gross weight growth. The P-38, as an example, saw engine power increase from 1,150 to 1,425 hp (858 to 1,063 kW, 24 percent) during its evolution, but airspeed increased by only 24 mph (39 kph) or 6 percent while GW went from 15,340 to 21,600 lb (6,958 to 9,798 kg) or 40 percent. The introduction of the jet engine, an entirely new aircraft propulsion means, again challenged teams to learn quickly and be agile in proposing and pursuing design solutions.

The NACA was selected to investigate the potential for jet propulsion but had not progressed far (see Chapter 5 for the ducted fan with augmentation research) before the revelation of the still-secret British progress and suspected German advances. The Special Committee on Jet Propulsion, formed in March 1941, provided the impetus to catch up. Even with the example of the British work, there was much fundamental research and development to perform assisting maturation of the new engine technology and integration into practical combat airplanes. The Committee helped establish the Jet Propulsion Static Test Laboratory at the Cleveland Center with new testing stands, completed in September 1943.

American engines with the compressor-turbine combination appeared the most promising to pursue, though working both centrifugal and the more challenging axial-flow compressor schemes plus afterburning. Eventually, Westinghouse Electric would carry forward turbojet development while General Electric focused on turboprop and Allis-Chalmers the turbofan (ducted fan). Each received War Department contracts. By the end of the war, the Americans were essentially co-equal with the U.K. in jet propulsion and rapidly closing on the Germans. However, the failure to foresee and lead this aircraft propulsion revolution was perceived as a "black eye" for the NACA.

The Americans played catch-up on jet engines throughout the war, beginning with British units and growing from there. This General Electric I-40 is being tested with a bifurcated afterburner section in a laboratory setting on July 7, 1944. Such resources permitted the U.S. to approach parity with the UK and close on Germany by the end of the war. (*NASA*)

Pushing the Old

An exceptionally useful experimental fighter platform for testing upgrades to existing radial engines was the Curtiss XP-42 (Model H75S 38-004). This was one of several spin-offs of the pre-war P-36 Hawk but was set aside in favor of P-40 production. Nonetheless, the singular example proved long-lived and fruitful as a research craft.

Delivered in March 1939, the focus was initially propulsion with a 1,050-hp (783-kW) Pratt & Whitney R-1830-31 Twin Wasp radial engine and three-blade propeller. It was unusual in having an extended propeller shaft and gear case such that there was a pressurized void (diffuser) behind the spinner and ahead of the cylinders. This contributed a somewhat streamlined nose for a round engine fighter and was believed to support engine cooling despite the small cooling air opening area between the spinner and lip of the cowling. The intent was to reduce propulsive drag to that of an inline, liquid-cooled engine. However, unacceptable temperatures, shaft vibration, and unsuitable carburetor ducting issues persisted. The weight of the extended-nose engine and cowling had to be balanced with tail ballast. Attempted remedies saw variations in cowling, cowl flaps, scoops, spinner, and propeller cuffs. While the changes sought improved performance without detrimentally high engine operating temperatures, weight and drag of the modifications continued to work against that goal. More advanced designs eclipsed the XP-42 in any event.

The XP-42 came to Langley in 1940 for full-scale tunnel testing. There it eventually underwent multiple cowl and spinner changes during trials. These saw the long nose eliminated. All the work chased just a few mph of speed gain. However, some of the features, such as an inlet fan, found its way into other advanced American fighter designs. Afterward, the XP-42 became one of Langley's test fleet and continued to have its propulsion system refined into 1943.

Pratt & Whitney got a Tomahawk II (H81A-1 c/n 17816) in September 1940 for power plant testing, eventually mounting an R-1830-SSC7-G. This made for an odd-looking P-40 (NX28990) with a big radial up front and reworked forward fuselage to fair the round cowling into the existing airframe designed for an inline. The engine was closely cowled but with a "jet exhaust" to draw thrust from the stacks by squeezing the pipes at their exits. It was operated from late 1942 to at least late 1943.[4]

Vought built an extra SB2U-2 as a company demonstrator they designated V-156, completed in October 1938. After the Vindicator became obsolete, this airframe was employed by P&W as an engine testbed and redesignated V-167. It was modified with an R-1830-S3C4-G and three-blade propeller replacing the P&W R-1535 with two blades, though apparently retaining most of the original cowling configuration.

Another valuable propulsion testbed was the pre-war YA-19, derived from the Vultee Model V-11 that was marketed successfully to several foreign air forces. The Air Corps purchased seven YA-19s in the lean years of the late 1930s; two served engine test purposes. Their voluminous interior lent itself to instrumentation installation and test observer stations. The single-engined attack aircraft was sold with a 1,200-hp (895-kW) R-1830-17 Twin Wasp. One of the closely associated designs was the Vultee AB-2, later V-12, powered by the R-1830. After flying for two years as a company demonstrator (NX18985, c/n 131), it was sold to P&W in fall 1940 as a Twin Wasp testbed with few modifications save for ducting added below the forward fuselage. This began an association between the firms that lasted throughout the war years.[5] The seventh YA-19 (38-555, c/n 138) became the XA-19C when sent to P&W in August 1941 where it was given a 1,200-hp R-1830-51. The engine and associated cowling tests were followed by general cooling investigations throughout the remainder of the war.

The XP-42 (at Langley Field on February 23, 1942) displays one of its propulsion modification configurations. The carburetor and oil cooler inlets are integral with the top and bottom lips of the cowling, a fan attached within the annulus behind the spinner, and propeller cuffs aid cooling. First the Army and then NACA reworked the installation many times from 1939 into 1943 before the testbed was turned to flight controls testing. (*NASA*)

This P&W testbed for the R-1830 is based on a Curtiss Tomahawk II (H81A) or P-40D. As that type had an inline engine with a narrow forward fuselage, adapting it for a large "round" engine required an extensive fairing aft of the firewall to blend into the existing fuselage. This did permit ready incorporation of a "jet exhaust" trough along the sides visible in the image. (*The Peter M. Bowers Collection/The Museum of Flight*)

Above: The first Vought V-156 demonstrator (leading to the U.S. Navy SB2U Vindicator) was turned to engine testing with an R-1830-S3C4-G to become the V-167. The Twin Wasp turned a three-blade propeller (first image from February 7, 1941) and later given a clear-vision forward canopy and many more flight test antennae seen in the bottom image. (*Vought Aircraft Heritage Foundation and The Peter M. Bowers Collection/The Museum of Flight*)

Below: Still with the expanded-area fin, the seventh XA-19A was passed to Pratt & Whitney in 1941 for testing the Twin Wasp. Here the XA-19C is seen at the engine maker's East Hartford facility with the R-1830-51 that did not see production. It nonetheless provided an invaluable testbed for optimization of the base power-plant that was used so widely it became the most produced aero engine of the war. (*San Diego Air & Space Museum*)

The second YA-19 (38-550, c/n 133) was turned over to P&W in June 1939, less than a month after delivery to the Air Corp. The engine maker reworked it into the XA-19B, equipped with an 1,800-hp (1,342-kW) R-2800-1 fourteen-cylinder radial and an oil cooler beneath the forward fuselage. It was first flown in this guise during July 1939. The Double Wasp became a power plant of enormous importance to the American war effort, installed on many fighters, bombers, and transports. Consequently, the XA-19B was kept very busy testing incremental improvements and so was operated by P&W into 1946. It was also periodically used by various contractors for individual tests.

More comprehensive testing of the R-2800 with supercharger and advanced propellers demanded a different aircraft. The prototype V-11 (Model V-11A, c/n 29) was sold to Pratt & Whitney in 1939 for the work, though Vultee performed the modifications. Swinging large diameter props demanded long main gear struts, fixed in the down position. Apart from the longer nose for the double-row engine, considerable volume behind the engine was essential for all the supercharger ducting. Consequently, the Vultee airframe was radically modified and weight went up 2,000 lb (907 kg). The cockpit was moved well aft and the chord of the rudder was extended. The resulting V-11T (NX-14980) flew again on January 19, 1940, and was delivered to P&W on the 21st. It was operated in East Hartford, Connecticut, testing various engines but most particularly the R-2800. The aircraft was damaged in an accident and grounded on March 20, 1945, but employed as a static test article thereafter, shorn of its aero surfaces.[6]

With the original vertical stabilizer, the second YA-19 was altered to serve as a testbed for the P&W R-2800 Double Wasp engine. This XA-19B proved very important in facilitating improvements to the engine supporting its many warplane applications. The aircraft was operated in this configuration beyond the end of the war. (*San Diego Air & Space Museum*)

Above: Vultee modified the first of its V-11A attack aircraft as an engine testbed for Pratt & Whitney. The V-11T was principally designed to accommodate the R-2800 and so had to assume a higher stance for prop clearance as well as provide volume for all the supercharger ducting. As a result, the airframe was modified beyond recognition. (*via Dan Schumaker*)

Below: The Vultee YA-19s proved surprisingly adaptable as dedicated testbeds for flight test of developmental aero engines. Here the outmoded airframe is again radically modified as the XA-19A with experimental Lycoming O-1230-1 "flat" engine in the close cowling. The exceptionally long nose (with drop-down lip cowl flap) drove a vertical tail extension. (*San Diego Air & Space Museum* and *National Museum of the United States Air Force*)

The sixth of the rare and outmoded Douglas B-23s (39-032) was bailed to Pratt & Whitney in August 1940 to operate through the end of the war as a testbed for the 1,850-hp (1,380-kW) R-2800-5 bound for the B-26 and XB-28. This saw the airplane flying with a four-blade propeller on the starboard engine and three-blade on the port at the same time.[7]

Inline development also demanded testbeds. Allison was loaned the second Curtiss P-40D (40-360) to serve as an engine development platform for their V-1710.

That seventh YA-19, mentioned earlier, had been initially finished as the XA-19A (38-555, c/n 138) with the 1,200-hp Lycoming O-1230-1 liquid-cooled inline engine. The long nose for the twelve-cylinder, horizontally opposed power plant lengthened the airplane to 38.3 feet (11.2 m) and requiring a compensating dorsal fin extension. First flight with the O-1230 was on May 22, 1940. The aircraft flew at Wright Field from June 1940 through March 1941, after which it passed to Lycoming. The engine, expected to be integrated within the wings of bombers, never entered production because the horsepower requirements of evolving combat aircraft outpaced the power plant.

Rushing the New

Many outmoded aircraft became a valuable testbed for new engine designs. Several such came from Vultee's disappointing Model V-72 dive bombers built for the RAF as the Vengeance II and then the USAAF as the A-31. These were normally powered by the 1,600-hp (1,193-kW) Wright R-2600 Cyclone 14. One of the aircraft taken up by the Americans (AF759, 42-35824, c/n 4115) was modified to take the Wright 2,200-hp (1,641-kW) R-3350-13 and become the XA-31C. Five others (AF756/782/845/887/904) were diverted to serve as YA-31C testbeds for the R-3350-17 engine with four-blade Hamilton Standard propellers. The large airframe, with a bomb bay and rear seat, was well-suited for testing big radials. The work they performed supported the ultra-important B-29 that relied on the Duplex Cyclone, which suffered protracted development challenges. Hence, they were kept busy at Wright Field and Paterson, New Jersey, through the latter half of 1943.

Flight testing of the R-3350 also included installation on the fifth twin-engined Lockheed Ventura I bomber (AE662, c/n 37-4005) to collect performance data. The testing was also intended to benefit the Lockheed C-69 Constellation transport being developed by Lockheed. Bearing the nacelles planned for the Constellation, the aircraft was dubbed the "Ventilation." The far more important B-29 and Consolidated B-32 programs were the principal benefactors of this work. Apart from the new engines and cowlings, the nose of the bomber had to be cut back for propeller clearance. It first flew near the end of September 1942 and was operated from the Lockheed plant in Burbank, California, with registration NX33626. The work on the Ventilation-assisted R-3350 development as testing could be done without interfering with bomber development work. In fact, more engine time was logged on the Lockheed plane (132 hours) during a critical four-month period, late 1942 through early 1943, than on the bombers. Two engines logged sixty hours each while there were multiple engine changes on the bombers.[8] The aircraft was subsequently employed by Wright for further engine development.

The prototype Vengeance II (USAAF A-31) intended for the U.K. (AF745, c/n 4101) was modified during 1942 as the Model 85 XA-31A (42-35824) to serve as a testbed for the R-2800. However, it was instead diverted to take the twenty-eight cylinder, 3,000-hp (2,237-kW) XR-4360-1 X-Wasp or X-108 (a security cover name) with which it first flew on April 25, 1942, as the XA-31B. This 3,670-lb (1,665-kg) engine had twenty-eight cylinders in four rows of seven that gave a low frontal area for reduced drag, although of unusual length that earned it the nickname "corncob engine." Vultee had an interest in the power plant as it was destined for their XA-41 attack aircraft program. A longer landing gear was installed on the A-31 to permit a larger prop to be swung. The gear sponsons were converted to oil coolers, so the gear was fixed down with diagonal braces. A large induction air scoop was affixed immediately in front of the windscreen. The vertical stabilizer and dive brakes were strengthened, the rudder covered in aluminum *versus* the original fabric, and a fuel tank was installed in the weapon bay.

The XA-31B first took to the air on April 25, 1942, at Vultee Field, Downey, under the hands of P&W test pilot Howard H. Sargent, Jr., to become the first airplane powered by the Wasp Major. The airframe and engine were then shipped separately to the manufacturer's flight test hangar at Rentschler Field, in East Hartford, where they were again joined and flight testing resumed on July 24. Sargent and F. A. Borsodi shared the piloting and the former was aboard during the final flight on September 15, 1942. The engine quit owing to a fuel pump failure and Sargent attempted a forced landing in a tobacco field near Bradley Field, Connecticut. Although the ship ended inverted, the pilot and observer, Richard G. Smith, escaped without injury. The XA-31B was written off.

Vought developed the VS-326 airplane (for Vought-Sikorsky, later just V-326) as an engine and propeller testbed for Pratt & Whitney, with the XR-4360 expressly in mind. It was conceived by two P&W engineers, Alfred Marshall and Rudolph Wallace, and the Vought project engineer was Russ Schwinn. The aircraft was more commonly referred to as a Pratt rather than Vought machine. The intent was to fly the aircraft to 50,000 feet (15,240 m) for altitude testing. This required an airframe with a pressurized four-place cabin. Elements of their XTBU-1 Sea Wolf aircraft were employed by Vought in building the aircraft in which the sealed cabin somewhat "floated" within the airframe such that its deformation under pressurization loads acted as little as possible upon the fuselage structure. Aircraft pressurization design was still in its infancy, so the best solution was to build this separate chamber. A large ram air duct in front of the tail fed long ducting forward to the engine for carburetion. The airplane was expected to reach 418 mph (673 kph) with the R-4360.

Above: The vital development work on the challenging R-3350, the key to the B-29 bomber, made a flight testbed necessary. Lockheed modified one of its Ventura bombers to take the nacelles from the Constellation airplane that was also to be powered by the Wright engine. The nose of the "Ventilation" had to be cut back to clear the arc of the propellers. (*San Diego Air & Space Museum and Gerry Balzer*)

Below: The prototype V-72 Vengeance II dive bomber was modified to serve as an engine testbed. This ultimately took the form of the XA-31B with XR-4360-1 X-Wasp in a long but slender cowling. The large air scoop in front of the windscreen and main landing gear stowage sponsons turned into oil coolers, such that the struts were fixed down, testifies to the experimental nature of the installation. (*San Diego Air & Space Museum*)

The Vultee XA-31B came to a bad end in a tobacco field in Connecticut on September 15, 1942, when the engine quit, prompting the forced landing. As luck would have it, the field was strung with wires across poles to support cheesecloth and so the ship flipped over. The airplane had just six hours in the log when lost. (*San Diego Air & Space Museum*)

Work began in 1941 on two examples: the V-326 with a deep cowling likely enclosing the supercharger, and the V-326A with a tight-fitting cylindrical cowling and inlets under the wings for twin turbosuperchargers. Several versions of the booster equipment were installed for testing. Wing and fuselage tanks had a total capacity of 700 gal (2,650 l). The aircraft was 43 feet (13.1 m) long, the wing spanning 57.8 feet (17.6 m), and it stood 19.3 feet (5.9 m) high with the tail up. It sat with an exceptionally nose-high stance to clear a large propeller. Weight empty was 11,242 lb (5,099 kg) and gross 17,176 lb (7,791 kg). There was volume in the aft fuselage for ballast to counterbalance engine variations plus accessories up front.

The Vought aircraft were among the most sophisticated engine testbeds to that time. The VS-326 first flew on June 18, 1943, as NX41861 with P&W chief test pilot A. Lewis McClain at the controls. Most of the subsequent flying was carried out by Harold B. Archer. Cabin pressurization difficulties usually kept it below 40,000 feet (12,192 m). The aircraft reached 418 mph (673 kph) at 29,000 feet (8,839 m). The 326A (NX41862) was first taken up on August 30, 1944, and delivered to East Hartford. There it apparently went into a modification period to change the turbosuperchargers from which it did not emerge, the need for the airplane having faded.[9]

One North American AT-6D (42-84241) had its 600-hp (447-kW) Wright R-1340 Wasp replaced by a 575-hp (429-kW) Ranger V-770-9 inline engine, in

The pressurized Vought V-326 is seen in flight with a deep cowling for the narrow R-4360 engine and likely supercharger ducting. The scoop ahead of the tail feeds the carburetor through long ducting. Despite the advanced appearance, the wing still had fabric covering aft of the spar and on control surfaces. (*Jay Miller collection*)

The engine mount of the Vought testbeds facilitated rapid engine removal and install while mounts for different engines could be substituted (the base R-4360 seen hanging). The V-326A is shown under construction with the "floating" cabin pressure vessel evident with its four hatches and turbosuperchargers on the bench. The cabin pressurization was developed by Garret Research and was pumped up by an electrically-driven compressor with warming by two combustion heaters. (*Jay Miller collection*)

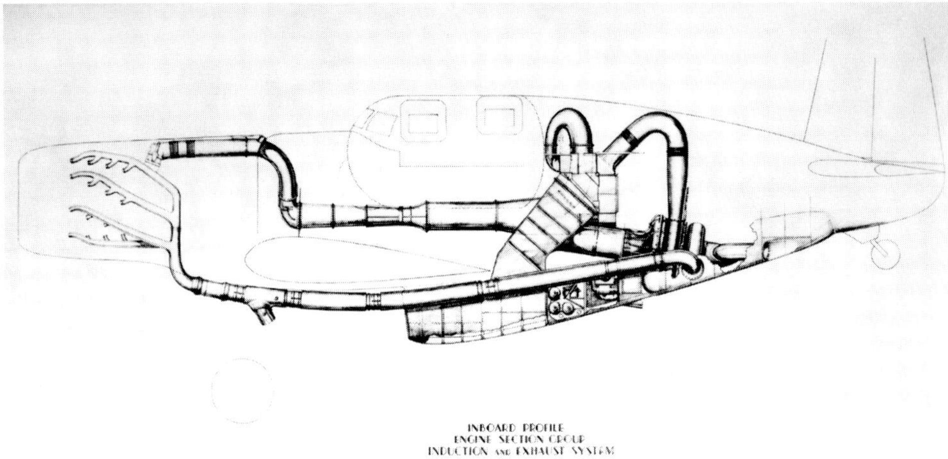

The high-altitude internal combustion engines required considerable ducting for carburetion through various stages of intercoolers and turbosuperchargers. Exhaust was ducted back to spin the turbos. The V-326A design also had a scoop ahead of the tail, so this drawing is either incomplete or for another configuration, but it illustrates the extent of effort required to operate advanced reciprocating aero engines of the day at high altitude. (*Vought Heritage Historical Foundation*)

The V-326A had a cowling that more closely followed the contour of the narrow R-4360 and it had a scoop under each wing, but was otherwise very similar to its twin, the V-326. This aircraft was flown very little and, like its companion, was scrapped in 1946, the V-326 with just 111 hours in the log. (*Vought Heritage Historical Foundation*)

an inverted "V" configuration, to become the XAT-6E. Any performance gain, or exposure of trainees to inline engines evident on some fighter types, was hardly the objective. Supplementing R-1340 production might have been beneficial. However, the idea came from Fairchild Aircraft who had manufactured the air-cooled twelve-cylinder Ranger until the last potential recipients—the Bell XP-77 and Fairchild AT-21—were canceled. It is noted that the higher-placed power shaft could permit the same diameter prop to be swung with sufficient ground clearance given shorter landing gear posts and so shallower deck angle for better visibility forward during ground ops. Similarly, a larger prop could be mounted for even more power extraction.

The project was approved with Fairchild performing the modification that altered all from the firewall forward making the trainer 2 feet (0.6 m) longer. This supercharged V-770 power plant significantly boosted performance due only to the more streamlined installation. Fontal area shrank from 13 feet^2 (1.2 m^2) to 5.2 feet^2 (0.5 m^2). Top speed of the XAT-6E went to 231 mph (372 kph) at 20,000 feet (6,096 m) and ceiling to 30,000 feet (9,144 m) compared with the standard Texan trainer at 172 mph (277 kph) for the same altitude (unsupercharged) or 208 mph (335 kph) at 5,000 feet (1,524 m) and 24,400-foot (7,437-m) ceiling. On the downside, the Ranger still had discouraging teething problems. Given the end of the war drawing near and the desire for a substantially higher performance trainer (see Chapter 12), the AT-6E had no future.

As B-17 Flying Fortress production was ramping up, there were proposals for improvements that included greater engine power. In 1942, the Vega Aircraft Corporation, building B-17s under contract in Burbank, investigated adding the developmental R-4360 as the Vega Model V-144 and the even more experimental R-3350 as the V-143. More practical was the idea of mating an inline Allison V-1710 for the V-134-1. The overall 900-hp (671-kW) power increase was expected to equate to a 30–50 mph (48–81 kph) boost. As a division of Lockheed Aircraft, builder of the V-1710-powered P-38, there was considerable experience with the Allison. The Air Forces agreed to explore the option as part of its ongoing efforts to employ liquid-cooled inline engines, in this case, a V-12, as an alternative to the radials with large frontal area contributing to drag. For inlines, the drag from the radiators required to carry away heat from engine coolant was the trade-off as well as the vulnerability of the radiator and coolant lines to battle damage.

Vega and the government began negotiating a contract on March 4, 1942, and signed on July 10 for three prototypes. This was to proceed initially with a single example as a new airframe (42-73515). Instead, it was decided to modify the Boeing-built B-17E pattern aircraft (41-2401), sent to Vega as they erected their production line. The usual four Wright R-1820-65 Cyclones of 1,200 hp (746 kW) were replaced by V-1710-89s of 1,425 hp (895 kW) to become the XB-38.

Lockheed-Vega (wholly owned after 30 November 1943) faced a considerable redesign of the wing structure to include the firewall and accommodating the

The Ranger V-770-9 inline, air-cooled, aero engine was manufactured by Fairchild Aircraft and had seen disappointing sales. By 1944, the production line was idle with all the aircraft powered by it canceled, prompting Fairchild's proposal it be installed on the North American AT-6 trainer, seen here. Note the exceptionally high-power shaft and the supercharger with ducting to the intake manifold. (*San Diego Air & Space Museum*)

The XAT-6E portrays the sleek engine installation in tight cowlings, large cowl flaps, and rare propeller spinner. Performance was markedly greater than the standard AT-6D from which the test aircraft was derived. However, it was not enough to fill the growing gap between the advanced trainer and period fighters and offered no other compelling justification for disrupting production lines for such a major design change. (*National Museum of the United States Air Force*)

coolant lines and radiators. The design was mocked up on a B-17 wing to serve as a test stand. Instead of a common welded steel tube engine mount, a riveted assembly was designed to save weight. For the testbed itself, the work in Burbank saw the wings pulled off for rework with large openings in the leading edges between the engines for the radiators. Oil cooling radiators were behind chin inlets in the cowlings. The Allisons spun a three-blade, 12.1-foot (3.7-m) diameter Hamilton Standard propeller behind a spinner. The General Electric (GE) turbosupercharger installation was unchanged. Outboard wing fuel tanks were also added with 1,080 gal (4,088 l) to greatly increase range.[10] A mock-up of the Sperry A-2 ball turret replaced the much-maligned remote-controlled Bendix belly turret. Extensive test equipment was added.

The aircraft was contacted to be delivered within ten months but work was slowed as personnel were occasionally pulled away to more urgent work. The XB-38 finally took to the air on May 19, 1943, with Bud Martin in the left seat and George MacDonald in the right. After six flights and seven hours over four days, the aircraft was put down to correct exhaust manifolds that were rapidly deteriorating. The ninth flight on June 16 was to focus on performance. However, the sortie was interrupted by an engine fire in No. 3 that could not be extinguished. After turning the stricken ship away from densely populated areas and setting the autopilot, the pilots abandoned the aircraft. However, both suffered parachute malfunctions such that MacDonald was killed and Martin badly injured. The XB-38 crashed near Tipton with twelve hours on the clock.

A B-17E was modified as the XB-38 incorporating Allison V-1710 inline engines, seen here during an engine run in Burbank, California. The large radiator openings in the leading edge between the engines as well as the chin oil cooling openings in the cowlings must have added drag that countered the benefit of the relatively sleek cowlings. Note also the two pitot probes moved above the nose to support flight test data collection. (*Lloyd Jones collection*)

Above: The XB-38 oil coolers are visible behind the chin inlets, the bottom cowl flap closed in this image. The cooling air duct over the exhaust manifold is also seen behind the small cowling intake, the exhaust directed aft and down out the bottom of the cowling. The engine mount is also visible as the riveted assembly under the engine with upper tube support, avoiding mounting loads carried through the crankcase. (*Lloyd Jones collection*)

Below: This angle on the XB-38, on its May 19, 1943, maiden flight (with outdated markings), emphasizes how the inline engines extended farther forward than the single-row Wright radial. This must have altered stability and control enough to prompt some changes to the flight controls and required careful flight testing to demonstrate suitable handling qualities. Note that the dome for the deleted Bendix belly turret remains in place behind the mocked-up ball turret. (*Jay Miller collection*)

The two additional XB-38s were being prepared and the design was considered for production. The V-140 was to have additional armament as a cross between the heavily armed XB-40 "bomber escort" (Chapter 12) and B-17F. However, this was curtailed by Gen. Arnold on August 12, 1943. He had doubts about the concept and by that point, the Cyclone-powered B-17s were proving effective despite being a nearly decade-old design. The engine supply was plentiful while P-38 demand for the V-1710 was adequate; the only aircraft that did well with the power plant that was otherwise disappointing. Introducing such extensive alterations to the production lines as a change in engine type was considered so disruptive as to negatively impact high delivery rates.

Failed Monster

Few of the monster recips reached flight tests. Those that did were usually in prototype aircraft that taught a hard lesson of mating an experimental engine to an experimental airframe—none went into production. One, however, saw experimental installation as an alternative power plant.

The need to have an alternative to the B-29's R-3350, in the event its troubles could not be resolved, led to consideration of the pre-war Allison V-3420. This was an enormous 2,600-lb (1,179-kg), twenty-four-cylinder inline, liquid-cooled power plant combining two V-1710s (90 percent parts commonality) seeking a hoped-for 3,000 hp (2,237 kW) at take-off. Development of the V-3420 had been halted in September 1940 so that Allison could focus on V-1710 production and improvements, but then resurrected in May 1942 for the B-29. However, no Superfortress airframe would be available for some time to support flight test. A C-46 conversion was considered, with the advantage of requiring just two of the rare experimental engines and so ready sooner.[11] However, the CG shift was unmanageable and an alternative had to be found. Consequently, the Douglas XB-19 (38-471) was turned to testing the Allison under MX-309—its originally intended power plant. This giant one-off bomber had a 212-foot (65-m) span and a 140,000-lb (63,503-kg) gross weight. It had first flown on June 27, 1941, but was underpowered with four R-3350-5s of 2,000 hp (1,491 kW) to give it a sedate 120-mph (193-kph) cruise airspeed. It was too big and underpowered to be useful as a practical long-range bomber and so served as an airborne laboratory for various projects, but especially as another mount for curing R-3350's ills.

The XB-19 had flown just 177 hours when modification began in November 1942 at Romulus Airfield in Detroit, Michigan, by the Fisher Aircraft Division of General Motors.[12] Allison was also a division of General Motors under which Fisher was attempting to build the XP-75 fighter powered by the V-3420, with much of the design work underway in Detroit. For that airplane, the amidships-mounted engine had two drive shafts to a reduction gearbox and coaxial propeller shafts in the nose. The bomber design had just a reduction gear case on the front of the engine. The Lockheed XP-58 was also in line to receive this engine in a similar arrangement. The turbosupercharged Allisons spun four-blade 16-foot (4.9-m) diameter Curtiss Electric propellers, the inboards reversible and all auto-synchronized. These were soon replaced with 18.2-foot (5.5-m) units.

After a prolonged modification, the bomber, relabeled the XB-19A, resumed flying in January 1944 as the largest and most powerful landplane aircraft in the world. Although the empty weight rose some 8,000 lb (3,629 kg) to 92,400 lb (41,912 kg), the aircraft finally approached its planned maximum airspeed with 265 mph (427 kph) and 185 mph (298 kph) cruise, although these were below the B-29 figures. One of the most advanced engine flight testbeds, with extensive instrumentation, it soon exhausted the Allison work and was employed as a transport until the end of the war.

The first YB-29 (41-36954) finally became available in late 1943 and was bailed to General Motors to continue the V-3420 test program with a lighter and sleeker airframe. This became the XB-39 (MX-230) with the four V-3420-11 engines shifted over from the XB-19A and fitted with four-blade propellers and spinners. Various models of superchargers were mounted. Although the YB-29 was flown to Cleveland in November 1943 (where the P-75 was intended to be manufactured), there were delays owing to greater priority for the fighter and shuffled turbosupercharger work at GE. In the meantime, cooling issues were addressed to include a revised nacelle design optimized with the benefit of data from full-scale tests in Langley tunnels.[13] So, the XB-39 did not make its maiden flight until December 9, 1944, and then without the turbos. It eventually demonstrated 405 mph (652 kph) at 35,000 feet (10,668 m) altitude *versus* the B-29's 358 mph (576 kph) at 25,000 feet (7,620 m), and with about 10 percent improvement in fuel economy. Although there had been discussion of ordering pilot production of 100 B-39s, this was not carried forward. The performance improvement with the Allison (still awaiting the intended turbos) was insufficient to warrant interrupting a production line to introduce a new B-29 model. Any such move was likely to use the Wasp Major.

Pratt & Whitney had proposed in September 1943 substituting the Wasp Major, promising 3,500 hp (2,610 kW), in the B-29 for markedly improved performance. This twenty-eight-cylinder monster was already flying in other applications and proving to be one of the pinnacles of air-cooled aero engines. Given the state of the Superfortress program with its troublesome if not hazardous R-3350, the proposal was welcomed. After approving a modification and flight test project in July 1944, B-29A (42-93845) was bailed to P&W to become a testbed for the R-4360 installation as the XB-44. Entirely new engine mounts and cowlings were required. Flight testing began in May 1945 and performance was indeed favorable, with 392-mph (631-kph) top speed and more than 500-fpm (152-mpm) initial rate of climb. Plans were laid for production as the B-29D that included other changes. An initial order was placed in July 1945 for 200 B-29Ds but waylaid by the war's end.

Douglas built the giant XB-19 for the Army Air Corp over several years before its first flight in June 1941, making most of its innovations outdated. Originally slated to get the equally massive Allison V-3420, this was delayed until 1943 after which it became the XB-19A seen here in flight. The re-engining did not change the assessment that the bomber was unsuitable for production and deployment. (*National Archives*)

Ground crewmen laboriously pull the enormous prop through on the No. 2 engine of the XB-19A on August 31, 1944. The narrow cowlings for the inline engine appears odd on the wings of a World War II American bomber. The aircraft was permanently devoted to flight test and so Wright Field, as denoted by the atypical logo beneath the pilot side window. (*National Archives*)

Above: The Allison V-3420 was created from the joining of two V-1710s, one of the few successful inline engines of the war. One of several "monster" power-plants evolved during the war, it weighed 2,600 lb (1,179 kg). Its size and complexity were indicative of the end of piston aero propulsion as jets emerged. (*National Museum of the United States Air Force*)

Below: The V-3420-11 testing eventually shifted to the YB-29 airframe to explore Superfortress performance improvements with the engine. The resulting XB-39 did not fly until the end of 1943 and did show speed gains. However, these were not significant enough to shift the production or shove aside the Wasp Major that was also a contender for an improved model B-29. (*National Archives*)

A B-29A was modified with the P&W R-4360 engine and began testing in the final months of the war as the XB-44. The performance improvement was most welcome, in addition to eliminating the temperamental R-3350. Although an order for 200 B-29Ds was placed in July 1945, this was reduced to sixty at the end of the war and ultimately completed in larger numbers as the B-50. (*Lloyd Jones collection*)

The unusually small cowling of the R-4360 in this censored image is testament to the small frontal area garnered from the four-row, seven-cylinder per row layout. The inherent power of the twenty-eight-cylinder giant was the appeal, despite the high weight of this one success from the "monster" engine effort. The testing on the XB-44 justified post-war piston-engined bomber production. (*Lloyd Jones collection*)

Turbo Boost

The turbosupercharger was one of American's most important and successful propulsion innovations of the war, supporting greater altitude performance of fighters and bombers by providing more compression for carburetion in the thin atmosphere. This greatly extended the capability of supercharging that was employed by all nations to one extent or another while also providing capacity for cabin pressurization. Although pioneered before the war, the device was only applied extensively in production applications during the conflict. There was continuing research into the best materials for the turbine in addition to developing automatic controls and improving operational safety. The equipment had to be carefully regulated to avoid surging the engine; developing and tuning the associated gear took much effort. Early production installations generated complaints about thrown turbine blades and fires that had to be addressed. Hence, flight testing was essential to continue perfecting the hardware.

One dedicated turbosupercharger testbed was created from a B-23 (39-050), bailed on February 20, 1942, to General Electric who was the principal developer of the turbine equipment. The modification and early flight testing were performed at the former American Airlines facilities at LaGuardia, New York. There, the engine nacelles were extensively modified to incorporate turbosuperchargers in a manner that allowed for ready alteration, four-blade propellers installed on the retained R-2600s although with revised cowlings, and the cabin altered to support pressurization (Chapter 8). The aircraft, dubbed XB-23 *The Robert E. Lee*, was ready for flight in December 1942. Early missions encountered heavy buffet from the nacelles that required revision. The work shifted to the Pan American Airways facilities in Brownsville, Texas, in spring 1944.[14]

The orientation of some turbosupercharger installations in the B-23 was such that the compressor output generated thrust. This may have been associated with the JB-1 (MX-543) program. The ground-launched "tailless" missile, with 2,000-lb (907-kg) bombs in the wing roots, was powered by two GE Type B1 turbosuperchargers connected to a combustion chamber in the center body. Each "engine" was to deliver 200-lbf (0.9-kN) thrust. Two prototype JB-1s were ordered in September 1944, and a launch on December 7, 1944, ended with the missile pitching up to stall and then crashing. The B1s were only producing about half their expected thrust and these were abandoned for a pulsejet engine.

The turbosupercharger was seen by some as the principal answer to outstanding performance and its inclusion in a design would attract praise from the military. This was simplistic, of course, and some models of successful types that included the weight and complexity of turbo boost found no benefit. The Grumman XF6F-2 incorporated the feature but did not proceed beyond flight test. Bell had been ordered to remove the turbosuperchargers from its original pre-production P-39s to shave weight, drag, and complexity. However, the compensating engine model with integral supercharger did not materialize and altitude performance suffered. Compromises were made and the production aircraft fell short of

Although this B-23 (39-050 *The Robert E. Lee*) retained its original Wright R-2600-3 engines, four-blade propellers were installed and the cowling and nacelles were radically altered to permit ready access to added turbosuperchargers and related equipment. Such draggy installations would only be tolerated on a testbed. The aircraft was operated by General Electric during the latter half of the war. (*National Museum of the United States Air Force*)

The new nacelles on the modified B-23 were the source of heavy buffeting that was never entirely corrected. The main gear doors appear to be made of wood slats and the normal cowl flaps have been removed for a fixed exit area along with changes to accommodate a duct that is probably to pass supercharged air to the carburetor. (*National Museum of the United States Air Force*)

These images show the Northrop JB-1 "powered bomb" under construction in a Hawthorne, California, shop. The staggered installation of the General Electric "jet engines" is evident along with an inlet and exhausts (the welded tubular assemblies are to simulate the bombs). The assembled missile of 28.3-foot (8.6-m) span looks clean and advanced but was destined for one failed flight before being redesigned for an actual turbojet engine. (*Gerald Balzer collection*)

expectations. Years later, Bell was compelled to test an added supercharger and then a turbosupercharger, each with intercooler, on a P-39D in a bid to improve the appeal of the notoriously anemic fighter. The podded arrangements added drag equaling or exceeded any gains and so the effort was to no avail. The SC-1 scout floatplane had the equipment in its first production model for no clear reason as the mission did not require it. The turbine was accompanied by safety hazards; it would occasionally throw blades and start fires. Operation was restricted and the operators usually removed the gear. The SC-2 model substituted a supercharger.

Above: By the time the Americans joined the war, the Bell Airacobra fell short of top-of-the-line performance. Efforts to improve the performance included increased boost from additional supercharging. This P-39D (40-6770) was modified to test additional supercharging and intercooler added as a saddleback fairing that cut speed by 45 mph (72 kph). (*Jay Miller collection*)

Below: Another supercharger modification saw the same P-39D carrying a turbosupercharger and intercooler in a belly fairing (mocked-up in this image). Seeking to raise the fighter's ceiling, the installation cut top speed by 40 mph (64 kph). This engineering trade-off was unacceptable to the operators and the idea proceeded no further. (*Jay Miller collection*)

Propelling Props

For high-performance military aircraft, there were just Aeroproducts, Curtiss Electric, and Hamilton Standard manufacturing propellers. Propellers were tested on outdoor whirl stands (static) and in wind tunnels (moving air), though the latter also introduced measurement errors from the presence of the tunnel walls. All props had to be optimized to an engine and airplane application. So, flight testing remained an essential regime for data collection verifying design predictions. Flow surveys or blade efficiency tests usually included an addition of pressure rakes installed behind the prop, typically projecting from cowlings or some other flight test rig. Multiple aircraft, suitably instrumented, were employed as flying propeller testbeds.

In the never-ending search for improved efficiency, especially as flight speed increased and tip speeds approached that of sound, several advances were pursued during the war. Designing propeller blades that retained efficiency to higher speeds as flow degraded from the tips in the presence of shocks was among the earliest supersonic work. Such efforts demanded flight test to augment ground-based data sources. Of the "simple" solutions were added blades to permit suitable thrust with a small diameter. Swept "scimitar" blades were also explored, with testing on a P-61.

Another innovation was coaxial, dual-rotation, or contra-rotating propellers ("contraprop") by which two propellers on the same engine, one behind the other, are turned in opposite directions on nested power shafts via a planetary gearbox. This seeks to take advantage of the air departing the forward propeller in a tangential orientation. This has the potential for improved efficiency by increasing the number of blades, reducing diameter, while also eliminating torque effects on aircraft handling. Detractors are greater weight and complexity as well as contributing additional vibration issues and noise. The first American example was a six-blade design developed by Hamilton Standard beginning in 1938 and eventually flown on the port engine of a B-23 from Rentschler Field. Of fighters, tests were performed on the XF4U-4 and a P-47D. The added effective area at the front of the airplane was destabilizing. Over a dozen American wartime airplane projects came to employ contra-rotating props, but none reached production. The added complexity of some potential solutions again pointed to the approaching end of the high-performance piston-engined evolution.

The reversible-pitch propellers were especially welcome on large aircraft like bombers in cutting stopping distance and assisting with ground movement in tight confines. A B-17F was modified with reversing props on the inboard engines and managed a landing roll of 900 feet (274 m) at 35,000 lb (15,876 kg) gross without the use of wheel brakes. This would normally have required something like 2,900 feet (884 m). A P-43 and P-47 with the Army, and F6F-3 with the Navy, tested reversing propellers to see their benefits.[15] Slowing fighters in flight with the props, especially in limiting dive speed without devices like flaps and brakes, was a notable interest. It held promise of such benefits as slowing after overtaking a bomber to extend gun firing time. There was concern with destabilizing influences of the props and the stress of going through zero when reversing.

This F4U-1A Corsair (49763 shown in Stratford, Connecticut) was one of two modified to test features of the F4U-4 that incorporated the R-2800-18W (water injection). This example, the F4U-4XA, has the new cowling plus square-tipped blades and spinner that were not adopted. Such work was the bread and butter of the propulsion test teams. (*Jay Miller collection*)

This P-39C has been fitted with a four-blade Curtiss Electric propeller for flight testing, replacing the standard three-blade unit. This was probably to assess candidates for the P-63. Seldom are such changes simple but they save time in the development of new aircraft types. (*Jay Miller collection*)

The Vought XF4U-4 (02460) (*left*) has been fitted with an Aeroproducts contra-rotating propeller consisting of two three-blade units. The blades are instrumented for vibration measurements during tests in summer 1945. Likewise, this P-47D (*right*) is prepared for an engine run with an instrumented dual-rotation prop. (*Jay Miller collection and The Peter M. Bowers Collection/The Museum of Flight*)

Jet Learning

The turbine engines were new to all and presented significant engineering challenges of efficient inlet design, heat of the exhaust, and extracting power for ancillary equipment. The power plants also demanded dedicated flight test for development and just allowing design teams to become familiar with the equipment and installation. All players contributed to the learning and documentation of findings. Particularly, NACA helped with basic studies of component efficiencies and engine operation in their altitude propulsion tunnels. It was there they found it advisable to bypass or bleed-off any boundary layer from a forebody ahead of the inlet, like the fuselage, to ensure suitable flow into the compressor—such was already being done for other inlets or intakes on existing recip designs to avoid pressure loss inside ducting. Of course, with the rush to build airplanes with these entirely new and immature propulsion systems, every airplane incorporating them became a *de facto* testbed. However, some surrogate airframes were used to test the jet engines while retaining the normal propulsion system as a safety measure. These particularly permitted air-start tests without inducing complete power loss.

Among the first applications of such engines for the Navy was to create hybrids with recips as the primary propulsion unit. This permitted the fuel-guzzling turbojets to be used only for heavy weight take-off and bursts of speed in combat. Another benefit was for wave-off during a carrier approach. The turbine engine took seconds to spin up on a throttle push and so power advance was too slow. The reciprocating engine and propeller were needed to ensure a safe wave-off. The turbojet's low-speed performance also gave distressingly long take-off rolls and it was accepted that catapult launch would be routine aboard ship.

Curtiss was tasked with developing one such hybrid as the U.S. Navy's XF15C-1 with R-2800 and J36. The goal of all these hybrid projects was a 500-mph (805-kph) fighter, and this kept up the chase after high-speed propeller efficiency.

This turbojet was an Allis-Chalmers development of the 2,700-lbf (12-kN) de Havilland Goblin engine. Since the jet engine was new to Curtiss as it began its XF15C work, and this airplane would rely upon air-starts while burning other than kerosene, the company sought an engine testbed to prove out these features and generally gain familiarity with the power plant. The Navy lent the firm a XTBF-3 Avenger (24141) to be modified in spring 1944. The J36 was housed in a fairing beneath the bomb bay and fed by two inlets under the forward fuselage. The navigator and radio operator stations were taken over with instrumentation and a monitoring position. The *Fertile Myrtle* flew with its new belly compartment in September 1944. The first Goblin was delivered from Britain and operated satisfactorily in ground tests on the Avenger during November 1944, flight operation following in December.[16]

Another turbine engine planned as a "booster" was the Westinghouse X19A Yankee turbojet, one of the first axial-flow turbojets and producing 1,000 lbf (4.5 kN). The first was run on a test stand on March 19, 1943. A Goodyear FG-1 Corsair was employed as a testbed for the second X19A with the first flight on January 21, 1944. The 19-inch (38-cm) diameter engine was fitted in a nacelle under the fighter's belly. The follow-on 19B Yankee turbojet at 1,600 lbf (7.2 kN) was installed for testing in the aft fuselage of a Navy Martin B-26 (JM-1 66599), with inlets in the sides. The modification was performed by Martin at their Baltimore, Maryland, facility and involved engine mount, firewall, fuel feed, engine control, fire suppression, and test equipment in the waist gunner's station. The engine was in the volume that normally constituted the tail gunner position. It was on a cradle free to move axially against a thrust measuring device. The fuel for the jet was in the long-range tank in the aft weapons bay.[17] The first operation aboard the JM-1 in flight was on September 28, 1944.

The AAF initiated jet bomber conceptual design efforts in the latter half of 1943 and formal projects were initiated in fall 1944. The goal was 500 mph (805 kph) top speed as a means of staying ahead of enemy fighters or reduce an intercept to a tail chase where tail guns became the only defensive weapons necessary. NACA developed a twin-engined jet nacelle with drag equal to that of a single-engined nacelle. This was almost certainly derived from calculations and wind tunnel, and not flight test. It was beneficial to all that flight tests with at least the new propulsion systems provide fundamental installation and operation data to bomber design teams. This was best achieved by an installation as a jet power plant nacelle in an existing prop-driven bomber.

The experimental installation goal was met by adding two podded jet engines to the experimental XB-42 under MX-880. This aircraft had two V-1710 engines driving coaxial pusher propellers at the end of the fuselage, leaving the wings free for a clean installation of the Westinghouse 19XB-2A turbojets. The 1.58-foot^2 (0.48-m^2) frontal area, 1,600-lbf (7-kN) unit could fit in a neat pod under each wing. Although entirely separate control and systems were introduced, the jets burned the same fuel as the XB-42's inlines. The modification as the XB-42A (43-50224) was still underway at the end of the war.

Among the dedicated testbeds for America's new jet engines was this Goodyear-built F4U (FG-1) of unclear Bureau Number. The Westinghouse X19A axial flow turbojet "booster" is attached to the belly for trials in 1944 (January 18 image). No doubt a separate fuel system was created to deliver the kerosene to the jet. (*National Archives and San Diego Air & Space Museum*)

The Navy also had this JM-1 (Martin B-26) modified with a booster engine in the extreme aft fuselage. Note the starboard inlet duct, another on the port side, for the Westinghouse 19B. The jet exhausted under the tail, although no jet blast warning stencils are evident in this June 28, 1944 photograph. (*National Museum of the United States Air Force*)

The odd XB-42 was rendered even more unusual at the end of the war with the addition of two 19XB-2A turbojets in "scabbed-on" underwing pods suggested by this author-retouched image. This offered early insight into jet engine integration and design challenges as the USAAF pushed manufacturers to begin developing jet-powered bombers. The extensive modification was still proceeding as the war reached its conclusion. (*Author's collection*)

Another hybrid saw a General Electric I-16-3 centrifugal-flow turbojet mated to a Douglas A-26B (44-34586), creating the XA-26F. This 1,600-lbf unit had a 4.1-foot^2 (1.3-m^2) frontal area. Mounting the 804-lb (365-kg) engine in the aft fuselage and exhausting out the end, an inlet was placed amidships where the gunner normally sat. A separate kerosene fuel supply drew from tankage in the bomb bay. The modification program began in July 1945 and the engine was operated installed during October, with flight following soon after. Similar work was performed by GE using B-24s to test turbojets—an inlet above the fuselage with an S-duct to the engine mounted within and exhausting out the aft end.[18]

The Americans were also developing a turboprop engine, then called the propeller turbine. The General Electric TG-100 (later T31-GE-3) also needed flight testing and, instead of a typical centerline mounting installation on a testbed aircraft, it was mounted to the starboard nacelle of a modified C-46G (44-78945) to become the XC-113. Design of the modification was still underway at the end of the war and modifications at Curtiss' Columbus, Ohio, plant did not begin until April 1946. The different thrust and throttle response characteristics of the two power plants on either side of the aircraft centerline made for quite problematic directional control characteristics. This led to a ground mishap that ended the program before flight.

Above: Testing the first turboprop also required a flight test platform and a C-46G was selected (note the stepped windscreen). Curtiss did the modification that was still in the planning stages when the war wrapped up (post-war image shown here). The first engine runs revealed the differences in thrust and reaction to the throttle that made directional control so haphazard that the machine never left the ground. (*The Peter M. Bowers Collection/The Museum of Flight*)

Opposite above: Also seeking integration engineering data was the motive behind mating of an I-16 turbojet to an A-26B. This hybrid is externally evident by the inlet above the aft fuselage and the jet exhaust out the aft end. The XA-26F modifications were still in progress as the war wrapped up. (*Ray Wagner collection*)

Opposite below: General Electric employed several B-24s as turbojet engine testbeds with the inlet above the fuselage, an s-duct to the engine within, and an exhaust out the aft end. The NACA used the same arrangement to test the effects of icing by spraying water onto the inlet in flight to induce ice formation. This C-109 (fuel transport / tanker version of the B-24) has been so modified. (*National Museum of the United States Air Force*)

4

Rocket Promise

The Air Corps had been investigating assisted take-off (ATO) devices since before the war. This sought to achieve a quicker take-off from short fields or take off at heavy weight for standard length fields, standard weight from a high density-altitude field, or clearing high obstacles in the climb-out path. It was also hoped that getting a heavy bomber off on a conventional runway and saving fuel would permit greater range and payload such that exceptionally large bombers like the Douglas B-19 would not be necessary. The service set a goal of reducing take-off over a 50-foot (15-m) obstacle by 25 percent, equated to reducing ground roll by 50 percent. Numerous concepts were explored and, with the advent of war, these received greater attention and funding.

A Boost Up

The Army assessed the potential of land-based catapults like those found on Navy aircraft carriers. This was rejected because of complexity and the heavy equipment that would need to be transported and erected. Adaptation for heavy aircraft like bombers appeared impractical, and any airplane would require modifications to interface with the equipment. A powered dolly, propelled by rockets or other means and presumably running on tracks, was similarly constrained. Additionally, a short take-off was expected to be followed by a short landing on the same field. The landing would require some manner of arrestment system that, again, bespoke heavy equipment and gross weight limitations resricting use to fighter-type aircraft. Realigning any of these devices with the wind, or at minimum an opposite direction take-off, was prohibitive.

Some aircraft could not be held by brakes while engines were run up to full power and so had to run down the runway consuming take-off distance while rpm rose. For these, a system of restraints was proposed to be released upon command or under a certain force associated with full power. Scaling all this up for a powered combat aircraft, especially a heavy bomber, appeared unworkable.

The adaptation of glider ground launch methods for powered aircraft was also examined. These included a winch or flywheel pulling the aircraft up to flight speed via a cable that was then released by the pilot, or a tensioned bungee that naturally fell away as the aircraft passed overhead. The idea of dropping a heavy weight down a deep well to provide the pull force was also posited, though not a technique used by gliders. In spring 1945, a contract was proposed with All American Aviation Corporation of Wilmington, Delaware, to develop some manner of winch system. Search for a powerful enough engine to pull the heavy cable came to focus on the Allison V-1710.[1] The effort appears to have been canceled with the end of the war. Apart from the danger of propeller entanglement on the cable, the time interval between take-offs was also seen as too great for launching a flight of airplanes.

A more daring scheme was the Merry-Go-Round or Picket Rope method by which the aircraft accelerated on a cable around a low mast until reaching flight speed and getting airborne upon which the pilot released. An attachment and release mechanism was necessary, and likely airframe strengthening for the radial forces for up to 1-*g* lateral acceleration (expected to be uncomfortable for the flight crew). The hazards of an early or unexpected release were obvious, discounting the problem of releasing into the wind or the crew becoming dizzy. For a 120-mph (164-kph) take-off speed, a cable of nearly 1,000 feet (305 m) would be required. The system was tested with an Aeronca light-plane piloted by Mr. J. A. Roche during which he flew the airplane around the anchor at 40 feet (12 m) before releasing.[2]

The AAC investigated means of boosting take-off performance to get off in a shorter distance or get a heavy airplane off in a standard length. Adapting glider winch tow was considered; an example mobile winch shown along with a Navy Schweizer LNS-1 (Army TG-2) being pulled aloft. The hazards of a propeller strike on the cable or failure to release, plus the heavy engine and cable mechanism, made this approach appear impractical. (*National Soaring Museum*)

A sloping runway permitted gravity to assist in accelerating the aircraft to take-off speed in a shorter distance downhill and in decelerating on landing uphill. An elevation change of 400–500 feet (122–152 m) over the length of the runway, or perhaps 29 percent grade or 15 degrees, was expected to be of best value and practical. A tractor or winch might be required to pull an aircraft to the top of such a runway if it could not taxi up under its own power. Of course, the landing would be in the opposite direction and, save for calm winds, only a headwind in any of the two reciprocal headings provided an advantage and otherwise a disadvantage unless another runway was built on the opposite side of the rising terrain. One motivation for the concept was intelligence about the Germans building inclined runways on the French coast during 1941.

An "accelerated" runway was built up a hill adjoining the Wright Field runway complex. With 10 percent grade (6.5 degrees), it was employed in 1942 for tests with heavy bombers. Nothing operationally feasible emerged from the trials. Later, the runway was used to aid brake testing that included use of a non-flyable A-20 (the outer wing panels removed).[3]

All of these ATO ideas were analyzed and some tested, but only attaching rocket boosters to the aircraft appeared practical for "super-performance." However, it was estimated that suitable ATO rockets would require two years to develop a fieldable device. Only a chemical rocket of liquid or solid propellants was likely to deliver the necessary thrust, compressed gases and liquids being dismissed. Between the wars, rocket motors had emerged as practical for at least projectiles. They appeared easy to operate since throttling might not be necessary and performance would be minimally affected by field elevation since the fuel included an oxidizer. Such a booster rocket could be dropped after take-off so as not to burden the aircraft with the drag and dead weight for the remainder of the mission.[4]

The modern rocket era had dawned in American with the pioneering liquid propulsion work of Dr. Robert H. Goddard who was largely funded by the Daniel Guggenheim Foundation. However, by World War II, he had grown reclusive and conducted his work in secret. The War Department engaged him in the effort to develop a booster motor, mostly with Navy sponsorship. They were particularly interested in assisting heavy flying boats up to lift-off speed and breaking free of the water. It was calculated that the Consolidated PBY could get off with an additional 5,000 lb (2,268 kg) if just 880 lbf (3.6 kN) of thrust was added for sufficient duration. The Army sought an 800-lbf (3.6-kN) unit burning for twenty seconds.[5] Goddard's tests in Roswell, New Mexico, were encouraging. However, while he demonstrated a liquid propellant motor, the unit was judged impractical. The effort ultimately proved fruitless while other options came to the fore.

As with many such endeavors, there was no shortage of eager civilian experimenters seeking attention for their ideas and prototype hardware. One such was the Myers Impulse Reaction Aircraft Engine offered by E. G. Hines and E. B. Myers of the Myers Motor Company in New York. Myers insisted it was not a rocket motor and wrote that "it differs in the essential detail of having controlled power thrust regulated to the speed of the aircraft propelled, altitude, and service desired." He calculated that the device could be scaled up to deliver the equivalent of 5,000 hp (37 kW) or propel an aircraft to "100% increase above full throttle at sea level—1,500 miles per hour at 40,000 ft," yet would weigh "one twentieth of a pound per thrust horsepower (installed)." While the liquid fuel motor produced thrust during Wright Field tests in January, February, and April 1941, it was far from practical as a combat aircraft propulsion unit or even booster. The propellants were also exceptionally hazardous to handle. The matter was set aside at a December 22 meeting as alternatives appeared much more practical.[6]

One manufacturer of rocket projectile propellants, Monsanto Chemical Company, suggested it could work towards a booster motor. One such compound was easy to handle, this consisting of equal parts ammonium picrate and sodium nitrate, plus 5 percent special urea formaldehyde as a bonding agent. Monsanto built a pilot production plant in Dayton, Ohio, and they continued to pursue ATO at a low level throughout the war. However, the Army found their best partner in Aerojet Engineering Corporation of Azusa, California.

The firm grew from a 1939 association of Caltech academics, though the foundational work dated from the preceding few years. These included Professor von Kármán, Frank J. Malina, Edward S. Forman, and John W. Parsons, joined later by Apollo M. O. Smith and Hsue-shen Tsien. Caltech's rocket work had begun in the latter half of the 1930s. While these men hoped ultimately to build sounding rockets, their initial focus (apart from Malina's Ph.D.) was ATO booster rockets. Their inspiration came from Ruben Fleet, president of Consolidated Aircraft, who encouraged the young researchers as he saw rockets someday assisting the take-off of his larger airplanes.[7] Professor von Kármán and Hap Arnold had previously discussed booster rockets. The General had visited Caltech in May 1938 and observed what the men were cooking up. Arnold was captivated by the potential and called on the National Academy of Sciences Committee on Air Corps Research, in the fall of that year, to explore the technology. With this push, the team was awarded $1,000 at the end of the year via the NAS and $10,000 in June 1939—the first federal investment in rocketry.

The Air Corps pumped in more money each year via the NAS grant as the booster rocket work showed progress. In February 1940, this U.S. Army Air Corps Jet Propulsion Research Project established the goal of developing an airplane boost motor generating 1,000 lbf (4.5 kN) thrust for sixty seconds to test within a year under MX-121. The researchers struggled with explosively rapid burning of solid "powder" propellants that would produce forces and accelerations much too great for aircraft applications. What was needed was ramp up to near-constant thrust for a sufficient number of seconds to assist a take-off until the motor burned out. Sustaining the burn became a matter of a constant ratio of nozzle throat and burning area of the fuel as it was consumed for a constant chamber pressure. After the Caltech researchers nearly blew up a lab, an experimental facility was improvised on leased land in the nearby Arroyo Seco dry gulch.

The Caltech team eventually arrived at a suitably evenly burning propellant of amidic black powder packed under 18 tons (16,329 kg) pressure as 1-inch (2.5-cm) layers into a steel chamber or "bottle" lined with incremented blotting paper and then coated with roofing tar mixed in its molten state with aluminum perchlorate. They soon had a cylindrical rocket motor 1.75 inches (8.9 cm) in diameter and 10 inches (25.4 cm) long that produced 28 lbf (0.13 kN) for twelve seconds when ignited by an electric spark. Unfortunately, although the fuel burned evenly down the length of the tube, it tended to expand and contract with temperature and to crack. This altered the burning area and occasionally produced an explosion. Nonetheless, the success won the team a further $29,000 from the AAC in 1940. This helped fund more permanent installations at Arroyo Seco that came to be called the Experiment Station for the Air Corps Jet Propulsion Research Project.[8]

Despite the difficulties, the Caltech team thought the boosters suitable if attached to a light airplane for an initial proof-of-concept demonstration. They fortunately had an AAC officer from Wright Field in their midst. Captain Homer A. Boushey, Jr., was a graduate student there, and so a student of von Kármán. Boushey was also a rocket devotee and proposed using an Engineering and Research Corp. (ERCO) Ercoupe 415C to test the rocket motors. This was among the lightest airplanes they could lay their hands on (753 lb/342 kg empty and with a 65-hp/49-kW engine) yet able to safely fly back under power when the rockets were expended. The Air Corps had acquired the Ercoupe on February 26, 1941, as the solitary YO-55 (41-18875, but still carrying the civil registration NC28655) to test its unique control system (aileron-rudder interconnect, no rudder pedals). Boushey collected the Ercoupe at Wright Field and flew it out to March Field, in Riverside, the closest air base to the GALCIT facilities.

Captain Boushey attended a demonstration of the rockets at Arroyo Seco only to see a nozzle fail and the motor explode. Regardless, he decided to proceed. Testing began on August 6 with the Ercoupe tied down and a pod of three rockets attached under each wing, these producing a combined 180 lbf (0.8 kN). During this static firing, another nozzle popped off and ricocheted off the pavement to pass through the skin of the empennage. Yet again, the intrepid experimenters chose to proceed to flight later that day. The aircraft took off and the rockets clusters were ignited while cruising above the field at 8,000 feet (2,348 m). All went well except for one motor failing to ignite.

Pondering the failures, Parsons realized the motors that failed had been loaded days before and had undergone several day–night temperature cycles. This would cause the propellant cracking and uneven burning. Only motors loaded soon before a test and rushed to the field would be used until the problem could be resolved. Again, Boushey elected to continue.

The August 12 test was to see the six rockets ignited during the take-off roll under engine power. The Ercoupe got off in about half the normal distance (300 feet/91 m *versus* 580 feet/177 m) and Boushey had to climb at a 50-degree angle to avoid overspeeding the aircraft. Several more such flights were executed that day. A take-off with a dozen rockets and engine idling attempted to cross above a streamer suspended 50 feet across the runway, but the Ercoupe failed to clear the "obstacle."

The first American aircraft to fly entirely under rocket power was the light YO-55 (Ercoupe 415C) on August 26, 1941, at March Field, California. This photo is of the attempt to fly over a 50-foot obstacle with engine idling (to permit a powered return) and twelve rockets firing. The rockets pushed the craft to such a high speed that the pilot had to climb at a steep angle to avoid over-speeding the airplane. (*National Archives*)

On von Kármán's suggestion, the propeller was removed and a take-off attempted on August 23 with six rockets under each wing providing the motive force. On the first attempt, the aircraft accelerated slowly and the motors burned out before reaching flight speed. Boushey proposed the aircraft needed a rolling start. He held onto a rope, tied to a truck, out the open canopy so that the Ercoupe was towed to about 25 mph (40 kph) at which point the rope slipped from Boushey's grasp and the pilot then lit the rockets. On August 26, employing this technique, the Ercoupe got off but only to about 20 feet (6.1 m) before the motors were exhausted. Boushey glided back to the runway. With the weight and drag of the empty rocket bottles, plus limited elevator travel, the landing wasn't pretty. Yet, it still marked America's first experience with aircraft rocket propulsion.

Much had been learned about handling the rocket bottles, and their capability in boosting airplane performance was proven. The propellant cracking issue was corrected after much effort. The team settled on a mix of 75 percent potassium or ammonium perchlorate, 15 percent asphalt tar, and 10 percent lubricating oil. Continuing interest at Wright Field saw trials in August 1941 with GALCIT 30-lbf (0.1-kN) solid motors. By November 1941, they were planning tests with a P-40K (42-10343) employing three 200-lbf (0.9-kN) motors possessing eight-second burn, followed by four eight-sec 500-lbf (2.2-kN) bursts, and then two eight-sec 1,000-lbf (4.5-kN) bottles.

The USAAF Aircraft Laboratory established a Jet Propulsion Branch and Wright Field was also building a rocket test facility expected to be ready by 1943. Most initial Air Forces flight testing was also undertaken in Dayton where nearly every USAAF airplane type was evaluated with the rockets. They and the USN evaluated

5-inch diameter British cordite four-second burn units (#5 MK 1/n) that initially delivered an average 1,500 lbf (6.7 kN). Storage requirements were less stringent than the Aerojet products and they generated less smoke.

The Aerojet and British rockets were evaluated in helping combat glider landing deceleration or to extend a dragged-in landing. Here again, for these very light and low-speed aircraft, it was important that all motors fire and do so near-simultaneously to avoid a possibly uncontrollable yaw. In one test, only one motor fired and the CG-4A glider abruptly turned a full 360 degrees to stop at the point of landing—a qualified success at best.[9] Although the glider test teams found the British rocket suitable, the wider AAF judged them unreliable and the burn too short for their purposes.

With encouraging results and Navy collaboration, the Engineering Division sought production of the GALCIT rockets and endorsed a proposal to build a plant in Arroyo Seco. The academics approached several manufacturers as prospective partners, but none were interested in the "Buck Rogers" technology. Consequently, the group decided to strike out on their own and Aerojet was incorporated on March 19, 1942. The core was von Kármán, Malina, Martin Summerfield, Forman, Parsons, and Andrew G. Haley (a lawyer with business experience). They continued to use Caltech assets for their development work and that caused some concern since the campus was supposed to be non-profit. This was eventually resolved.

Aerojet's immediate two contracts, totaling $3 million, was to develop a production solid-fuel ATO. By December 1942, they had 150 employees and initial deliveries were in early 1943. The government began work on a $149,000 pilot plant in Azusa. By summer 1943, the firm had $500,000 worth of business and could barely keep up. In January 1945, they became a division of General Tire and Rubber Company. It remained largely an R&D organization, with most actual manufacturing performed by subcontractors. Aerojet attracted mostly young, imaginative, and adventurous engineers, and this proved beneficial.

The Navy had conducted trials of ATO systems since 1940 at the Navy Engineering Experimental Station in Annapolis, Maryland. These included liquid and solid propellants, the later with devices similar to Aerojet products. Liquid propellants were not welcome aboard ship and so were more suitable for flying boats and large land-based aircraft. One of the Annapolis team's earliest tests may have been the take-off on May 25, 1942, of a F2A-3 Buffalo by Lt (jg) C. Fink Fischer aided by five British solid-propellant rockets. The take-off distance was cut by 49 percent.[10] The USN employed Aerojet rockets to assist heavy aircraft off carrier decks (presumably not part of a catapult launch). The service concluded the 200-lbf (0.9-kN) bottles were the most promising, reducing take-off roll by 50 percent and improving handling via good take-off airspeed.

The 200-lbf rocket weighed 41 lb (19 kg) and burned for eight seconds (8AS-200 or "8-seconds Aerojet Solid 200 pounds"). They were 1.3 feet (0.4 m) long and 0.5 feet (0.2 m) in diameter. The Navy also had a five-second version of this motor manufactured. Some 8AS-500 units were also produced for service trials, weighing 110 lb (50 kg) when loaded; they were 2 feet (0.15 m) long and

These shots show the Aerojet 200-lbf ATO rockets and possibly the British 5-inch motor in tests with CG-4A and CG-15A gliders involving both rapidly slowing with forward firing and boosted final approach through rearward firing. These helped avoid excessive landing speeds or an extended landing approach. These tests did not yield a fielded capability, especially as the failure of one motor to ignite could have dire consequences. (*National Soaring Museum and The Museum of Flight*)

An extension of the glider tests with ATO was used with the experimental powered gliders. These were so underpowered that the take-off assist was important for them to carry much of a useful load. Here the Waco XPG-3 is helped aloft by what are likely two 200-lbf (0.9-kN) bottles installed under the wings at the attach point for the struts. (*The Museum of Flight*)

The U.S. Navy had been working along a parallel path as the Army on booster rockets, similarly finding the Aerojet products superior and began to buy quantities for flight trials. A test of a Grumman F6F Hellcat fighter with two 200-lbf 8AS-200 motors shows it flying off a carrier deck without the aid of the catapult. The sea service soon became the largest purchaser and user of the Aerojet ATO bottles. (*Naval Aviation Archives*)

Flying boats could particularly benefit from the use of ATO rockets. Although they ostensibly had miles of water on which to take-off, they required almost that in surface run to get airborne and this could be hazardous in anything but modest swells. A heavy boat (PBM shown) could have particular difficulty getting on the "step" and breaking free of surface suction, but this was made easier with rocket ATO. (*Naval Aviation Archives*)

0.7 feet (0.20 m) in diameter. Likewise, 15AS-750 units (3.3 kN) units weighed 227 lb (103 kg) when loaded.

Although the Aerojet motors produced a jet of hot gas for propulsion, the ATO name was actually adopted to avoid ridicule from using "rocket," which was considered a subject of pulp fiction and not a serious academic or industrial pursuit. The designation RATO was seldom used at the time and JATO only post-war.

Aerojet's development soon yielded a 1,000-lbf (4.5-kN) motor that became the most widely used ATO solid propellant unit. AWith a twelve-second burn, this was the equivalent of about 330 hp (246 kW) at 90 mph (14 kph). The 1,000-lbf units were manufactured with five-, eight-, ten-, twelve-, twenty-, and thirty-second durations, though 8AS-1000 and 12AS-1000 were the most common. Longer burns meant no abrupt change in acceleration during a take-off if the motors cut off, complicating the pilot's task. The thrust produced depended on the area of the propellant burning and the nozzle dimensions. Long burn times eroded the solid copper nozzle and degraded performance. A burn time of thirty seconds or more generally required a steel nozzle with carbon throat insert. A burn from soon after brake release to a point during the climb (beyond 50 feet) would be ideal for a land-based aircraft while a carrier-based machine just had to get off the deck at flying speed.

The 12AS-1000 steel bottle was 36 inches (91 cm) long and 10 inches (25 cm) in diameter, weighing 205 lb (93 kg) when loaded. The 8AS-1000 weighed 190 lb (86 kg) loaded and 115 lb (52 kg) empty; it was 30 inches (76 cm) long and 12 inches (31 cm) in diameter. The 15AS-1000 (twelve produced) weighed 267 lb (121 kg) when loaded and the 30AS-1000 weighed 459 lb (208 kg). Each bottle cost $200–300.

The Aerojet ATO motors were ignited with an electric squib fired by command from the cockpit using the common aircraft 12- or 24-V system. The squib was a black powder igniter or "flash cap" screwed into the base of the motor to produce the required 700 degrees F (371 degrees C). The motor reached full thrust in less than half a second. Propellant burned at a rate of about 1 inch (2.5 cm) per second with an internal pressure of 1,800–2,500 psi (124–173 bar). A safety blowout device near the nozzle prevented bottle bursting if internal pressures exceeded safe limits (1.5 times operating pressure). This was a frangible diaphragm under a deflector cap that slowed particles to prevent aircraft damage. The bottle had three mounting lugs for attachment to fittings that had to be specially installed on the aircraft, along with installing the ignition electrical elements. The motors had to be placed and oriented carefully so as not to produce unwanted aircraft pitching and where uncontrollable yawing would not result if any of several motors failed to light. The fittings could be made to drop the empty motor after exhaustion. The bottle could be reconditioned and reloaded if recovered intact (very seldom done). The Navy preferred to drop the expended bottles over water for recovery. They usually suffered no damage and floated upright, about two-thirds submerged.

The motor burned with a load hiss and produced a prodigious cloud of dense but harmless greyish-white smoke visible from quite a distance and required five to fifteen seconds to disperse depending on wind conditions. This could settle on objects as a non-injurious water-soluble deposit, containing potassium chloride and carbon monoxide (comparable to the output from the aircraft engine). The 3–4-inch (7.6–10.2-cm) flame was generally only visible at night and not blinding. Aerojet was working on a "smokeless" propellant called Aeroplex. It was also observed that piercing the bottle with a .50-cal round ignited (not detonated) the propellant. The bottles had to be stored nozzle-up, with a cap over the nozzle, and at no less than 10 degrees F (-12 degrees C) or more than 120 degrees F (49 degrees C). The fuel shrank and cracked along the bottle walls if too cold. On ignition, this presented a larger burning surface and generally blowout of the pressure release. Too hot and the propellant could flow very slowly over time like tar such that a flat burning surface was not present. Although reduced from an initial 40 degrees F lower value (9.4 degrees C), the storage temperature requirements proved difficult to meet in some field scenarios and was the source of most criticism.

Aerojet prepared for mass production but got few large orders from the Pentagon. Through tested at Wright Field and with field units, AAF operational interest was weak. Aerojet was close to disbanding in spring 1943. Yet, a demonstration launch of a Grumman fighter from the deck of the escort carrier USS *Charger* (CVE-30) in Norfolk with 200-lbf units went well save for the smoke annoyingly obscuring

What were probably the most common 1,000-lb (4.5-kN) ATO boost units are seen attached under a boom of the Fairchild C-82. The image shows the nozzle, the electrical igniter connection, the safety pressure release plug, the flat base for lifting and storage with the nozzle up, and attachment brackets. Most such installations permitted the bottles to be dropped immediately after take-off at propellant exhaustion to cut weight and drag. (*Air Force Test Center*)

the flight deck for a short period in addition to washing across the Navy brass and discoloring their uniforms. The USN subsequently went for the rockets in a big way as their Pacific island-hopping campaign expanded, using them to get heavy airplanes off the short "jeep" carrier decks, for heavy flying boats, and other activities. The service began placing orders for thousands of units, with most going to Hawaii for service trials. The USN mounted one 8AS-1000 unit on the belly of the F4F but two on all other fighters and dive bombers. The Grumman TBF required four. Take-off distance was reduced anywhere from 33 to 59 percent (without catapult).[11] They also had Aerojet develop 15AS-1500, 25AS-2000, 45AS-1500, and 62AS-1200 motors.

The Azusa facility expanded tremendously and employees rose to 1,600. Capacity reached approximately 1,100 8AS-1000 and 12AS-1000 bottles per annum with a goal of loading 400 bottles per day.

GALCIT also began pursuing liquid propellants on July 1, 1940, with Dr. Summerfield the principal researcher under von Kármán's supervision. Their efforts through 1942 initially focused, like many others, on gasoline and kerosene mixed with liquid oxygen (LOX). The LOX was objectionable to the services and so red fuming nitric acid was substituted as an oxidizer. When this proved unsatisfactory, they substituted monoethylaniline (aniline) as the fuel on the advice of Navy Lt Robert C. Truax and Ensign Ray C. Stiff of the Annapolis station. The spontaneous hypergolic combustion was steady and spontaneous. Compact and self-contained 1,000-lbf motors were built for testing as an aircraft booster. The USAAF was unhappy employing the toxic aniline (also used in explosives and so production was carefully regulated), just as they had been adamant that LOX was impractical in tactical environments. However, ground testing was so successful they quieted their opposition.

The Army was quite interested in the Aerojet liquid rocket booster because of the promise of greater thrust and longer burn times, plus the ability to throttle and restart the motor. Weight and servicing would be the trade-off. The first practical Aerojet unit was completed in February 1942 and one each was installed in the aft end of the engine nacelles on a Douglas A-20A Havoc medium bomber. A sphere of compressed nitrogen (1,800 psi/124 bar) forced the two propellants, at a ratio of 1.5:1 nitric acid to aniline, from their tanks and into the combustion chamber at a pressure of 300 psi (20.7 bar). Each unit weighed 650 lb (295 kg), was under a new nacelle tail cone, and burned for 35 sec.

The test aircraft was flown from Wright Field to Burbank and then on to Muroc by Maj. Paul H. Dane, another former student of von Kármán who would remain involved in rocket motor development. After several ground runs with the installation, the first flight test occurred on April 22, 1942. Dane followed a line laid in oil on the lakebed surface and the rockets were operated on board by Beverly Forman. The recip engines were started and then the rockets. From a standing start, the aircraft roared off in a short distance and climbed out at an astonishingly steep angle. Take-off distance had been cut by 32 percent.

Other tests followed and the USAAF ordered sixty units to equip thirty Havocs for service trials. Assembly was underway in November 1942 and all had been

Liquid propellants offered potentially for greater thrust and longer burn time for ATO, plus the ability to throttle and restart the motor, though weight and servicing would be the trade-off. The Douglas A-20A is seen with the motor on the aft face of one engine nacelle and then in take-off from the Muroc dry lakebed on April 22, 1942. The motor operated by the man visible at the aft gunner's station. (*Air Force Test Center*)

delivered and were engaged in testing by the end of 1943. The 25AL-1000 motor burned for twenty-five seconds, weighing 240 lb (109 kg) empty and 397 lb (180 kg) loaded. They reduced the take-off distance over a 50-foot obstacle by 33 percent and improved climb rate by 15 percent. They were also seen as a means for a bomber to accelerate away from attackers, increasing the A-20's level flight speed from 150 to 197 mph (241 to 317 kph) at burn out. The exhaust from the rockets was less pronounced than with the solids but were hazardous to personnel until it dispersed. At very low altitude, the hot carbon particles emitted by the motors could start brush fires.

Aerojet then developed a podded unit to be fitted under wings and so reduce the extent of aircraft modifications. The 25ALD-1000 (Aerojet liquid droppable) included a 24-foot (7.3-m) diameter parachute for recovery after release. Weighing 382 lb (173 kg) fueled and 225 lb (102 kg) empty, they were 6.2 feet (1.9 m) long and with 1.1 × 1.8 feet (0.3 × 0.6 m) in frontal dimensions. Six experimental units were ready by June 1943. The AAF then ordered 100 production motors for delivery by December and 100 for delivery early the following year. The motors cost $3,000–4,000 each and were entirely self-contained save for pilot controls. The motor could be started and stopped repeatedly but was not considered low drag enough to be retained after take-off for use.

Testing was performed on several types during 1943 and 1944. A heavy B-25C bomber with two, then four, of the motors mounted under the wings measured take-off distance reduced by 30 percent. Two were installed under the wings inboard of each inboard engine on B-24D 41-1125 for testing in fall 1943 through spring 1944, which reduced the take-off run by a third. A similar installation

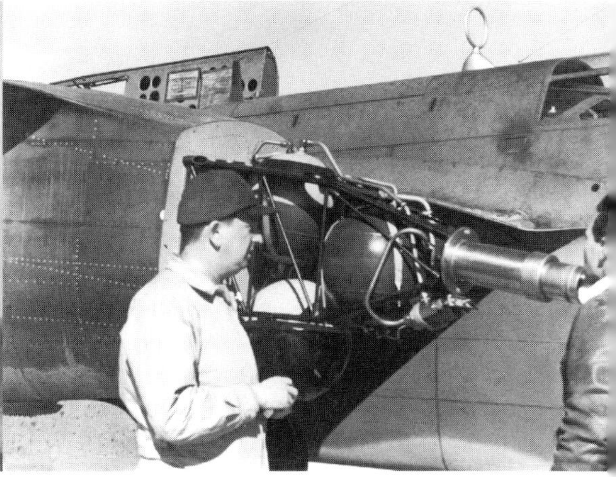

Above: A production design of the 1,000-lbf liquid propellant motor for the Havoc was procured to convert thirty airplanes. The 25AL-1000 is seen under test aboard an A-20B (41-2990) at Wright Field. The pilots were enthusiastic about cutting take-off distance by a third or briefly adding 45 mph (72 kph) to their level flight speed, but the capability simply was not vitally needed. (*Air Force Test Center and National Museum of the United States Air Force*)

Below: A podded version of the Aerojet 1,000-lbf liquid-propellant ATO was created to greatly reduce the extent of aircraft modifications to employ it. The 25AL-1000 motor is shown without the outer fairing and aerodynamic nose cap. Visible are the three tanks for propellants and pressurizing gas, and propellant lines to the combustion chamber ahead of the nozzle. (*Air Force Test Center*)

Above: Flight-ready 25AL-1000 motors are shown in pairs under a B-25C (41-13039, photographed on February 21, 1944). Also seen are the flight deck controls for the four motors (top panel between sunshades). Widely tested (a September 25, 1944 flight trials image), the system was practical and safe but simply not worth the effort of adopting it for operational application. (*Air Force Test Center and National Museum of the United States Air Force and National Archives*)

Below: The Aerojet 1,000-lbf liquid propellant motor was revised to be dropped and recoverable. This saw the casing lengthened to include a folded parachute over the nozzle housing and a cushioning nose cap. This 25ALD-1000 model was purchased and tested aboard several models of Army aircraft, and the burn time plus thrust altered for additional variants. (*Air Force Test Center*)

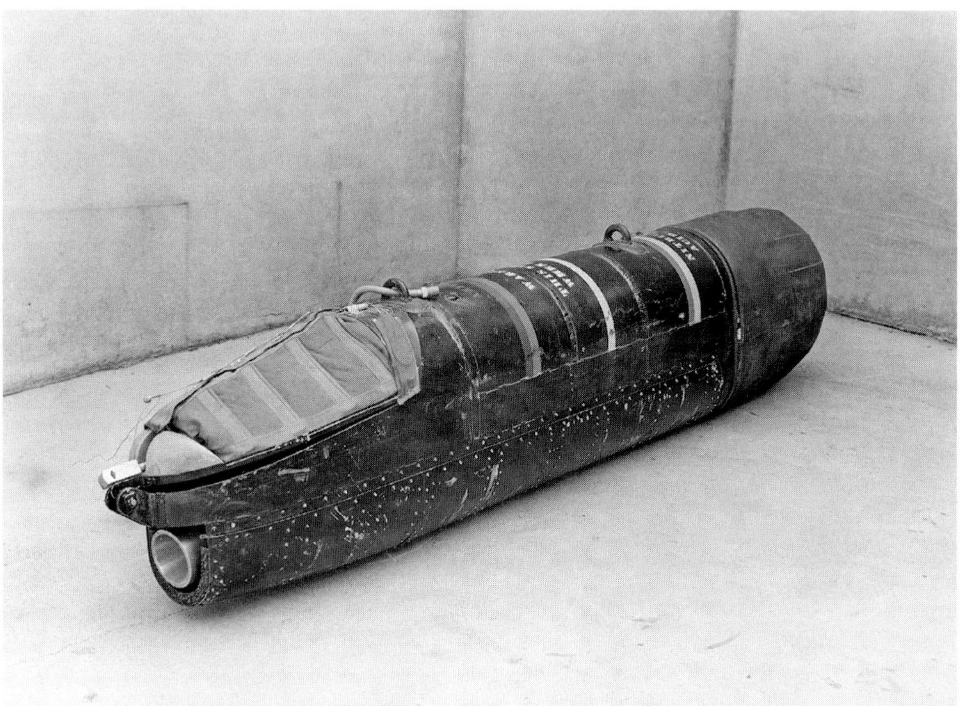

of four motors was made on B-26B 41-17545 with the conclusion a single 40ALD-3000 under each wing would be more desirable. Two 25ALD-1000s were also attached under the belly of XC-47C (42-5671), a Skytrain equipped with floats, for trials. The take-off distance was reduced by approximately 35 percent. Tests on P-38G 42-12690, with a unit on the drop tank fitting under each wing, included firing just one to find no yawing resulted. A Consolidated OA-10A Catalina (44-33994) air-sea rescue flying boat was modified at Wright Field in early 1945 with two of the 25ALD-1000s mounted internally to assist when taking off from rough water. Four combustion chambers and nozzles were mounted under the keel at the rear step. It also had fittings for two solid motor bottles adjacent to the rear gunner blisters.[12]

The Navy took interest in the Aerojet liquid motors and placed their own orders for examples supporting test. This includes a single X35AL-6000 for testing on a PB2Y-3 with an auxiliary engine-driven pump and the thrust chamber initially submerged. Also developed was a single X40AL-6000 with pumps and 100 45ALDW-1500 (the "W" perhaps indicating Water-recoverable). Two of these last were tested in the aft volume of a PBM-3 engine nacelle for shorter take-offs.[13] All droppable units floated.

Both War Department users were pleased with the longer burning time and higher thrust of the liquid-propellant motors but disliked the challenges handling the fuels. Trailers and carts to service the installed motors were being procured. The X40ALD-3000 (1,050 lb/476 kg empty and 1,750 lb/794 kg fueled) was tested by the Army and featured nozzle throat and chamber cooling via circulated propellants. Aerojet proposed 6,000- and 12,000-lbf (26.7- and 53.4-kN) units for very heavy bombers (B-29 and B-32) and 12,000-lbf for the B-36. In summer 1944 an AAF requirement for a 4,000-lbf (18-kN) motor with a sixty-second burn was formulated, but lack of suitable test facilities slowed progress. Engineering Division sought units that were rapidly attached, added little drag, and were readily jettisonable. Ideally, the system would permit the aircraft to get off a paved runway at 115 percent of maximum take-off GW in 5,000 feet (1,524 m) over the 50-foot obstacle in no-wind conditions.[14]

By March 1944, Aerojet had delivered 1,600 ATO units to the AAF and 2,845 to BuAer with more orders outstanding. By May, the Army had signed some $3 million of contracts and, by July, it had taken delivery of 600 8AS-200, 500 8AS-500, and 500 8AS-1000 units. Just about every Army aircraft had been tested with rocket ATO to include pursuit, medium and heavy bombers, light-planes, and gliders, but all trials had proceeded at an apparently leisurely pace. Only 214 motors had been expended. Engineering Division had been recognizing it had too many projects underway and there was slack interest from operational units for the ATO capability. The A-20 program had been dropped in December 1943 by direction of Materiel Division. Rapid airfield construction answered most requirements. War emergency power for engines was also introduced while higher octane fuels also improved performance. All these measures rendered solutions like booster rockets of marginal combat value.

By contrast, Navy contracts, which included some 18,000 ATO (never all delivered), brought the Aerojet backlog to some $6 million. The Army eventually resold 400 of its 8AS-1000s to the Navy who had made this their standard unit, adapted to most of its aircraft. Oversight of government property in Azusa transferred from the Army to the Navy in summer 1944. Whereas, previously, the Army had been concerned with Navy orders slowing its own rocket motor acquisitions, soon the tables were turned and the Navy set the priorities.

By February 1945, all Army contracts with Aerojet had been concluded with none on the horizon. This, however, was short-lived and investment continued through the end of the war as boosters were expected to be especially helpful with the first turbojet-powered bombers and ground-launched winged missiles. The USAAF was especially eager to boost a B-29 with a powerful ATO and had initiated a project on September 26, 1944. Ultimately, they hoped to attach four droppable 40ALD-3000 liquid-propellant rockets. While awaiting delivery, twelve 30AS-1000 units (407 lb/185 kg each) were employed. This appears to have been the selection of the highest thrust motors available as specific take-off requirements were not provided. Flight tests were performed at Eglin in May 1945 with B-29A 43-93921 fitted with two racks of three rocket clusters each attached to mounts fitted under each wing between the engine nacelles—where the liquid rocket pods were to be installed—for a total added weight of 5,100 lb (2,313 kg). Three assisted take-offs were compared with four unassisted at the same GW. Ground-roll distance was cut by 38 percent, and take-off distance by 34 percent over the 50-foot obstacle. The effort was shelved with the end of hostilities.[15]

Aerojet's liquid propellant ATO technology provided an emergency solution to an urgent operational need. It was important that the principal escort fighter for the strategic bombing campaign over Germany, the P-51, have a greater edge during engagements with the much faster Luftwaffe jet aircraft like the Me 262 fighter or Ar 234 reconnaissance platform. The podded ATO was unsuitable for a fighter, but a rapid development program offered an alternative. A small fumic acid and aniline rocket was built, identified as the X60AL-1300. This was mounted below the aft fuselage of a Mustang carrying the propellants in two 75-gal (284-l) underwing tanks. Tested in spring and early summer 1945, it gave the fighter a burst to 513 mph (826 kph), or 76 mph (122 kph) over the advertised maximum level flight speed.[16] War in Europe ended before this capability was deployed.

While being acknowledged as successful, the impracticality of the P-51 solution was immediately evident. Movement and storage of the hazardous fuels were not welcome. The more practical alternative was the use of War Emergency Power to boost the fighter's engine performance, adding roughly 20 mph (32 kph) to the P-51's top speed.

The NDRC, Monsanto, and Allegany Ballistics Laboratory were also pursuing alternative solid propellants with less stringent storage requirements and less smoke, and possibly reloadable in the field. These were generally intended for ordnance rockets but also airplane ATO, though not tested as such during the war.[17]

Aircraft like heavy bombers could benefit from ATO since they generally used much of a runway when fully loaded and had little margin for clearing obstacles, yet no such capability was fielded. This late-war Navy PB4Y-2 (59640, likely a test asset given the instrumentation fitted above the nose) has four rocket motors per side, but the proximity of the hot exhaust flame to aircraft airframes was seldom a difficulty. (*San Diego Air & Space Museum*)

Rocket assist helped rescue this B-17G from a field in which it had to make an emergency landing in March 1945. After removing all unnecessary weight, six rockets were mounted on fabricated racks under each inboard wing segment—large motors such as the Navy acquired. The bomber cleared the obstacles after a ground roll of just 372 feet on steel matting placed over the plowed ground. (*San Diego Air & Space Museum and National Archives*)

Boost to catch German jets was the goal of a formic acid and aniline motor of 1,300 lbf (5.8 kN) fitted under the aft fuselage of the P-51 Mustang (photos from April 7, 1945). Propellants fed from two 75-gal (284-l) tanks under the wings, likely via a pump within the fuselage. The 60-sec burn added an astounding 76 mph (122 kph) to the top-level flight speed but was not deployed operationally. (*Air Force Test Center*)

Monsanto did produce rockets to propel ground-launched winged missiles off rails, but these were not perfected for aircraft mount. The Navy performed tests using rockets to launch an L-4 off a short catapult rail. This "jet catapult" consisted of a twin-rail wooden shell track with a steel I-beam runner between, all 100 feet (31 m) long. The main gear wheels rode in the shell track and the aircraft's tailwheel sat in the runner in which the catapult also rode. The catapult rode in the I-beam. A rocket bottle was attached to the catapult, but under the runner, and ignited by ground personnel. The aircraft was connected to the catapult via a cable loosely looped to a fitting at the top of main undercarriage V-brace and also around the rear of the tailwheel. Erected by two individuals, it took only eight–ten minutes to launch and prepare another aircraft. The Piper was usually airborne at 50 mph (81 kph) in 75 feet (23 m). While this permitted spotter support where a runway was impractical or yet to be built, it did not support aircraft recovery.[18] It is doubtful this device was produced and deployed.

Reaction Motors of Pompton Lakes (later Pompton Plains), New Jersey, was founded on December 16, 1941, by four members of the American Rocket Society. Under a Navy contract, they set out to develop a liquid-fuel motor designed by James H. Wyld that employed regenerative cooling by which fuel was circulated around the combustion chamber for cooling but also improved performance via

The Northrop JB-1 missile sits ready on December 7, 1944, at Eglin for its one and only test flight. It is mounted on a carriage running on rails propelled by solid propellant rocket motors, a technique used for several years post-war for ground-launched missiles. These are probably Monsanto ACL-1 4,000-lbf (18-kN) solid propellant motors, weighing approximately 220 lb (100 kg), used to launch the JB-2. (*National Archives*)

heating of the fuel. The firm built a 100-lbf (0.5-kN) motor that employed a mixture of ethyl alcohol, diluted with water, and LOX. They then created a 1,000-lbf motor, operated successfully in November 1942, burning gasoline (with some cooling water added) and LOX. This was intended to serve as a lift-off booster for heavy flying boats. A 3,400-lbf (15-kN) variant, first fired in May 1943 and burning for forty-five seconds, successfully assisted the take-off of a PBM-3C Mariner on January 12, 1944, from Severn River near Annapolis. The filled motor weighed 1,300–1,400 lb (590–645 kg). This, too, saw no production follow up.

Engine Option

The successes developing rocket motors naturally lead to discussions of extending this from ATO to the primary propulsion system for aircraft. Eliminating propellers and the cooling requirements of reciprocating engines held promise for great reductions in drag and so increase in speed. Rockets were conceptually less complex and possibly lighter, with greater thrust-to-weight ratio than air-breathing engines. However, their fuel burn rate is many orders of magnitude greater. The fuel mass keeping a reciprocating-engined aircraft aloft for hours is consumed within seconds by the rocket motor. The greatest hurdles were then carrying sufficient fuel and oxidizer for a meaningful mission duration without excessive weight and providing the ability to throttle the motor. Pre-war German work on rocket-powered aircraft was known and it was assumed such was continuing behind the veil of secrecy engendered by war. There were plenty of visionary American engineers and scientists willing to confront these challenges. The war provided the impetus as the Army's Jet Propulsion Research Project.

Although the Army saw solid propellants as easier and less hazardous to handle than liquids, the later held more promise for high thrust and long burn time in addition to being throttleable, all requirements for an airplane's sole propulsion unit. Aerojet's aniline and fuming nitric acid technology appeared the shortest path to achieving such an aircraft motor. The imperative came with a rocket interceptor development called simply "Project X" for security reasons. Aerojet undertook the engine development along two parallel paths, authorized in January 1943.

The Aerotojet XCALR-2000A (or simply "Rotojet") was to generate 2,000 lbf (8.9 kN) with four combustion chambers. Two auxiliary chambers at 250 lbf (1.1 kN) served for cruise and were mounted to a longitudinal shaft. They were canted 20 degrees such that a portion of their thrust caused the shaft to rotate. This, in turn, drove centrifugal pumps via a gearbox to feed two boost chambers of 750 lbf (3.3 kN) each that were regeneratively cooled (ignorant of Wyld's patent). During development, problems were encountered in sealing the rotating interfaces to prevent propellant leaks. The best that could be achieved was minimal leakage, but the acid corroded wiring and even the smallest mixing of the propellants could be catastrophic. Design of the pump was most challenging because it ran at a then-remarkable 8,000–12,000 rpm. Finally, after many delays, an attempt at operation in 1944 produced an immediate and violent explosion from which nothing was learned.

The USAAF abandoned the XCALR-2000A but development of a two-thirds scale version termed the Centrojet, at 506 lb (230 kg) for 500 lbf (2.2 kN), was started in June 1943. This had just a single chamber at the end of the shaft but with initially four, then two, nozzles, angled to generate the shaft torque and turn the gearbox at a more modest rate (started with an electric motor). The engine did finally prove the concept in 1945, though leakage remained unresolved. However, the technology could not be scaled up.

The identified alternative to the Aerotojet was the Reaction Motors XLR-7-AJ-1. This was very similar in terms of the four regeneratively cooled chambers, each 1,500 lbf (6.7 kN), burning for five minutes, but was to use a gas turbine pump for the twin combustion chambers. Such pumps there then still in their infancy. The engine weighed 425 lb (193 kg) unfueled. This development, as well, ran long and was not tested until August 1945.[19]

In the early years of American involvement in the war, there was a concern with enemy bombers appearing across the borders of the USA. The Army was keenly interested in a high-speed interceptor that could quickly get up to the bombers' altitude and engage them, then just as rapidly get down to rearm and refuel. Among the concepts was a tailless rocket plane offered on September 15, 1942, as an unsolicited proposal from Jack Northrop. He had for years researched "all wing" designs with experimental airplanes. Likely with some encouragement from Northrop's friend Dr. von Kármán, Arnold chose to pursue Northrop's idea. When taken up by Materiel Command, it became the XP-79 under MX-365.

The initial concept was the Model 14 Jet-Driven Interceptor that would be boosted to altitude but then, with propellants exhausted, glide back to landing. The airplane would have very high acceleration and so a prone pilot position was conceived that was to offer greater *g*-tolerance. The smaller frontal area this offered also supported the low-drag flying wing layout. This point-defense interceptor was defined in an April 1, 1943 specification. It would be powered by the XCALR-2000A fed by 8,200 lb (3,720 kg) of propellants for a loaded weight of 11,400 lb (5,171 kg) and 35.5-minute endurance. If achieved, with the planned 2,000-lbf thrust, this would be a true rocket primary propulsion system supporting the narrow mission. To conserve fuel, the aircraft was expected to be boosted aloft on a trolley or rails powered by droppable ATO rockets, and the unpowered landing would be on four retractable skids. The aircraft was to top 540 mph (869 kph), a remarkably high speed at the time, and reach 40,000 feet (12,192 m) in just 6.2 minutes while possessing a 454-mile (731-km) range.

With so little data on flying wings, Materiel Command lacked the insight to assess the technological risk of the Northrop proposal. Consequently, the service insisted Northrop build mock-ups for wind tunnel testing and flight trials as proof-of-concept. The company had no spare capacity to undertake this work and so the Engineering Division began on November 1, 1942, designing the assets under MX-334. Northrop then, under a $149,542.50 contract, assembled the three mock-ups of plywood over steel tube frames with a blended wing-body profile. The first was completed in May 1943. They had a 36-foot (11-m) span of 252 feet^2 (23 m^2) area and 21.8 degrees quarter-chord sweep, 11.3 feet (3.5 m) length (wing root chord), stood under 5 feet (1.5 m) tall, and weighed 2,600–2,800 lb (1,179–1,270 kg) when flight-ready. They would go from the wind tunnel to flight as gliders to perfect flight control before introducing the rocket motor for powered flights.

The wind tunnel tests at Langley in summer 1943 found inadequate directional control, among other issues, and so a wooden vertical tail was added, held erect by wires. The basic flying wing flight control surfaces had to be operated by the prone pilot via novel means (see Chapter 9). Flights of the unpowered MX-334 began on August 27, 1943, towed aloft behind an automobile and then behind a P-38 beginning on September 30, from various dry lakebeds at and near Muroc. The aircraft were flown in brief free-flights and dives reaching 305 mph (491 kph). The team had to move to wheels on the skids, then a droppable dolly, and finally fixed landing gear. Flight controls also evolved as deficiencies were uncovered and corrected. All was not without hazards, and all the machines were damaged, one written off.

The XCALR-2000A motor was running well behind schedule, but a single 200-lbf (0.9-kN) auxiliary chamber could be used as the XCALR-200A.

A mock-up of the Aerojet XCALR-2000A lies within the mock-up of the XP-79 rocket interceptor. Visible are the two primary thrust chambers with a pair of auxiliary units. The auxiliary chambers are mounted canted on a shaft such that when firing the shaft rotates to operate the propellant pump via the gearbox seen forward. (*Gerald Balzer*)

Attempting to develop a flying wing rocket-powered interceptor, the USAAF insisted Northrop build mock-ups for wind tunnel and free-flight testing. The three MX-334s were initially unpowered for tow and gliding flight to perfect the flight control system and prone pilot position. This example is fitted with the smallest of three vertical tails and a wheeled dolly affixed to the skids, ready for towing off a dry lakebed in Southern California's Mojave Desert. (*Gerald Balzer*)

Non-throttleable, this would operate for just five minutes. It was fitted to the MX-334s, which then became the MX-324 Rocket Wing. The combustion chamber and nozzle lay between the pilot's legs while the propellant tanks were outboard on opposite sides. Any leaking of the propellants into the pilot compartment or mixing outside the combustion chamber would be disastrous and so neoprene shields were installed. The entire propulsion system added 427 lb (194 kg) to bring flight weight to 3,495–3,600 lb (1,585–1,633 kg) depending on any added ballast, and 4,252 lb (1,929 kg) fueled.

Some towed flights with the engine inoperative preceded powered flight during which a data telemetry system was installed. The first ground run of the motor was performed on June 22, 1944, before the first powered flight on July 5 with Harry Crosby doing the honors. The glider was towed to 15,000 feet (4,572 m) by the P-38, flown by Capt. Martin Smith. After release, the motor was ignited and the craft became America's first "rocket plane." The meager thrust merely extended the glide and permitted brief 120–130 mph (193–209 kph) level flight. On the next flight, Alex Papana dived to 350 mph (563 kph) with power. Six more powered flights followed through July 27.

Plans to modify the gliders to match the XP-79 configurations as it had evolved and to install the full XCALR-2000A were not fulfilled. The point-defense interceptor idea had faded with any fear of enemy bombers appearing over the United States. While Northrop remained enthusiastic about flying wings, there

With the full liquid propellant engine running late, a single auxiliary thrust chamber was installed in the MX-334 gliders. The pilot couch is at the top of the picture and his legs would lay under the arrangement of lines and back to either side of the 5-inch (13-cm) diameter combustion chamber. The spherical tanks are likely compressed nitrogen vessels to move the propellants. (*National Museum of the United States Air Force and Gerald Balzer*)

America's first purely rocket-powered flight was actually an MX-324 glider towed to altitude and with a motor of meager thrust for demonstration purposes. The July 5, 1944 event, with Northrop's Harry Crosby at the controls, was part of a rocket-powered interceptor program. That effort had already been adapted to jet engines and so the MX-324 had become a technology demonstration effort. (*National Museum of the United States Air Force*)

were other projects satisfying this lust and more vital defense programs that consumed all the firm's resources. The MX-324 effort was ended in September 1944 after expending $403,187. The XP-79 was redesigned for twin turbojets as the XP-79B. This flew once post-war, the first flight ending in a crash that claimed Crosby's life.

Under a Navy contract, Reaction Motors developed an alcohol and LOX motor, ignited via an electric spark, weighing 210 lb (95 kg). This 6000C4 was to produce a maximum 6,000 lbf (27 kN) with four 1,500-lbf (6.7-N) thrust chambers that were operated either individually or in combination as crude throttling. The development was fraught with problems and the motor did not operate as an integrated unit until just after the war. It would be employed in propelling the XS-1 research aircraft (Chapter 5) to supersonic speeds.

By January 1945, the Navy was seeking an answer to the Japanese kamikaze threat. With access to early information on the Germany Me 163 rocket interceptor, BuAer performed a preliminary design of two rocket fighters and began seeking prospective manufacturers. The 6000C4 was perhaps the intended propulsion unit. The war's terminus brought that effort to a halt.[20]

5

Sonic Reach

Compressibility effects were impeding progress to high speeds that equated to a tactical advantage. The never-ending push for speed, through drag reduction, engine performance improvements, and propeller design had all contributed to the most advanced fighter aircraft approaching or just exceeding 500 mph (805 kph) or Mach 0.6 in a steep dive and so touching the transonic regime where air compresses into shocks. This increased drag and affects stability and control owing to the rearward shift in the center of lift. The speed at which shocks first form is termed the critical Mach number and is unique to each aircraft design. Propellers rotate at speeds faster than the aircraft flies and so supersonic flow occurs first at the tips of the blades, causing separated flow and reduced propeller performance. A dive into the transonic regime could produce Mach tuck or inability to recover until very low altitude.[1] Aircraft, as then designed, were simply not suited to flight into such conditions that were little-understood.

The loss of Lockheed's test pilot Ralph Virden in the fatal dive of YP-38 39-689 on November 4, 1941, has one of the most notable tragedies illustrating this lack of knowledge. General Arnold grounded the type, already in production and early service, as solutions were sought, and full-rate production of the type was in doubt until resolved. This was one of several P-38s to be lost in this manner, but the death of a highly experienced test pilot suggested the Lightning was just too dangerous. Working to ensure the aircraft could pull out of a Mach tuck dive, the elevator had been made more effective, but this only contributed to the aircraft's break up. Yet, something had to be done quickly. The aircraft was one of the fighter types the USAAF was counting on to help win the war which that the U.S. soon found itself a part.

Work by the NACA on understanding the phenomenon and devising a solution, in concert with Lockheed, pushed all other projects to the side for a time. A P-38 tail assembly was flown to Wright Field for testing in their 20-foot tunnel. Some tail buffet was alleviated with a carefully designed wing root fillet. Distortion of elevator fabric was also a player and this was another motive to move towards making metal covering standard. Langley helped to puzzle out the locked-in steep dive or Mach tuck phenomenon via analysis and high-priority wind tunnel testing during early 1942. Langley had at first balked at Lockheed's use of the tunnel, fearing damage if the model came apart, until Arnold ordered compliance. The priority was that great. Having dismissed tail flutter, and with the collaboration of Caltech's Dr. von Kármán, it was concluded compressibility was the culprit. Shocks were forming on the inboard wing segments at Mach 0.65 and causing flow separation with loss of lift and lessened downwash on the tail that produced the locked-in dive. The NACA suggested several solutions in April 1943 that included the dive recovery flap that restored the lost lift only at high speed and was the immediate solution for the P-38. This was applied to many other high-speed fighter types.

Testing the dive flaps required many hazardous high-speed dives with instruments photographed over the pilot's shoulder (the "photo panel" method) and with airframe stresses measured and recorded. Lacking a Mach meter, the team used dive angle measured with an attitude gyro turned on its side for data consistency. Some 400 modification kits for aircraft already in Europe were hurriedly assembled and placed on a C-54 for priority shipment to the U.K. However, mistaking the transport for a German patrol type, a flight of RAF fighters shot it down as it approached Ireland. Lockheed's designer "Kelly" Johnson wrote a technical paper on the P-38 experience and presented it at a January 1943 conference, providing copies to other design teams, before the War Department classified the document and recalled all copies.[2]

Most of the leading, high-performance fighters suffered from compressibility effects and contributed to fatal accidents throughout the war.[3] Pulling to maximum lift promotes flow separation on the wing that impinged on the empennage, but this is exacerbated by shock formation. During development tests of fighters, particularly heavy empennage buffeting was being experienced with alarming oscillations. Structural failures with fatal crashes had occurred. It was learned that testing from high to low altitude reduced risk to the pilot, and some dive tests were performed under remote control because of the great hazard. Structural alterations could move the buffet boundary, but the fundamental problem remained unresolved, with compressibility clearly a factor. The F4F was one of the last naval fighters to meet the requirement for the mandatory dive to limit speed with an 8-*g* pull-up. For all subsequent developmental aircraft, the participants agreed to abandon the trials in the interest of safety. Aircraft were being delivered to combat outfits without the condition having been fully explored.[4] The manufacturers and BuAer agreed on the safe limits to which the aircraft was to be operated, and production marched on. The national emergency did not permit any alternative course of action. However, fleet pilots would occasionally push the limits such that damage and deaths continued to be suffered.

Lack of suitable means for collecting data in the transonic regime was hampering understanding the aerodynamic influences that had to proceed in devising solutions permitting safe flight to greater airspeeds. There was doubt that driving to and beyond the speed of sound was possible or that anything but

Above: Lockheed's chief designer "Kelly" Johnson (right) and test pilot Tony LeVier (left) hold a segment of the P-38 dive recovery flap shown deployed behind the two men. The Lightning became suspect in the eyes of many pilots because of several deadly compressibility dives until the dive flaps were introduced. This altered the aerodynamics enough to permit less stressful recovery at higher altitudes. (*Air Force Test Center*)

Below: Most of the hottest American fighters got the dive flaps. The Grumman F8F had a smaller and single panel dive flap under each wing just behind the landing gear (post-war F8F-2 shown). The simple device probably saved several aircraft in the Bearcat's service life. (*The Peter M. Bowers Collection/The Museum of Flight and Northrop Grumman History Center*)

a rocket engine would facilitate the feat. This brought forth the misleading phrase "sound barrier." However, there were knowledgeable and influential personalities who insisted supersonic flight was possible. With the propeller-driven airplane clearly reaching practical limits of airspeed, and as jet fighters were introduced, the armed forces desired to explore this potential.

Push to Mach

In practical applications, one has to fly through the transonic "sound barrier" to go supersonic. The fundamentals of flight into the transonic region were understood by aerodynamicists and solutions were being investigated in the U.S. by NACA and private laboratories to a modest degree. It was known that high-velocity projectiles exceed the speed of sound and generated shocks. Lockheed even conceived the L-133 jet fighter in 1941 with features to fly deeply into the compressibility region and achieve 602 mph (969 kph) at 40,000 feet (12,192 m), but this was not taken up by the military services. It did, however, show that design teams were thinking about how to deal with compressibility to achieve a substantial speed increase.[5]

This model of the Lockheed L-133-02-01 design *circa* 1941 suggests bold concepts for achieving transonic airspeeds given the limited understanding of the aerodynamics at the time. Low drag was achieved with a canard layout, a high degree of body blending, and judicious choice of airfoil augmented with boundary layer control. Most notable was use of then-notional turbojet engines to eliminate propellers. (*Tony Landis collection*)

Until soon after the war, the U.S. (and everyone else) lacked wind tunnels that could achieve transonic speeds on any practical scale. The major challenge to sonic research was that a conventional tunnel produces a standing shock reflecting off the walls where Mach 1.0 first occurs and no further speed increase is possible. This is called choking and will likely occur where the model and mount is installed. This normally prevents sustained transonic flow over the model. By careful design changes, the NACA was able to achieve Mach 0.9 in a standard high-speed tunnel. Supersonic tunnels, operating in the U.S. since 1943, produced good results above approximately Mach 1.2 or 1.3, but data in the transonic region was lacking. This impeded progress in understanding and overcoming compressibility effects.

The laboratory limitations inspired innovative means of collecting transonic and supersonic data informing aircraft design and validating analytical results. These techniques included placing airfoils projecting from parts of an aircraft over which the airflow approached the speed of sound at high flight airspeed. Limited forces and pressure data could then be collected. One such was on the upper surface of the P-51 wing at the point of maximum wing thickness. Although the wing proved disappointing in service with respect to sustained laminar flow, it was an excellent high-lift design had a marginally higher critical Mach number than more conventional airfoils. This proved one of the principal benefits of laminar flow wings during the war.[6] Under rare lighting conditions, Mustang pilots had observed the shadow of a shock becoming visible at this "bump." Airfoil shapes just inches long were mounted vertically above the wing of a P-51B (43-12094) and near the end of the war, a P-51D (44-84900, NACA 127). The data were recorded by gear in the ammunition bay during dives at speeds up to Mach 0.81 that produced transonic then supersonic conditions at the bump.[7] The ammunition bay door had to be replaced with a thick panel to avoid distortion and with some surface shape change to help straighten the flow over the portion above which the model was mounted.[8] The "bump" was replicated in the Langley 7 × 10-foot tunnel for more controlled test data before the tunnel choked.

Another approach to transonic research by NACA, arrived at in consultation with British researchers, was dropping a weighted, unpowered streamlined aerodynamic shape. The drop-body accelerated in freefall under the pull of gravity to very high velocity. Its purpose earned it the name "locomotive." Airspeed, forces, rates, and pressure data were recorded on board. This was followed by digging the wrecked shape out of the ground and hopefully recovering the recording. Initial drops in 1943 near Langley were not entirely satisfactory. Drops were pushed to higher altitudes and, for safety, directed into the mud of Wallops Island off the Virginia coast. Testing resumed in May 1944 from B-17s flying at 30,000–35,000 feet (9,144–10,668 m), but the shapes still did not achieve transonic speeds before impact. Drops from a B-29 flying above 40,000 feet (12,192 m) reached the desired speeds momentarily. By this time, radio telemetry was introduced to transmit the data to the ground and provided a more reliable collection method. Determination of altitude and speed also used a radio beacon for radar tracking augmented with innovative slaved phototheodolite optical tracking. Various body

Lacking a suitable wind tunnel with which to explore transonic aerodynamics, the NACA sought data via flight test. In high-speed dives, it was known that flow over the top of a Mustang wing reach the critical Mach number and shocks began to form. This led NACA researchers to place small models on the wing of a P-51B to collect forces, rates, and pressures data using instrumentation within the gun and ammunition bays inside the wing. (*NASA*)

Another source of transonic data were test articles dropped from high altitude, rapidly reconfigurable with such things as various wing sweep angles. Data were transmitted to the ground via early telemetry before the shape plunged into the ground. The example shown—a 1,350-lb (612-kg) steel model of the XS-1 to test elevator effectiveness—was dropped from a B-29 flying near 40,000 feet (12,192 m) to permit the projectile to accelerate under gravity to transonic airspeeds. (*NASA*)

and wing shapes were tested to include carefully tapered bodies and swept wings of very thin airfoil section.

A third transonic research technique employed rockets to fly aero shapes to supersonic speeds, data again telemetered to the ground. On June 13, 1945, the Navy boosted a ramjet engine to operating speed with four 5-inch (12.7-cm) rocket motors from air-to-ground rockets. Under the thrust of the engine, the projectile flew to supersonic speed and more than 6 miles (10 km) down range from launch on Island Beech, New Jersey.[9] The BuAer encouraged NACA to undertake similar tests via projects and funding to develop the aerodynamic data collection technique.[10] This work was performed at remote Wallops Flight Center, an auxiliary field associated with Langley on Wallops Island where rockets could be safely launched across the coast and end at the bottom of the ocean. While the establishment of the missile test range was largely in response to the growing number of guided missile and sounding rocket projects, it also offered a research opportunity. For the booster rocket, they chose a Monsanto solid propellant composed of 45 percent ammonium picrate and 45 percent potassium nitrate with a resin binder.[11] The high-speed rocket-boost testing did not begin until October 1945.

Researchers also built rockets with various wing and fin shapes to collect data at high boost speeds, the first launch on June 27, 1945, being this 3.25-inch rocket to check tracking stations. The data were transmitted via a telemetry system (shown in the nose) before the rocket dropped into the ocean. They were flown from Wallops Island, Virginia, where a test facility was erected supporting shots beginning in the final months of the war. (*NASA*)

X-Planes

It was clear that exploring aircraft controllability at transonic and supersonic speeds would require a full-up piloted experimental airplane. Although Langley had always worked under the guidance that it was not an aircraft design or development organization, the war left no others with the resources to undertake a supersonic research aircraft project. With a conventional propeller-driven airplane clearly unsuitable, alternatives were explored.

A small conceptual design effort was launched based on the published research of Italian engineer Secondo Campini. He developed an augmented ducted fan that powered the experimental Caproni-Campini CC.1 and CC.2 airplanes, which first flew in 1940. This employed propellers, driven by a conventional piston engine, encased inside a duct within the fuselage. These propellers served to compress the airflow before it passed into a combustion chamber where fuel was added and ignited for a tremendous boost in pressure. This air then passed through a nozzle at the end of the duct and fuselage to produce thrust. Once in flight, the reciprocating engine could be shut down and the propulsion system operated as a ramjet, though with appalling fuel consumption rate for an unimpressive maximum airspeed. Langley only expected to use this augmenter (today called an afterburner) for supersonic dashes or assisted take-off while the propeller provided suitable propulsion at other times. For a supersonic application, the duct would initially slow the supersonic flow to subsonic speeds via a standing shock at the entrance. The walls of the duct would also reduce or eliminate the tip sonic speed issues of the propeller.

A ground test rig, nicknamed "jeep," was built at Langley in 1940 to optimize this "motojet" propulsion system with Eastman Jacobs the principal engineer. This included a two-stage axial compressor (two coaxial propellers) and efforts to keep the intense flame near the center of the duct to allow a sheet of air along the duct walls for structural cooling. The hot engine exhaust was employed to vaporize and ignite the fuel, which then provided the primary flame for the combustor chamber. This arrangement proved relatively successful by summer 1942, measuring 2,900 lbf (13 kN) of thrust though burning 3 lb (1.4 kg) of fuel per second with the afterburner. Thoughts then turned to flight applications. Original plans explored converting existing designs with the propulsion system. First considered was to modify a Martin B-26 Marauder bomber with each of the two engine nacelles extensively altered to accommodate the system. The engineers calculated that a 50-mph (81-kph) boost in speed could be realized when the afterburner was employed, although with a 300 percent increase in fuel flow.[12] Later, a Bell P-39 was suggested as a candidate testbed.[13]

An entirely original craft that might approach the speed of sound was also proposed. The preliminary design, built as a wind tunnel model in 1942, was a tubular fuselage with a shallow canopy ahead of the shoulder-mounted straight wing. A V-tail with ruddervators was featured. The 450-hp (336-kW) P&W R-1535 Twin Wasp Junior and propellers, along with the minimal cockpit, was nestled within the duct, airflow passing to the sides. The aircraft was to be small, accommodating only pilot, test instrumentation, and minimum essential fuel. The

Left: In seeking means of achieving wing-borne transonic flight, engineers at Langley considered a ducted fan propulsion system augmented with an afterburner. The inlet would decelerate supersonic airflow into the centerline duct where a reciprocating engine drove propellers that compressed the flow then passing into the combustion section. This December 1942 wind tunnel model illustrates the aircraft that included a shallow canopy, variable exhaust exit area, roll spoilers atop the straight wing, and a V-tail. (*NASA*)

Below: An interior profile drawing of the ducted fan research aircraft proposal (31.4-foot/9.6-m length) illustrates the hybrid jet engine. Although NACA normally did not develop aircraft, this was considered a wartime special case that still required War Department support. The concept's originator, NACA's Eastman Jacobs, sought such support but the project was rejected because of secret jet aircraft programs already underway. (*NASA*)

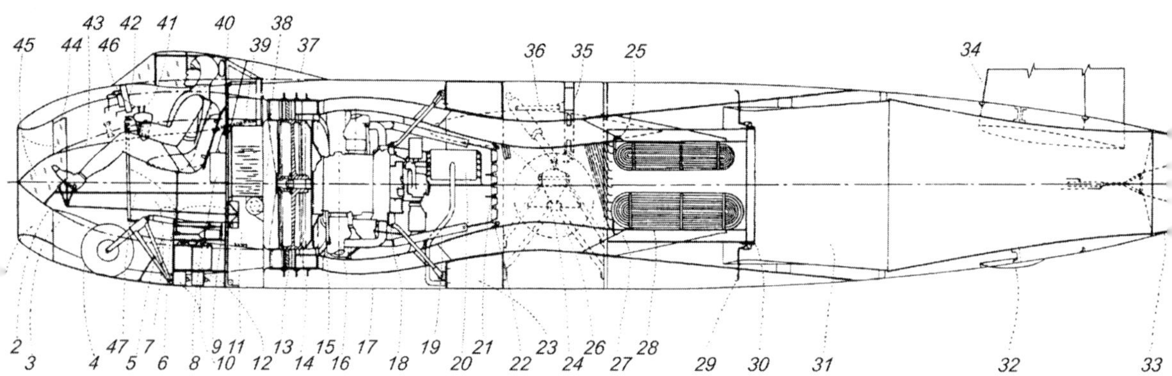

1 NOSE AIR INTAKE
2 INNER CONE
3 NOSE-WHEEL WELL
4 NOSE WHEEL
5 INTERSECTION WELL AND CONE
6 FLIGHT CONTROLS
7 INSTRUMENT SPACE
8 RADIO
9 NOSE-GEAR RETRACTION
10 TRANSFORMERS FOR SPARK IGNITERS
11 OIL TANK
12 BATTERIES
13 BLOWER MAIN STAGES
14 BLOWER ENGINE-COOLING STAGE
15 ENGINE-COOLING DUCT
16 P. & W. R-1535 TWIN WASP, JR., ENGINE
17 MAIN AIR DUCT
18 ENGINE MOUNTING RING
19 EXHAUST BOILERS FOR PRIMARY FIRE
20 FUEL PUMP
21 PRIMARY BURNER
22 SPARK IGNITER FOR PRIMARY FIRE
23 FUSELAGE GASOLINE
24 MAIN BOILER SPIRAL SECTION

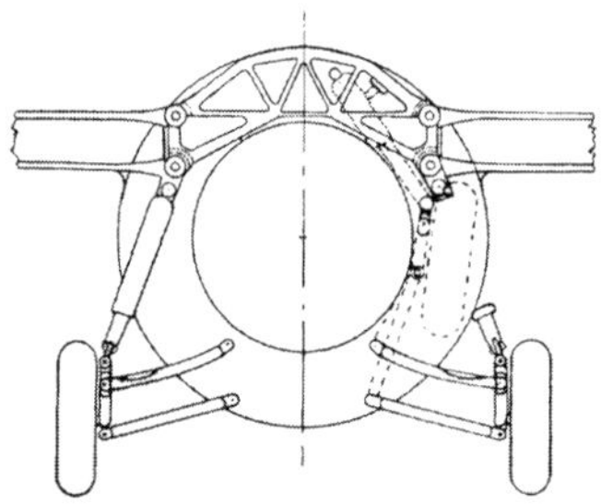

MAIN LANDING GEAR AND WING CARRY-THROUGH TRUSS

25 23 GAS-VAPOR JETS
26 MAIN LANDING GEAR
27 MIXING DUCT
28 MAIN BOILER PANCAKE SECTION
29 SPARK IGNITER FOR ANNULAR IGNITER
30 ANNULAR IGNITER
31 MAIN COMBUSTION CHAMBER
32 TAIL BUMBER
33 VARIABLE-AREA NOZZLE
34 VEE-TAIL
35 WING CARRY-THROUGH TRUSS
36 WING ROOT SECTION
37 CANOPY
38 CO_2 EXTINGUISHER
39 DUCT-SURFACE OIL COOLER
40 TURN-OVER PYLON
41 ENGINE CONTROLS
42 INSTRUMENT BOARD
43 INTERSECTION PILOT'S WELL AND CONE
44 PILOT'S WELL
45 TRANSPARENT SECTIONS
46 BURNING CONTROL
47 FLOOR

exit of the centerline duct came to include two flaps actuated from the sides to expand or contract the exit area for optimal thrust.[14]

The decision in late summer 1942 was that both modification and new design paths were to be pursued. However, the NACA charter did not clearly allow for aircraft development, and actual construction of the unique testbed would require military backing of a contract to a suitable manufacturer under wartime priorities. The Army was duly approached, with their initial reaction being to suggest an aircraft more easily reworked to combat purposes.

Secrecy surrounding the jet propulsion efforts in the U.S. meant that the Langley engineers worked in ignorance that turbojet engines and American jet aircraft were already a fact. While the associated aircraft development projects were not supersonic vehicles, the engines were clearly superior to the ducted fan in potentially propelling an aircraft to such airspeeds. The military leaders who prioritized Langley's wartime workload was unable to inform the lab of the largely dead-end path they were on in the ducted-fan research aircraft project. Hence, the USAAF ultimately declined to back the NACA development project and soon both services turned down the modification option. The ducted fan research project was canceled in March 1943, months before the reason became clear when jet progress was divulged.

The NACA requirement for a research aircraft remained. Industry and others working on the first generation of turbojet-powered airplanes were also making it clear that the compressibility problem would very soon be a major challenge for jets. Langley formulated other plans during summer 1943, championed by John Stack. Using turbojets and pushing out to supersonic speeds might require a fighter-size aircraft with as many as four engines, the Westinghouse 19XB recommended.[15] The military showed immediate interest when the NACA initially approached them informally during the latter half of 1943, but little action ensued. Major Ezra Kotcher, chief of aeronautical research at Materiel Command and an Engineering School senior instructor, and Captain Walter S. Diehl of BuAer were the principal supportive voices. Kotcher was formerly a civilian drafted into uniform, but he was posted back to his Wright Field job. He had recommended a research aircraft as early as 1939 in a report summarizing impediments to aeronautical advancement. The Army had finally begun considering transonic research in early 1943 under Major Kotcher's emphasis and von Kármán's sponsorship. This yielded preliminary designs for jet- and rocket-powered aircraft. Coincident with this movement, the Chief of the Engineering Division, Brig.-Gen. Frank O. Carroll, had asked von Kármán if it was possible to build an aircraft capable of flying to 1,000 mph (1,609 kph, about Mach 1.5). After a weekend of working with a group of Wright Field engineers, the answer was in the affirmative.

It was March 1944 before the War Department and NACA finally stirred themselves into vigorously addressing the compressibility problem via a flight research aircraft. In two separate meetings at Langley that month, between the services and NACA, it became clear that a dedicated experimental airplane was required to provide data that could not be gathered in wind tunnels or using existing airframes. The NACA was the natural center of the effort, but with the services playing essential roles.

Langley had to overcome its long-held belief that a rocket motor was unsafe for manned flight propulsion. Their preference was evident when NACA submitted a proposal for their 19XB-powered transonic jet to the AAF on July 10, 1944.[16] In January 1944, the Material Division's Development Engineering Branch had directed study of a high-speed research aircraft. Kotcher labored with the Design Branch to work up "Mach 0.999" concepts of turbojet- and rocket-powered machines. By April, the report was out, concluding that rockets were superior. It was recognized that rocket fuels were more difficult to work with and flight time so brief as to be of questionable operational practicality. However, the high fuel consumption might still permit the test objectives to be met provided the aircraft was towed to altitude or carried internally and released from a bomber.[17] As jet engines began to emerge from test cells and from behind the veil of secrecy there was a question of their superiority over rockets in attaining high altitudes and exceptionally high airspeeds. By that time, rocket boosters had established a good safety record and the MX-324 had flown with a rocket motor. A turbojet engine was likely to achieve only transonic velocities but with a longer data gathering period. However, at the state of the technology at the time, there were uncertainties associated with a jet engine inlet designed for transonic and supersonic flight. The turbojet's thrust also decreases with altitude, unlike a rocket.

Another principal debate was whether to seek only transonic speeds or go for supersonic, this driving the debate on the propulsion system. Despite identical goals, after lengthy discussions and examination of available technology, the three organizations decided in December 1944 to pursue two courses. One would be a rocket-propelled aircraft sponsored by the Air Forces that might be pushed supersonically and the other a transonic jet-propelled machine sponsored by the Navy.

As an interim solution to obtain transonic data by mixing the two approaches, the NACA pursued the idea of diving a Lockheed P-80 to very high speed, accelerated with auxiliary rockets. To help ensure the structural integrity of the aircraft during the subsequent pull-out, a specially strengthened wing was built to withstand 18 *g* and installed on the first YP-80A (44-83023). However, investigating available rockets to fit within the available fuselage volume (external mounted rejected owing to drag) found none that were suitable for the task. The idea of using the YP-80A as a transonic research vehicle was abandoned in the latter half of 1944.[18]

The Army/NACA project was designated MX-524 High-Speed Flight Investigations (changed to MX-653 in summer 1945) and several contractors were approached at the end of 1944. In mid-December, Bell Aircraft was judged the better choice for what became the XS-1 (S for Sonic). With specifications for the Model 44 drawn up the same month, a $4,278,537 contract was signed on March 16, 1945, for three aircraft taken through initial flight testing. The requirements were daunting, calling for achieving 800 mph (1,288 kph) for two to five minutes

A spring 1944 comparative study of jet *versus* rocket propulsion included preliminary designs such as this "Mach 0.999" experimental rocket-propelled aircraft designated MCD-520. Similarity to what would later become the Bell XS-1 is striking. As a research testbed propulsion system, the rocket had many superior performance characteristics compared with the first generation of turbojets, but its operational practicality was questionable. (*Air Force Test Center*)

at 35,000 feet (10,668 m) or above, equating to about Mach 1.2, while carrying 500 lb (227 kg) of instrumentation gear. The paucity of aerodynamic data in the region of interest created uncertainty in the design effort. Under Chief Engineer Robert Stanley and Project Engineer Stanley Smith, the design team focused on a sleek fuselage intentionally following the shape of a .50-cal bullet that had been shown to exceed the speed of sound. The windscreen conformed to this shape to reduce drag and avoid asymmetrical shock formation, and so visibility was bound to be marginal.

The XS-1's structure was designed very strong to withstand loading associated with 18-g normal load factor to cover all potential contingencies—approximately 50 percent greater than any aircraft known to have flown. Lacking a suitable wind tunnel, the pressure distributions on the surfaces and movement of the center of lift was essentially a matter of conjecture. Two thin-section wings were built, one of 10 percent and the other of 8 percent chord length-to-thickness ratio (a compromise between disagreeing engineering camps at Langley) that sought to delay shock formation to high speeds and lessen adverse controllability effects. By comparison, the P-38 wing tapered from 16 percent at the root to 12 percent at the tip and the P-51 from 15 to 11 percent. The Me 262's root thickness was 12 percent. Meeting the airframe strength requirement in a thin wing saw an unusually thick skin tapering from 0.5 inches (1.3 cm) at the root. This also worked against skin wrinkles under air loads that could corrupt test data.

The MX-524 was a joint Air Forces and NACA program to explore the transonic and supersonic regimes with a rocket-powered research aircraft. This is a Bell drawing dated 3-1-45 showing this aircraft, with the development effort kicked off in March 1945. The unique aircraft was initially much smaller than the final design owing to a change from a mechanical pump to pressurization in delivering fuel to the motor. (*Jay Miller collection*)

The drawing and wind tunnel model show the final configuration of the XS-1 after a redesign for pressurized fuel tanks. The conformal windscreen gave limited pilot visibility but was acceptable for the research aircraft where sources of shock formation were discouraged. The mid-set horizontal tail with trimming stabilizer were intended to ensure suitable pitch control in the transonic regime. (*Jay Miller collection*)

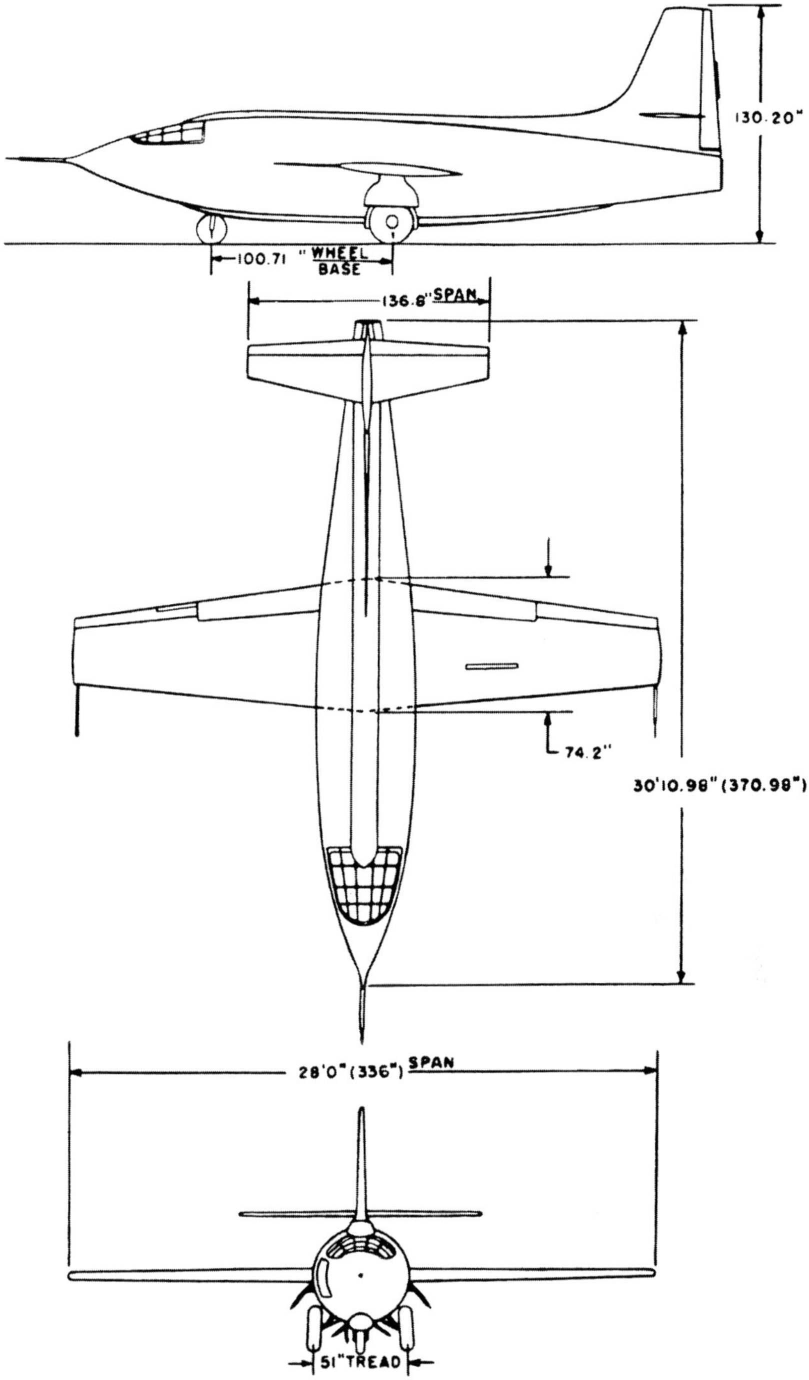

The dimensions of the Bell XS-1 as it entered construction are shown in this period drawing. The fuselage shape intentionally followed that of a .50-cal bullet that was known to exceed the speed of sound when fired. The aero surfaces were thin and exceptionally strong but otherwise conventional for the period. (*Author's collection*)

NACA dive tests with the XP-51 had revealed wing surface distortion that varied chord-wise pressures. At transonic speeds, this could contribute to unpredictable trim changes in an already dangerous realm.[19] The thin wings, with ailerons, flaps, and spoilers compelled main landing gear stowage in the fuselage and so a narrow track.

The horizontal stabilizer was mounted above the plane of the wing to avoid turbulent wake. This surface, with elevators, had variable incidence to 15 degrees via an electric jack screw. It also had a thinner airfoil than the wing (6 percent for the 8 percent wing and 8 percent for the 10 percent wing) to ensure longitudinal control authority would be retained should wing airflow be seriously disturbed. The variable incidence horizontal stabilizer, as added insurance for suitable pitch trim authority, was considered a security-sensitive design feature. The elevator could also be locked in trail such that the entire horizontal tail could move as a stabilator.[20] Controls were otherwise not boosted.

A yoke control was chosen over a stick in the event two-handed strength needed to be applied. Test instrumentation was built into these aero surfaces and the rest of the airframe. The data recorder and engine ignition switches were located on the yoke so that the pilot's hands need not be removed during a speed run. The cabin was pressurized before launch and the slow leak rate meant this did not need to be maintained during the brief flight.

Observing that existing and envisioned turbojets would not push an aircraft supersonic, and combining with rockets would be prohibitively heavy, Bell agreed with Kotcher that pure rocket propulsion was necessary. The 6,000-lbf (27-kN) Reaction Motors 6000C4 (military designation XLR11) rocket motor was chosen over the Aerojet Rotojet because the latter was still suffering developmental difficulties and its propellants were less safe for a manned aircraft.[21] A production-representative 6000C4, weighing 345 lb (157 kg) dry, would first be fired on August 30, 1945. Although it consumed fuel very rapidly, it delivered tremendous power for a high acceleration and rate of climb, and firing one or more of the four combustion chambers for throttling. Endurance was just sufficient to meet the specific mission objectives. The ethyl alcohol and LOX were stored within the fuselage. The ethyl alcohol was diluted with water before being circulated in a cooling jacket around the combustion chamber and then injected into the chamber. A stream of fuels was ignited by a spark plug before full fuel flow was established. The original intent to use a turbo-pump to move the fuels was causing a schedule slip and so was replaced with 4,500 psi (311 bar) nitrogen in a dozen small spherical tanks. The nitrogen turbine was driven by steam from the catalytic decomposition of hydrogen peroxide. Regulating this pressure to each propellant tank with cockpit controls was another means of varying thrust in flight. The pressure also provided motive power, usually supplied by hydraulics, for moving control surfaces and lowering landing gear (with gravity assist).

The change to nitrogen pressure to move the propellants, intended to be temporary, meant they had to be stored in the heavy spherical tanks instead of cylinders. Aircraft size increased and empty weight went up 2,000 lb (907 kg),

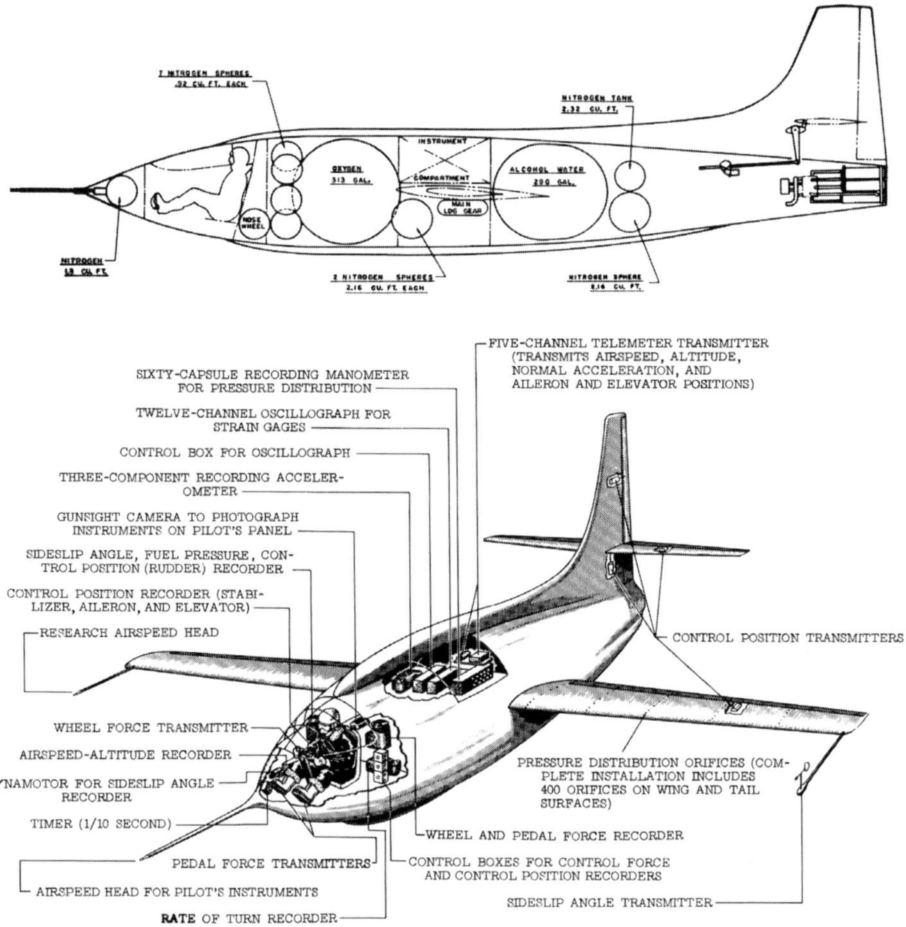

These period cutaway drawings show the internal details of the XS-1 as finally manufactured. The spherical tanks were necessary because of the pressurization fuel delivery to the engine. Ultimately, the propulsion system fuel was some two-thirds of the aircraft gross weight. (*Author's collection*)

with two-thirds of the aircraft gross weight consisting of propellants. Fuel capacity was nearly halved and powered endurance went from 4.2 to just 2.4 minutes with all chambers firing. This, in turn, drove the team to choose an air-launch mode, dropping from the bomb bay of a B-29 at 30,000 feet (9,144 m). Langley, again, had to accept deviation from a long-held principle that a research aircraft should be as conventional as possible. Furthermore, the rocket engine and air launch meant flight testing at Muroc and so far from the close supervision of Langley.

Preliminary design of the XS-1 was well along when the war ended, the mock-up being inspected in October 1945. The wing area was 102.5 feet^2 (9.5 m^2). The final design grossed 13,034 lb (5,912 kg) but landing at 6,785 lb (3,078 kg). Landing would be unpowered and around 170 mph (274 kph) after any remaining fuel was jettisoned for safety.

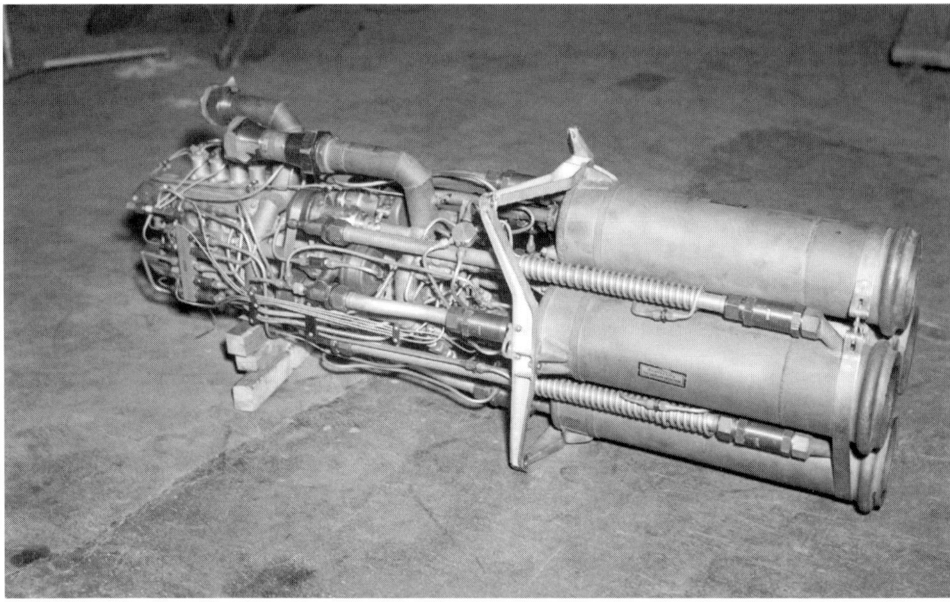

The XS-1 was powered by the Reaction Motors 6000C4 rocket motor generating 6,000 lbf (27 kN) thrust. The motor had four thrust chambers that could be fired individually or in combination as a form of throttling. Diluted ethyl alcohol and liquid oxygen were combusted within the chambers. A turbopump for the fuels lagged in development and forced a major change in the aircraft design. (*Air Force Test Center*)

The Navy/NACA jet-powered research aircraft was also defined by a specification compiled in late 1944. The formulation was complicated by Navy efforts to ensure the resulting aircraft might have some military value as a warplane. This included seeking bifurcated side inlets *versus* the nose axial inlet proposed by NACA such that gun integration at a future date would be possible. The specification required the machine to take off and land conventionally, powered by a General Electric TG-180, carry 500 lb (227 kg) of instrumentation, and fly to Mach 0.8–1. The GE turbojet was then the most powerful jet engine available in the U.S. at 4,000 lbf (18 kN).

Douglas got wind of the War Department's interest in transonic flight. They had been in discussions with individuals, including Kotcher, since early 1944 and had been performing aerodynamic studies.[22] Under the guidance of designers Ed Heinemann and Leo Devlin, project engineer Robert Donovan's team drafted a proposal, presented in February 1945, for their Model 558. Of several design options, with back-and-forth between the three parties, the team ultimately chose a three-phased approach. Phase one (six aircraft) would employ just the TG-180 with annular inlet for transonic flight research; phase two (two aircraft) a Westinghouse 24C turbojet (later J34-WE-7) fed by bifurcated inlets (for take-off, climb, and return) plus a trio of podded Aerojet 40AS-1000 rocket motors (high-speed dash) for an assault on Mach 1 in a 25-degree dive; and phase three development of a combat model of the aircraft for which a mock-up would be assembled.

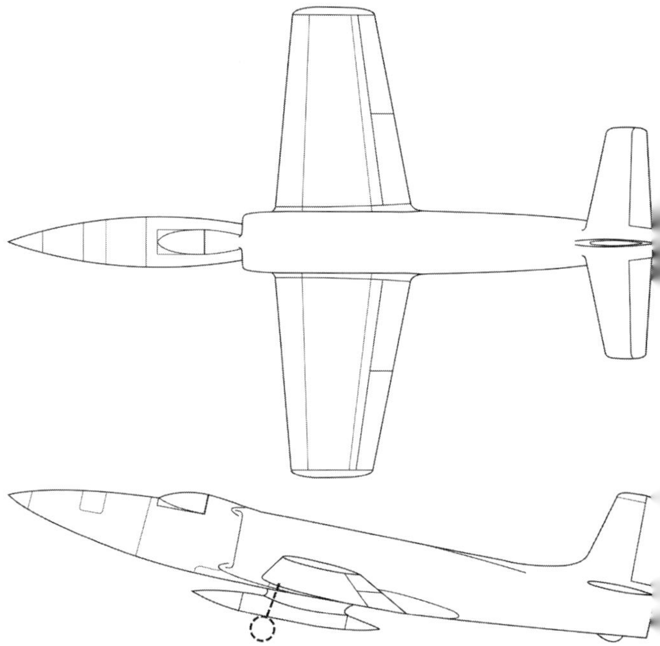

Among design concepts explored for the D-558 was this turbojet-powered 'tail-dragger' with one of three rocket booster units on the belly (the aft cone separating for firing). Changes in the D-558-1 mock-up included switching from flush inlets to annular and canopy alterations, suggesting this design may have been reflected in the mock-up initially. However, the horizontal tail was to be mid-mounted based on early NACA guidance and the final design possessed a tricycle undercarriage. (*Drawn by the author*)

Douglas was given the go-ahead on June 22, 1945, with $6,888,444.80 funding six airplanes. The requirements for 18-*g* normal load factor was also applied to the Douglas design that featured the horizontal tail set mid-span of the vertical. A V-tail was investigated as another alternative, based in Bell's testing of a P-63 so configured, but the conventional design was felt to be the least technologically risky. It was agreed to develop an afterburner for the Phase I machine to push it deeper into the transonic regime. An unusual degree of equipment and cockpit cooling was incorporated.

The mock-up inspection was on July 2–4 in El Segundo, California, featuring submerged 'cheek' inlets. A follow-up inspection on August 14–17 reviewed change to an axial inlet and canopy revisions that were all found satisfactory. It was also decided at that time to drop Phase III and have three aircraft built for each of Phase I (D-558-1, 37970/2) and Phase II (D-558-2).

Detailed design of the three D-558-1s (37970/2) with the Allison J35-A-11 (Allison having taken over production of the TG-180) yielded an aircraft that was largely conventional in layout, although careful aerodynamic choices were made to ensure speed goals could be safely achieved. The goal was conventional take-off and landing with a flight to at least Mach 0.75–0.85, 40,000 feet (12,192 m), and about thirty minutes in duration. Going after the smallest airframe wrapped around the largest engine, the straight wing spanned just 25 feet (7.6 m) with 150.7 feet^2 (14.0 m^2) compared with a length of 35.7 feet (10.9 m) and maximum weight of 10,105 lb (4,584 kg). Optional wingtip tanks were planned. The wing had a 10 percent section and the horizontal stabilizer was all-moving for trim.

The thin wing required the development of particularly narrow wheels and tires to retract into the contour. That contour was carefully maintained in assembly with a thick skin, magnesium in the case of the fuselage. Very stiff jigs with metal contour forms permitted assembly from the skin inward to help minimize surface irregularities.

As with the XS-1, a control yoke was selected over a stick as it was feared the pilot might need the strength of both arms at times. The stabilizer trim switch was on this yoke. The aft fuselage also featured airbrakes on each side to assist in deceleration but could also assist in pull-out from a dive by generating a tail-down pitch rate. Another innovation was a detachable forward fuselage for pilot emergency egress as ejection seats were then still in their infancy and employed shells to boost the seat up and out. It was feared this abrupt acceleration would cause injuries.

Construction of the first XS-1 in Niagara Falls, New York, was finished in December but the motor was delayed. The XS-1 conducted separation and glide testing beginning in January 1946 and the first powered flight in December before Ship 1 was flown supersonic ten months later. The first D-558-1 Skystreak was completed in January 1947 with a maiden flight in April. It went on to establish new speed records. A military variant of the Douglas aircraft was wisely forgotten.

Langley continued to pursue a separate course in avoiding rocket propulsion for a transonic research aircraft capable of reaching Mach 1.4. A proposal was

The joint Navy and NACA supersonic research aircraft project took an initial step with the Douglas D-558-1 as the first of a planned three iterative designs. As this concept art suggests, the first aircraft was conventional in appearance save for the then still new jet engine. It sought only to explore the transonic region short of Mach 1. (*National Archives*)

Unlike the XS-1, the Douglas airplane employed the powerful General Electric TG-180 turbojet engine with an annular inlet. The firm was placed on contract in June 1945 and this mock-up was approved as the war wrapped up. It was initially a "tail dragger" with "cheek" inlets when first inspected in July 1945. (*Tony Landis collection*)

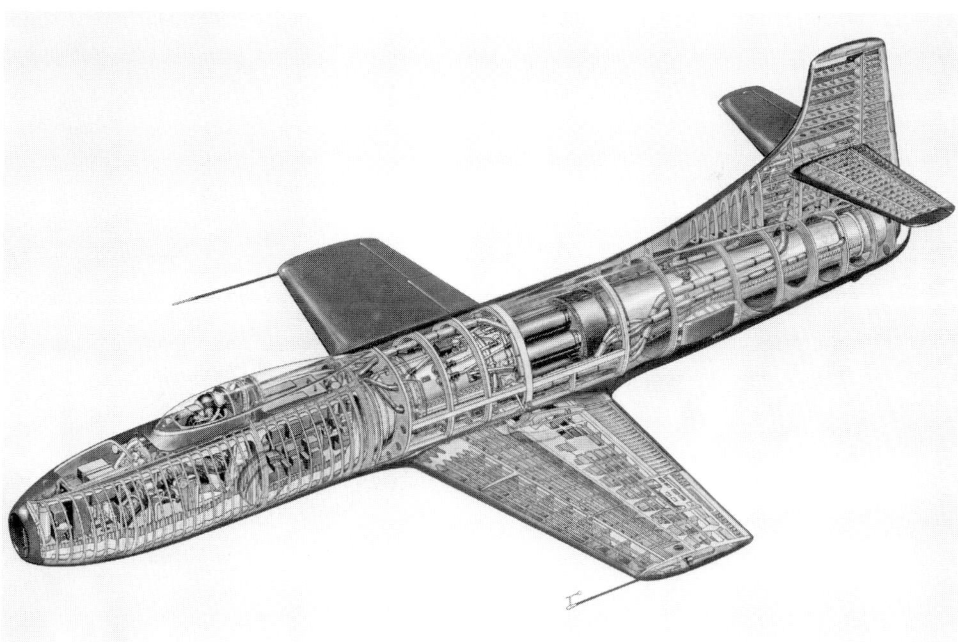

Detail design of the D-558-1 was well underway at war's end. The TG-180 engine was the most powerful American turbojet at the time. The low-profile bubble canopy eventually gave way to an equally low enclosure with V-windscreen and flat transparencies that provided better roll-over protection for the pilot but was even more confining. (*National Archives*)

under developed at war's end for a ramjet-powered vehicle with rocket motors to boost it to the transonic airspeed at which the ramjet could function. Air-launch or towing aloft would be required, this and the rocket motors again departing from NACA dictum. This project was ultimately rejected.[23]

Sweeping Controversy

Within a few months of Germany's surrender, its application of swept wings in advanced jet aircraft designs was common knowledge within the American aircraft development community. As the XS-1 and D-558 Skystreak configurations emerged, the natural question was why their wings were straight.

Research into aero surface sweep was being undertaken in the U.S. only as low-level efforts late in the war, whereas, in Germany, it had been a subject of research since 1939. Swept wing aircraft had been featured on some American experimental aircraft and a few production designs such as the DC-3, but for stability reasons. Leading aerodynamicists appreciated the benefits of the sweep in delaying compressibility effects for higher critical Mach numbers and lower drag. However, swept surfaces complicated structural design. They moved flow separation at stall to the wingtip and the ailerons for degraded roll authority and with a pitch-up tendency (hence the outboard slats on the Me 262). In dealing with these problems, little analytical or empirical information was available. By early 1945, Robert T. Jones at Langley was leading serious research into the advantages of wing sweep for high-speed flight that he had shown analytically several years before. This remained constrained by the limits of testing in the transonic regime. It progressed slowly as few initially saw the advantages or leadership felt such a radical idea required substantive empirical data was required to support the conclusions.

It was evident to German researchers that once the speed–performance limitations of the propeller were eliminated by the introduction of the jet engine, the critical Mach number at which shocks formed could be extended significantly only by sweeping the wing. Nearly all their jet designs after 1941 possessed swept surfaces. There was a tendency in the United States during the war years to pursue anything the Germans were doing because they were clearly in the vanguard of military aviation technology and had been frightfully successful in employing such resources. Although few details were known of the German wartime programs, that they were developing swept-wing aircraft was clear. The twin-jet Me 262, with 18.5-degree wing sweep, had a typical 100 mph (161 kph) speed advantage on its prop-driven, straight wing adversaries. Yet, the U.S. military made no effort to specifically direct the use of swept wings on advanced aircraft projects and, consequently, NACA did not give such research priority. For that matter, no one else in the world made any appreciable investigation or use of swept surfaces for high-speed advantages apart from the Germans. It was only at the end of May 1945 that analytical results were coupled with wind tunnel and flight test data to substantiate the swept wing benefits to the satisfaction of senior engineers. Findings were also gleaned from technical inspections of German aeronautical test and research sites following the end of the war in Europe, along with studying seized documents and interviewing leading German scientist and engineers. These yielded preliminary findings that were just reaching Langley and service personnel associated with the transonic aircraft development during fall 1945.

Despite some opinions to the contrary, both the USAAF and NACA agreed the XS-1 aero surfaces would be straight but with a moderately thin section. There was simply insufficient swept wing research to support fast-paced wartime design programs. Later in 1945, the design had advanced to a state at which accommodating such a rework could not be borne by budget and schedule.

The depth of Allied under-appreciation of the importance of swept wings for high-speed flight is readily evident in the first generation of jet aircraft. These machines were pursued to build beyond the speed limits of piston-engined/propeller-driven combat aircraft. Yet, all of them until the last months of the war were conceived with straight wings of conventional thickness. This was partially

After the XS-1 detailed design effort had begun, results of the investigation into German swept wing research became available to engineering organizations within the United States. This immediately suggested the Bell aircraft should have swept surfaces to reduce compressibility effects, as confirmed by wind tunnel testing. However, the decision was made not to hold up the program for such a fundamental change. (*National Museum of the United States Air Force*)

an intentional effort to introduce a limited number of major new design features into aircraft that had to enter production and service rapidly yet were already radical in fundamental aspect. However, when the Americans began planning for research aircraft to explore the problems of high-speed flight with a goal of exceeding Mach 1, even these designs lacked swept surfaces.

In the summer of 1945, after NACA testing had demonstrated the advantages of wing sweep, Bell was tasked with considering this change. Following Germany's surrender, the Allies sought out the records, equipment, and individuals associated with the country's pioneering research into swept wings and supersonic aerodynamics. The initial output of the investigation was shared with the American aircraft industry in late summer so that benefits could be realized in the continuing struggle with Japan and to ensure U.S. post-war lead in aeronautical science. The NACA and the War Department were criticized for being overly-conservative in failing to explore wing sweep sooner.

Had MX-524 started in fall 1945, the design would certainly have been different.[24] As it was, wind tunnel testing confirmed the potential benefits of swept surfaces for the XS-1, but the USAAF decided not to suffer the long delay to affect the substantial design change. In fall 1945, the move to explore wing sweep benefits at high speed led to a proposal that the Phase II D-558s include this option. This was eventually adopted for the clean nose/bifurcated inlet design with supplemental rocket engine.

6

Undercarriage Variations

A sideline story is the efforts to make fighters and other aircraft more flexible in terms of operating environments. This included large tires and skis. Although many of these "funnies" and experiments were successful, none were employed in any substantial and meaningful way during the war. Yet, they show a willingness to entertain such significant modifications and the technical acumen to successfully carry them out.

Alightment Refinement

In the few years prior to the war, the U.S. Army and Navy had become familiar with tricycle landing gear, though NACA and civilian organizations had also been experimenting with this configuration. The commercial aircraft and airline industries were already moving firmly in that direction as evident with the newest models emerging as war arose. The benefits for aircraft control and safety during ground operations and potentially shorter take-offs were evident. It was clearly the wave of the future. But, more technical details were necessary if design and evaluation criteria were to be developed for future military aircraft.

A Navy pre-war BT-1 was modified with fixed tricycle gear for testing and given the unofficial designation BT-1S. With Douglas developing the tricycle gear XB-19, the Army bailed an OA-4B seaplane to Douglas who added a nose gear for flight trials. The Air Corps operated a modified cabin-class Lockheed 12A Electra Junior twin designated C-40B with a non-retractable tricycle gear for testing in 1939–1940. During the same period, the Naval Aircraft Factory tested the similarly modified Lockheed 12A (1267) but added an arrestment hook. This XJO-3 flew eleven take-off and landings aboard USS *Lexington* in August 1939 off the Coronado Roads.[1] For the USAAF, tricycle gear was featured with almost all new fighter designs plus all bombers and transports ordered after the war began. The exception suggests this was not a firm policy and some design teams chose to stick with what they knew. Nose wheel steering, however, was initial rare.

Both the Army and Navy modified Lockheed Electras to a tricycle gear configuration for testing and familiarization. The USAAC was already deep into adopting nose-gear aircraft while the USN was more leery of the feature, especially for carrier ops. Note the arresting hook under the aft fuselage of this Navy XJO-3, giving aviators exposure to twins, nose gear, and associated arrestments all in one testbed. (*Naval Aviation Archives*)

In the case of the Grumman XP-50, they insisted on a nose gear for the Air Forces spin-off of the Navy's tail-dragging XF5F-1 Skyrocket.

The U.S. Navy's attitude toward tricycle undercarriage was evolving, but integration into carrier ops remained a great concern that was cause for hesitation. The principal worry was the nose gear sheering off on a landing cable or in a crash barrier, risking the pilot in an overturn. Trials with the XJO-3 were encouraging, but more needed to be done to convince the decision-makers of the feasibility of operating "trics" aboard ship. Within two years, the Navy was readily accepting concepts with tricycle gear. They knew this was going to be the norm and most of its new designs incorporated the feature, especially with jets on the horizon. They had to adapt if they were to remain relevant. The same evolution was evident with twin-engined aircraft.

The USN put one tricycle type into production during the war. The Grumman F7F, incorporating both tricycle gear and twin engines, was ordered in summer 1941 and some 250 had been delivered by war's end. However, only the Marines deployed with the type, arriving in theater just at the cessation of hostilities. The Navy appears to have intentionally delayed incorporating the F7F into carrier air wings until after the war. All of its jet fighters and mixed jet-recip types in development had, by necessity, nose gear so that jet blast did not strike the surface immediately aft of the aircraft. Wooden carrier decks were also incompatible with jets. All the other developmental fighters and attack machines were a mixed lot of conventional and tricycle gear types. This suggests the USN was ready to accept

The first Grumman XF7F-1 is seen in flight on December 23, 1944, over NAS Patuxent River, Maryland. The type was ordered into development in summer 1941 and then production in 1943. Although many squadrons had worked on the Tigercat by the end of the war, carrier integration was left until after the war. (*Naval Aviation Archives*)

This Piper L-4A has been fitted with experimental main gear struts to accommodate high-flotation tires on swiveling wheels with bungee shock chords for a greater wheel track in an arrangement referred to as "crosswind gear" as it also permitted landing in a crab or forward slip. The castoring wheels also permitted agile aircraft movement in close confines by ground personnel, such as under concealing trees. (*The Peter M. Bowers Collection/The Museum of Flight*)

a mixed fleet on its decks. The service showed no hesitation in accepting tricycle undercarriage for its land-based aircraft.

As discussed in Chapter 2, operating liaison airplanes on soft ground, in concert with their ability to take off and land on short, unprepared fields, was a priority. This became a challenge as weight increased with complexity to meet the ever-growing number of missions demanded of the light-planes. Balloon tires assisted, or at least ones of greater width and diameter (footprint). There was also a need for ground movement in tight areas, either taxiing or shoved about by ground personnel. To these ends, an experiment was performed with Piper L-4A NX-42049 fitted with large tires on castoring wheels. As the loads on the undercarriage from such an arrangement were much different than those for the standard lightweight gear, entirely new struts had to be fashioned. These also permitted a wider wheel track to be introduced. Crosswind landings in a crab or forward slip could be performed without final alignment to runway heading prior to touchdown, while avoiding an overload of the gear. The equipment was quite heavy and so, like many good ideas, considered a cure worse than the disease. However, the castoring main gear wheels were adopted for the XL-13 (Chapter 2).

The conceptual first generation of jet bombers was to have thin wings. These and the engine nacelles did not readily lend themselves to storage of retractable landing gear. This suggested a tandem or bicycle landing gear with two main gear posts and wheels extending from the fuselage and outboard outrigger stabilizing gear of low enough profile to fit in the wing. Before the end of the war, Martin, designing their XB-48, sought to experiment with such a gear to determine design variables and gain practical operational experience. To this end, Wright Field obliged with a contract and TB-26G 44-68221. The bomber was modified with B-26 main wheels installed on twin posts within the fuselage. The steerable forward wheel retracted into the forward fuselage while the aft, behind the bomb bay, was fixed. The brakes in both wheels where operable. Castoring B-17 tailwheels were adopted to long-post outriggers retractable into the engine nacelle wells.[2] This XB-26H they named the *Middle River Stump Jumper*. The month beginning May 4, 1945, saw the earliest testing of the modified aircraft in Baltimore by E. R. "Dutch" Gelvin, and more was to follow.[3] Handling was assessed and gear loads were measured. All was not ideal, particularly landing in a crosswind, but it could be made to work and it eventually did for the XB-48 and Boeing XB-47.

Ensuring floatation on mud and slush saw the adoption of large balloon tires, such as tested on a P-40. Other landing gear concepts were also tested, to include dual tandem wheels and multi-wheel trucks tested on the P-40. None of these arrangements appeared to be retractable.

Operating bombers and transports from soft fields led to the idea of a caterpillar track-laying or tread gear replacing the wheels, such as found on a tank but light in weight. It had to withstand abrupt rotation on landing, go to higher speeds than for land vehicles, and sustain side loads such as in a crosswind landing without throwing the track. Installation of a small Firestone track on a P-40 fighter showed the promise in the concept.

The coming jet bombers would need innovative solutions for landing gear given the expected thin wings and turbojet engine nacelles. A tandem undercarriage offered a solution for which experimental testing was performed with this modified B-26G (post-war image). The XB-26H had longitudinal stiffeners installed to assist in distributing loads from the landing gear in a "quick and dirty" modification. (*Jim Hawkins via The Norm Taylor Collection/The Museum of Flight*)

An early model P-40 has had its landing gear modified for not two but four balloon tires offering greater floatation on soft ground. The Curtiss fighter's wheels were normally mounted outboard of the strut, reaching half the height, so the added large-diameter wheels are inboard. Photographed on September 14, 1943, it is clear the gear is no longer retractable. (*National Museum of the United States Air Force*)

Above: A similar P-40 is equipped with another arrangement of multiple tires but on a truck arrangement. Shock absorption for truck rotation appears to be provided by fore and aft bungies. Seen on August 12, 1943, this was one of several experimental gear designs evaluated on the fighter during the period. (*National Museum of the United States Air Force*)

Below: This early P-40 (apparently the same aircraft as shown above) has been fitted with experimental Firestone tracked main landing gear trucks. The continuous track is a treaded rubberized band, and the pivoting truck has a shock cylinder joining the aft face if the gear post. Retraction of the trucks was clearly impractical on the P-40, though the well doors are retained. (*National Museum of the United States Air Force*)

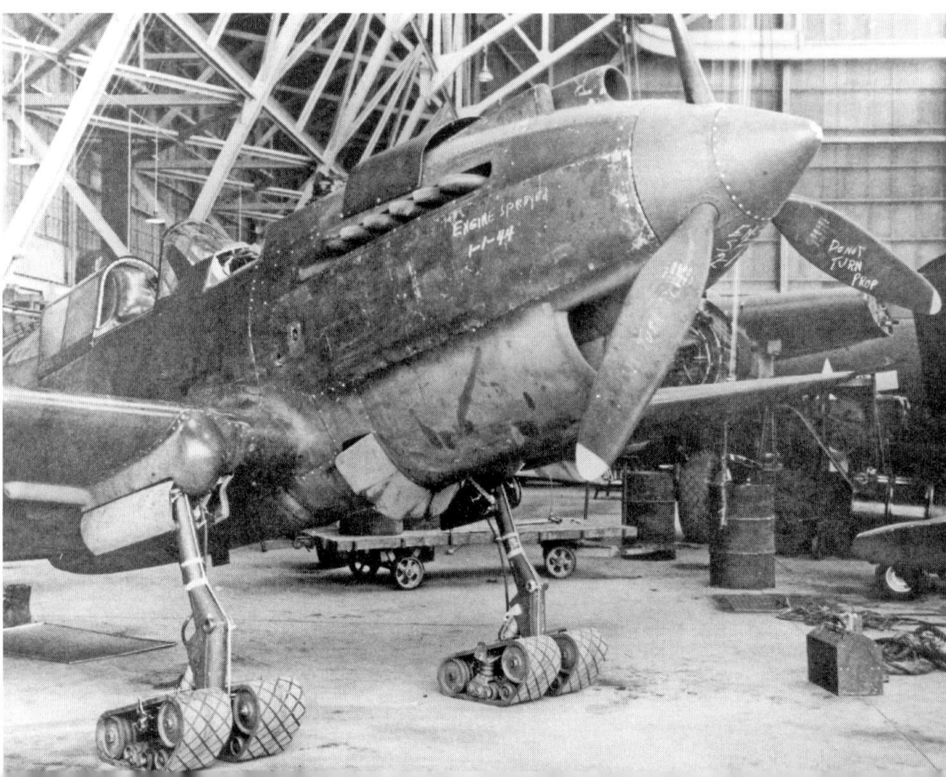

A larger, more complex endless track was tested on an A-20C (41-19158) bomber followed by an A-20H (44-466). This featured grooved rubber belts, reinforced with steel wires, running over bogies and rollers, and supported by shock absorbers.[4] The main gear strut arrangement underwent considerable change on the A-20 and was non-retractable. It permitted the track to hang "heel down" as do common aircraft multi-tire trucks to lend an energy absorbing shock strut acting in the rotation axis. The Firestone track was an endless band nearly 3 feet (0.9 m) wide. It had ridges on the inside surface that rode in grooves on the wheels to resist side loads and lateral slipping. It was tested in landings up to 120 mph (193 kph) and increased the footprint area three times for superior floatation on soft ground.

Although many of these designs and experiments were successful, none were employed in any meaningful way during the war. Experimentation continued after the war with the TA-20H and similar tracks installed on a C-82, B-50, and B-36. Still, no operational applications emerged.

Of Skis and Things

Skis on aircraft had a long history before the war, especially in northern climes like Canada where skis for production airplanes were manufactured and sold. In the U.S., Federal Aircraft Works of Minneapolis, Minnesota, manufactured skis adaptable to many light airplanes built in American such as the Piper Cub. Of course, the principal disadvantage of skis is that they have no brakes and are seldom steerable (if this would have any effectiveness). Directional control from prop wash over rudder or varying thrust for P-factor yaw or differential thrust of multiple engines were generally the only means of control. These might also produce a ground loop to help stop an airplane, but all were poor substitutes for proper directional control and braking. Consequently, skis generally remained a choice only for light aircraft or larger machines under special circumstances.

Shipment of warplanes to Canada and the Union of Soviet Socialist Republics (USSR) had to occur year-round, and so operations on snow were mandatory. For example, some North American AT-6C trainers bound for the northern neighbor were equipped for skis.[5] The design allowed the tires to project through the bottom of the ski and perhaps offered some improvement to the directional control limitations. Some Lend-Lease recipients of the Texan also attached locally produced skis.

American operations in the wintery Alaska and Aleutians suggested that skis would add operational flexibility. These would have to apply to support aircraft as well as fighters. However, the latter would also support shipments to the Soviet Union if German submarines made ocean vessel delivery too costly. The concept appears to have been explored with skis installed in a P-36A tested at Ladd Field in 1942. As the cold weather testing base, Ladd hosted the majority of such work. This was followed by trials with all the major American fighters. Operational

Above: The Havoc tracked gear testing continued with this A-20H. The equipment appears little changed from the C-model installation and apparently represents a considerably added drag increment. Note the "heel-down" attitude of the truck, done to assist in landing energy absorption. (*National Museum of the United States Air Force*)

Opposite: Continuing the search for means of operating aircraft on unprepared ground suggested track-laying gear for large aircraft. This A-20C, photographed on August 3, 1943, was modified with such an arrangement, though clearly non-retractable. The close-up image shows the complex yet rugged equipment. (*National Archives*)

This AT-6C, photographed near Dallas on January 29, 1943, has been fitted with fairly simple wooden skis on the main gear and tailwheel. Notice the cant of the tailwheel ski with the weight off wheels. The exhaust is evidence the machine was bound for northern climes (Canada and Greenland). (*National Archives*)

The P-36A (*right*) was photographed at Wright Field on February 20, 1942, with experimental Luscombe skis on the main gear and tail. The painted airplane (*left*) on May 14, 1942, at Ladd Field (where snow was scarce the day of the test) gives a better view of the elegant but complex and no doubt heavy nature of the enclosed main gear skis. (*National Museum of the United States Air Force and National Archives*)

evaluations were also performed in the northern regions. Although the system appeared to work well enough, by 1944, the Aleutians campaign was winding down and the Nazi threat at sea was receding. Other motivations may have been to prepare for ops in Europe once the Allies re-entered the Continent. This was sure to include one winter and there was no certainty that enemy airfields could be consistently seized intact or runways readily cleared of snow. However, none of the fighter applications are known to have been employed operationally by the Americans. There appeared little future for the concept, but designs were retained if requirements developed.

Fully retractable but flimsy-looking skis were tried on a P-40 during tests at Ladd. A P-38G (42-13444) was fitted with retractable experimental Federal Aircraft skis replacing the wheels. The skis, appearing very light affairs, enclosed the gear well when retracted and so doors were removed. These were tested at Ladd in winter 1943–1944 during which, on January 15, 1944, there was a mishap when one ski collapsed. More successful trials, possibly with a P-38J (42-13565 *Ice Cold Katie*) possessing a slightly different ski configuration, were performed in March 1944. A P-47G (42-24964) also received a ski installation. This was aerodynamically refined, with fairings around the fixed-down gear posts and faired-over skis that added weight. Two P-51As (43-6003 and 43-6005) were fitted with skis in place of the wheels such that the landing gear could still be at least partially retracted. This was tested in Fairbanks by Lt-Col. Randy Acord and a few other pilots. The P-63 was supplied to the USSR that had long and severe winters. Ski-equipped airplanes were valued, although combat types employed them largely for internal movement only. The Kingcobra skis could be partially retracted to decrease drag and extend range.

Utility and liaison aircraft especially benefited from the addition of skis given the need for them to operate from unprepared fields close to combat units advancing across the country in all weather conditions. The L-1, L-4, and L-5 applications were employed in European combat ops. There, the L-4 skis were assembled locally but found to excessively stress the undercarriage, leading to gear collapses.[6]

Seven Beech AT-7A navigation trainers were fitted for Edo water floats that could be swapped for skis. Nine AT-7Bs were specifically built for winter operations of which five were supplied to the Royal Navy. The skis appeared to be similar to the aerodynamic P-47 units.[7] They looked like compressed water floats and so were probably built by Edo Corporation of College Point, New York, maker of most aircraft floats employed by the United States. The AT-7 was essentially a Model 18 twins stripped to essentials for training and so had minimal utility compared with a C-45. Flight training was normally conducted in southwestern locales where operations could be conducted year-round. The need to equip a handful with skis is unclear. Operation on skis was normally taught on fielded types and picked up quickly.

Larger applications also had value where fields could not be cleared of snow yet urgent operations had to be performed. For personnel transport and light freight, ski installations were made to several transports. On a large scale was

Above: Even after the tough early months following the U.S. entering the war, there was a desire to operate fighters in extreme environments. The P-38 was the subject of tests with skis replacing the wheels, and with gear doors removed. Here, a P-38G operates with Federal Aircraft skis during tests on January 15, 1944. (*National Museum of the United States Air Force and Ray Wagner collection*)

Below: In flight, the P-38J's skis looked ungainly and draggy, likely requiring the fighter to fly well below its normal cruise airspeed. This particular design had the benefit of being retractable. The ski surfaces were apparently designed to exactly fit the openings of the gear wells without the usual doors. (*The Peter M. Bowers Collection/The Museum of Flight*)

These images of the P-47G on skis give little hint of location and date other than the national markings that appear to have the red surround from summer 1943. The skis are unusually refined, with enclosed aerodynamic fairings. Even the gear posts, fixed down, have fairings to reduce the drag of the installation. (*National Archives*)

The first P-51A, seen here, and another P-51A were employed in testing skis to allow the fighter to operate on snow and ice. The skis were mechanized to permit the landing gear to be retracted. The aircraft was deployed to Ladd Field, Alaska, for testing. (*National Museum of the United States Air Force*)

The P-63 was not employed in combat by the USAAF, instead most being exported to the USSR. The Soviets valued ski-equipped aircraft, if only for delivery and internal movement, and so such equipment was developed. A P-63As with partially retractable skis is shown. (*Jay Miller collection*)

This poor photo on a Stinson L-5 (probably 42-98275) on skis was shot on January 30, 1945. Little is known of the configuration but it was most likely created to support winter operations in Europe. The nature of the tailwheel ski on the Sentinel is unclear. (*National Archives*)

Skis also adorn this Stinson L-1A (41-19031) photographed on April 18, 1944, in a wintery setting. Like others, the ski is designed to fit onto the axle of the strut after removing the wheel; this also permits rotation as a stress-relieving measure. A cable runs from the nose of each ski to the base of the strut, likely to prevent excessive nose-down rotation. (*National Archives*)

Right: The rugged Noorduyn Norseman UC-64 could operate out of semi-prepared runways and some unprepared. Extending this utility by permitting operation on snow was advantageous, with laminated wood skis by several manufacturers being prominent. These images reveal two designs for such a fielded installation plus details showing shock absorbing features, cables restraining over-rotation, and designs with and without the tailwheel retained. (*The Peter Bowers Collection/The Museum of Flight and National Archives*)

Below: Among the largest ski-equipped aircraft was the C-47. Being able to operate the ubiquitous tactical transport on snow was a great boon, but was probably seldom employed during the war yet used for decades after. The skis are a complex assembly with an aerovane on the rear and permitting the tires to protrude out the bottom for operations in the absence of snow. (*The Peter M. Bowers Collection/The Museum of Flight*)

the ubiquitous C-47 with a complex design that permitted the wheels to protrude through the skis. This supported ops with and without snow. A couple of C-46s were also reported to have been subjected to ski trials, these probably the largest aircraft so-equipped. Other large aircraft included a B-25 and a P-61.[8]

The Waco CG-4A assault glider was initially built with main gear that could be dropped after take-off under tow. This permitted landing on skids at the sides of the flat-bottomed fuselage. Ultimately, fixed gear struts were adopted but the skids remained in the event the gear sheared off during landings on unprepared fields—an all-too-common occurrence).

As helicopters were developed during the war, all the military types had wheeled undercarriage. It was clear that the ability to alight just about anywhere made it beneficial to adopt something that would spread the weight of the aircraft over a broader surface area to ensure floatation. At the extreme, this permitted floating on water. Very early in the evolution of the first production American helicopter (the Sikorsky R-4), inflatable floats were attached to the bottom of the aircraft. Skids were post-war innovations.

Portable Runway

Farther afield was eliminating a landing/take-off surface entirely where runways were not yet available or impractical given the terrain. The idea was light airplanes launching and recovering from a suspended cable via a hook atop the aircraft such that it never touched the ground or a deck. Based aboard a ship, it could permit even medium-size cargo vessels the ability to operate a submarine scout that might also drop a depth charge. This last was extremely important because air cover for convoys crossing the Atlantic initially had a gap the U-boats were exploiting with deadly effectiveness. Such a system was proposed by 1Lt James H. Brodie, a Field Artillery officer and engineer. He had sketched out the design by March 1942, a time when many people were coming forward with concepts for rapidly improving American air power. Brodie offered his concept to the National Inventors Council and the U.S. Navy, but without success. However, the Army's Transportation Corps found it worth pursuing and Brodie was appropriately assigned.

The basic idea for the land-based system was a "cableway" suspended at each end between an angle of bridle cables attaching to masts. This created openings at each end into which the airplane could enter or depart. The pilot was to fly in under the bridles at one end and snag a sling suspended from a wheeled trolley, riding on the cable, with a hook mounted above the aircraft. The trolley would be braked to a stop and drawn back to one end where the aircraft was lowered for servicing or cargo exchange. Once raised back up, the aircraft could depart in a similar manner, riding the trolley as it accelerated until the pilot released the overhead hook and flew out between the masts on the far end. Where level ground was not available, the cable could be strung between canyon walls. Installed on a ship at sea, the cable would be suspended from booms projecting off the side of the vessel.

Right: The early jettisonable wheel assembly can be seen under the CG-4A assault glider in the bottom image with skids ahead and behind, while the top image shows men appearing to be prepared a Waco for tow aloft on skids. A fixed gear was eventually adopted though the skids were retained on the CG-4As to provide support when the undercarriage sheared away on a rough field landing. (*National Museum of the United States Air Force and The Museum of Flight*)

Below: In yet another test at Ladd Field, this Sikorsky R-4B performs operations on its floatation bag undercarriage. This form of support on soft surfaces was developed very early in the history of the helicopter and carried over to the present day. The now-common skids did not appear until after the war. (*The National Museum of the United States Air Force*)

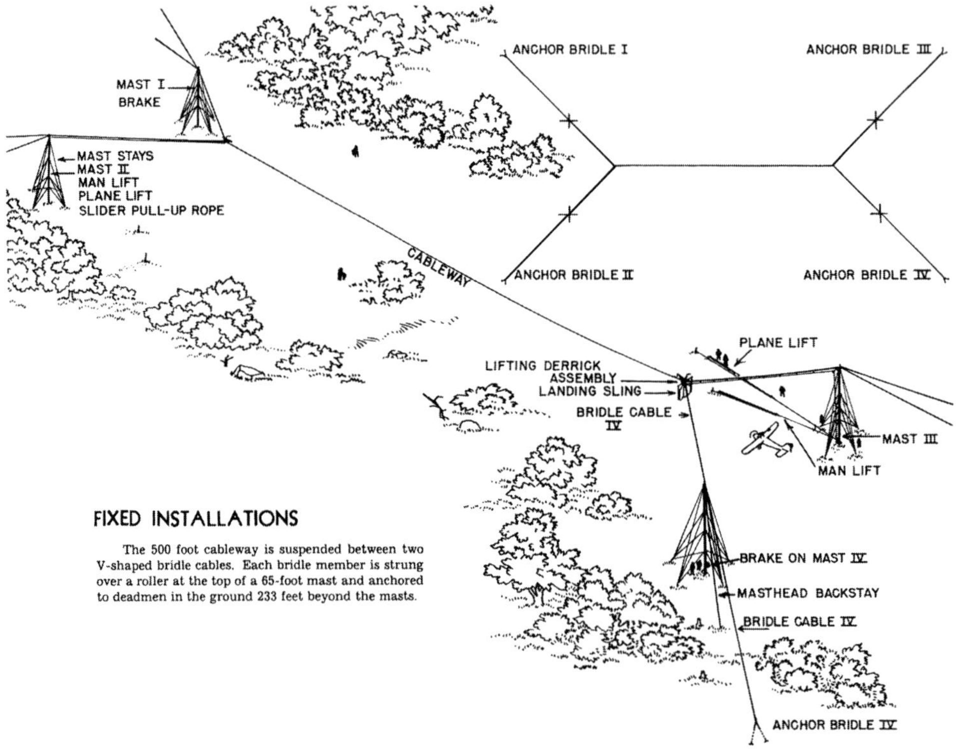

This diagram from a presentation to the Office of Strategic Services shows the rudiments of the Brodie system. While it permitted light aircraft such as the L-4 and L-5 (no more than 2,100-lb/953-kg gross weight) to take-off and land without a runway, it was not a simple device. The approximately 7,000 lb (3,175 kg) of equipment required hundreds of man-hours to erect and encompassed a considerable area of terrain. (*Author's collection*)

The lieutenant was given $10,000 and permission to construct and test his Brodie Device. It was soon evident that the devil was in the details, but he pressed ahead. Brodie had to work on the system after his regular duties redesigning cargo transport ships at the New Orleans, Louisiana, port had been completed for the day. In about a year, he had the first prototype of his system completed. The design was suitable for aircraft weighing up to 2,250 lb (1,021 kg). Tested were the L-4, commonly grossing about 1,220 lb (553 kg), and the L-5 at 2,020 lb (916 kg). The Brodie Landing System soon earned names like "Shoestring Airport" and "Clothesline Runway."

In the final design, the masts could be installed such that the 500-foot (152-m) cable was aligned with the wind (only when initially erected) to prevent the higher speeds of a tailwind engagement or challenging handling in a crosswind. The masts extending to 65 feet (19.8 m), a pair 160 feet (49 m) apart at each end, 600 feet (183 m) away, and supported by guy wires. Bridles from each pole pair met in a "V" to support the 1¼-inch (3.2-cm) steel cableway that ran between the pairs. With supporting anchor cables, the entire rig encompassed an area of 1,000 feet (305 m) by 500 feet (152 m). This was not a factor for a seagoing vessel as the deceleration or acceleration distance on the cable would be less given the air velocity created by the ship's passage.

To "land," the pilot lined up on a 6 × 8-foot (1.8 × 2.4-m) target frame containing an 11/16-inch diameter nylon rope sling arranged in three loops. A loop had to be engaged by a hook attached about 6 feet (1.8 m) above the airplane via support tubes that also served to guide the rope into the hook. The hook on the fixed braces had to be positioned above the approximate center of gravity so that the aircraft hung relatively level. On definite hook-up, the pilot cut power as the trolley slid forward. The trolley's lower half swung forward on contact before forward motion began and the hook was on an arm that rotated aft to a horizontal attitude and telescoped out about 2 feet (0.6 m) on contact. Along with the elastic characteristics of the nylon line, these motions ensured that the engagement and deceleration to a stop would be smooth and would not permit the aircraft to swing dangerously. A line ran from the trolley to a reel and hydraulic braking mechanism such that the aircraft was automatically slowed to a stop as it ran along the cable beneath the trolley and before reaching the far end. Line tension had to be adjusted to the aircraft gross weight but maximum braking occurring after about a 50-foot (15-m) run, reaching about one-third *g*. Design of the drum braking mechanism was among the greatest challenges Brodie had to overcome and he received assistance from All American Aviation who had worked up similar systems for glider snatch (see Chapter 10).

It was important for the pilot to push the stick forward on contacting the sling (opposite the normal landing technique) so that the aircraft would not pitch up and the propeller strike the cableway. An error usually only resulted in damage or loss of the wooden prop. If the pilot mistakenly felt he had hooked up and pushed the stick forward while throttling back, there would be a surprising dive towards the ground that was recoverable.

A pilot that could reach out and manually turn the aircraft in the sling to then "taxi" back to the starting bridle cables or drop a line so that ground personnel could pull it backward. This line was coiled up within the airplane and led out a window aft where it was tied off to the lifting handle on the rear fuselage. At the bridle cables, the "Hooker" was manually raised 65 feet off the ground seated on a man-lift line. This person attached a lifting ring to the aircraft hook. Lifting the aircraft slightly allowed the landing sling to be unshackled from the trolley and the aircraft lowered to the ground manually or via a motor-powered winch.

For take-off, a 4-foot (1.2-m) length of nylon line was fitted into a stirrup atop the hook and closed by a release finger to support the aircraft hanging below. The landing line was removed from the hook. The line in the stirrup extended from a lifting ring in the middle and then to an eye and shackle at the top. The aircraft was lifted by the ring via the lifting derrick so that the shackle could be attached by the Hooker to a different wheeled trolley on the cableway. A separate line and winch pulled the trolley and aircraft to the far end of the cableway, if necessary. The pilot powered up and pulled a lanyard to release a clutch lever and disconnect the trolley from a holdback line. A spring-loaded trip mechanism released the holdback only under the tension of full power. Alternatively, a person could do this from the ground with a rope. The take-off run was some 50 percent shorter

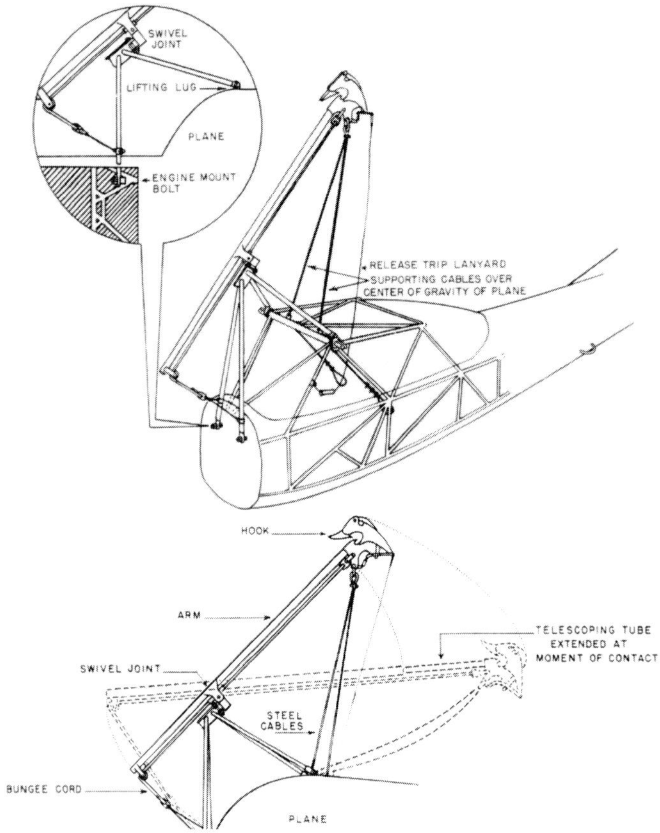

The hook atop the aircraft was integrated with the welded steel tube structure and placed it above the approximate center of gravity. The bottom opening of the hook was to snag the landing sling and the top held the launch sling until opened for release by the pilot once flying speed was attained. The articulation indicated helped relieve the shock and abrupt lurching of the airplane during the snag and slowing on "landing." (*Author's collection*)

A Piper L-4 "Grasshopper" liaison airplane snags the nylon sling of the Brodie device during testing at Wright Field. The frame that had held the sling open for the hook above the airplane to snag is seen just collapsing. It hangs at the bridle end of the cableway that has an arrangement of plane lift derrick tripod and man lift davit. (*National Archives*)

than on the ground because of the lower friction to overcome and the aircraft was already at flight attitude (no need to lift the tail). At flight speed, the pilot pulled a chain to release the hook top stirrup. An emergency release let go the airplane's hook near the end of travel if the pilot had not released manually by that point. The take-off run along the cableway was approximately 200 feet (61 m) into the wind and 400 feet (122 m) in calm conditions.

The ship assembly was less than 8,000 lb (3,629 kg) and consisted of fore and aft booms of about 50-foot (15-m) height angled outboard fore and aft, catwalks, kingposts, and bracing struts for the 300-foot (91-m) cableway paralleling the port side of the vessel. A hoist lifted the aircraft from the deck or deposited it on same. As with an aircraft carrier, the ship was expected to steer into the wind and sail at full steam for maximum headwind. The rolling and pitching of the ship moved the target frame and nylon loops around with as much as 30 feet (9.1 m) vertical motion. The pilot had to try and match this motion or time the approach accordingly. With practice, most were able to snag the sling consistently. Once the trolley rolled to a stop and was pulled to the end of the cable beside the forward boom, the support personnel would transfer the airplane to a cable strung inboard so that it could be lowered to the deck. Departure was essentially the reverse of this process, the aircraft mounted on the trolley pulled to the far end of the cableway. When the pilot powered up to full throttle, he signaled the crew who would release the trolley. The pilot was to release at about the 250-foot (76-m) point and, if lacking full flying speed, would descend the precious tens of feet above the waves to gain airspeed. The crew boarded the aircraft by moving out on the catwalk and then being lowered down via ropes to ease in through the doors from above. Deplaning was the reverse of this. A take-off cycle (mount aircraft and launch) could be performed in ten to fifteen minutes and a landing cycle (land and lower to deck) in five to eight minutes.

Erection of the initial rig in New Orleans began in April 1943, and it was ready in July along with a modified L-5. Brodie then worked to entice transient pilots to give it a try. Most begged off after seeing the "contraption," but there were a few takers. The first take-off was performed by a Lt C. B. Wheeler in late August. The first complete cycle from take-off to landing was executed by a B-26 pilot, Maj. James D. Kemp, on September 3. By the middle of that month, the assigned test pilot, S/Sgt Raymond A. Gregory, had arrived and he applied himself with vigor. During one test, with Brodie aboard the L-5, Gregory approached too high and the prop struck the sag in the middle of the cable. He was able to execute a forced landing beneath the rig.

Development of the prototype ship-based system was also completed during this period. The "suspension landing apparatus" was installed on the 5,800-ton motor ship USS *City of Dalhart* (IX-156), a general transport and barracks ship. Sea trials employing the L-5 in December 1943, on the Mississippi River and in the Gulf of Mexico, were successful. The L-5 had an engine starter while the Piper had to be "hand-propped." The latter required the pilot to place one foot out on the adjacent wheel, hold onto the door frame, and reach forward to flip the propeller while the airplane dangled 50 feet up. Although there were thoughts the undercarriage could be removed from the airplanes operating from ships, this was not done.

The success of the device became generally known in fall 1943. The Navy had little interest and the Air Staff was resistant, many officers considering it too hare-brained. It was offered with an anti-submarine application as a major selling point—a mission that had passed to the Navy who was unlikely to suggest their current capabilities were deficient. The Office of Strategic Services, the forerunner of the Central Intelligence Agency, foreseeing use in clandestine operations, acquired an experimental Brodie rig for familiarization and training. They then assumed responsibility for system development and production; they set out in January 1944 to acquire eighteen land rigs plus spares with the intent of employing them in the China Burma India (CBI) Theater. They contracted with Maryland Engineering Company of Pikesville and All American Aviation with a delivery schedule of two sets per week. As finally amended, this $690,737.36 contract included 204 aircraft conversion kits for the L-4 and a similar number for the L-5.

The commander of Army Ground Forces, Lt-Gen. Leslie J. McNair, grasped the Brodie System's potential for field artillery spotting airplanes. However, when on February 6, 1944, he sought to acquire sets for testing, he encountered opposition from Air Staff. This was likely part of the continuing contention between the Air Forces and the separate air elements directly supporting ground troops. However, the USAAF still saw little value in the device, observing that a short airstrip could be prepared as quickly as the device could be inserted and erected, with the coming helicopters removing the need of an airstrip altogether. Seeing the lack of commitment, AGF suggested that procurement fell under the Corps of Engineers since it was essentially a "synthetic airfield" while the AAF countered that it was aircraft equipment.

As the OSS rigs began to be delivered in February 1944, they were lent to the Army at their request. A demonstration on May 23, 1944, at Fort Belvoir, Virginia, employing two of these sets, brought a clearer understanding of its capabilities. General McNair's staff was able to borrow two more sets for operational evaluations at Fort Sill, Oklahoma, during fall 1944. There the AGF conducted advanced training for artillery spotting pilots and observers. Many individuals were trained on the system with great success. It seemed so "easy" that one student cut his engine 1,000 feet (305 m) above the rig and performed a dead-stick approach to hook-up. Another executed hook up at the bottom of a loop. Capt. Tony Piper flew a cycle in an L-4 with its undercarriage removed, fortunately without mishap. McNair had requested 22 sets of the rigs and conversion kits in June 1944, but his death at Normandy in July 1944 brought such high-level sponsorship to an end.[9]

In July, the Air Staff became jealous of such development work being performed beyond their purview and Arnold ordered responsibility for the Brodie Device be assumed from the OSS. Materiel Division oversaw the technical aspects for the ongoing procurement as MX-561 and began the process of acquiring the twenty-two sets for the AGF. The OSS agreed to provide ten of its eighteen kits to the AAF as compensation, saving the service six to nine months obtaining the gear. These eighteen were substantially completed by September 1944 and all delivered by January 22, 1945. By that point, the "spooks" had no further use of the device and yielded all assets to the AAF.[10]

Brodie, then a captain, was assigned to Wright Field where he and Gregory, then a flight officer, were to optimize the design for production, to include development of C-46 and C-54 airdrop options, of what was formally the Brodie suspended cable landing and launching system. Along with the original experimental rig, four sets were retained at Wright Field for testing. There they employed an L-4B that Brodie also flew. The extensive use of the system by AGF revealed deficiencies reported to Dayton for correction. Two events saw premature release during launch before full flying speed: one due to the unauthorized release of the hook top stirrup and the other the emergency release let go too soon. One aircraft was damaged in these events.[11] Brodie and Gregory also assisted in training at the several locations. The captain proposed further development to handle up to an 8,000-lb (3,629-kg) airplane, but this was not taken up.

The entire land set weighed less than 7,000 lb (3,175 kg), could be transported in two 2.5-ton trucks, and erected with 250–350 man-hours under favorable conditions.[12] Crated for shipment by sea, it was 10,000 lb (4,536 kg) and consumed 700 feet^3 (19.8 m^3). It could also be packaged with all necessary tools, weighing less than 9,000 lb (4,082 kg), for airdrop along with a nine-man crew parachuting into the location. Using just hand tools, the device could be erected in less than twenty-four hours. The rig was said to be difficult to spot from above 500 feet (152 m) or destroyed by bombing. Probably conceived at the instigation of the OSS, it was thought possible to rig the device with bullseye lights for night ops, but it is unclear this was ever developed.[13]

As knowledge of the device became more widespread, more potential operators came forward. All expressed urgency for accelerated delivery and each would require several L-4 and L-5 conversion kits per set. In August 1944, the Navy sought two sets for evaluation, which OSS agreed to provide. One was sent as soon as available to the amphibious training base in San Diego. Interest remained high within several AGF units such that training at Fort Sill continued, with demonstration teams formed to accompany kits sent overseas where there was an urgent need perceived in the European Theater of Operations (ETO). The Mediterranean Theater also requested two sets and a training team for an in-theater demonstration. An example, along with training personnel, were sent to India in November 1944 along with eight kits each for L-4 and L-5 aircraft. Army and OSS personnel erected a rig at the Royal Air Force base in Jessore, where it was demonstrated using an L-5. The British saw possibilities it could support special forces operations in places like Burma. They were also impressed with the shipboard device after one was sent to England for evaluation at the Royal Aircraft Establishment (RAE), Farnborough. They planned to install it on two hospital ships operating off Burma so that wounded personnel could

Captain James Brodie and Flight Officer Raymond Gregory stand at Wright Field before the modified Stinson L-5 they employed in the trials of the Brodie Device. This rig allowed light aircraft to transition to and from flight without a runway. The major portion of the unique aircraft equipment is shown as the truss placing a hook a suitable height above the machine at the approximate center of gravity. (*National Archives*)

A RAF Lend-Lease L-5 (KJ-403) performs a take-off from the Brodie device during demonstrations at Jessore, India, on April 14, 1945. Testing also followed in England. As with many field organizations, the Allied forces in Indian saw potential in the Brodie and sought sets to equip ground forces and two hospital ships. (*National Archives*)

be transport to them more rapidly. This was forestalled by the collapse of the Japanese campaign in Burma.[14]

Production of the twenty-two Brodie sets ordered by AGF was to begin on March 1, 1945, and be completed in six weeks. Along with a six month's supply of spare parts, each set included conversion kits for six L-4s and six L-5s. However, delays due to material shortages ensued and Capt. Brodie was sent to the contractor's plants to help expedite matters with hopes shipments would begin in February 1945. Fourteen had been completed by June 16.[15] Each Brodie Device cost approximately $13,600 and an aircraft conversion kit $670.[16]

Despite all the eager potential operators, the Army Air Forces Board in Orlando issued a report on May 29, 1945, declaring the AAF had no requirement for the system, though it acknowledged AGF might have a need. It judged the system still immature, night ops (probably never demonstrated or defined as a requirement) likely hazardous.[17] By that point, the war in Europe was over and AGF eyes turned to the invasion of Japan as deliveries continued. In summer 1945, the AAF agreed to provide to the Navy six of its land rigs, and a seventh created from spares, plus aircraft conversion kits.[18]

By the time the system was ready for ship employment, the Battle of the Atlantic was waning and the submarine scourge reduced to manageable levels. It appeared the best use would be to provide spotter planes for amphibious landings where onshore airstrips had yet to be established but it was too dangerous to bring "flattops" close to the beach. The system was installed on 316-foot (96-m) Landing Ship, Tank (LST) vessels in support of amphibious landings. The LSTs had shallow keels so they could maneuver closer to shore, but they were also especially subject to rolling in even moderate seas and full speed was a mere 8 kts (9 mph/17 kph). Plans included twenty-five LSTs to be equipped to take the Brodie system; eight were completed by March 1945.

Only the USS LST-776 was fully fitted with the Brodie Sea Rig in New Orleans and used it during operations in the Pacific. Installation was approved in June 1944 and crew were trained in its use during September at Coronado Island, near San Diego, where a demonstration for Navy officials was conducted on October 5–6. A team of two officers and two mechanics from Fort Sill erected a land-based device and provided instruction. They then took it to Hawaii for further training of naval and Army personnel.[19] Marines of VMO-4 and VMO-5 trained on the system in Hawaii with their OY-1s (L-5s) and then on the LST's system. Three of the aircraft were lost during the LST training because of the ship roll, dropped into the sea after successfully "landing."

At Iwo Jima, the LST simply launched OY-1s to land shore once an airstrip had been established—the first Allied airplanes on the island. They would otherwise have had to be lowered onto barges and brought to shore in a laborious and fraught exercise that was, nonetheless, played out hundreds of times elsewhere. The USMC pilots and LST personnel were still little experienced with the device. Four aircraft were launched with one going into the "drink." They came away with a poor impression and passed this along to the Army pilots that followed.[20]

The Tenth Army artillery air officer, Maj. Norman E. McKnight, wanted to employ the Brodie device for his L-4 spotters during the Okinawa landings. The XXIV Corps artillery air officer, Maj. Charles Ernest, had trained with the Brodie in Hawaii and brought one of the land systems to Leyte, in the Philippines, training other pilots there. This duty was taken over by several personnel from Fort Sill. However, in typical Army fashion, the 77th Infantry Division was chosen to operate from LST-776's Brodie and given no training. Two Pipers were modified with the hooks while in the Philippines and several of the division's liaison pilots were shown the LST's gear, told how it operated and what was expected of them. The ship set sail with several pilots while two others, Maj. John C. Kriegsman and Lt Earl B. Montgomery, had to fly out and hook up with no other instruction or training, which they did successfully.

The Brodie system is shown in use with three Piper L-4s on the USS *LST-776*. This view reveals storage of one aircraft atop a structure beside the forward Brodie boom and another on a launch platform, and there appears room on the deck for the aircraft on the sling (likely not left there indefinitely). Although eight LSTs were fitted with the Brodie ship rig, only 776 was fully completed and employed in combat. (*Author's collection*)

The LST supported the securing of an anchorage at Kerama Retto about 30 miles (50 km) from Okinawa, the landings on March 26, 1945. The Grasshoppers spotted shoreline caves and tracks leading from each into the water; these caves were then destroyed by shelling.[21] The L-4s then spotted artillery falls during the Okinawa landings and battle, beginning on April 1. In one instance, shore-based spotters were grounded by fog but the LST was able to launch its two aircraft to provide observation during the amphibious operation. In total, twenty-five take-offs and landings were performed, with two smashed propellers as the only casualties, before an airstrip ashore was ready to take the airplanes in two days.[22]

Four more LSTs were to be readied for the Operation Downfall invasion of the Japanese home islands, and pilots trained with LST-776's system in Manila Bay.[23] However, the operation was fortunately canceled following Japan's surrender and further LST rework was halted. This and the Brodie land rig became another footnote in aviation history.

7

Range Extension

Facing a world-spanning war and theaters covering vast distances, there was an urgent need for the U.S. to extend the range of all military aircraft, from fighters to transports. At the same time, the requirement for protection with "leak-proof" tanks worked to reduce fuel tank volume. Thus began a progressive effort to add fuel quantity while maintaining favorable aircraft weight and balance plus avoiding excessive complexity. Some transports sacrificed cargo deck area for auxiliary tanks plumbed into the fuel system. Bombers could carry extended-range ranks in bomb bays at the expense of weapons. External droppable tanks came into wide use for fighters and scout machines. Other more exotic measures were explored.

Drop Tank Hustle

External fuel tanks for fighter aircraft were a rare feature on U.S. aircraft up until the war, and almost invariably centerline "belly" installations. External fuel tanks had been introduced in the 1920s and so design standards existed. External bomb mounts could also accommodate tanks provided the fuel couplings were incorporated. In the 1930s, the Navy scout aircraft had an option for a centerline tank to extend endurance. An alternative loading was a bomb to hit targets encountered and posing a threat to the fleet. The Navy mission also mandated torpedo bombers carrying a centerline torpedo and dive bombers a centerline bomb. Some American manufacturers were familiar with the incorporation of the feature. However, the Army contributed little fostering of the resources. The USAAC was pushing for an expanded bomber fleet and so pursuit or attack aircraft with extended range and carrying bombs would undermine their case. The larger Army forces saw pursuit types' primary role as keeping enemy air at bay and so 200 miles (322 km) was the only necessary radius of action. Although the range and endurance extension or external tanks were welcome, there was a general dislike for the drag increment and added complexity. For retractable gear aircraft, the potential for a belly landing with the tank attached represented an intolerable hazard. Giving up external weapons mount points was an additional element of angst. The drop option—"cleaning up" before combat—was seen as wasteful in a time of sparse resources.

As war dawned, there was the example of German fighters routinely carrying drop tanks during the Spanish Civil War. Other nations adopted the feature while the Americans continued holding to old notions. By 1940, it was evident from ongoing combat abroad that flying missions of extended range would soon be an imperative. When the U.S. had to move quickly to a war footing, drop tanks became essential for the bomber escort as the new-found vital role was adopted in Europe during 1943. Operations over the vast expanse of the Pacific Theater also demanded the capability. Ferry delivery to theaters across trans-oceanic distances was another mission motive as sea transport became precarious owing to the submarine menace.

Some new USAAF types had accommodations for drop tanks included, but only at manufacturer's expense as the service resisted adding it to contracts. Some firms did what they could while others adhered strictly to contractual obligations, Lockheed and their Lightning being one example of the former.[1] The Navy had no such prohibitions, but they moved slowly as a matter of organizational inertia. In time, drop tanks were incorporated into advanced models of existing designs and from the start for new. All the combatant nations followed the same course.

When the American industry had to adopt drop tanks rapidly, the design history and specifications to guide design teams were meager. Consequently, many solutions emerged, some drawing upon examples observed overseas and Lockheed's P-38 hardware. The centerline mount was easiest while the underwing required more lines, values, and pumps, not to mention strengthening the structure to carry the load. Some were "slipper tanks," flush mounted to the belly and generally not jettisonable. More practical teardrop shapes on pylons saw many forms as well, especially in an effort to reduce drag. Safe separation when jettisoned occasionally required rear fins to generate the necessary aerodynamic forces or just reduce buffeting. Demand for more and more fuel led to various quantities and ever-larger tanks. Some tanks were suitable only for ferry as they limited maneuvering. The expectation that fighters would jettison the tank before engaging in combat (reducing drag plus the hazard of the tank being pieced and flaming) demanded a manufacturing and logistics pipeline. Littering the sea and land with discarded tanks was of little concern in war, and hazard of falling tanks to other aircraft and individuals on the ground likewise accepted.

The early war years in the U.S. were accompanied by a shortage (perceived or real) of aluminum. Seeking alternatives, some tanks were made of molded plywood. American officers in England observed the British employing compressed paper-and-glue tanks and sought the same for their escort and attack fighters. Wright Field dismissed this as impractical and unsafe, despite the evidence. It was true that the tanks were not robust, but they were light, did not involve strategic material, and were seldom brought back. So, the GIs in the field units ignored the engineers and adapted the British products to press on with winning the war.

These images document the evolution of external fuel tanks for the P-40. Common was the 52-gal centerline teardrop tank introduced with the P-40C (seen on a P-40K). P-40Es model experimental flattened wing tanks, likely for ferry, including 170-gal and 225-gal versions, and a similar "plastic" belly tank of 150-gal capacity. Even larger were "dirigible" ferry tanks that also did not enter production. *(Jay Miller collection, Museum of Flight, and San Diego Air & Space Museum)*

The P-51D displays a pair of papier-mâché drop tanks. These 110-gal compressed paper and glue tanks were manufactured in England at the instigation of local American officers after Wright Field dismissed the concept. What appears to be a metal equivalent is mounted on a Mustang fitted with a camera blister, likely to record jettison tests exploring safe separation conditions. (*National Museum of the United States Air Force and the San Diego Air & Space Museum*)

Not much is known of the project installing wingtip fuel tanks on this second prototype of the F4U-4 Corsair (F4U-4XB) photographed on March 31, 1945, at Stratford, Connecticut. All manufacturers retained prototypes and service aircraft bailed back to them for flight tests. Wingtip tanks have structural and aerodynamic benefits as well as freeing up wing hardpoints for weapons carriage, and they were all the rage with the new post-war jets. (*Vought Historical Archives*)

In seeking to provide external tanks but not take up underwing stations, the benefits of fuel tanks mounted at the tips of the wings were explored. Vought went so far as using an F4U-4XB (50301) to demonstrate the design option. This also held promise for altering wingtip vortices created by the high pressure below the wing spilling around to the low pressure on top. This generated drag that might be reduced by the presence of the tanks. The far outboard mass could also have structural loading benefits. The wingtip tanks did not see application during the war, but soon appeared on Vought's XF6U-1.

Airborne Filling Station

Aerial refueling (AR) had been of interest to the Air Corps since its earliest days. (This was and is variously called air-to-air refueling, in-flight refueling, and flight refueling. This text will use the now-common phrase of aerial refueling.) Apart from prolonging a flight to an almost indefinite duration, an aircraft could be fueled to above its take-off gross weight, take-off with a greater payload fraction followed by refueling, or take-off on a short field enabled via a light fuel load (low GW) followed by a fill-up once at altitude. Flight testing was carried out in the U.S. during 1923 and 1929 with a fuel hose dragged behind a tanker aircraft so that it could be manually grappled into a fuel fitting in the rear cockpit of an aircraft flying below and behind. Exceptionally long flights were demonstrated as well as fill-up beyond a gross weight at which the machine could have taken off. This work then entered hiatus with the economic downturn, but similar activities were afoot elsewhere.

Britain, particularly, carried AR to a high level, pioneered by Alan Cobham. His system had a trailing hauling line of flexible steel cable from the receiver's fuselage aft end (Figure A in accompanying illustration). The line had a 25-lb (11-kg) sinker weight at the end for stability with pawl grapnels attached above this. The tanker maneuvered such that its similar contact cable crossed the receiver's and rode the curve of the hauling line before hooks at the end engaged the pawls. An innovation was the ejector method in which the tanker firing a "harpoon" projectile trailing its line across the hauling line, wrapping around or at least riding down until the hooks engaged the pawls (Figures B and C). The line casting gun was similar to that used at sea to shoot rescue lines to persons in the water. The lines contacting also electrically bonded the aircraft. Any difference in potential might cause a spark, but well away from the airplanes. For these activities, the tanker flew in the rear starboard quarter of the receiver. The tanker then reeled in the joined lines where it was secured in a vice while personnel removed the weight and pawls to attach a 2-inch (5-cm) fuel hose and nozzle to the receiver's cable (Figure D). The hose was made of fuel-resistant synthetic rubber with integral helical steel wire reinforcement and outer woven sheath. A drogue above the nozzle held the hose steady as it was reeled out. The tanker climbed to the upper rear starboard quarter of the other aircraft. The tanker allowed the hose to unwind as the receiver reeled the hauling line into the throat of a bell mouth reception coupling. The coupling had adjoining bifurcated fuel lines running out to the tanks (Figures E and F). To avoid damage, the tanks were modified with a valve for automatic shut-off of the supply as they filled. The ball end of the nozzle seated into a fuel-tight flexible seal and engaged hydraulic latches while also automatically opening the fuel valve in the coupling. These latches would automatically release with sufficient tension in the hose and nozzle if the two aircraft moved apart, perhaps in turbulence. A guillotine could also cut the cable or hose at either end in an emergency. Fuel flowed from the tanker's supply through a valve into the center of the hose drum via a rotating seal. The fuel valves opened for gravity feed from the tanker, approximately 120 gpm (454 lpm). Before refueling, the tanker sent a charge of nitrogen down the hose, exiting via the receiver's tank vents, to purge explosive fumes. Prior to release, the hose was again purged, plus a methyl bromide charge flushed into the coupling. The tanker would reel in the hose and the still-attached hauling line that extended to a weak link that broke under high tension as the aircraft moved apart (Figures G and H). This, of course, meant the receiver could perform the AR evolution only once unless a new hauling line and weight/grapnel assembly were attached via a hatch in the mouth of the coupling funnel. The receiver carried some 250 lb (113 kg) of AR gear and the tanker approximately four time this weight.

This system was marketed by Cobham's Flight Refueling Ltd. (FRL) of Littlehampton, England, and employed commercially very briefly on a modest scale until the war.[2] Yet, it attracted the attention of the USAAC, which was determined to pursue long-range strategic bombardment. In August 1939, Arnold received a description of the system from Maj. Jimmy Doolittle (then a civilian working for the Shell Oil Company), having gone to England to investigate the capability at the request of the General. Although Materiel Division studied the possibilities of increasing bomber range that included aerial refueling, no action was taken until entry into the world war.

Following Pearl Harbor and alignment with Allied nations, range deficiencies to reach some targets were starkly evident. The Materiel Center was tasked with exploring AR and initiated project MX-204 on January 10, 1942, along with the more general MX-192 performance and tactical utility improvement study. It was concluded that making a retaliatory attack on Japan with B-17 or B-24 heavy bombers would be exceedingly difficult. All the proposals required a "continuous sequence of miracles" and made them impractical or lacking an adequate margin of safety. Consequently, in-flight refueling was considered. To avoid a prolonged "gadgeteering" phase of development, the service sought to procure the FRL system as quickly as possible. Yet, adapting the AR system to an operational level, plus manufacturing sufficient quantities of the equipment (yet to be even inspected) while modifying enough aircraft for trained crews, made the option infeasible for the short-term objective of striking Japan.[3]

Despite AR being rejected as an immediate solution, procurement of the Flight Refueling gear went ahead and it was decided to proceed with aircraft

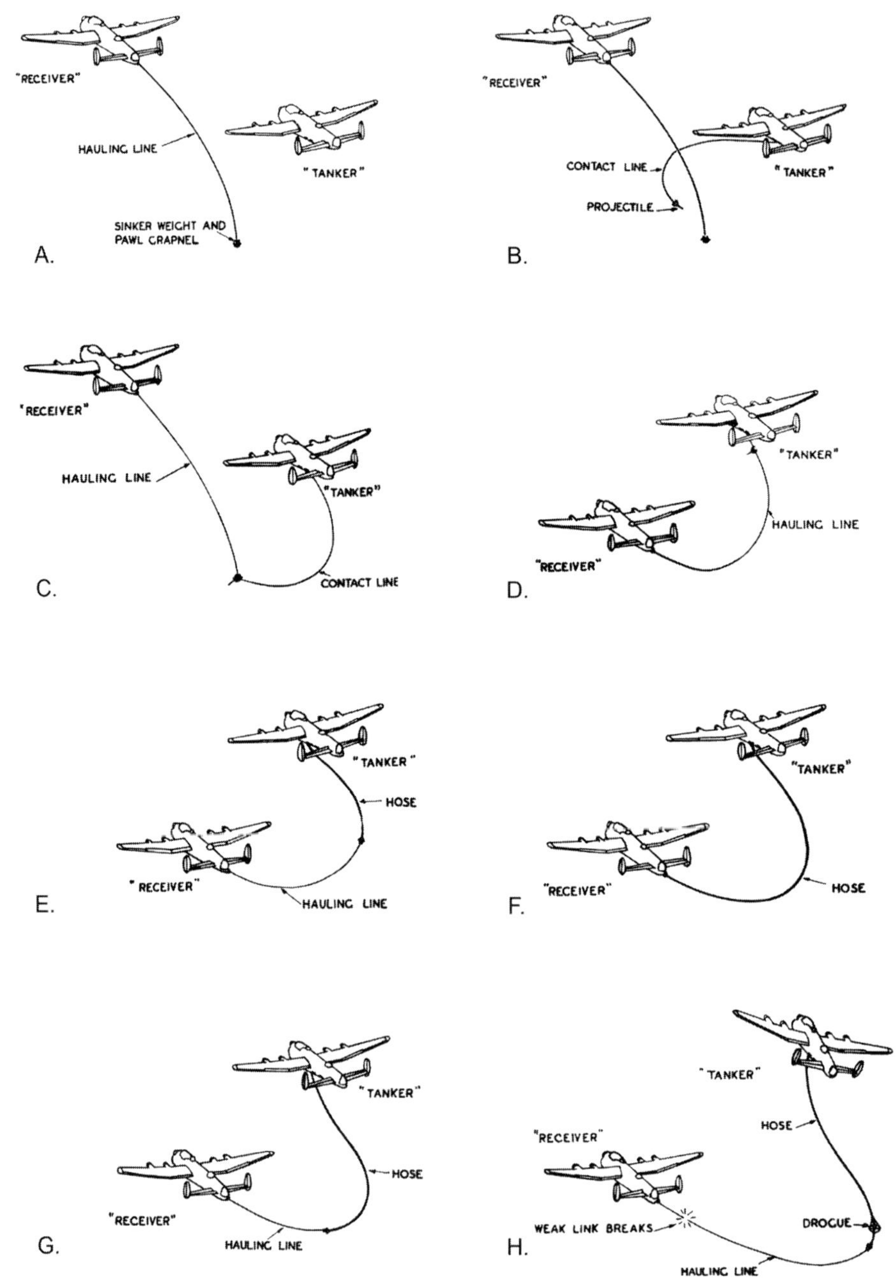

This series of period drawings illustrate the Flight Refueling Ltd. aerial refuel technique the UK firm named the Ejector Method. This was the most successful pre-war system and available to the Americans in 1942 for experimentation with their heavy bombers. Although appearing complex and even wasteful, especially by comparison to modern equipment, the method was reliable and permitted a refueling to be performed in under twenty minutes. (*Author's collection*)

modifications and flight testing. While longer range bombers were planned as upgraded models or new types (B-29 at 5,333 mi (8,583 km), XB-32 at 4,450 miles (7,162 km), and the intercontinental B-36), the introduction of self-sealing fuel tanks further cut fuel capacity of existing machines. Some targets would always push the performance limits of the fleet. By summer 1942, Air Materiel Center had contracted with FRL and acquired a near-complete AR kit, with drawings and specifications, from materials in Canada and Britain. An arrangement with the Royal Canadian Air Force brought Squadron Leader Hugh C. Johnson to Wright Field in March 1942 to serve as a consultant for the trials. This man had been Flight Refueling's chief test pilot before the war.[4]

The ejector method was adopted and the equipment was installed in a B-24D (40-2352) with a B-17E (41-2539) as receiver. The basic kit had to be adapted to these aircraft with the installation designed and fabricated focusing on structural and systems interfaces. The modification to the design and installation was performed by Pennsylvania Central Airlines with assistance from FRL personnel. The tanker cable and hose reels were in the bomb bay of the B-24 along with long-range tanks while the B-17's nozzle coupling was in a pronounced fairing on the starboard side of the tail gunner's station. Some alterations to the gear were necessary owing to the greater speed and wing loading of the bombers when compared with the pre-war civilian customers. Among these was the extension of the AR hose to 235 feet (72 m), stronger cables, carbon dioxide substituted for the nitrogen purge, and motorizing the previously manually operated reels (electrical for the B-24, hydraulic for the B-17).[5]

The flight tests were conducted at Eglin Field over seven weeks from April through early summer 1943. The Liberator was piloted by Capt. Fred C. Bretcher and 1Lt M. K. Norton while the Fort was flown by Capt. Ralph C. Hoewing and 1Lt John A. Kelting. Initial trials led to further adjustment to technique while building up to contacts and fuel transfer. This saw such harrowing events as the harpoon-fired cable being cut by the B-24 propeller while laying of the gun was being worked out. Ultimately, 1,450 gal (5,489 l) of fuel (of 1,500 gal/5,678 l available) was transferred at 150 mph (241 kph) on seven flights. Only five minutes were required to establish and then break the contact, and 13.5 minutes for fuel transfer. On the last contact, the receiver was filled beyond full, with fuel steaming from the vents. The test personnel assessed that aircrew with normal training and skills could execute the task.

The Materiel Command report of June 30, 1943, recommended adopting the equipment as standard for bomber range extension, and Johnson had gone to the U.K. to explore production potential. An estimated six months would be required to modify aircraft, train crews, and stand up a mission-ready force. The capability was then demonstrated to the AAF Board. By this point, mass bomber formations were becoming the norm and refueling on this scale would be cumbersome. Additionally, bomber production had reached mammoth numbers, as had aircrew training. So, sending hundreds of aircraft with a reduced bomb load rather than fewer with more ordnance requiring refueling *en route* was acceptable.

This B-17E was modified for the aerial refueling trials, the obvious evidence being this coupling funnel beside the gunner's station. A weighted cable emerged from the funnel to grapple a line cast by the B-24 tanker. The lines were reeled into the funnel, drawing in the fuel line with a fitting in the end that coupled with a fitting in the base of the funnel, valves then opening to permit fuel to flow. (*Author's collection*)

The sole USAAF B-24H tanker and B-17E receiver are shown in 1943 with hose joined to "pass gas." The aerial refueling trials that year employed a British pre-war system with some modifications. While this proved entirely practical, the tactical situation coupled with prodigious American bomber production made deployment of the capability unnecessary. (*via Dennis Jenkins*)

The gear also increased vulnerability to combat damage. Given that the B-29's entry into the force was imminent, the Air Staff saw no tactical requirement for aerial refueling. On September 27, they ordered the work suspended and in January 1944 directed the aircraft be "demoded."

The Board recommended the gear be sent to Gen. George C. Kenny, Fifth Air Force commander who was running the air campaign in the Pacific Theater, for combat trials. Although the general urgently requested five kits be sent to him in Australia, only the flight test equipment was available. It was decided to install this in two B-24Js to be sent along to the Fifth AF. This was apparently never consummated.

The struggle to get B-29s over Japan by mid-1944 created monumental challenges of which range was but one. The initial missions from China and India were near the limits of the bomber's fuel capacity, and so weapon loads were comparatively light. Aerial refueling was studied as an option, with B-24s as tankers. However, the onload capability and fuel burned during the transfer made the benefits meager: 1,500 gal (5,678 l) extending range by just 830 miles (1,336 km). Furthermore, the projected six–eight-month modification period would also take the valuable bombers out of action for a discouragingly long period. Some AR equipment redesign was also projected. The idea was shelved in August 1944.

Top Off

Bomber range extension raised the question of escort fighters keeping up. Fighters had initially been unable to go the distance with the bombers in Europe and the very long-range B-29s exacerbated the problem. There was an urgent operational need for fighter range extension and several solutions were explored. Fighter AR was requested in November 1943 as a high-priority effort. The P-38J was the first platform targeted and with the developmental P-82 Twin Mustang close behind. The capability was developed and testing in 1944 under MX-522 and founded on an initially rejected concept proposal by Armored Force officer Capt. Smiley. Range to 2,500 miles (4,023 km) was anticipated.

The Inland Manufacturing Division of General Motors was tasked with preparing a preliminary design. Inland's concept was judged satisfactory and they were subsequently granted a contract for two P-38J kits and twenty modified drop tanks. All American Aviation performed the aircraft modifications and flight testing.[6]

Their basic scheme was rigging a P-38 to snag the nylon line trailing from a B-24 on which hung a fin-stabilized fuel tank. The fighter pilot would position his craft above the tank, the line falling in the angle between the starboard wing and tail boom. The line would ride on a rope affixed between the wingtip and tail in a "V" to a point on the boom aft of the wing. Descending caused the tank to slide onto a securing mount on the boom. This action automatically disconnected the tow line and caused a nitrogen bottle inside the tank to discharge, forcing the fuel into the fighter's tanks, and then the tank to drop away.

Prior to actual hardware fabrication, the scheme was altered to ropes between the starboard nacelle and nose with the "V" ending on the fuselage below the canopy, the associated structure strengthened to take the weight of the tank. This made the maneuver to engage the trailing cable easier but added the hazard of a potential propeller strike. Mirrors were added to P-38J test aircraft's nacelle inboard face to allow the pilot to see the position of the tank as he descended onto it, riding the tow line. A means of cutting the line in an emergency was also installed. The B-24H had the tank released from an improvised mount between the fuselage and the port inboard engine nacelle. The tow line was taped and clipped along the fuselage to a hole in the bomb bay doors. A glider pickup winch was installed within (see Chapter 10).

Flight trials began in July 1944. The team arrived at a proper tow line strength and a stable tank design after attempting ten configurations. The first flight contact attempt was made on September 2, but new problems arose. Initially, the starboard engine was shut down and the propeller feathered, but positive tank contact could not be made. The next attempt had the engine operating and a good contact was nearly made before the prop cut the line and the tank dropped away. More alterations and trials followed with six tests through December 20 without a completely successful contact.

Assessing progress, the basic approach was deemed too hazardous, requiring considerable pilot skill, and the hardware too unreliable. An alternate approach of letting the line ride onto rollers within a slot in the wing leading edge was discussed but not pursued. In their March 20, 1945, report, the Engineering Division's attitude was largely negative and Air Technical Service Command closed the project.

Another concept was offered by Republic Aviation for ferrying their P-44 fighters over great distances. A fuel tank in the shape of a wing would be mounted above the aircraft on struts to make it a biplane. The lift generated by the wing helped compensate for the added weight, at least once the over-weight fighter got off the ground. When exhausted, the wing would be released and discarded, its lift assisting safe separation. Should the aircraft have to ditch in the sea, the upper tank/wing would provide added flotation.[7] The P-44 had been ordered soon after the war began, but a year later, it was clear the type would be second rate before any were delivered and the order was converted to other purposes. The creative range extension idea gained no traction for the abortive P-44 or any other airplane owing, no doubt, to the extensive modifications of the baseline aircraft to add the struts, fuel system alterations, required strengthening of the undercarriage, and dramatic change to the flying qualities.

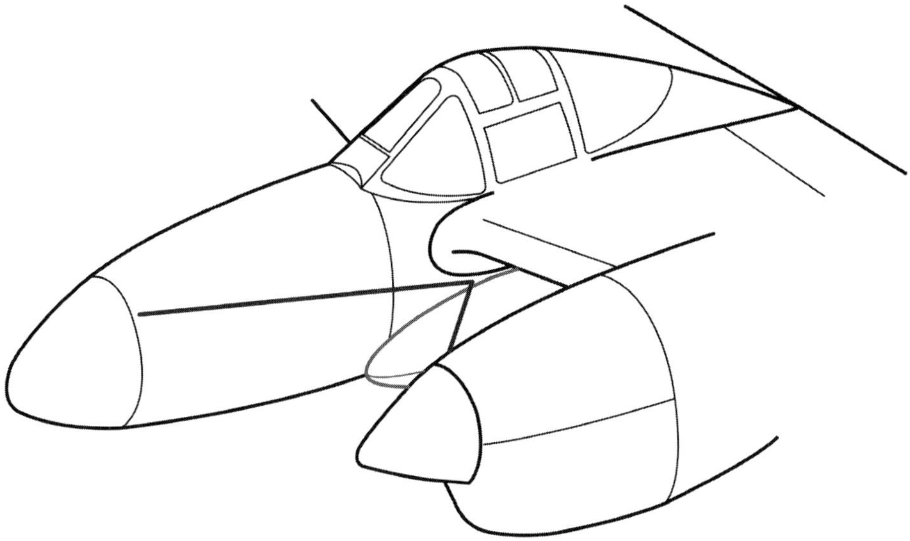

With a tank trailing below on a tow line, the P-38 pilot was to guide his aircraft such that the line slid between the ropes attached to the fuselage and nacelle, just inboard of the propeller. The tank would automatically couple with a fuel fitting in the side of the fuselage. Tests in fall 1944 with the propeller feathered were unsuccessful in making contact, and with the prop turning it cutting the line. (*Author's collection*)

With the goal of transferring a drop tank to a P-38 in flight, this B-24 was modified as the "tanker" in 1944. The tank, with added stabilizing fins, was held on an improvised wing mount with a towing line leading to a reel inside the bomb bay. Multiple flights were required to devise a suitably stable tank design and optimal flight conditions for extension and towing. (*National Museum of the United States Air Force*)

Republic conceived another scheme for providing long-range fuel by mounting a high wing/fuel tank to create a biplane but with the added wing jettisoned when empty or the fighter was engaged by enemy forces. The wing would generate lift to help compensate for the added weight. Proposed as a feature for ferrying their P-44, the idea disappeared when the Republic fighter was canceled. (*Author's collection*)

Dragging it Out

Towing unmanned fuel tank gliders was first considered immediately after Pearl Harbor. Much effort was expended in seeking a naturally stable glider tow arrangement such that a pilot was unnecessary or workload would be much reduced. Wind tunnel work at Langley arrived at a Y-tow line in which the single line from the tow ship branched to a line attaching at each wingtip of the glider or, better yet, two parallel lines from the tow-plane. No action was taken until American Aviation Corporation approached the Aircraft Laboratory on April 30, 1943, with a proposed 2,000-gal (7,571-l) glider. The USAAF conducted a feasibility study of the concept as MX-151 and decided that it held merit. By that time, military glider ops had been developed to a practical routine and it was known how to automatically stabilize a glider on tow. The glider was to be towed behind a long-range aircraft on a "tow hose" through which fuel was passed via a wind-driven pump. Once the fuel was drained, the glider would be released and discarded. The service chose to contract with Cornelius Aircraft Corporation of Dayton, Ohio, with the aircraft derived from their aborted XBG-3-towed bomb glider.[8] Under project MX-416, a $273,420 Army cost-plus-fixed-fee contract dated October 4, 1943, funded the effort. Cornelius was to deliver a static test article and the first of two gliders in March 1944.

The company's leader, George W. Cornelius, was a long-time promoter of innovative aircraft designs.[9] Their XFG-1 was a "tailless" aircraft with a 15-degree forward-swept wing at quarter chord and the dihedral was ground-adjustable between 2 and 8 degrees. The design was expected to be naturally stable on tow and for basic free flight. It was to provide 764 gal (2,892 l) from two fuel tanks as part of an 8,000-lb (3,629-kg) all-up weight. The undercarriage would serve only for take-off after which it would be jettisoned.

Development saw wind tunnel testing and static loads trials during summer 1944. Langley looked particularly at the spin characteristics in their 20-foot (6.1-m) Vertical Spin Tunnel during July 1944 with a 5.6-percent model, subsequently offering very specific techniques for recovering from the unconventional spinning behavior that was observed.

With Cornelius lacking construction facilities, Spartan Aircraft Company in Tulsa, Oklahoma, built the two gliders under subcontract. The fuselage was steel tubing and wood framing while the nose and tail cones were poplar plywood, the rest of the fuselage covered in fabric. The wings were wooden in structure with plywood covering, the aft spar being steel tubing. These were manned aircraft with fixed gear to support flight testing. The initial XFG-1 (44-28059) was towed aloft and released for the first time on October 11, 1944, probably in Tulsa, before being moved to Clinton County AAF. Although it flew quite well, it was lost on March 14, 1945, during spin tests. It entered a flat spin from which Spartan test pilot Alfred Rietherman, not employ NACA's recommended procedure, failed to recover. He bailed out at too low an altitude and was killed.

By this point, $249,990 had been spent on the project with the benefit bypassed by the progress of the war. Additionally, it had been learned that static electric build-up on the aircraft or radio transmissions could ignite fuel vapors during any in-flight transfer (inerting being either not incorporated or dismissed for some reason). Yet, the glider was likely the first large aircraft with a forward swept wing flown outside of Germany, and the project continued as an aerodynamic testbed.

Wright Field conducted scale-model testing (Chapter 2) and NACA spin tunnel work to identify the spin modes and develop recovery techniques. With the insight provided, the spin characteristics of the XFG-1 were judged safe to resume flight testing. The second prototype XFG-1 had a "spin chute" installed at the aft end of the fuselage to be deployed in the event a recovery-resistant spin developed. Parachute inflation could cause the aircraft nose to drop, breaking the stall and allowing recovery after which the chute was jettisoned. The testing at CCAAF continued post-war, finding spin recovery quite tricky (the spin chute saving the aircraft from one potential mishap) and likely beyond the skills of the average pilot. Yet, valuable data on the unusual configuration may have been deemed worth the additional $237,420 expended by cancellation.

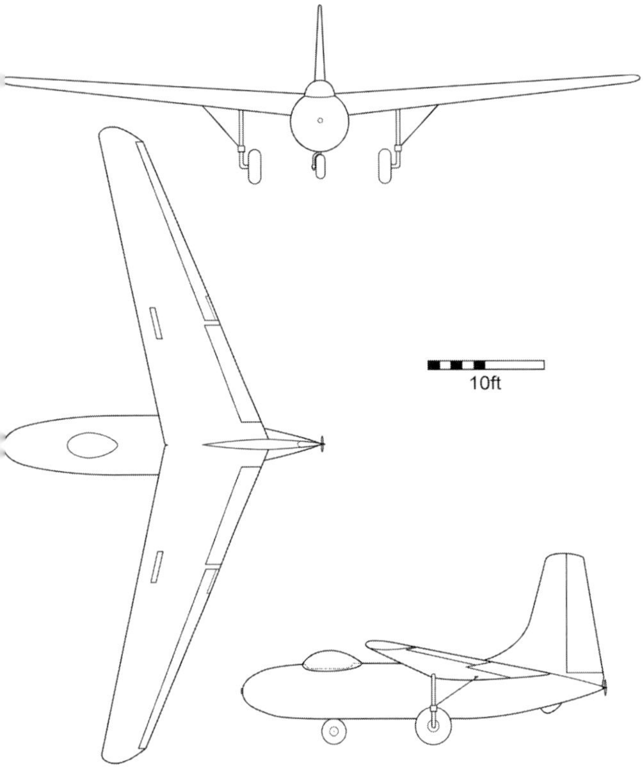

Left: The FG-1 glider was to serve as an unmanned towed fuel tank from which fuel would be pumped to the receiver before being discarded. This unmanned version was never built (note wind-driven generator propeller at the fuselage aft end). The bubble canopy would be installed for optionally manned tow, such as repositioning the aircraft for an operational mission, for which the canopy would be removed and the cockpit covered over with a fairing. (*Drawn by the author*)

Below: The XFG-1 was built as two manned gliders to refine the aerodynamic design, seeking natural stability on tow. The "tailless" configuration with a forward swept wing was an aerodynamic curiosity for which the NACA wished to collect data apart from the USAAF's towed fuel tank project. The first example is shown here under tow with the pilot distracted in the cockpit. (*National Soaring Museum*)

The initial XFG-1 was lost in a fatal crash after entering a flat spin, the pilot not employing the recommended recovery procedure. Note the emergency spin recovery assembly under the tail with lanyards to the parachute beside the wreckage (apparently extracted by the personnel). Another look at the spin chute installation, and the wood plus fabric finish of the aircraft, is afforded by the image of the second aircraft. (*National Soaring Museum and Jay Miller collection*)

Tipoff

Yet another approach to extending range was conceived for the Douglas C-54 strategic transport. Almost every new model introduced had additional fuel capacity, initially via tanks on the deck of the forward cabin which reduced cargo volume. This evolution was prolonged and the USAAF sought to advance the process with a novel concept of flying wingtip tanks, one on each side. These were hinged wingtip-to-wingtip such that the tanks flew via their own lift without adding to the wing loading of the C-54, yet they were coupled for fuel transfer. Each tank also had an outrigger gear to support its weight on the ground. Although the development of the flying wingtip tank was undertaken, new transports with greater range were just appearing and such measures were not necessary.[10]

Possibly as part of the flying wingtip fuel tank effort, a Fairchild PT-19 trainer was modified with a “trailer” of wing and tip vertical stabilizers attached via hinged booms. While it appeared designed to fly free without elevator, cables ran along the booms to tip sails that contained rudders and so suggested directional control from the cockpit.

Further flight tests of efficient towing appear to have included this "trailer" suspended from hinged booms off the PT-19A. Cables permit operation of the rudders but no elevator is evident. Nothing more is known of this experiment but was likely part of seeking a flying wingtip tank for the C-54 transport. (*National Archives*)

Off You Go

If one could tow a fuel glider, then a combat airplane could be towed with engine temporarily shut down as a range extension measure. Apart from repositioning small aircraft with ailing engines to locations better equipped to perform the maintenance, bombers towing escort fighters would help relieve that range issue. However, a conventional tow from the ground, as with gliders, was infeasible. The higher wing loading of a fighter meant it would not lift off until near the point the bomber tug became airborne, or even later. This placed the fighter in the worst of the bomber's downwash that would likely flip over the smaller craft. The only practical way to tow a fighter airborne was with an airborne pickup of the aircraft from the ground ("snatch"), although in-flight joining was also explored.

Snatch had been thoroughly developed supporting heavy combat gliders, and operational kits were in the field (see Chapter 10). This still challenged the power output of the bomber to climb away and tow without engine overheating. Finding a suitable towing airspeed acceptable to both very disparate airplanes (different wing loading, again) was another difficulty that might also mean a less-than-economical cruise.

Towing experience began with light-planes and training sail-planes, then grew to fighters with medium and heavy bombers and transports doing the task. Each required modifications. On the towed airplane side, it consisted of metal jaws opened from the cockpit via a lever. The jaws were closed over a pin captured in a metal thimble around which the nylon towline was looped. The towing loads had to be carried to the tow-plane's structure via attachment to an aft bulkhead. The release cable was run to the cockpit lever mounted in a convenient location. Experiments yielded double and triple glider tows, and two tow-planes in tandem, joined by another tow rope, hauling heavy gliders aloft. Training taught the rudiments of towing from take-off into flight, flying slowly so as not to overspeed the glider or overheat the tow-plane's engines, and hitting the release point or arriving over the landing zone at altitude and on time.

Experimentation on towing fighters began with towing small single-engined aircraft like trainers and outmoded types. The propeller was removed and a towline attachment installed on the prop shaft, secured so as not to turn, and a release cable run to the cockpit. The aircraft was either towed off the runway by the tug, of modestly greater power, or snatched by the passing tow-plane. Released over the destination, the aircraft would be glided down to landing. The Army experiments were performed with at least a Vultee BT-13, All American Aviation's Stinson (XC-81D), a P-47B, and a P-51B. The tests with fighters were performed at Muroc AAB in October 1944 under project MX-200.

The Naval Aircraft Factory also undertook such tests, including a May 16, 1943, flight from Akron, Ohio, to Philadelphia using the Army design to haul a Curtiss XSBC-3 (9225) via a PBY-5A (08065) on a 300-foot (91-m), 5/8-inch (16-mm) nylon rope. To compensate for the removed propeller, 80 lb (36 kg) of lead shot bags were placed in the aircraft's nose. Preparation for the flight required just 1.5 hours. The NAF reportedly performed several more such tows at the request of nearby units with stranded aircraft. As described in Chapter 1, in 1944, the NACA used a P-61 to tow a P-51 to altitude and then release to collect aerodynamic data in the absence of prop wash.

The first range-extension fighter tow experiment using airborne snatch was by the Navy in late 1941 with a Grumman F4F towed by a Grumman TBF torpedo bomber. On May 10, 1942, two Wildcat pilots, Lt-Cdr William H. McClure and Lt-Cdr Robert W. Denbo, snagged lines trailing behind a Douglas BD-1 (A-20A Havoc). The two fighters were then towed for an hour at 7,000 feet (2,134 m) and 180 mph (290 kph). The propellers could be feathered after the engine was shut down and then, using battery power, the pitch coarsened to begin turning for engine restart when desired. This success was later repeated with a B-17C borrowed from Wright Field for an eight-hour tow. Also during 1942, an F4F towed an Army Cessna UC-77 Airmaster from Philadelphia to the nation's capital.

These photos show P-47B 41-6038 being prepared for a snatch take-off behind a B-17 from the dry lakebed at Muroc AAB. The first shows an aircraft with the feathered propeller but with this heavily restrained in a non-operational manner (could not retract the landing gear) to prevent it spinning. The others show the aircraft, without the propeller, being snatched and then inflight under tow. (*National Archives and The Peter M. Bowers Collection/The Museum of Flight*)

The U.S. Navy did considerable work in towing fighters and similar-sized aircraft, though principally to relocate them for engine maintenance. Shown is the tow line installation on the restrained power shaft of a XSBC-3 and a release mechanism (not shown) provided the pilot. After being towed aloft behind the tug, the pilot would hold position until releasing at the destination for a dead-stick landing. (*National Soaring Museum*)

To eliminate the inconvenience of the ground snatch, the Army also experimented with airborne snatch for long-endurance towing. This was perhaps first done with a B-17C towed a P-39 for over ten hours on August 31, 1942. The Airacobra pilot engaged the towline with a hook at the tip of his wing, the line stabilized with a drogue or streamer, and then drew away until the hook set against a stopper at the end of the line. The hook was attached to a pendant that ran through spring clamps to an attachment on the spar near the root of the wing and outside the propeller arc. When the pendant released under towing loads, the aircraft needed only slight rudder trim to maintain position slightly to one side of the tug. Once on tow, the fighter engine could be shut down and the propellers feathered, later restarted via windmilling. A cockpit control released the pendant and line. A second hook-up could be made using a pendant on the opposite wing. The potential for towing a P-80 jet was explored in Langley wind tunnel tests but without results by the end of the war.[11]

The fighter tow capability was never carried forward to field use. For the Navy, the tests served to collect data supporting their glider bomb program. For the Army, the work gave encouragement to an even more ambitious application of towing a B-29 suffering engine trouble or other malady. The idea was to get a towline on the stricken aircraft in flight and assist it in reaching its destination—in this case, Tinian Island—across the very long over-water route following a bombing strike on Japan. These Assist tests in spring 1945 used two C-47s before being successfully executed with two B-29s. The tow subject closed on the line, stabilized by two sleeves, trailing from the tow ship. The pilot snagged the towline

This montage of images (viewed clockwise from upper left) shows the testing of a large, multi-engined aircraft (C-47s for this trial) towing another as envisioned for a B-29 towing another Superfortress out of combat. The technique took advantage of the equipment and skills built up in the combat glider efforts of the USAAF. The tow line had to attach outside the propeller arc of the towed airplane, but this was found tolerable. (*National Soaring Museum*)

with a wingtip hook. He then shut down his engines and feathered the propellers. The aircraft glided easily in trail to one side of the tug, requiring only slight rudder trim. The technique proved practical and was deployed just as the first atomic bomb was dropped.

Interestingly, the British independently hit on a similar airborne pickup methodology pioneered by Alan Cobham. Testing during 1943 showed the feasibility of a fighter snagging a trailing rope to be towed by a bomber, but it was judged as requiring skill beyond the average fighter pilot and went no further.[12]

The YL-13 under design by Consolidated-Vultee at the end of the war (see Chapter 2) was designed to be towed at up to 150 mph (241 kph) with the propeller in place and then released followed by engine start.[13] This was still a relatively slow towing speed that would limit the choice of tugs. However, the requirement showed that the Army considered the capability a proven, practical, safe, and useful technology.

Little Buddy

The problem of escort fighters for long-range bombers appeared intractable when it came to the intercontinental behemoths being conceived at the end of 1942. Even the extant World War II long-range heavy bombers executed missions as long as eleven hours that posed difficulties for escorting fighter pilots sitting on parachutes in a confined cockpit with limited environmental control—exhausting despite their youth. Autopilots for fighters was virtually unknown given the weight sacrifice. In the South Pacific, with its long over-water missions, aircrew fatigue was assessed as the cause of more accident than losses to enemy action.[14] For missions potentially lasting more than a day, a fighter might be so heavy with fuel and the pilot so fatigued, even at the mid-point, that engaging in aerial combat was unrealistic. The poor fuel economy of the early turbojet engines worked against the desire to employ a jet escort. The pre-war "composites" or piggyback of smaller airplanes launched from atop a larger at some point in a flight, saving on fuel for the smaller that continued on to the destination, brought forth similar ideas for range extension.

The USAAF examined the problem under project MX-472 Unconventional Fighter Escort beginning in December 1942. This concluded a 'parasite' fighter was the best solution. The idea envisioned launching a few small, remotely controlled drones powered by ramjet engines, but this was beyond the state of the

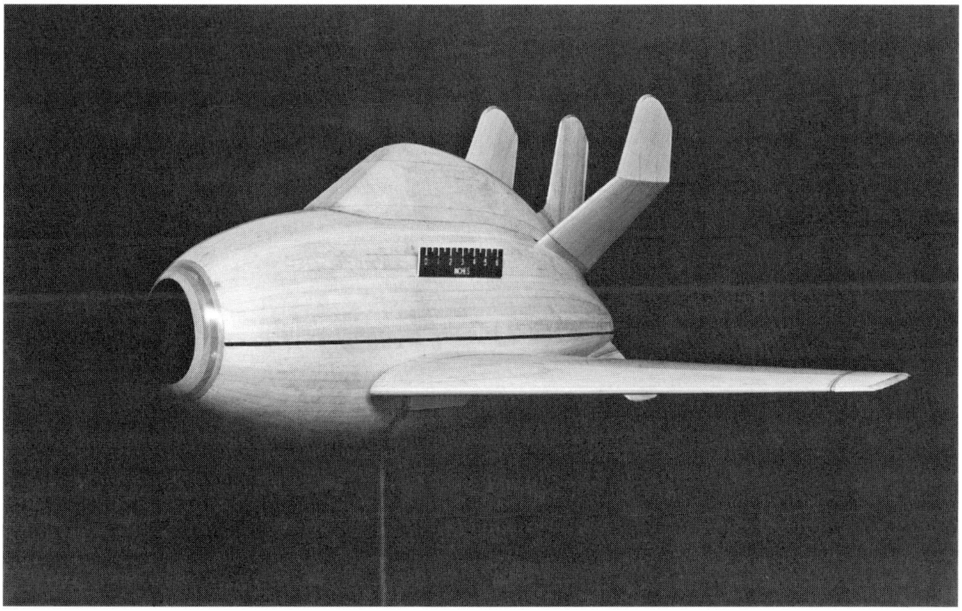

Range extension for escort fighters exceeded practical limits with the very long-range B-29 and the intercontinental B-36 in development. Expecting a pilot to sit in a tiny cockpit for a day or more, then also fight, was unreasonable. In seeking a solution, the idea of a "parasite fighter" carried by the bomber was conceived and found expression in the McDonnell Aircraft XP-85, shown in one configuration as a wind tunnel model. (*NASA*)

art. Only a manned aircraft seemed potentially feasible. The bomber could carry its escort with it as a small aircraft that would detach from and then return to "mother." With the XB-36 intercontinental bomber growing close to realization, the parasite fighter requirement was finally issued on January 20, 1944.

Only McDonnell Aircraft of St. Louis, Missouri, responded in autumn 1944 with four Model 27 concepts. To partially nestle the tiny fighter within the bomb bay of the B-29, B-36, and Northrop B-35 required an unusual design. The Air Forces then decided the machine must fit entirely within the B-36, dictating dimensional limits of just 15-foot (4.6-m) length and 5.5-foot (1.7-m) width, sending the McDonnell team back to the drawing board in January 1945. They returned on March 19 with their Model 27DE concept that looked much like the final design.

The tiny egg-shaped fuselage was armed with four 0.50-cal guns, had multi-element tail surfaces, and a folding wing swept at 37 degrees. The envisioned power plant was the Westinghouse 3,000-lbf (13 kN) 24C axial-flow turbojet. This engine was projected to power the little aircraft, which ultimately grossed 5,600 lb (2,540 kg), to 581 mph (935 kph) at 35,000 feet (10,668 m), albeit with fuel for just thirty-two minutes. It was to have an ejection seat and pressurized cockpit, a perforated speedbrake under the fuselage, and an enormous hook projecting from the nose substituting for landing gear. Once the pilot boarded, the aircraft would be lowered from the bay, engine started and wings extended, and then unhook to engage the enemy. At the end of the combat, the fighter would rejoin and hook onto the trapeze arrangement, shut down, fold the wing, and be raised into the "mother ship."

Although the USAAF was pleased with the design they labeled the XP-85 (MX-667), little more was done before the end of hostilities. It flew years after the war to find that the engagement of the trapeze was most challenging and the need for such measures was rapidly fading given airpower evolution.[15]

8

Piloting Diversions

A subset of research projects was directly aimed at improving the "working conditions" of aircrew. These ran the gamut from safety, flight effectiveness, and comfort. Some followed the example set by allies and enemies, while others were innovations inspired by specific needs of new aircraft or unique circumstances presented by the war. They all pushed the "envelope" of available technology and kept up the pace of aviation advancement.

Vision Revisions

The British began introducing bulged frameless canopy elements to their fighters to improve pilot all-around visions—a benefit in combat. They adapted such to their Mustang IIIs as the Malcom Hood to improve headroom and vision, though there was speed lost to drag. American units copied the innovation and passed word back to the States regarding the advantages. This and the other U.K. examples, with full 360-degree bubble canopies, compelled work on blown plexiglass transparencies (*versus* molded) in the U.S. To incorporate the feature on new models of existing types required major alteration to eliminate the "turtle deck" spine behind the earlier greenhouse sliding canopies. The change in CG also had to be addressed. It also gave concerns about reduced overturn protection, but the fighter pilots were enthusiastic with the bubbles. The P-47Ds and P-51Ds were the most famous examples to adopt the feature. Many American fighters were built originally with canopies possessing minimal framing and good vision to the rear without the turtle deck, examples being the P-38, P-39, and P-63.

The substantial redesign to eliminate the turtle deck degraded directional stability in going from a deep, flat-sided aft fuselage to a shallow and rounded structure with much less restoring effect in a yaw. The initial P-51Ds, with the bubble canopies and the four-blade propellers associated with the Merlin engine, suffered notably reduced directional stability and even rudder reversal (reversed control sense) at high yaw angles. This became another Langley research project seeking a cure. They recommended extending the height of the vertical stabilizer that was ultimately featured on the P-51H. This is evident on NACA's P-51B 43-12105, though this model possessed the earlier "greenhouse" canopy. An interim solution for the Ds was fitting of a vertical tail leading edge extension and a reverse rudder boost tab (opposite the normal motion) to help preclude pilot over-control in yawing maneuvers. Kits were created so that field units could make these changes. This dorsal fin was also added to earlier models that had experienced the directional "snaking" that had always plagued the aircraft.

The P-47D suffered the same directional stability deficiencies when adopting the bubble canopy. Langley tested a P-47D-30 (44-33441) in 1945 to explore the flight characteristics. The Thunderbolt eventually added a dorsal "strake" ahead of the vertical tail. When Goodyear incorporated a bubble canopy into the Corsair for the F2G, they also lengthened the vertical tail and added an independent and automatic sub-rudder to counteract torque effects at low speed and high-power settings, such as take-off and wave-off, to compensate for the loss of the stabilizing turtle deck. They also included a headrest armor plate that reduced rearward vision to little better than the standard F4U with its quite nice canopy.

These P-47Ns are late-war examples with bubble canopies for superior all-around pilot vision, though the feature was adopted as early as the D-model. The Thunderbolt, like the P-51D, had to undergo major aft fuselage "surgery" eliminating the "turtle-deck," and this degraded directional stability. The cure for the P-47 was the addition of the shallow strake ahead of the vertical tail while the Mustang added a leading-edge extension. (*Jay Miller collection*)

The NACA insight helped guide design teams that employed the canopy. Almost all experimental or prototype propeller-driven airplanes begun mid-war had the bubble canopy as standard to include the XP-40Q, YP-60E, XP-63D, and P-75A. When bubble canopies were incorporated into the new jet fighter designs, the engineering lessons had been learned. Additional problems requiring attention was solar heating of the interior (mandating canopy tinting), vision distortion, distracting reflections during night flying, ease of operation, safe jettison, and rain and fogging removal.

The introduction of jet engines caused a similar problem. The prop wash over the empennage on power advance gave immediate controllability in a go-around scenario lacking on the jets. This required new rules of thumb for tail sizing. Most of the earliest jets experienced directional "snaking," making them poor gun platforms. In many cases, this appeared to be due to flow separation off the vertical tail and rudder oscillation from the periodic separation. The lack of propeller slipstream uncovered these deficiencies. More careful design and tighter manufacturing tolerances were the solutions for some, while others introduced electric yaw dampers, among the first stability augmentation systems. The lack of vibration also saw some cockpit instruments sticking that previously had not been a problem.

For large aircraft, designers had begun to adopt smooth forward fuselage enclosures for improved vision and drag reduction. The C-46 had wrap-around transparencies while the B-29 had a multi-pane "greenhouse." The XB-32 and XB-36 also had expansive greenhouse enclosures over the flight deck. These "advanced" features contrasted with the common stepped windscreens of two to four panels at an angle such as found in the B-17 and B-24. While the smooth fuselage forebody gladdened the hearts of the aerodynamicists seeking to reduce drag and the structural designers who had to accommodate pressurization loads (although the C-46 ultimately did not feature pressurization), the pilots soon learned to detest the vast transparencies. All the multiple panes or the curved panels tended to reflect interior lights or exterior glare at different angles and only a few could be fitted with sunscreens, defog blowers, and wipers, leading to vision distortion and irritation. They could also make the flight deck quite hot with the sun beating down and crewmen naturally seeking to cover some panels and so defeat the purpose of the wide-field vision. Consequently, reports from the field expressed desire for the more normal design that would likely also simplify construction.

Redesign of the B-29 to a "discontinuous nose" was considered but rejected due to cost and time of introduction to the production line, potentially impacting delivery rate. The extensive changes to the Consolidated XB-32 to arrive at the production B-32 included adopting a stepped windscreen. Curtiss investigated the change to a stepped windscreen via a modification in St. Louis during 1944 of C-46A 43-46953, generating the XC-46B for flight testing. The nose appearing much like a Douglas C-47. This was not programmed into the production schedule until the C-46E built in St. Louis and the C-46G in Buffalo. Both lines closed at the end of the war with just seventeen C-46Es and one C-46G completed.

Above: Boeing's B-29 was initially praised for its low-drag forward fuselage and excellent pilot view owing to the multiple vision panels. In service, the design was widely disliked for the hot flight deck, multiple reflections, and rain distortion. Redesign to a "discontinuous nose" was contemplated and a mock-up built, but the need to maintain a high production rate meant this change was never incorporated. (*National Museum of the United States Air Force and Tony Landis collection*)

Below: The Curtiss XC-46B featured the stepped windscreen common with most transport and bomber aircraft, this looking much like the Douglas C-47. The wrap-around transparencies of the standard Commando (C-46A shown) were, like the B-29 and other World War II aircraft, so panned by aircrew that such a major design change was made. However, it came too late to be seen on but a handful of airplanes before production was shuttered. (*The Museum of Flight and National Archives*)

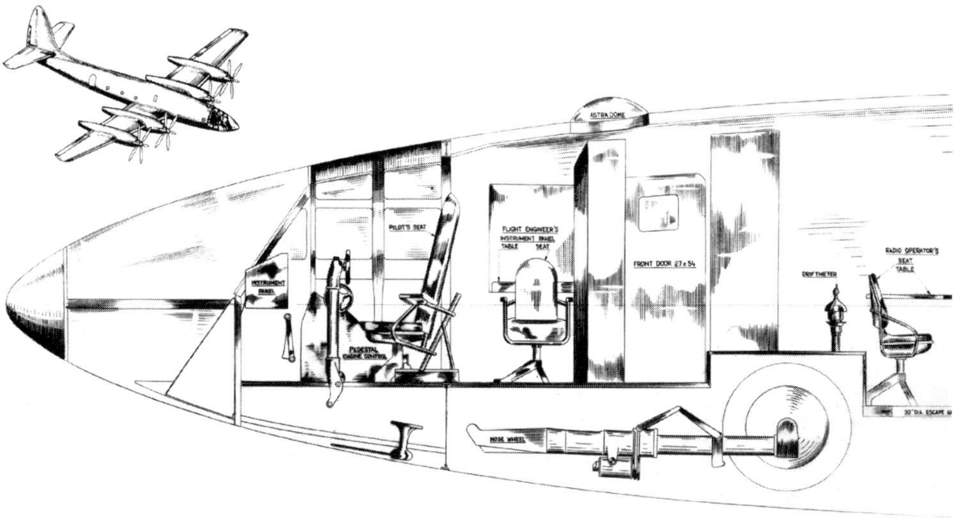

The XF-12 long-range, high-altitude photo reconnaissance aircraft was originally designed with an aerodynamically clean ogive nose consisting mostly of transparency. Concern with distortion, especially in rain, compelled a design change. For take-off and landing, the curved panels ahead of the pilots were to slide down to expose the slanted flat windscreen seen in this illustration. (*National Archives*)

When Republic was developing the XF-12 long-range photo reconnaissance aircraft, concern was expressed by the USAAF about vision problems through the ogive nose transparencies and would have been a pressurization challenge. A test program had a mock-up nose with pilot seats mounted at representative height on a truck. This was run up and down the runway at night and in rain. It led to a design in which the curved panes retracted into the unpressurized nose fairing for take-off and landing to expose flat windscreens at the forward end of the pressure vessel. The wrap-around and greenhouse enclosures have been seldom seen since the war.

Better Position

All countries pursued the prone pilot position in an effort to reduce aircraft frontal area and to increase pilot *g*-tolerance.[1] It required innovative pilot control while also complicating emergency egress from the aircraft. The semi-reclined position was better in these respects but also found wanting by most test pilots for vision and effective control via reach.

The challenge of the prone piloting position is that the arms and legs are somewhat restrained in supporting the body and so limited in providing sufficient leverage to affect control movements. An arrangement supporting the body comfortably was sought that left sufficient range and fidelity of motion for piloting without being fatiguing. Looking forward required the head be rolled back and this quickly led to neck aches. Supporting the head was possible but if employing a chin rest the pilot might experience difficulty speaking and the chin muscles could get sore. Suspending the head on a spring was another solution but raised questions of restricting all-around vision and impeding safe bailout, and compromised crash survivability.

Grumman sought a half measure with the XF4F-6 (7031) that served as a testbed for various projects. In one trial, the controls and seat were reworked to permit the pilot to fly in a crouched position during a high-*g* pull-out. Tested in February 1942, this was expected to reduce the potential for pilot *g*-induced loss of consciousness. While this may have been observed, the practicality of changing the seat and control arrangement in combat and prior to a pull-out, and then back to normal after to continue an engagement, was clearly questionable. The data was collected and everyone moved on.

Vought had explored a prone pilot position for their V-173 testbed of an all-wing airplane, with two counter-rotating propellers blowing over same. Expected drag reduction was the motivation. Yet, after lab demonstrations with pilots in the prone position, it was dismissed because of the common fatigue and vision problems. A reclined seat was then considered but also dismissed because of back pain from the pilot leaning forward to fly the airplane. The follow-on XF5U-1 program also considered alternate pilot positions, but all were set aside.

Northrop, however, was determined to make prone piloting work. The planned XP-79 flying wing, rocket-propelled interceptor (Chapter 4) would benefit greatly from the reduced drag and improved *g*-tolerance. The flying wing design required novel flight control means and moving those by a prone pilot required equally novel cockpit design. These were explored in the MX-334 gliders.

The MX-334s had an unusual assortment of aerodynamic surfaces and cockpit controls. Elevons on the wing's tailing edge operated symmetrically with fore–aft motion of the pilot's control bar produced pitch and asymmetrically with differential motion of the bar for roll. Further inboard, combination rudders/speedbrakes ("brudders") split to rotate both above and below the wing for directional control.[2] Force to deploy the brudders was provided by bellows fed by ram air from intakes under the wing root leading edges and modulated by pilot pedals. To permit single-hand control of the bar, the brudders were ultimately modulated by pilot pedals for rudder effect and a handle for speedbrakes. Leading edge slats were added near the tips to improve elevon roll effectiveness as stall was approached. Flight testing found stability and controllability problems that were addressed through a number of design changes, including eliminating the slats and adding a fin. Three different fin sizes were eventually tested.

The MX-334 gliders were built primarily of wood over steel tube frames. The wing cross-section alone was found inadequate to accommodate the prone pilot in a manner allowing suitable operation of the aircraft. Consequently, the center-section was thickened by 20 percent and an extended canopy added. As suggested above, the pilot flight controls consisted of pedals for his feet and a bar for his hands. He lay on a "couch" with his arms free and legs supported

This XF4F-6, photographed on October 22, 1940, was built with a single-stage, supercharged R-1830. Nothing came of this configuration, but the aircraft served as a testbed for several subsequent projects. One was an adjustable pilot seat and controls permitting a crouching position for high-*g* pull-outs, believed to improve *g* tolerance. (*Grumman Historical Archives*)

The XP-79 rocket interceptor was planned with a prone pilot station to enhance g-tolerance for the high accelerations anticipated. Here a man has climbed inside a wooden mock-up of the aircraft, probably in summer 1943, to demonstrate the position and the poor visibility. It does not appear that a support coach or controls are included as these had yet to be designed to any level of refinement. (*Gerald Balzer collection*)

enough to permit extension motion. A means of supporting and counterbalancing the pilot's head under *g*-loading was considered. The pilots ultimately requested a simple chin rest. The directional control was originally to be manipulated via "bobsled steering motion" of the control bar before pedals were adopted.

Test data were collected during 1944 and 1945 with maneuvers on tow and free flight. During one test flight in which the aircraft entered an inverted spin, test pilot Harry Crosby recovered but then had a difficult landing with the glider bouncing hard several times. This ended with the nose gear collapsing and Crosby knocking out two teeth on the chin support after his shoulder restraint slipped. The chin support was subsequently revised to a V-brace that supported the head under all maneuvers.

During all this, to collect fundamental data on the prone pilot position and associated control system design options, a CG-4A glider was modified in early 1943 with the right-hand pilot station converted for a prone pilot while the left seat and controls remained unaltered for a safety pilot. This assisted in establishing basic design guidelines for the pilot "couch" and restraint system. Testing during late 1943 at Clinton County AAF was followed by orientation flight training for prospective XP-79 pilots.

It was concluded that the CG-4A control forces, particularly for roll via aileron, were too high and so the training may have conveyed negative learning. Instead, a TG-6 training glider was modified by Taylorcraft as the XTG-33. The forward and middle pilot stations and the nose enclosure were altered to accommodate the prone pilot and the revised controls. The aft station was retained for the safety pilot. The XTG-33 was flown at CCAAF from summer 1944 for testing and to serve as a trainer for project pilots.

The XP-79 transitioned to the jet-powered XP-79B also with a prone pilot station, carrying over many of the design lessons from the glider work. The flight control surface layout was similar, but with three wing trailing edge devices per side. The outboard split surfaces served only to generate drag to yaw the aircraft for directional control. These were called "decelerons" and were still operated with ram air pressure modulated by the pilot pedals. The XP-79B flew once immediately after the war that ended in a crash and Crosby's death.

Northrop was able to develop the prone pilot station to a functional level but it was not popular and its operational suitability remained to be proven. The ultimate conclusion, as arrived at then and many times after by other researchers in multiple nations, is that the position was generally uncomfortable for the pilot over a long duration and greatly degraded the ability to check visually all around the aircraft. Prone is a good position, but not necessarily for flying airplanes.

Another concern was pilot operation far removed from the aircraft centerline. Would he receive the usual cues and be able to respond appropriately, and would fighter-like maneuvers cause debilitating discomfort? During 1940, the first P-38-LO (40-744) was given a pilot station and canopy on the port boom, both turbosuperchargers removed, to become RP-38 *Jollie*.[3] The added cockpit, far off centerline and behind the wing (and so degrading vision in the forward lower quarter), unlikely containing even minimal controls and instruments. During tests, it was usually occupied by a

Right: This Taylorcraft T-6 glider trainer has been modified for prone pilot testing as the TG-33. The forward two seats and flight controls have been removed to make room for a coach and revised controls plus instruments. Bernie Driscoll demonstrates in preparation for a towed flight ending with a glide to landing. (*National Museum of the United States Air Force*)

Below: Test pilot Harry Crosby stands in the bottom and top hatches of the Northrop MX-334 glider. The glider helped in perfecting the flying wing stability and control for the XP-79 rocket fighter plus the prone pilot cockpit accommodations and controls (notice the padded chin rest inside the cockpit). Crosby was instrumental in this process and flew many of the MX-334 and MX-324 flights. (*Gerald Balzer collection*)

Above: The XP-79 evolved during the war to a twin jet engine design, though still with prone pilot station. This XP-79B had pilot controls and support similar to the MX-334 gliders, but they were refined. These photos illustrate the top entry/escape hatch and the forward cockpit control (chin support and couch removed). (*Gerald Balzer collection*)

Below: The turbosuperchargers were removed from this P-38-LO to permit an auxiliary cockpit to be installed in the port boom, necessitating exhaust stacks added to the cowlings. The cockpit may have had basic controls, permitting some assessment of the "asymmetrical" cockpit location on pilot performance. Results may have supported the development of the XP-82. (*National Museum of the United States Air Force* and *National Archives*)

flight surgeon and so discomfort from feeling and seeing aircraft motion so offset may have been the objective.[4] The motivation in 1940 for the project is unclear. The resulting data was helpful in the development of the North American XP-82 Twin Mustang years later. This aircraft had pilots in the two P-51 fuselages offset from the centerline and joined by wing and tail center segments.

Safe Separation

Just bailing out at the front of a bomber could see a person bounce along the bottom of the fuselage and encounter protuberances like antennae that could cause harm. Jumping from a fighter risked a harmful encounter with the empennage. Egressing ahead of a pusher propeller was an even greater concern. University research showed that the centrifugal forces experienced in a spinning aircraft could inhibit bailout. Additionally, as airspeeds increased, any bailout risked some injury and, if rendered unconscious, the crewman had no hope of deploying a parachute. Separation at high altitude risked oxygen deprivation and exposure to extreme cold. While all this was well understood and crewmen were briefed on the hazards and the best bailout methods for their aircraft, the hundreds of life-threatening in-flight egresses during the war emphasized that better solutions were greatly preferable, especially for an injured and impaired crewmen. Service labs looked for solutions. Arguably the best oxygen systems, cold-weather garb, harness, parachutes, and survival gear were developed; the fundamental problem of separating from the aircraft remained among the greatest challenge. This began to be addressed in the U.S. during the war.

One of the first pushers was the pre-war Bell YFM-1 Airacuda with props at the ends of nacelles manned by gunners who faced a dire choice on bailout. Some later designs introduced means of separating the propellers as part of the bailout procedure. The Curtiss XP-55 Ascender had an electrically actuated link and compressed air charge to release and separate the prop. The Northrop XP-56 employed an explosive charge to blow off the propeller. Such unfamiliar systems were looked on with suspicion by aircrew.[5] Just having a system that could, with a stray electrical charge, disabled the propulsion system must have engendered some disquiet. The trajectory of the wildly cartwheeling propeller, while the pilot fell away from the machine, was perhaps more worrying.

The Vultee XP-54 offered another alternative for separating the pilot below the arc of the pusher propeller. The pilot pulled a lever that depressurized the cabin and armed the ejection system. He then pressed a bar with his feet to initiate the automatic sequence. The floor rotated down at the rear and the seat pitched forward, the harness releasing to dump the pilot out. The cockpit was arranged to ensure against anything in the bottom egress path, including having the control yoke pivoted off the sidewalls. Due to the high stance of the airplane on the ground, owing to the very large propeller, the system was also used to enter the aircraft. The panel lowered with the seat into which the pilot climbed and an

The Army program for fighter drag reduction produced some unique designs, all with pusher propellers that complicated pilot bailout as he risked passing back through the prop. This XP-56 is typical of these with contra-rotating propellers ready to chop the pilot into mincemeat. As with others of this ilk, Northrop devised a means of separating the propellers (explosives in the XP-56 case) as part of a bailout procedure. (*Gerald Balzer collection*)

electric motor lifted it up into the cockpit. This permitted a cleaner canopy design simplifying accommodation for cabin pressurization. The deficiency of the system was that it relied upon gravity to affect the jettison, requiring that the aircraft be upright (though airflow ram pressure would assist the opening once the panel began to rotate). The system was never exercised in flight.

What appeared the most effective technique for safe separation at high speed was propelling the pilot, in his seat, clear of the aircraft where the speed would very quickly decay and the pilot release from the seat to pull the parachute ripcord. This ejection method had been investigated previously but never with the motivation of war and many thousands of aircraft in harm's way. The Americans observed British development of similar systems since 1944. This was led by Martin-Baker Aircraft Company, which performed a scientific approach to the problem through analysis and experimentation. Much work was required to ensure the mechanical system did not harm the pilot in an effort to save his life, such as spinal compressions from too abrupt an ejection. Much ground testing was performed and, in the final months of the war, ejections of seats with sandbags or dummies were made from aircraft in flight over Britain. Although the USN took the earliest interest in Martin-Baker's work, the efforts only yielded practical systems years later.

During the war, the Germans (principally Heinkel) had employed an ejecting seat in some aircraft, especially their early jets. The procedure was relatively

Another pusher design was the Vultee XP-54 that faced the problem of safe separation of the pilot in an emergency. Given the cockpit positioned in the long, unobstructed nose, Vultee chose to use a bottom bailout technique. This also facilitated pilot boarding from below to assist cabin pressurization design. (*National Archives*)

Upon initiating escape procedures, the bottom panel jettisoned and the floor panel on which the seat was secured pivoted down. The seat rotated at the end of the panel to dump the pilot well clear of the propellers and to be carried away in the slipstream. Note how the yoke and pedals do not impinge on the escape path. (*National Museum of the United States Air Force and San Diego Air & Space Museum*)

simple. After the pilot jettisoned the canopy, he commanded the ejection which released compressed air or fired an explosive charge to propel the seat up rails. The pilot would pull a release to separate from the seat when forces permitted and pull the parachute ripcord. The allies had captured some of these devices and a few made their way to the U.S. for careful examination.[6] More was learned at the end of the war in Europe when original data and individuals came to hand.

New American jet fighter designs at the end of the war had ejection seats installed or planned. Although some design teams remained leery of the explosive charge for ejection, few alternatives appeared suitable. One of the very earliest U.S. ejection seats was designed into the Consolidated-Vultee XP-81. This aircraft was a hybrid with a turboprop in front and a turbojet engine in the rear, though when flying in February 1945, a recip engine had to be substituted in the nose. The airplane was designed to reach 500 mph (805 kph), a speed making safe separation by conventional bailout quite hazardous. Consequently, Convair incorporated a seat propelled out the top of the cockpit by a catapult gun. This typically meant a cartridge within a tube that, when fired, propelled the seat up a rail or rails on the slanted seat bulkhead. The pilot jettisoned the canopy, which armed the gun. He then positioned himself in the seat for safe egress and squeezed the eject handle.[7]

As the D-558 was designed at the end of the war, the team faced the highest speeds yet for potential bailout: high transonic. The entire forward portion of the fuselage, including the cockpit, separated on command. Pulling an ejection handle released four hooks and the nose fell away. The pilot would then separate from this segment by jettisoning his seat back and falling out the open aft end.

Pressure's On

The American commercial aviation industry had begun experimenting with cabin pressurization in the 1930s. The advent of superchargers, and in America particularly, turbosuperchargers provided the pressurized exhaust that could be diverted to a sealed cabin. The incoming air is also heated to warm the cabin in the chill at high altitude. Pressurization permits flight at a higher altitude than the cabin pressure altitude, passing above weather and gaining favorable winds but where oxygen is rarefied and the air very cold. For the military, operating as high as possible also held promise of getting above enemy fighters and flak. There is a hazard of accidental depressurization during which persons are impaired or lose consciousness from lack of oxygen and suffer from the low atmospheric pressure once the cabin equalizes. Even supplemental oxygen delivered via masks was limited by gas cylinder capacity and encumbered the user, and paying passengers could not be expected to wear them.

The B-17 and B-24 heavy bombers were unpressurized and unheated, primarily because of the defensive gun ports and turrets, leaving aircrew to wear bulky electrically-heated clothing and oxygen masks, but still suffering from the extreme

The XP-81 was a high-speed jet aircraft that first flew in February 1945, though shown here in an early post-war photo. It sought a 500-mph (805-kph) maximum airspeed via a turboprop in the nose and turbojet in the aft fuselage. This raised questions about safe pilot separation in an emergency and led Consolidate-Vultee to choose an ejection seat for the fighter. (*Tony Landis collection*)

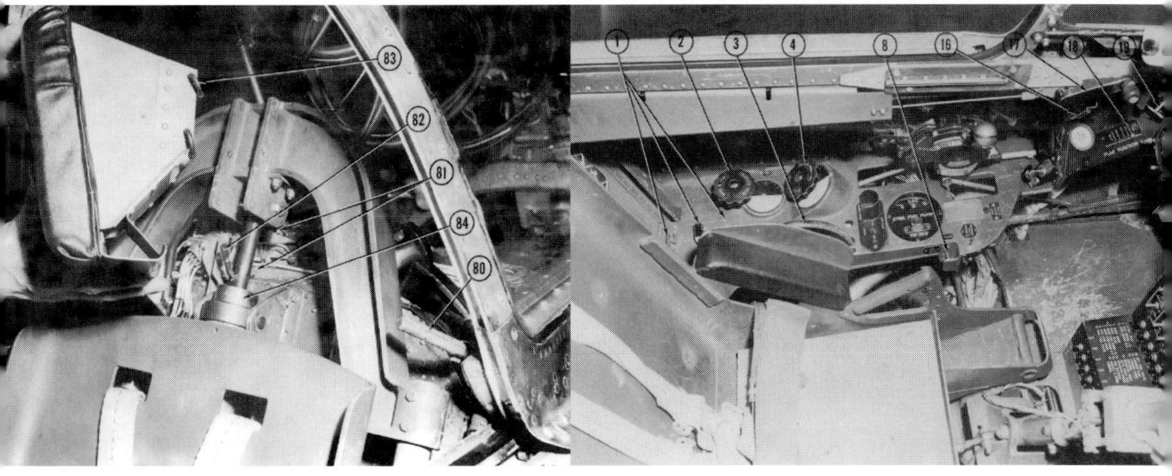

The ejection seat of the XP-81, among the first adopted by the Americans, was a classical catapult design. These flight manual illustrations show, in the cockpit, the seat stirrups and ejection handle with squeeze trigger. At the top of the seat, with the headrest removed, is seen the end of the catapult mechanism in the slanted seat bulkhead. (*Tony Landis collection*)

cold at high altitudes. The continuous-flow oxygen system in use at the beginning of the bombing campaign in Europe required 1,800 psi (124 bar) pressure cylinders that posed a combat safety risk. Its use could be problematic and deaths were occurring. During the war, 45,000 feet (13,716 m) was the altitude limit without pressurization, though on pressure breathing equipment, wearing heavy clothing, dependent on mechanical equipment, and with an ever-present debilitating hazard.

A demand oxygen system was developed and introduced in 1943. This reduced the required supply, with only 450 psi (31 bar) pressure bottles, was easier to use and was more reliable. Deaths and injuries decreased. However, more could be done to create a friendly "shirt-sleeve environment" to improve personnel performance. The greatest concern with pressurization, apart from power extraction from the engines to operate air compression equipment, was the effects of rapid decompression should the cabin be holed in combat.

The military supported exploration of cabin pressurization with the XC-35 (36-393), a heavily modified Lockheed Model 10 Electra. Its "supercharged" interior supported 10 psi (0.7 bar) differential pressure at the cost of 1,486 lb (674 kg) added weight.[8] This project, begun before the war, permitted standards of construction and system safety to be established. Both the Army and, beginning in 1941, NACA experimented with the instrumented craft, making improvements in the design and systems. Some commercial applications were already underway as war arose. The commercial precursors of the C-46 and C-54 were to be pressurized, but the Army chose to leave the capability behind when they moved rapidly to military production. Later, Douglas was contracted for a pressurized model of the C-54 as the XC-112 with R-2800 engines. This, however, moved slowly and did not emerge until after the war. Much remained to be learned about efficient design and manufacturing techniques plus operating and repairing pressurized combat aircraft in service and combat. The Army felt it knew enough and began contracting for pressurized bombers and bomber escorts in 1939. Despite that apparent confidence, experimental work continued into the war years.

A pressure cabin was added to the XB-23 introduced in Chapter 3 with respect to turbosupercharger flight testing. The team was led by N. F. Frischhertz and was assisted by American Airlines personnel under Marvin Whitlock.[9] The pressurized volume extended from the nose back to the bomb bay. It was created by reinforcing the existing structure then sealing it with various rubberized materials and sealants. The superchargers added to the engine provided the heated pressurized air ducted to the cabin. Automatically regulating this flow during altitude and power changes, and in the presence of necessary ventilation and cabin leaks, was the real trick that required careful design of hardware and then repeated adjustment during flight testing in the early portion of 1942.

The USAAC contracted for a pressurized twin-engined bomber in 1939 with the Martin XB-27 and the North American XB-28. Only the latter went to prototype stage, flying in April 1942. Although it was an excellent airplane, it simply was not needed and production plans were shelved in summer 1943. The surviving

The route to a pressurized cabin airplane was methodical and encouraged by Air Corps R&D dollars. One expression of this was the XC-35 "sub-stratospheric" research aircraft built from a Lockheed Electra and first flying in 1937. It helped establish design and construction methodologies that made possible the very high altitude, pressurized B-29 bomber, while later being turned to thunderstorm research with the NACA. (*Jay Miller collection*)

A wartime supercharged cabin research aircraft was this XB-23. The added flight testing turbosuperchargers provided the pressure source, but other work regulated the flow and sealed the cabin back to the bomb bay, proving a substantial project for General Electric. There is little external evidence of the cabin modification, but internal changes were significant to seal the structure not originally intended for pressurization. (*National Museum of the United States Air Force*)

XB-28 (40-3056) was held at Wright Field, its outer wing panels shorn off, so it could serve as a ground-based pressurization test article. Martin had another opportunity with the XB-33, but this also did not leave the drawing board.

The new very heavy four-engined bombers were seen as especially benefitting from pressurization and heating, facilitated by remote-controlled gun turrets. These were placed on contract in 1940. Being a large aircraft, Boeing was able to employ common pressure vessel design characteristics for the B-29. These included cylindrical fuselage with hemispherical ends translated into lightweight aircraft structure. The occupied spaces were also built as pressure cylinders. The Consolidated XB-32, competing with the B-29, was also pressurized. The second prototype's system was fully functional when it flew in summer 1943. However, the production B-32 discarded the feature in a near-sighted assessment that it was tactically unnecessary. The new technology was proving quite challenging for most of the industry, lacking design standards and experience, and its practicality in battle remained to be proven. In combat during spring 1945, the B-32 crews noted lack of pressurization as an impediment for operations above 20,000 feet (6,096 m).

Cockpit pressurization never played a significant role in B-29 combat as originally anticipated, largely because of the changing circumstances of the air battle. The Superforts began by bombing from 33,000 feet (10,058 m) but

The B-29 was to operate to at least 30,000 feet (9,144 m) and a desired 40,000 feet (12,192 m). This demanded cabin pressurization that presented a challenge given the bomb bays in the middle of the aircraft. The solution was forward and aft pressurized compartments joined by a crawlway tube and pressurized by the turbosuperchargers within the engine nacelles. (*National Archives*)

soon brought it down to 24,000 feet (7,620 m) to save on fuel in the climb and because flak was not as great a threat over Japan as over Germany. The cabin was unpressurized or pumped down to a modest altitude, the crew donning oxygen masks, so that battle damage that penetrated the vessel would not produce explosive decompression. Discovery of the jet stream meant disruption of bomb patterns and dispersal, forcing the planes even lower, and low-altitude firebombing was adopted as the most effective tactic as Japanese aerial defenses dwindled.

The intercontinental Consolidated-Vultee XB-36 was designed for pressurization, flying after the war. All the jet bombers ordered into development were to have pressurization, the turbojets offering pressurized air the same as the turbosuperchargers. The Navy found a need for the supercharged cabin in the patrol-bomber mission as this grew in complexity by war's end and as land-based aircraft. Such was sought with the Martin XP4M-1 that flew after the conflict. The same was true for the Lockheed R6O heavy transport. Of Army strategic transports, only the Lockheed C-69, flying in January 1943, had pressurization given its derivation from a planned commercial airliner. The Boeing C-97 was derived from the B-29 and so was also pressurized, first going aloft in November 1944.

Fighter pressurization was more challenging in that accommodating common pressure vessel features was usually impractical while sealing around the canopy was notably difficult. An inflating rubber seal tube was the solution for the canopy. This usually drove accepting a heavier structure, which was anathema to aircraft design. Either a dedicated "blower" or extra burden on the supercharging system and ducting was required. Some of these elements required armor to prevent explosive decompression if penetrated in combat. Tests were performed via the P-47E (a modified B, 41-6065) with an added supercharger. Although the work began in fall 1941, it was July 1943 before pressurized flight was achieved, and testing continued for more than a year.

The September 1939 contract for the first production Lightnings included terms for an experimental cabin pressure version as the Lockheed XP-38A (40-762). This was tested in the latter half of 1942. As with similar modifications, the canopy was heavily reinforced, sacrificing some transparency area and vision to the rear. As with many such programs, results of pressurization experiments were being released as new fighter projects were already compelled to face and solve such problems in holding to schedules.

After 1940, pressurization was considered for every new design intended to operate at high altitude. Lockheed's XP-38A testing informed the company's XP-49 design, a spin-off of the Lightning. That was to be a bomber escort version delayed waiting for the promised engine and so did not fly until November 1942. Lockheed struggled with fundamental system problems and damage from forced landings. The final configuration was so late that it achieved little not already being performed by P-38Js. While contemplation of production went no further the aircraft was passed to Wright Field for use in "stratospheric research" above 40,000 feet (12,192 m) to take advantage of the rare cabin pressurization. A second seat was fitted for this purpose. However, the airplane continued to

There were experiments with fighter cabin pressurization, but combat never demanded this be taken to production during the war. One such testbed was the Republic XP-47E, the modifications suggested by the reinforced canopy. First pressurized in flight during July 1943, it was the source of valuable test data. (*San Diego Air & Space Museum*)

The XP-38A, with a pressurized cockpit to explore the bomber escort capability, was built with the first production example Lightnings that lacked the feature. Flying in May 1942, America was then at war and could not interrupt Lockheed production by introducing a feature of questionable value. Ultimately, the P-38 did well without pressurization, as did all other American fighters. (*American Aviation Historical Society*)

be plagued by engine and fuel system issues during 1944 and stent prolonged periods in the maintenance shed until set aside. A long-range escort, the Lockheed XP-58, also carried over pressurization and much the same unfortunate history of waiting for the intended power plant. The engine and mission were altered, and the airplane was so late and heavy that it was not needed when it flew in June 1944. The XP-54 was designed for pressurization but it is unclear whether this was installed in the overweight airplane when it began flying in January 1943. The feature was specified for the Curtiss XP-62, contracted for in summer 1941 and flying two years later. It was February 1944 before the pressurization components were ready to be installed by which point interest in the aircraft had dissipated and nothing more was done. The XP-67 that started flying at the beginning of 1944 was to incorporate pressurization. However, work just getting the basic airframe operating safely meant this was never installed. The conceptual Curtiss XP-69 and XP-71, and the Hughes XA-37, were all specified with pressurization.

The Navy mission did not benefit much from pressurization and so it was not as vigorously pursued. However, Brewster tried pressurizing a F2A-3 (1388) as the XF2A-4 near the end of 1941 using a supercharged engine. This appears to have been more an effort to color the fighter "advanced," but this was not enough to save the much-maligned Buffalo or the company. The Navy requested the feature for the XF14C-3 before project cancellation.

Jets have the advantage of a power plant from which high-pressure air could be bled off for cabin pressurization. All the Army jets projects had the feature specified and the Navy soon followed. Wartime flying examples included the production Bell P-59As and service test Lockheed YP-80As, plus the prototype XP-81 and Bell XP-83. The last three of these are additionally noteworthy in combining pressurization with bubble canopies, showing the rapid advance in design application. A bubble canopy was also planned for the P-59.[10]

No fighter seeing combat during the war was pressurized. More could have been achieved in those years, but American warplanes were doing well enough without the added complexity. The new designs incorporating the feature promised it would soon become common.

Unlike bomber and transport aircrew, fighter pilots are confined to their seats throughout a flight. This makes it more practical for them to wear partial pressure suits covering portions of the body, most importantly the head and chest. This protects them from the effects of very low atmospheric pressures as an alternative to cabin pressurization or as a safety measure in the event of depressurization. Such suits had been developed and some flown before the war in altitude record attempts. Both the Army and Navy undertook work to perfect such gear. "Stratospheric research" above 40,000 feet (12,192 m) during the war included pressure chamber trials of such suits. Academia, government labs, and industry participated. During Lockheed's pioneering work in the field, in support of their P-38 efforts, the company lost a senior test pilot, Marshall Headle, who was fatally injured during a chamber accident. The suits did not see routine use during the war. A full pressure suit was also secretly developed by the Americans, though there was no application. There were no aircraft then flying high enough to require such pilot protection, though such were on the horizon.[11]

As the jet engine drove fighters faster, the skin heating generated by friction with the air combined with solar heating through the canopy, heat generated by electrical equipment, and a naturally hot day could make pilot stations intolerably hot. Temperatures of 150 °F (66 °C) were measured inside a P-80 cockpit on a 90 °F (32 °C) day. Yet, the sealed, pressurized space meant the end of gaspers and other vents for outside air to help keep the pilot cool. Fans just moved the already hot air and took up too much volume in a fighter cockpit. Air conditioning would become the next priority.

Even with cabin pressurization, the pilot had to survive depressurization, such as from battle damage, and so partial pressure suits were developed. They were generally only used for research projects but were the forerunners of those to gain wider use in coming decades. Here Milo Burcham descends from the YP-38 in February 1941 wearing gear for safe operation at high altitude, illustrative of Lockheed's work in this field. (*Air Force Test Center History Office*)

9

Mission Support

The services had an ongoing effort to improve flight safety and characterize aircraft behavior for the flight crews in support of mission execution. This, however, took a definite backseat to expanding combat capability. Field units did their own transferring of information from experience and this made the rounds of the units operating an aircraft, though sometimes this was misleading or amounted to dangerously misinformed "scuttlebutt." Generating and disseminating accurate information to improve efficiency and save lives was the goal of the "smart guys" in the development and test agencies.

Of large formal efforts, investigating the water ditching behavior of aircraft was one significant project in the area of crew safety. In the area of operational safety, improving de-ice and anti-ice systems was another. The latter affected aircraft deliveries as well as combat ops.

Ditching

In 1943, NACA was given a new urgent task by the Pentagon to study airplane ditching as part of a wider program of ditching survivability.[1] Many of the emergency ditchings were ending badly, the aircraft breaking up, flipping over, flooding rapidly, or impacts leading to severe injuries and death even short of the drowning hazard. Many lives were being lost. It was hoped Langley's work might provide insight into ideal techniques for pilots to use in executing a survivable ditching. These would include attitude, speed, configuration (flap setting, undercarriage position, and bay doors open or closed), and orientation with respect to waves at impact.

Langley's tow tanks were put to new use, possibly employing repurposed wind tunnel models, to observe the basic hydrodynamic characteristics of the design, none intended for water landing and seldom if ever a design consideration. Data were collected in various configurations, weights, CG locations, and scale speeds. Waves were created in the tank to check the effects of encountering these at various points (crest, trough, etc.) and attitudes. These results were coupled with analysis of loads imparted to the aircraft structure during a ditching and lab tests on actual airplanes with simulated loads applied and reactions measured. These data might also aid in more suitable structural design or modifications.

Assisting in the research was a catapult erected to launch models into the Back River beside the lab. This appears to have started with a small assembly before moving to a much larger catapult. The flight and impact were photographed during repeated launchings and in various configurations and conditions, as in the tanks. Wave impact (river eddies on the scale of waves) at various orientations were a matter of chance. Nearly every military landplane type was subject to the evaluation.

To help substantiate the ditching study results, performing an actual ditching with one of the more numerous over-water aircraft, the Consolidated B-24 bomber, was deemed necessary. The Liberator was particularly notorious for digging in, breaking up, and rapidly flooding, with an average 24 percent personnel fatalities. Crews had gotten into the habit of personally buying lumber to reinforce the bottom of their aircraft to prevent immediate collapse on touchdown in water. The chosen B-24D was instrumented by NACA to collect acceleration and other data. Weighing 44,100 lb (20,003 kg), the bomber was guided onto a river by two pilots because of the proximity to homes on the banks. The shallow water was important for aircraft recovery and study. The intent was to collect data for comparison with the model results. So, in addition to ensuring the safety of the pilots, it was acceptable to reinforce the airframe with wood and steel ribs such that it would not immediately break up. Non-essential gear was removed and resulting exterior holes patched over. Steel plate covered the bombardier nose windows, the bomb bays, and absent belly turret gap.

To validate the modeled aircraft ditching data, it was necessary to collect data from an actual ditching. A B-24D was selected and modified with test instruments and reinforced so that it would not suffer such catastrophic damage as to endanger the essential aircrew of two pilots. The aircraft is shown here with lifting cables installed to permit the machine to be lifted from the water following the test. See pp. 264–265 for more images. (*NASA*)

Above: Many aircrew forced to execute emergency ditching were coming to grief as their aircraft somersaulted or broke up to sink rapidly. The armed forces turned to NACA Langley for assistance, running models of the aircraft through their hydrodynamic water tanks, built for flying boat and seaplane development, to test for water impact behavior. Here a B-29 model is prepared for a session in tow tank No. 2. (*NASA*)

Right: An effort to investigate ditching characteristics of various aircraft included NACA catapulting models (possibly former wind tunnel subjects) across water and filming the results for analysis. They began with the fixed catapult (B-26 model being launched) and then built an arched support permitting models to be launched at various orientations to the waves. Nearly every American military aircraft type was subjected to this testing. (*NASA*)

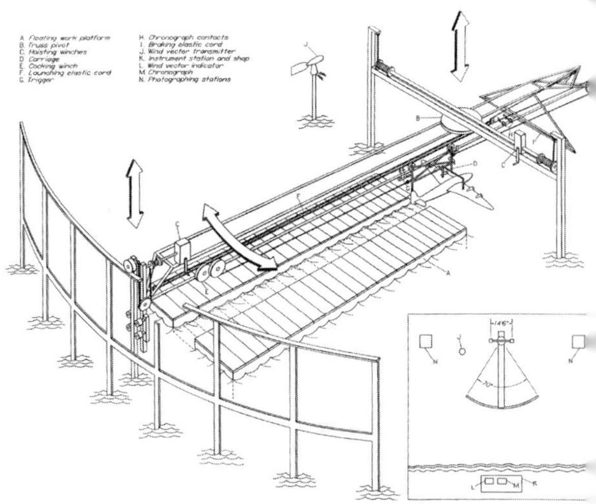

The ditching was conducted by the AAF on September 20, 1944, on the James River, near Newport News, Virginia. The selected area was adjacent to the James River Bridge to permit good observation and filming of the event. The pilots were Maj. Julian Harvey and Col. Greene, the latter commanding Langley Field. Contact was with flaps at 40 degrees and 97 mph (156 kph) ground speed. Despite the reinforcement, the bottom of the aircraft still suffered severe damage and the fuselage broke both in front of the wing and ahead of the tail assembly. When the nose touched down, the nose gear doors collapsed and the pressure forced the gear up through the floor between the pilots. Yet, the brave airmen emerged unharmed. Dynamically, the recorded data matched the one-sixteenth scale model results well. Another Air Forces B-24, lightly modified with the lumber addition combat crews were installing, was slated for a 1945 ditching test in Choctawhatchee Bay, Florida. A third entirely unmodified airplane would then be ditched to complete the program. However, the two later tests were canceled given the dire results of the initial event.[3]

Based on the B-24 study results, Wright Field designed and tested ribs that could be installed in preparation for a ditching to give the bomb bay doors additional strength and increase survivability. The four ribs could be installed in minutes and weighed only 40 lb (18 kg). These were produced and supplied to operational units beginning in 1944. However, the word was out not to ditch a B-24. Crews were diverting damaged aircraft to neutral countries rather than risk a water landing.

The intentional ditching of a B-24D into the James River, Virginia, occurred on September 20, 1944. Due to the risk to homes along the shoreline, it was necessary that the bomber be manned with a minimum crew of two pilots. These men executed the maneuver following published procedures with gear up, flaps down, and settling in at minimum airspeed accounting for the nose-high attitude. (*San Diego Air & Space Museum*)

Above: The bomber was immediately met by motorboats to ensure the safety of the aircrew and to prepare the aircraft for recovery. The pilots are seen after emerging from the flight deck's overhead ditching hatch, just forward of the where the airplane's spine has been broken. Divers are attaching lifting cables and inflating buoyancy bags beneath portions of the structure. (*San Diego Air & Space Museum*)

Below: After being lifted from the water, the Liberator's damage was graphically evident—testament to why the bombers flooded and sank quickly during actual ditchings at sea. The reinforced nose survived but the belly aft to the bomb bay doors was shredded. The doors were buckled as well. (*NASA*)

The CG-4A assault glider would be making many flights over water and so its ditching characteristics were of particular importance. Given the large number and low cost of the Waco, a ditching test was authorized and a willing crew stepped forward. Executed on July 30, 1943, at Laurinburg-Maxton AAB, North Carolina, it is seen on initial impact and later partially supported by drums as the crew tries out with the inflatable raft. (*National Soaring Museum*)

These Langley research found that types commonly had many adverse ditching characteristics owing to fundamental design. The lab had also performed static loads testing to destruction of a B-17, B-24, and B-26 to assess the structural survivability in a water landing. Based on the test results and stress analysis, NACA designed a "ditching flap," "hydroflap," or "hydrospoiler" that could be tailored for any aircraft type to provide more survivable ditching behavior. Such modifications were considered too extensive and disruptive to the high rate war production to introduce.[2]

Inflight Icing

Flying through clouds or rain showers risked ice accreting on the aircraft. The ice added weight that robbed the airplane of performance, distorted lifting surfaces such that the aircraft risked stalling, and altered handling characteristics or jamming controls. Ice on antennas disrupted communications and navigation. Carburetor and pitot probe heating were by then common while electrically heated windscreen panels were just being introduced. De-icing "boots" were also production articles on commercial airliners. These rubber bladders were installed on the leading edges of flying surfaces to be pneumatically inflated and deflated to break away accumulated ice. The de-icing boots had to be operated correctly and were not entirely effective depending upon conditions. They were considered unsuitable for high-speed aircraft. Additionally, they could be cut by anti-aircraft artillery (AAA) shell splinters with the rubber strips flapping violently in the slipstream. After the ferry to theatre, some bomber crews were cutting the boots away before going into combat to avoid the hazard of damaged rubber beating on the wings and tails.

With an emphasis on strategic bombing and the need to support forces across the globe, the AAF sought safe all-weather operations. In fall 1938, Gen. Arnold had challenged the National Academy of Sciences to assist the USAAC at ensuring suitable vision through the windows of bombers in the presence of icing.[4] The AAC also sponsored an extensive NACA program to better understand aircraft icing and investigate more effective anti-ice (preventative) and de-icing (in-flight removal) methods. Langley had been operating an icing wind tunnel since 1938 in which ice formation on aircraft wings and other components were studied. Water droplets were injected into the chilled airflow to observe ice formation on aircraft models in the tunnel. Flight data augmented these results and permitted practical demonstration of various technologies. Fake but non-melting ice shapes, informed by tunnel observations, were attached to leadings edges such that the effects on aircraft handling and performance could be measured in flight. Langley had done this as early as fall 1937 with sponge rubber shapes cemented to the wing leading edges of a DC-3.[5]

Construction of the enormous propulsion altitude tunnel in Cleveland offered the opportunity to use the same air chilling plant to supply a far more capable icing tunnel. It could deliver 300 mph (483 kph) air to the 20-foot (6.1-m) diameter test section with a water spray system and air chilled to -45°F (-43°C). When activated in 1944, actual elements of an aircraft would be accommodated to include windscreen, engines and propellers, and entire wing sections.

Research had come to focus on heated leading edges of aero surfaces to prevent ice accretion (anti-ice) or to melt the ice (de-ice). The heating had to be such that any ice was vaporized, as simply melting to a liquid risked this flowing aft on the surface and refreezing. The ready source of heat was the waste exhaust from the engine, though redirecting it risked back-pressure that could harm the engine or reduce efficiency. It also contained corrosive elements and could be so hot as to weaken the structure. The structure also had to be designed to accommodate the hot ducting.

By the late 1930s, Langley was flying a biplane with a section of a test wing installed between the struts. Onto this, water droplets could be sprayed during flight at cold temperatures aloft and ice photographed as it built up. Hot air was pumped into a pipe running within the test wing section leading edge and effectiveness in melting or prevent the formation of the ice photographed. This Martin XBM-1 (9212, an obsolete Navy dive-bomber) was still providing test data at the beginning of the war. An old North American O-47A (37-323) served as an intermediate platform for testing elements of a system bound for a more comprehensive test platform.

The two services each provided additional flight test platforms. The Navy had a PBY modified, beginning in 1939, with the wing leading edge thermal system, which they then tested. This was such a great success that they sent the flying boat to support the Aleutians campaign. The Navy found an added benefit of greatly reduced exhaust flame and muffled noise.[6]

The Army provided a Lockheed 12A Electra Junior (NC17396, NACA 97) for the extensive modification and becoming available for flight trials in 1940 when it was passed to Ames. Initial testing was during the winter of 1940–1941. It had heated wing leading edges via the engine exhaust pipe that ran span-wise. The tails retained the boots. Fresh air was inducted through leading edge openings, circulated around the heating pipe that served as a heat exchanger, and flowed to the wingtips where it was expelled. The exhaust flowed aft inside the wing to be drawn out louvers farther aft on the wing upper surface. An alternative was also tested in which fresh air was mixed with the exhaust and this combination flowed directly into the ducts. The exhaust was thusly cooled to tolerable levels and the proportion of contaminants reduced acceptably.

Electrical heating was also investigated via resistive wires bonded within the structure or heating pads applied externally. Wires embedded in windscreen glass could be an alternative to the method of hot air blown between twin panes then in use. Both methods were tried with propellers, the hot air blown into internal cavities and expelled out the tips. Alternatives to carburetor anti-ice systems (usually by drawing air from within the cowling rather than from outside flow), such as heating and alcohol, include shaping the intake such that the heavier water particles were bypassed or impacted and iced in an area not critically blocking the intake area. Fuel injection, of course, eliminated the carburetor entirely.

Seeking less crowded skies than near the San Francisco Bay area, the Lockheed 12 was taken to Minnesota for the winter of 1941–1942. This locale seemed so suitable that, on the advice of NACA Ames, the Army established the Icing Research Base at Wold-Chamberlain Field in Minneapolis. Operated by Northwest Airlines under contract but also with United Air Lines participation, it began test support in earnest during the winter of 1942–1943.[7] With America plunged into war and combat aircraft flying in icing condition, the Air Forces and Navy launched a program seeking to turn the results of the year of R&D into operational practice.[8] To this end, the NACA established a subcommittee focused on these problems. Participating was the Civil Aeronautics Authority,

Right: This Martin XBM-1 has been modified by the NACA with a metal airfoil mounted between the main wings on the starboard side. Water droplets could be sprayed on this such that ice accreted in flight while being photographed by the camera above. Then, hot air was pumped into the section leading edge to check the effectiveness of this as an anti-ice and deicing method. (*NASA*)

Below: The Army's pressurized cabin testbed, the Lockheed XC-35, 36-353, was employed by the NACA in high-altitude weather and contrail formation research. All were important for ferry and bomber combat operations in most weather. It is seen here at Langley on February 3, 1943, without the long nose boom and instrument installed to collect rain samples. (*NASA*)

the Weather Bureau, National Bureau of Standards, manufacturers, Northwest, several universities, and the British Royal Aircraft Establishment.

The team began working with more vigor, leveraging off the earlier NACA efforts. This moved to testing the prototype heated-air systems on in-service types with production-representative installations replacing de-icing boots. It required each exhaust to be ducted through a heat exchanger and the heated air directed into the wing leading edge, if not also to the empennage leading edges. The air was also passed to the cockpit for windscreen de-ice and defrost, for carburetor heat, and to the propeller for anti-ice. Such represented a substantial alteration to an existing design, but the work was considered a priority.

Ames developed de-ice systems for the Army's heavy bombers, seeking reduced weight and volume in addition to thermal efficiency. Prototypes were available by the end of 1942, typically adding just 300 lb (136 kg) to the aircraft compared with the 230 lb (104 kg) of de-icing boot equipment removed.[9] A B-17F (42-5474) and XB-24 (41-11678) were then operated in Minneapolis for tests of ram air heated for circulation via exhaust heat exchangers. The testing was conducted in the winter of 1943 and production applications followed. To collect more fundamental data, a C-46A (41-12293) was modified in 1943 with a full suite of the most advanced de-icing systems and comprehensive data collected. It was also fitted with an airfoil shape above the cabin for further testing of de-icing techniques with instrumentation installed to collect data on icing formation. The aircraft was flown into natural icing conditions to provide data, collected at great peril, for predicting icing and how quickly it accumulates.

Further exploring production-representative leading-edge hot air de-icing, a B-25C (42-32281) was modified. It was redesignated XB-25E when first flown on February 4, 1944. Martin did the same in 1942 with a B-26 (40-1380) to become the XB-26E. Both passed hot engine exhaust gases through a heat exchanger to warm ram air then passed into ducts. The B-25 installation made the leading edge so hot that it succeeded in vaporizing the water droplets. However, neither were felt worth the added complexity and interruption of production lines to make these standard features. Consolidated retained a B-24D (42-41003) in San Diego to explore potential production thermal de-ice installations for the Liberator that also were not adopted.

A Douglas BTD-1 (04968) later joined the program as well as a P-38J (43-28519) to test electrically heated "gloves" on the wing and empennage.[10] The Lightning also collected data on turbosupercharger effects on carburetor icing.[11]

The NACA developed the process of spraying isopropyl alcohol or ethylene glycol "antifreeze" solutions over a surface or injecting it from the root of propellers to migrate across the span under centrifugal acceleration. Alternatively, it could be expelled out a feed shoe along the propeller blade leading edge, though this degraded aerodynamics. The glycol could also be directed over windscreens and carburetor. However, it was inflammable and so the tank or tanks presented a hazard in combat if holed by an enemy round or shell splinter.

The Army's XC-35 was again employed by NACA for high-altitude weather and turbulence investigation as what may have been the first "storm-chaser" airplane.

The wing-like surface (covered) atop this C-46A was employed in observing ice accumulated and testing de-icing methodologies in flight (see also the modification to the exhaust adjacent to the wing leading edge). The aircraft was fitted with the most comprehensive suite of de-icing equipment then developed. Note the bulged window by the ladder under the top appendage for photographing the wing leading edge that lacks a de-icing boot. (*Jay Miller collection*)

The XB-24F was employed in inflight icing trials by NACA. A number of test installations are visible on the aircraft, including sensors on the fore-body and above the flight deck, and a tail fin to collect ice, observed via added blisters. The NACA testing, that included hazardous operations in natural icing conditions, also collected basic data on temperature and water droplets necessary for various types of ice to form. (*NASA*)

An alternative to the de-icing boots was explored with leading-edge hot air de-icing on a modified B-25C-10, becoming the XB-25E. Note the revised cowling for the engine exhaust gas heat exchangers. Although successful, the system was not judged worth the cost and complexity of production application for the Mitchell. (*San Diego Air & Space Museum*)

This investigated gusts, lightning, and heavy rain effects of thunderstorms on aircraft flight. Towards the end of the war, a project to more fully explore and understand thunderstorms was authorized but barely began organizing as the conflict concluded. The NACA also investigated contrail (condensation trail) formation with the XC-35 after the British reported this as a hazard in high-altitude bombing. The RAF initially aborted missions if contrails were observed, fearing they simplified enemy fighter intercept. The NACA suggested changing altitude to an air mass where the water vapor did not condense, and changing configuration, like cowl flap settings, to promote more rapid contrail dissipation. In time, the contrails were accepted since they could not be entirely prevented or avoided, and German fighters were vectored by radar.

While anti-ice and de-icing systems development were laudable and certainly improved the safety and effectiveness of transports, the benefits to combat aircraft such as bombers was arguable. Many teams felt the weight and hazards of the systems did not balance the disadvantages, and they had them removed. They could often simply change altitude to avoid icing conditions.

10

Special Missions

A number of special missions emerged or grew enormously during the war as demanded by the circumstances and by example of those who had already been fighting for years. These missions were typically serviced by existing aircraft types, which were modified as required. They were then under a continuous process of improvement as new equipment became available or GIs identified a need. Field work on the aircraft was common in this domain. Again, all combatant nations did the same but the American effort was, as always, on a larger scale.

To the Rescue

The Americans probably took a more intensive interest in helping downed aircrewmen survive until rescued, especially at sea, than other countries. Aircraft were fitted with more numerous and better equipped inflatable rafts, rations, survival gear, and rescue radios. These were improved based upon combat experience.[1] Although the Navy originally had floatation bags that would pop out of wings to help keep a carrier aircraft afloat long enough for aircrew rescue, these were discarded early in the war as too heavy and complex for rapid production and ready sustainment in the field, in addition to taking up volume that could be used for fuel and contributing weight that could be lent to weapons. A survival raft and inflatable life preserver vest was considered suitable with the expectation a naval aircraft would be close enough to the fleet that rescue by a vessel would occur within a few hours or a seaplane could pick them up.

The Army Air Forces had a more challenging ocean rescue scenario. Long-range bombers could operate well away from friendly vessels. Searches were mounted with aircraft at hand, crews augmented with visual scanners. Dedicated C-47s were assigned air-sea rescue (ASR) duty with the ability to shove an inflatable six-man life raft out the troop door to survivors spotted in the water. The Americans also dropped inflatable rubber dinghies from bomb racks on fighters and bombers, as did the British.[2] For a man with a life

Left: The Navy initially specified flotation bags in fighter-type aircraft (like this XF4F-2 Wildcat) to assist in keeping the ditched machine afloat until rescue. During the war, the services came to rely on flotation vests, inflatable rafts, and other survival kits as the unfortunate Marine F4F-3 pilot is about to field-test after a cat shot went wrong. (*American Aviation Historical Society and United States Navy via The Peter M. Bowers Collection/The Museum of Flight*)

Below: The Vought OS2U Kingfisher could landing in the open ocean under low sea states to take aboard survivors in the water. There were few places within the aircraft for these persons and so clinging to the exterior for water taxi was one option as shown in this image of one historical 1944 event. (*Vought Historical Archives*)

preserver and a one-man raft, this would be a godsend provided he could reach it.

The Navy's Consolidated PBY flying boat could set down in moderate seas and, sitting low to the water, affected rescues few other seaplanes could hope to perform. Rough seas would break up or swamp the boat. The service developed a platform that could be extended out an open gunner's blisters (after dismounting the guns) to allow crewmen to lean out and assist survivors into the boat.[3] The APS-3 radar mounted above the flight deck, which became common late in the war, assisted in locating aircraft still afloat. Other seaplanes could rescue personnel in the water, and accommodating them became specific design features, the Grumman J2F and Curtiss SC-1 being examples. However, even more than the PBY, deep-sea surface operations were too hazardous.

The USAAF's ASR organization and activities were modeled on the RAF example, but rapidly evolved to greater proportions. The service did not then routinely operate flying boats, but the Navy and Coast Guard were too focused on anti-submarine operations or shipping emergencies to lend the Air Forces the necessary support. Despite the slow Catalina's limitations, its recues were legend and the AAF acquired amphibious variants as fifty-four PBY-5As from the USN in 1942–1943 and 230 Canadian-built PBV-1A, all designated OA-10A. It was learned that Canadian Vickers altered the Consolidated design such that the aft fuselage had fewer stringers in the rear step making it prone to collapse.[4] This was another factor discouraging open-sea landings, but it was occasionally unavoidable to save airman or sailors. The boats, named Dumbo for search and rescue operations, were frequently brought back with damage.

Bombers were also turned to ASR because of their long endurance (especially with long-range auxiliary fuel tanks), safety of multiple engines, and ability to carry a large payload. Another attraction was that the heavy bombers had been adopted to carry advanced radar that could assist in location downed aircraft while they remained afloat. However, apart from finding survivors and directing rescue vessels to the location, the bombers could do little more. The Americans observed the British employing Lockheed Hudson and domestic light bombers (such as the Vickers Warwick) to carry a boat under the belly. Introduced in early 1943, this 20-foot (6.1-m) motor dinghy used carbon dioxide bottles to inflate floatation chambers upon parachute opening. On water contact, rockets fired rescue lines to either side of the boat as well as deploying a sea anchor.

Along these lines, the U.S. Navy augmented Catalina capabilities in late 1944 and early 1945 by developing the means of dropping a well-equipped and sea-worthy boat, parachute retarded, to survivors in the water. Weighing 1,500 lb (680 kg), the boat fit snuggly under a wing outboard of the struts where there was a hardpoint stressed for 2,000 lb (454 kg).

The USAAF also took an early interest in the British air-dropped boats. One of the RAF's Mark II lifeboats was brought to Wright Field in November 1943 as the impetus for creating a similar capability. A mocked-up boat hull was built for carriage and drop tests from beneath a B-17E.[5] However, the Mark II

The PBY was legendary for air-sea rescue and the Navy created this boarding platform (*left*). Faced with large numbers of aircraft crossing vast ocean distances, the Air Forces adopted the Catalina as the OA-10 (Observation Amphibian). This OA-10A (44-33879) from the 2nd Emergency Rescue Squadron is seen at Labo in Mindanao on the Philippines during early 1945. (*San Diego Air & Space Museum and National Museum of the United States Air Force*)

The Catalina could not land in even moderate sea states and so might locate survivors (note APS-3 radar radome) but be unable to effect a rescue. This PBY-6A carries an air-droppable rescue boat under the starboard outboard wing segment, descending under parachute once released. The 1,500-lb (680-kg) boat was equipped with much survival gear and supplies, enough to sustain survivors beyond that found in their life rafts. (*The Peter M. Bowers Collection/The Museum of Flight*)

accommodated just seven persons and did not do so well in deep-sea scenarios. A larger and sturdier vessel could easily be fitted under the heavy bomber. Requirements were drafted and released on May 26, 1944. Higgins Industries of New Orleans, a noted manufacturer of wooden boats, was selected on June 10 to build 600 A-1 Airborne Life Boats (later reduced to 300). The project was given high-priority and twenty were delivered by October then 75 by December.

The 3,300-lb (1,497-kg) laminated mahogany and birch plywood craft was 27 feet (8.2 m) long and was self-righting and self-bailing. The twenty water-tight compartments made it virtually impossible to capsize or sink. It could stand up to 20-ft (6-m) waves and 40-mph (64-kph) gales. Outfitted for twelve survivors, it had heavy clothing, blankets, food for twenty days, and navigation gear. The two inboard motors could manage 8-kts progress with fuel for up to 500 miles (805 km), but the vessel was also equipped with sails. The boat was suspended from four cables attached to the bomb shackles such that the aircrew needed only pull the bomb salvo lever to drop. When released at 1,500 feet (457 m) and 120 mph (193 kph) directly over the survivors, three 48-foot (15-m) parachutes were deployed by static line for descent at a 50 degrees nose-down angle. Fins on both sides of the stern helped stabilize the boat on release and descent, but these appear to have ultimately been deleted. On splashing down, three rockets automatically fired to deploy 600-foot (183-m) lifelines in three directions. Carbon dioxide bottles inflated the self-righting chambers. The parachutes settling into the water acted as sea anchors to reduce drift while the survivors worked to reach the boat.

Boeing was contracted to convert 130 B-17Gs to H-models to take the A-1 boats, to include some training TB-17Hs, with work beginning in 1945. The initial B-17Hs, also called Dumbos, were first deployed to the U.K. in March 1945. The first rescue was in April off the coast of Denmark. All the Hs were fully armed but soon the chin turret was replaced with an ASV search radar in a non-retractable radome. As the war situation improved, all weapons were deleted in the interest of endurance, further augmented with a long-range fuel rank in the bomb bay. With the war in Europe winding down and the B-29 seen as more suitable for the Pacific, the B-17H contract was terminated with only twelve machines completed and none of the trainers.

The very long over-water missions flown by the B-29 for their attacks on Japan made ASR particularly challenging. For missions from the Marianas, there were "lifeguard" submarines and surface vessels scattered along the route to help retrieve crews who ditched. Aircraft listened for distress calls and PBY Dumbos were ready to respond in any search. Aircraft were still the best means of locating the crew and dropping a boat with supplies. The B-17H Dumbo could go out just 350 miles (563 km) before turning back. However, a B-29 could go the full mission distance and hold off the enemy coast to return with the formation. It could remain on station for up to fourteen hours, usually carrying a long-range fuel tank in a bomb bay, searching for ditched aircraft and survivors, and directing rescue efforts. So, the Superfortress itself appeared the best means to address the Pacific Superfortress ASR challenge.

An even larger boat could be carried by the Superfortress (the normal B-29 combat crew complement was eleven men). The A-3 Airborne Lifeboat was

This image of a B-17H of the 6th Emergency Rescue Squadron, photographed on Luzon on June 27, 1945, shows the proximity of the boat hull to the ground (note wheels for ground movement of the boat). The boat coaming was shaped to match the bomber's belly and the rubber cushion added to create an air seal. This aircraft has had the chin turret removed to accommodate an ASV radome for the search radar. (*National Archives*)

This B-17G deploys its A-1 survival boat in a test. This bomber retains all its armament, and the parachute static lines appear to be contacting the extended belly turret (possibly mounting a camera). The boat descends at a steep angle to water impact with one of the two stern fins visible (which appear to have been deleted later). (*National Museum of the United States Air Force and The Peter M. Bowers Collection/The Museum of Flight*)

manufactured in aluminum by Edo. The 2,800-lb (1,270-kg), 30.6-foot (9.3-m) boat was maneuvered under the aircraft with beaching gear that also jacked it up for securing. It was carried stern forward. Rubberized-fabric chambers at the bow and stern inflated on release from the aircraft to right the boat in the water, aided by twenty sealed compartments. An inboard engine drove a single propeller, with fuel for a 500-mile (805-km) range. Also on board were rations for twelve men over thirty days, water distillers, clothing, heaters, and radio. The release was either pneumatic or manual, and commanded from the bombardier's station. A displaced linkage guided the boat safely away from the aircraft and a static line deployed the single 100-foot (31-m) parachute to descend at a 50-degree bow-first angle. Two fins at the bow helped stabilize the boat on release and descent.

A B-29A (44-616171) was modified for the role, first dropping a boat from its belly in May 1944. As the boat would cover the retractable AN/APQ-13 radar radome location between the weapon bays, the radome was relocated to the lower forward gun turret position. The aircraft were otherwise fully armed, but with some guns or turrets removed at the discretion of unit commanders. With additional radio gear installed, the radio operator's station was moved aft to behind the bays. There was an additional operator and an extra navigator. As few as three bombers were modified for the mission by the end of the war.[6] These B-29s held no special designation during that period but were referred to as Super Dumbo. They were not fully operational during the conflict.[7]

This B-29 carries the Edo A-3 Airborne Lifeboat. The boat and the search radar mark the bomber as a Super Dumbo air-sea rescue asset. Only a handful of these conversions were completed by the end of the war but were important in supporting the large B-29 offensive flying long distances over the Pacific to bomb Japan in the final six months of the war. (*Warren Thompson via The Peter M. Bowers Collection/The Museum of Flight*)

Helicopters held promise for ASR work. A United States Coast Guard (USCG), Navy, and Royal Navy team at Floyd Bennett Field, Brooklyn, began working on the potential in December 1943 using Sikorsky HNS-1s (YR-4Bs passed to the USN). After trials with a number of devices through late summer 1944, they hit on a hydraulic winch with a personnel rescue harness lowered to the survivor in the water or raft while the helicopter hovered above. With this gear, they began training for ASR and performed some stateside saves (mostly civilians) before the war ended. However, aside from the couple of "true believers," there were few in control of resources who envisioned the helicopter's future and none who worked to see it to fruition.

Rotorcraft ASR remained largely the aspiration of a handful of USCG visionaries who had great enthusiasm for the new capability. The Navy would not even consider helicopters integrated aboard their carriers. The Army was quite keen to apply helicopters to ASR but the only applications were some Sikorsky R-4Bs equipped with pontoons operating from Tinian and Saipan in 1945 to rescue B-29 crewmen that ended their mission's take-off or landing in the sea, relatively close to the islands as the helicopter's radius of action was just 65 miles (105 km).[8] Yet the seed was planted for what would eventually supplant all other means as the primary ASR platform and carrying forward the methods pioneered during the war.

Urgent Care

The importance of getting a casualty under the care of a medical professional in the shortest time was well-appreciated by the time of World War II. While there were many transport airplanes that could be configured to carry litter patients to hospitals out of the combat theater (becoming a common contract requirement), getting the wounded person out of the frontline area remained a challenge. Combat took place in some of the most remote and hostile regions of the planet. Days of travel by ground vehicle, if that was even an option and the soldier could survive the rough journey, was sometimes necessary to get to the most basic aid station much less a hospital. Air transport was possible if the aircraft could get into the area to carry out a casualty. If ambulatory, the wounded person could climb aboard an airplane and sit in a seat. If not, the aircraft had to be able to accommodate a litter, securing it and the patient from movement during the flight. Labeled an air ambulance, this compelling need saw variants of liaison airplanes and then helicopters adapted to carrying a litter.

Four Stinson O-49s were modified as O-49B (later L-1B) ambulances. The arrangement for the litter was revised for the 113 L-1Cs converted from L-1As, and seven more for versions on floats as L-1Es. Smaller liaison models were also modified to transport a litter-bound soldier. At AAF behest, Stinson modified the L-5 fuselage in spring 1944 to accommodate a litter or 200 lb (91 kg) of freight through a fold-down hatch that included the passenger door. Unfortunately, there was no room for an attendant. The service procured 730 of these L-5Bs, rushed to production in anticipation of the invasion of western Europe.[9] The USMC operated twenty-nine of these as OY-2s.

A Coast Guard HNS-1 (Sikorsky R-4B) performs the first hoist test of an individual at sea on September 26, 1944. It was the USCG that principally looked to helicopters for air-sea rescue roles, so they developed the rescue hoist and personnel harness. This role would expand post-war and eventually supplant all other ASR means. (*National Museum of Naval Aviation*)

A flight surgeon stands before one of the four L-1B ambulances (40-208), modified O-49 Vigilants. The alterations to accommodate the litter are clear in the photo. However, the internal platform appears uncomfortably high off the ground for those personnel loading the patient. (*National Archives*)

The Navy had acquired 100 HE-1s (Hospital, later AE-1, 26196/425) from Piper in 1942. These were converted J-5C Cub Cruisers, a three-place machine powered by the 100-hp (75-kW) Lycoming O-235-2 in an enclosed cowling, modified for casualty transport. The aft fuselage decking behind the wing was hinged at the front so it could be raised and laid atop the wing. This permitted a litter to be placed on a platform beneath and the cover lowered.

In 1943, the AAF let a contract to Piper to create an ambulance airplane from their available designs. The firm again chose their J-5C. As the aircraft also had to serve liaison duties, the approach was different from the HE-1. The aircraft had the aft fuselage decking cut down and the cabin transparency extended farther aft. This could be raised to permit a litter to be loaded from behind the wing. The first machine was a converted Cruiser, NX41552 (s/n 5-1387) with an O-235-3. The aircraft first flew on June 16, 1943, and tested into 1944. Further alterations included an enlarged windscreen and other changes to the transparencies, plus modifications for high lift and landing on unprepared fields. A second prototype was created from another J-5C, NX33529 (5-3001), though a 130-hp (97-kW)

The Navy acquired 100 HE-1 Hospital variants of the Piper J-5C in which the top of the aft fuselage swung up to reveal a platform for the litter. Later redesignated AE-1, crew was reduced to just the pilot. The fittings to secure the litter are evident. (*National Archives*)

Lycoming O-290-A was substituted. Its maiden flight was on September 9, 1944, and was referred to as the L-4X and later the L-4K.[10] The rest of this story is related in Chapter 2.

There was also an attempt to develop an ambulance plane from the L-4J, initiated in October 1944. Although a mock-up was inspected in November, nothing more is known to have come of this effort.[11] The developmental L-13 (Chapter 2) was designed to carry two litters.

Several Waco CG-4A gliders were modified to carry six litter patients each. Although the gliders could alight in quite small, unprepared fields, extracting them was more difficult. This entailed the snatch or aerial pickup technique described later. A team had to erect the snatch rig and then collect it all up later. However, extracting casualties for lift to a rear aid station where no other aircraft could get into the location proved invaluable on occasion. Such arose with an isolated bridgehead in German territory opposite Remagen, on March 22, 1945. Only the gliders could make it in and out expeditiously, getting the critically wounded GIs to a field hospital in thirty minutes.

The difficulty in operating even the liaison light-planes or gliders in remote areas to extract a casualty made the maturing helicopter an attractive rescue platform. The early models were two-seat affairs with little power margin,

Above: The Army had yet another solution with the CG-4A for what would come to be known as medivac. The glider could land in unprepared fields within a few hundred feet and then be snatched out by a passing tow-plane. It was natural that some would be modified as shown here with litter stanchions. (*National Archives and National Museum of the United States Air Force*)

Below: Pointing the way to the future, a Sikorsky XR-6A helicopter demonstrates casualty evacuation with an enclosed litter pod mounted off each side. The pods devised for the R-6A prevented the rotor downwash from buffeting the patient. From the first, the light helicopters produced during the war had more potential for battlefield casualty extraction than offensive action. (*National Museum of the United States Air Force*)

making them suitable for little beyond liaison missions, though rescues of mobile individuals were affected. The Sikorsky R-6 had more lift capacity but was unable to accommodate a litter inside the cramped interior. A side litter mount was devised but the rotor downwash onto the casualty would be intolerable. So, enclosed pods were created, with as many as two per side (though carrying that much payload would seldom be practical). These helicopters were deployed to China in the search and rescue role near the end of the war.

Smoker

As did all combatant nations during World War II, the U.S. military used smoke to conceal the movement of personnel and equipment from enemy observation and targeting. Aircraft smoke laying could more quickly cover a large area and this was adopted early in the airplane's evolution. This might also serve to lay insecticide or herbicides, and it provided a delivery means should the war devolve to chemical attack. Each U.S. service pursued aerial smoke laying that matured during the war to well-developed equipment, supply chain, and trained personnel. Fighters and medium bombers were the most common delivery platforms, flying in formations for denser or wider dispersion.

The smoke agent was developed by the Chemical Warfare Service (CWS). It was produced by release of a liquid chemical from a tank on the aircraft in flight, which then reacted with water vapor in the air to create a dense white cloud that remained suspended for some time.[12] The liquid flowed out an orifice and was automatically atomized in the slipstream until the tank ran dry.

At the time of America's entry into the war, the standard USAAC aircraft smoke tank was the 30-gal (114-l) M10 of 550 lb (250 kg) manufactured by Douglas Aircraft with the external shape recommended by NACA. Two of these units were common on fighters but as many as four were observed on A-20s and six on B-25s. The release was via ram air entering an orifice in an intake pipe above the tank and the chemical exiting a pipe at the rear, normally at the bottom to assist with gravity feed of the liquid and help keep the fluid stream away from the airplane surfaces. Both orifices were opened via a small charge fired electrically from the cockpit to shatter glass disks. Duration of smoke generation was a function of airspeed, running from 5.5 minutes at 175 mph (282 kph) to four seconds at 325 mph (523 kph). Dispersed at 300 feet (91 m) altitude, the "smoke curtain" could tower to 400 feet (122 m) along a 2,000-foot (610 m) trail.

Although some 90,000 M10 tanks were produced, the method risked leaving harmful acid residue on the aircraft, and aircrew were required to don gas masks when operating the generators. It was desirable to increase the volume of liquid and have a means of interrupting the application if desired. The Navy developed 30- and 50-gal (114- and 189-l) external tanks based on the original design but pressurized by compressed carbon dioxide in a cylinder, delivered via a valve opened or closed on command from the cockpit. These were adopted for the Army as M20s and M21s for bomb bay installation, although the M21 was also mounted externally. During 1942–1943, some 6,000 of each tank were manufactured for the USAAF. However, they were not satisfactory owing to the thin cloud and difficulty supplying the CO_2 bottles, and so replaced in 1944.

Tanks were developed for carriage in bomb bays, the delivery pipe extending out the bottom of the bay. This held risk to the aircrew should the tank be hit by ground fire. The M33 held 70 gal (265 l) but there was a variant (M33A1) for external mounting. A M40 200-gal (757-l) tank, or 2,000 lb (907 kg), was developed for internal mounting in heavy bombers but ultimately not produced.

The United States did engage in chemical warfare during World War II, but against insects. Insecticide was sprayed from aircraft to reduce the insect population, in advance of Allied forces moving into an area, to combat malaria and typhus. Powdered DDT (dichlorodiphenyltrichloroethane) was sprayed at about 600 feet (183 m) with the aircraft flying parallel to the wind. The aircrew had to wear gas masks from before the application began until the aircraft returned to base. The usual means was a 200-gal drum suspended in a bomb bay with a hose or tube leading out into the slipstream. A method common with crop dusting involved tubes run along the wings with nozzles spaced along the length to distribute the chemical across a broad swath. Combat aircraft involved in this mission included the A-20 and B-25, but also the C-47 and likely others.[13]

As a means of combating disease, the Americans delivered insecticide over jungle and forest areas troops were about to pass through or occupy. This F4U-1D is dispensing DDT from two underwing tanks during tests on July 12, 1945. This may have been a developmental tank as the photographer noted that the tanks were with short tubes. (*Naval Aviation Archives*)

This P-39D carries a M21 tank under an inboard wing station on 11 November 1942. Not a fine aerodynamic shape, the dispensing pipe is a hose meant to exit a bomb bay. The same aircraft is seen in flight generating a smoke screen, though at a higher altitude than typical in actual combat scenarios. (*National Museum of the United States Air Force*)

In the bottom image, USAAF P-47Ds carry both the M10 smoke tanks (foreground) as well as the new M33A1 tank on the distant machine. The M10 was a 30-gal tank while the M33 carried 70 gal. The M10 is shown in close-up mounted under the wing of a P-38F on a clearly modified pylon with improvised sway-braces for flight testing. (*National Museum of the United States Air Force and The Norm Taylor Collection/The Museum of Flight*)

Aerial Delivery

At the beginning of the war, the Americans had very little experience dropping anything but bombs from airplanes. In a few years, they were executing mass paratroop and glider assaults, with hundreds of aircraft, assisted with the airdrop of weapons, ammunition, and other supplies. They followed the German example and took lessons from the British, but quickly evolved their own tactics and developed their own systems. The principal tow and jump airplane was the Douglas C-47 Skytrain, a civilian aircraft at hand and ready for mass production as a military transport with few changes. It proved adaptable to many tactical airlift missions. Others, like the Curtiss C-46 Commando, were adopted while aircraft like the Fairchild C-82 Packet were developed specifically for tactical airdrop and glider tow.

Paratroopers jumped out the aft personnel door of the converted civilian transports, though the door was soon widened and set in an even larger cargo door. Their parachute release lines were attached to a static line strung along the aircraft sidewall leading overhead to the door. The same mechanism was employed to shove and kick bundles or containers out the door to be lowered to the ground by parachute. This was eventually facilitated by a roller-conveyer system, installed in the floor, to make the movement of the heavy cargo to the door more efficient such that only one pass over the drop zone (possibly under fire) might be necessary to deliver the load.

The American combat gliders were initially conceived as also delivering paratroopers jumping from the troop loading door, and possibly the tow-plane simultaneously. This was quickly set aside as inefficient use of the tow/glider combination that was usually operating near the limits of performance. The same applied to dropping cargo packets under parachute. One requirement for the new large glider, the Waco CG-13, was to deliver four parachute-recovered packs (parapacks). These were supported in a chute at the aft end of the cabin. A lever opened bottom doors and released each pack. Although built into the preproduction machines, the feature was not carried to production because such a mission was inefficient use of a glider. However, a similar feature was introduced into the first purpose-built tactical transport, the C-82, with an internal hatch and bottom doors to permit the drop of more rigid containers (paracontainers) from overhead rails. This aircraft was just being delivered at the end of the war.

More efficient than all these internal delivery means was to drop the parachute-recovered load from beneath the aircraft. Mounts were created for the belly of the C-47, along with standardized parapacks or paracontainers. The ripcord was attached to the shackle and remained with the aircraft, releasing the chute as the pack fell away. When dropping paratroopers, as many as four paracontainers with their support equipment could be dropped from the Skytrain's belly mounts as well. Any fighter or attack aircraft with external store stations, or bombers with shackles and release mechanism, could perform such duties. This mission could be as vital as dropping bombs or firing rockets. If the freight was simply

In cooperation with the British, the U.S. armed forces developed its own paratroop techniques and equipment. The C-47 was the principal paradrop platform and static line release the most common means (note parachute release lines trailing out the door from the interior static line). The same methodology was employed to drop parachute-recovered packs of rations, ammunition, medical supplies, and clothing. (*Author's collection*)

Interior of the thirty-place Waco XCG-13A assault glider shows a vertical chute in the rear of the cabin for dropping parapacks out the bottom of the aircraft. A lever was used to release each in turn or as a salvo. The feature was the poor use of a glider, better serving by landing the freight directly to the troops, thus not carried to production. (*National Museum of the United States Air Force*)

boxes of rations, they could be tossed into the bomb bay and dropped by simply opening the doors, falling without significant harm. Simple small parachutes could be attached to slightly heavier boxes for gentler lowering to earth, but again just stuffed into the bay and released by opening the doors. Even the mighty B-29 performed the duty. At the end of the war, it dropped food, clothing, and medical supplies into prisoner of war camps all over Asia.[14]

Under the motivation to supply troops in *extremis* or behind enemy lines, the GIs employed much innovation. However, the difficulty was encountered in carrying parachute-recovered bundles inside liaison light-planes and shoving them out the door without damaging the aircraft. Consequently, the field units adapted a light bomb shackle for attachment to the wing struts with a release mechanism added (mechanical rather than electrical desired). The initial motivation was to drop parachute-recovered cases of rations to combat teams in remote areas where routine supply was impractical—the planes subsequently dubbed "biscuit bombers." This expanded to dropping ammunition and 5-gal (18.9-l) cans of fresh water. Standard AAF parachutes were used but the ripcords reduced to 6 feet (1.8 m) from 15 feet (4.6 m), and a safety release on the line if the chute failed to deploy and the load dangled from the aircraft. These bundles approached 40 lb (18 kg) in weight for the L-4 and 200 lb (227 kg) each for the L-5 and leaves one wondering how this undermined the structural integrity under flight loads, and handling with the lateral CG, especially if one of the bundles got hung-up. No doubt, severe flight restrictions were imposed. In one European action, 5,000 lb (2,268 kg) of supplies were dropped by repeated flights of L-4s. On Leyte, seven L-5s and nine L-4s dropped an average 21 tons per day during a troop advance.[15]

Carrying bundles under the wings of fighters, at their much higher airspeeds, risked them being torn and shredded. They had to be carried within some container from which they could be easily dropped. Such a "paradrop container" was developed as a rectangular box open at the bottom with aero fairings at front and back. The compartments within the container could apparently be tailored in the field to the bundles to be dropped by moving the bulkheads. The entire arrangement may have been subject to much modification in the field.

Above: These GIs prepare parapacks for mounting below a C-47 in Guadalcanal on or before November 24, 1943. The packs and mounts were standard equipment by that time. Note the ripcord for the parachute awaiting attachment to the mount. (*National Archives*)

Below: Aerial delivery was very important for supplying forces behind enemy lines or virtually inaccessible by road or sea. Many types of aircraft were turned to this mission, even torpedo bombers like this Marine Corps TBM-3 performing a practice drop over Oahu in July 1945. Notice how the parachute ripcords are attached either to the aircraft bay or to another container. (*Grumman Historical Archives*)

Above: These GIs prepare parapacks for drop from the L-5 seen in the background in Burma. The aircraft is already fitted with the dense packs, a parachute atop each, hanging from a bomb shackle. Such delivery was more certain than higher volume drops from C-47s and was sometimes the difference been life and death for troops far from surface transport. (*National Archives*)

Below: Carrying parachute-recovered bundles hung exposed under the wings of pursuit airplanes, at fighter airspeeds, was prohibitive. An alternative was this container with aerodynamic fairings at the front and back. This A-24 (SBD 41-0492), photographed on April 18, 1945, carries such a "paradrop container" and is a good use of obsolete combat aircraft. Presumably, a mechanism allowed the release of some or all of the bundles from each bay within the container. (*National Archives*)

These aircraft carrying larger containers have more refined aerodynamic nose fairings. The P-47D (43-25426) and F-5E (P-38J 43-29008, photographed on May 31, 1945) carry containers with two to three exposed compartments. (*San Diego Air & Space Museum and National Museum of the United States Air Force*)

Airborne Pickup

Using a low-flying, slow airplane to pick something off the ground and carry it aloft without landing was a stunt from the earliest days of aviation. All American Aviation extended this to an actual service in "snatching" mail sacks off the ground from a community without an airport or otherwise little in the way of level ground. The sack was secured to a loop of nylon rope clipped between the tops of two poles to create a suspended line above the ground. The aircraft would trail a hook and rope on a polearm projecting below the fuselage and undercarriage to snag the line that pulled free of the poles and arm. The nylon had sufficient elasticity to resist breaking under the shock of the sudden motion and load. Once up and away, the lines and bag were drawn into the cabin.

This pickup method was used by American forces with light-planes collecting mail, dispatches, or other light material. In that case, it was a line with a weighted hook at the end and a reel inside the aircraft to draw it in after snagging the line with the dispatch bag attached. Even simpler was the airplane line with a weight at the end wrapping itself around the ground line on impact. The observer in the rear seat then drew the bundle in through the side window hand-over-hand.[16] Extension of the pickup method to snatch a glider was explored. Gliders could alight in very small fields where a tug aircraft could not land or where there was insufficient take-off distance in a tow configuration. It was desirable to recover the glider from such circumstances or tow it aloft for a combat mission.

The exploration began with light-planes snatching training gliders, their tow rope creating the nylon loop to be snagged by the tow-plane hook. Heavier gliders required more robust equipment aboard the tug. It was so successful that a kit was created to convert C-47s and other aircraft for snatch and tug duties. This consisted of a winch on the cargo deck or in the bomb bay. The snatch gear was adopted to transports and bombers, and gliders up to 25,000 lb (11,340 kg) were picked up by the method. The hook to engage the loop was slid into the end of a 20-foot (6.1-m) wooden channel lowered electrically to trail below the aft end of the aircraft. A steel cable ran from the hook through a pulley and guide tube into the aircraft and to the winch. On pickup, the hook pulled free of the channel and hundreds of feet of cable payed out on the winch drum before a hydraulic brake slowly brought this to a stop. All this happened in seconds as the pilot "poured on the coals" and climbed away with his charge in tow. The glider was airborne in about 200 feet (61 m) and three seconds. The system was reliably used thousands of time in training and combat. It was also extended to towing fighter-type aircraft as described in Chapter 7.

If a sack, glider, and airplane could be snatched off the ground by a passing aircraft, it was speculated the technique might also be used to retrieve a downed airman in inaccessible surroundings or behind enemy lines. The person would assemble the snatch kit parachuted to them and await the return of the airplane for pickup. The idea was the brainchild of Col. Rudolph Fink, heading Wright Field's Equipment Laboratory. It was explored at Clinton County AAF during mid-1943.[17]

In preparation, bundles up to 200 lb (91 kg) were snatched for practice and to get settings on all the equipment correct. The snatch in July of a container with accelerometers and recording equipment showed as much as 17 *g* on the standard snatch gear. This was too great, risking harm to the person. The equipment, including an inertia reel in the airplane, was modified until the accelerations were reduced to 7 *g*. It was also seen that the snatched bundle would drag on the ground initially. This was resolved by the pilot pulling up sharply as soon as snatch tension was felt.[18] The idea of snatching a chimpanzee as a build-up to a human was vetoed when it was realized how powerful this animal was and how dangerous it could be when aroused. The team settled on sheep, selected because of their docility and supposed fragility. The first attempt did not go well when the harness slipped and the tow line wrapped around the neck of the animal. It was strangled or suffered a broken neck. This was resolved and sheep were successfully snatched to be brought aboard the aircraft in flight.

In preparation for the first human pick up, the normal parachute harness was modified to permit the legs to be secured against the chest to prevent flailing. The subject wore goggles and a crash helmet, plus a chest parachute. The lines from the shoulder parachute attach points were attached to a transverse rod and the tow line to this. The man carried a knife to cut away anything that would prevent a safe parachute recovery if the snatch went wrong. A check was required of the harness, sensations trailing from the aircraft, and the ability to be winched aboard. On September 4, 1943, paratrooper Lt Alex Doster clambered out the door of a Stinson XC-81D (NX2311, later UC-81D 43-7280) in flight and was lowered out on the winch line to trail behind the aircraft. When being winched back in, a problem with the harness was uncovered and he could not be drawn up to the door. With sheer determination and body strength, Doster pulled himself to the door where winch operator Winters assisted him aboard.

For the actual snatch the next day, the harness was revised to eliminate the uncovered issue. Doster lay on his back facing away from the route of flight. The Stinson had been used for such work at Clinton County and was flown by crews long engaged in such work—pilots Norman Rintoul and Flt Off. Ralph I. Mickey, with Winters on the winch. The picked-up of Lt Doster went off exactly as planned. He was pulled aloft on a 150-foot (46-m), 3/8-inch (1.0-cm) diameter line at 125 mph (201 kph). Winched up to the airplane, he was left to dangle for a time. He was unable to repeat his feat of hand-over-hand climbing the rope against the wind blast. After three minutes in flight, he was finally winched to the door and assisted aboard by Winters.

The human pickup capability lay dormant for a year before being revived. The CCAAF team again snatched deadweights and sheep weighing up to 180 lb (82 kg) in preparation. The harness had been revised so that it could be donned without assistance. On September 23, 1944, two men were snatched separately at Wilmington by a Noorduyn UC-64A Norseman (43-5388) flown by Lt Norman S. Benedict. These were S/Sgt Harry C. Conway and Capt. John Peter Lee-Warner, the latter of the British Army, with each about 180 lb.

Apart from the pickup gear, the Norseman had a deflector ahead of the tailwheel to ensure a snatch line did not snag there. Ahead of the main gear posts were deflecting bars with cutting edges for the same purpose. Dragging a man snagged on a wheel would certainly have ended very badly. For the September 23 snatches, each first pass had a strut cut the line and so it had to be replaced and rerigged before the successful second attempt.

The feat was repeated on October 7 with Sgt Constantine Stiakatis taking flight at the end of a rope trailing from a C-47 flown by Rintoul and Lloyd Santmyer (both of All American Aviation, though Santmyer had been drafted but stayed with the pickup program). With sufficient elasticity in the system, the pull off the ground was not violent and the ride was thrilling.

With the advent of helicopters, the need for such devices as human pickup was not seen as necessary. However, the British used the capability to retrieve clandestine operatives from occupied Europe.[19]

The ability to snatch a person off the ground by a passing aircraft, employing the same system as aircraft pickup, was developed by the USAAF in 1943. After nearly a year of inactivity, this was revived in 1944 and demonstrated with a Noorduyn UC-64A. Here the paratrooper volunteer is pulled aloft on September 23 on an elastic line with only mild acceleration. (*United States Air Force via The Peter M. Bowers Collection/The Museum of Flight*)

At the final stage of the "flight," the snatched person clambers aboard with assistance. The snatch harness had the man's knees held against the chest, but could be released once "airborne." Note the still lowered snatch pole and the cutting blades ahead of the fixed undercarriage should the pilot misguide the airplane such that the snatch line risked snagging on the gear. (*United States Air Force via The Peter M. Bowers Collection/The Museum of Flight*)

The human pick-up was repeated on October 7 with a C-47. The system held promise for recovery of clandestine operatives from behind enemy lines. The pickup kit would be air-dropped to the person for assembly and awaiting the pickup ship, though a night snatch would be problematic. (*The Peter M. Bowers Collection/The Museum of Flight*)

11

Shipboard Duties

Since the U.S. Navy first adopted aircraft carriers, they insisted these could respond more effectively to foreign crises requiring the application of airpower than Army bombers who required basing privileges in some distant land. Even if the Army found such a base, they had to get the airplanes there by either laborious ferry flights or seaborne transport, along with all the support equipment and personnel. However, the Navy shipboard combat aircraft were of meager bomb delivery tonnage compared with Army bombers. World War II offered many opportunities to test all these arguments. The Navy found cause to adapt Army aircraft to their decks and the Army needed to fly aircraft off the carriers given various imperatives. Some of the special projects under these motivations reveal more evidence of American ingenuity and chutzpah under the pressures of combat.

Getting to Tokyo

During planning immediately following the Pearl Harbor attack, flying a medium bomber off an aircraft carrier was soon seen as the only practical means for America to strike Japan for the purpose of shocking the enemy and raising morale at home. The range of carrier-based aircraft meant the ships would have to approach so close to the islands that they would be vulnerable to land-based attackers. Bombers could take off with sufficient range to keep the carriers reasonable safe, fly over Japan to bomb, and fly on over the Sea of Japan to China and a base 70 miles (113 km) inland. The range (with expanded fuel load), wingspan, and take-off distance of the B-25 won it the honor. It was larger and heavier than any aircraft to have been flown off a carrier to that date. The project was undertaken with as small a team as practical and as a top-secret effort.

Exploring the feasibility of the concept was Jimmy Doolittle, then a lieutenant colonel working as Director of Operational Requirements, or essentially working special assignments for Arnold. Doolittle was later approved to lead the mission and overcame any "roadblocks" by invoking the authority of the Chief. The aircraft just fit on the Yorktown-class aircraft carrier with the left wheel running along the edge of the deck and the right wing clearing the island by approximately 6 feet (1.8 m). After practicing ashore, two lightly loaded B-25Bs were flown off the USS *Hornet's* (CV-8) 814-foot (248-m) long flight deck on February 3, 1942, to prove the feasibility. The first bomber flew from a position forward on the deck where the first of a group of attacking aircraft would have to take off. It became clear that, while the wing would clear the island, if the bomber rose too high too soon, it could strike a structure projecting over the deck.

The Mitchell bomber was still new at the time with a large percentage of the operational machines to be committed to the strike. The twenty-four low-time B-25Bs of the 17th Bombardment Group from Pendleton Airport, Oregon, were selected. The design still had teething problems and Doolittle consulted Wright Field regarding improvements. Beginning at the end of January, each aircraft was rotated through Mid-Continent Airlines in Minneapolis for modification.

Each bomber had an autopilot and leading-edge de-icing boots installed, a post-strike camera added in the tail of several machines, and non-essential equipment removed. They also received an extensive fuel system modification. This consisted of lines run to manifolds, drains and filters, shut-off or selector valves, tank vents, plus level sensing and indicators. Testing ensured against air bubbles being introduced into the lines. A 225-gal (852-l) self-sealing rubber

The project to attack the Japanese home islands following the Pearl Harbor attack came to center on flying North American B-25B Mitchells (like that shown) off an aircraft carrier deck. This was the largest and heaviest airplane ever to fly off a carrier to that time and required pilot special training. The long-range mandated special modifications to the bomber that saw the bottom turret removed. (*The Peter M. Bowers Collection/The Museum of Flight*)

cell in the bomb bay replaced an initial 265-gal (1,003-l) steel unit that leaked excessively. Bomb shackles had to be revised because of this bay tank installation. Another rubber tank of 160 gal (606 l) was installed in the crawlway at the top of the bay. Once empty, it could be collapsed to permit the men to move between the forward and aft ends of the aircraft. The ventral turret, that never worked well and would be of no value in the planned low-level mission, was removed and the opening faired over. A self-sealing 2-foot (0.6-m) square cube auxiliary (aux) fuel tank of 60-gal (227-l) capacity was created to occupy the volume. Five 5-gal (19-l) fuel cans were to be loaded in the radio operators compartment aft of the bomb bay to be emptied by hand into the auxiliary tank as its level drew down. This top-off was to begin soon after take-off. The empty cans were to be punctured then dropped all at once so as not to leave a trail of debris back to the carrier. With the 646 gal (2,445 l) in the wings, total fuel capacity became 1,141 gal (4,319 l), though the mechanics chased leaks until the date of the mission.

Although the modifications were performed quickly, not all were complete when the aircraft moved on to Eglin Field between February 27 and March 3. The few weeks of special training was aided by a Navy instructor Lt Henry "Hank" L. Miller. Unsuitable weather meant fewer flying hours than Doolittle had planned. The top-secret Norden bombsights were removed because it would be ineffective at the low bombing altitude planned and because it could not be risked falling into enemy hands. Substituted was a simple, jury-rigged, lead-drop sight fashioned in the base metal shop for $0.20 each. The crews (five men per twenty-five aircraft plus twenty ground personnel, 140 individuals) volunteered consistently when asked. The training included low-altitude bombing (1,500 feet/457 m) and especially short, low-speed take-offs from an auxiliary field. With a stiff headwind, they were getting off at maximum GW in as short as 300 feet (91 m). Instead of the usual 80–90 mph (128–145 kph) take-off speed, the aircraft were being pulled off at 55–60 mph (89–96 kph) with full flaps. The elevator trim was set three-quarters nose high and the yoke held full back until the nose rose to the point of the tail skid approaching the surface until unstick when it was pushed forward and the flaps raised. The machines had the carburetors specially adjusted to optimal settings by Bendix and the crews developed best endurance power settings.

Following the training, the aircraft were flown to McClellan Field, Sacramento, California, on March 23–25. There the aircraft were inspected with great care and "squawks" corrected. Work included receiving new props, removing the 230-lb (140-kg) liaison radio, working to get the gun turrets operating properly, completing the "mods" not finished in Minneapolis, and having another go at the fuel leaks. At first, the aircraft and parts delivery were not getting priority until Doolittle asked Arnold for help instilling a sense of urgency in the depot supervisors. Once motivated, the mechanics kept exceeding their orders and doing work like readjusting the carburetors back to their common settings or replacing others. Doolittle was furious with the poor service and did not hold back his criticism.

The team then moved on to Alameda, California, where only the optimal sixteen machines were hoisted aboard the USS *Hornet* (CV-8) beside the pier on April 1, 1942. The original intent was to take fifteen aircraft but a sixteenth was added with the intent that it fly off early and return to shore as a demonstration to the crew of the feasibility of the take-off and to carry any vital messages back. Ultimately, the aircraft remained aboard and participated in the raid. The ship put to sea the next morning and was joined by the carrier *Enterprise* (CV-6), four destroyers, two cruisers, an oiler, and with two submarines patrolling well ahead of the task force. The two carriers represented a significant portion of the country's remaining naval striking power, emphasizing the risk the operation entailed. A blimp came over the *Hornet* to deliver a few last-minute spares plus glass navigation windows for the Mitchells to replace plexiglass models.

Four 500-lb (227-kg) demolition bombs were carried, or fewer in a mix with incendiaries depending on target—essentially, the maximum bomb load. The bombs were especially filled with more explosives than normal. The 500-lb incendiaries, with 128 bomblets, were also specially assembled for the mission and served as the basis for those that followed throughout the war. The aircraft retained the .30-cal nose gun on a ball mount and the upper twin .50-cal turret. Like others flying the early B-25s into combat, the crews added two short poles made from broom handles, painted black, affixed to the aft end of the aircraft to make it appear the bomber had a tail gunner. With the 5-gal cans of fuel, gross weight rose to 31,000 lb (14,061 kg)—2,000 lb (907 kg) over the advertised maximum.

The targets—Tokyo and other major cities—were selected while at sea. The plan was for five flights of three airplanes each to attack targets across a 50-mile (80-km) front to give the impression of a larger formation. No fuel would be wasted in forming up; each airplane flew back over the ship to align with the sailing bearing towards Tokyo and then continued on at best-economy airspeed. The team had hoped to launch at a 450-mile (724-km) distance at dusk on Sunday April 18, Doolittle leading by three hours to start fires to guide the others bombing at night. However, the *Hornet* was sighted by a picket ship on the morning of April 18. Although the vessel was destroyed by gunfire, it was feared a radio alert had gone out. Consequently, the crews immediately manned their aircraft and promptly launched at 620 miles (998 km) from Japan. The Navy men topped off all tanks, rocking the aircraft to eliminate air pockets and get in every gallon possible. They also added five more 5-gal cans of fuel.

A white line had been painted near the left edge of the deck and the pilots were to roll with their left tire on this line. Each pilot was signaled to begin the take-off roll to correspond with an up-pitch of the ship. They saw as little as 67 mph (108 kph) on the airspeed indicator, well below the usual 110 mph (177 kph) for maximum GW. Although they were to use full flaps, one aircraft managed a good take-off with flaps mistakenly left up.[1]

The first aircraft, flown by Doolittle, had just 467 feet (142 m) to get off and an hour was required to get all the bombers into the air. The aircraft had about

50 kts or 58 mph (93 kph) wind over deck, allowing Doolittle to get off in under 400 feet (122 m). The technique developed at Eglin was probably overly conservative, with the aircraft barely above stall on leaving the deck and the pilot struggling to put the nose down and retrim after passing over the bow.[2] It received low marks from the naval aviators observing on board. If any single bomber had had problems and held up the process, it would have been shoved over the side. Likewise, if the task force was engaged by the enemy, the Mitchells would have been "deep sixed" to permit the *Hornet's* aircraft to be brought up onto deck and launched.

The aircraft were flown just above the surface and all but three of the B-25s made landfall off course. They climbed to 1,500 feet (457 m) for the bombing phase. Except for some ineffectual anti-aircraft fire, the bombers went unchallenged. All but one crew found and hit their targets, the one that never determined its location hitting a target of opportunity. All then flew on to the Asian mainland with some heading changes to throw off possible pursuit and plotting of their course to the recovery sites. A fortunate tailwind aided in all making landfall, although with darkness, weather, and lack of the expected homing beacon, the landing sites could not be found. After about thirteen hours in the air and covering roughly 2,250 miles (3,261 km), each crew was forced to bailout but for one landing in Russia. One man was killed in the egress and two more drowned while three others were seriously injured. Eight men were captured by the Japanese of which three were executed and one died of malnutrition during captivity. The crew that came down in the USSR were interned for a year before escaping.

Despite the losses, the Doolittle Raid was considered fantastically successful. The morale boost at home was enormous and the Japanese were compelled to keep fighters at home for defense plus deciding to launch their disastrous Midway attack. Doolittle was decorated and promoted to brigadier general, going on to further command of combat forces.

Exactly a year later, another blow avenging Pearl Harbor was struck when a flight of sixteen P-38s, acting on decoded radio intercept traffic, shot down a bomber carrying Adml Isoroku Yamamoto, the architect of the attack. The fighters flew what was then a very long fighter intercept mission at 435 miles (700 km) outbound in 2.5 hours, and a total of 4.5 hours. New 310-gal (117-l) external tanks were mounted after a quick modification. The lead aircraft was also hastily modified to carry a large navy ship compass for more accurate readings during the unusually long flight based solely on dead reckoning.

Above: The sixteen B-25Bs were initially parked on either side of the deck, angled forward, except for two parked on the fantail. As the bombers were launched, the aircraft were pulled out and aligned on the deck (this scene probably an *en route* rearrangement for engine runs). Note the Dauntless dive bombers to be launched, (after shoving some Mitchells overboard) to defend the ship if discovered by the enemy. (*National Museum of the United States Air Force*)

Below: The famous Doolittle Raid on Japan was flown off the USS *Hornet* on April 18, 1942, each aircraft carrying 2,000 lb of bombs and extra fuel. The results on morale at home and the reaction in Japan far exceeded the physical damage. The effort illustrated the leadership and skills inherent in the U.S. military as it ramped up to meet the worldwide challenge of the war with more maturing warplanes like the Mitchell. (*USAF*)

Delivery

Delivering large numbers of aircraft to distant theaters of operation was a significant challenge for the Americans in the early years of the war. Bombers and large transports had the range to fly extended over-water routes once intermediate airfields were established or leased, weather stations erected, and training for such operations (rare even before the war) was enacted. Smaller aircraft (that could not be crated) such as fighters did not have the range for such undertakings and the journey would be too wearing on the equipment. These were delivered aboard ships, usually lashed to the deck. They were then lifted off via crane and deposited dock-side. They might then be transported to an airfield where any assembly and preparation for flight was performed. However, during the early period, there was a paucity of suitable ports, much less close to airfields. Alternatives were lowering the aircraft onto barges or rafts to be landed on the most acceptable beach. The aircraft then had to be laboriously dragged across planks and roads to an airfield.

Flying Army fighters off Navy decks was a means of delivery sometimes adopted when circumstances did not allow for dock-side unloading. They were loaded aboard, not flown, owing to the specialized skill required for a deck landing and arrestment (a "trap"). Many could just fly off without the catapult, as did the lighter naval aircraft, but some required this assistance. The U.S. Navy carriers were equipped with steam or hydraulic catapults that moved a long piston that slid a shuttle nearly flush in the deck. A steel cable launch bridle fit around this shuttle and the ends looped onto two hooks in the belly of the aircraft. A holdback at the end of the aircraft restrained movement until catapult pressure built up and a frangible link in the holdback broke. For the Army aircraft, the bridle attachments had to be specially engineered and installed as a modification. The holdbacks were more challenging and do not appear to have been routinely used, instead accepting perhaps lower end-of-deck speeds since the aircraft were likely launched at a modest weight. The Navy, naturally, had grave misgivings about such activities from their vessels, but accepted that getting off the deck was much less problem-prone than flying on. By 1944, the USN had fabricated catapult equipment for every Army pursuit type, suggesting all had been tested as well.[3]

The first experience was probably P-36s delivered to Hawaii in February 1941. The 33rd Pursuit Squadron's thirty P-40Cs, three primary trainers, and eight O-47As flew off the USS *Wasp* (CV-7) to alight at Reykjavík, Iceland, in summer 1941. The USS *Ranger* (CV-4) carried sixty P-40s to Accra, on Africa's Gold Coast, to fly off *en route* to Karachi, India. These aircraft were loaded aboard in Norfolk on July 25, 1941, and sailed two days later. The *Ranger* made four trips across the Atlantic through February 1943 ferrying Army aircraft. In July 1943, it carried P-40s within 100 miles (161 km) of Takoradi, Ghana, from which they continued across Africa to Cairo. It also hauled sixty-eight P-40s to the CBI Theater, these flying 125 miles (201 km) to their initial destination. Midway Island received 73rd Fighter Squadron's twenty-five P-40Es in June 1942 via the *Saratoga*. Also in the Pacific, P-40Ks were delivered to Wheeler Field, O'ahu, Hawaii, on December

Above: Bringing fighters to distant theaters aboard sea transports before the war was difficult, especially given the relatively small numbers of vessels. With assets heavily tasked and some ports in enemy hands, the vastly growing movement requirements of World War II made innovation in getting aircraft from ships decks to an airfield essential. This P-38 is resting on a barge made from piping and planks fixed between two DUKW amphibians. (*National Museum of the United States Air Force*)

Below: Carriers turned to transport, with aircraft either in the hangar deck or above decks, was common for moving fighters between theaters as ferry was generally impractical. In this case, a deck is crowded with Mustangs, plus a Fairey Swordfish, to be off-loaded via crane as there is clearly insufficient room to fly them off. Such vessels represented rich targets for marauding submarines and many aircraft were lost being moved across the water. (*Naval Aviation Archives*)

The Navy found itself transporting and launching so many Army aircraft off its decks that it ran a program to support the operations. By 1944, it had developed the necessary equipment and techniques to catapult all Army fighter types. Likely as part of this effort, this P-39Q has been prepared for a land catapult shot with holdback cable and launch bar. (*The Norm Taylor Collection/The Museum of Flight*)

Among the first experiences of Army aircraft flying off U.S. Navy carriers was P-40Cs delivery to Iceland in summer 1941 to protect Allied assets engaged in North Atlantic Neutrality Patrols. Flown off the *Wasp* (CV-7), they were likely not catapulted. Three primary trainers and eight observation aircraft were also brought along. (*United States Navy via The Peter M. Bowers Collection/The Museum of Flight*)

10, 1943, catapulted off the USS *Breton* (CVE-23). The *Wasp* twice ferried RAF Spitfires to defend isolated Malta by flying off the vessel.

The first combat operation was likely the seventy-seven P-40Fs of the 33rd Fighter Group launched off the escort carrier USS *Chenango* (CVE-28) at the beginning of the North Africa operation. They flew into Port Lyautey airfield, Morocco, beginning on November 10, 1942. The fighters were catapulted with one ending up in the sea. A holdback was fitted behind the tailwheel and fittings for the launch bridle cable under the wing. The first two aircraft found the field in bad shape but could not hold up the launches. Several cracked up upon landing and so the launches were eventually suspended for two days, the rest of the aircraft going to Cazes airdrome, Casablanca. Days later, thirty-five more of the Group's P-40Fs were catapulted off the HMS *Archer* in November 1942 and flew into Port Lyautey. In mid-January 1943, the *Ranger* brought in seventy-five replacement P-40Fs from the 325th Group, flown to Cazes. Then it carried seventy-five P-40Ls to Casablanca, arriving on February 23. In November, it was the 79th Group's airplanes going to Egypt. It is understood that in none of these instances had the pilot been given any practice in the catapult launch.

Bell P-39Qs of the 72nd Fighter Squadron, 318th Fighter Group, were catapulted off the USS *Nassau* (CVE-16) in December 1943 to land on Butaritari Island in the Makin Atoll. That same month, Airacobras of the 45th Fighter Squadron also flew off a carrier to Kanton Island. Similarly, seventy-one Army P-47Ds of the 318th Fighter Group were loaded aboard the escort carrier USS *Manila Bay* (CVE-61) and USS *Natoma Bay* (CVE-62) in Pearl Harbor (O'ahu) and sailed on June 5, 1944, *en route* for Saipan. Approaching the island on June 23, the *Manila Bay* was attacked by a pair of Japanese fighter-bombers that dropped four "eggs" that fell wide of the ship. The captain launched four of the Thunderbolts as combat air patrol (CAP), the airplanes recovering to Saipan. One would be hard pressed to find a similar event of Army fighters flying CAP for a Navy carrier in a war zone. The following day, the remaining fighters were catapulted off to land on Saipan. In the meantime, the *Natoma Bay* shot off its P-47Ds on the 22nd and 23rd.

For the American World War II combat debut, in North Africa, the *Ranger* carried three L-4A spotters along with its Wildcats, launching the light-planes with 35 kts over the deck on November 9 to fly the 60 miles (97 km) to shore and support the troops. Approaching the coast, the Grasshoppers were engaged by U.S. Navy gunfire and, crossing the beach, by U.S. Army anti-aircraft gunners. One Piper was shot down, its pilot wounded, while another, badly damaged, landed near French forces and the crew taken prisoner. Only the third managed a landing at the intended destination.

Operation of light-planes off Navy decks continued later in the war such as during the Pacific island-hopping campaign. During fall 1944, operations in the Philippines, Marine OY-1s were launched off the USS *Sangamon* (CVE-26). This was repeated at Saipan and Okinawa, with the Stinsons flying off as many as seven "Jeep Carriers" in the latter case.[4] The numbers on each vessel were kept

Above: This P-40F of the 33rd Fighter Group is poised on the catapult of the USS *Chenango*. The holdback behind the tailwheel is visible but the bridle for the shuttlecock, propelled in the slot under the airplane, is hidden by the wing. The aircraft is one of seventy-eight launched off the carrier at the beginning of the North Africa campaign and America's combat debut of WWII. (*San Diego Air & Space Museum*)

Below: P-39Qs from the 72nd Fighter Squadron, 318th Fighter Group, catapulted from the escort carrier USS *Nassau* (CVE-16) in December 1943 to land on Butaritari in the Makin Atoll. The catapult bridle attaches to a special fitting on the fighter, the cable discarded at the end of the deck. Note how the bridle length allowed it to connect to the catapult shuttlecock such that neither interfered with the nose gear. (*Jay Miller collection*)

These P-47Ds were transported from Hawaii to Saipan in summer 1944 aboard the escort carrier USS *Manila Bay*. They were modified for catapult from the vessel with the bridle attached to fittings on the landing gear struts and a holdback attached at the aft end of the fuselage. Four of the Thunderbolts were launched (flaps down) to fly patrol above the carrier before landing on Saipan. (*National Archives* and *San Diego Air & Space Museum*)

Another group of P-47s prepare for take-off from an aircraft carrier. In this case, they are simply being flown off without the aid of a catapult, presumably at a light weight and suitable wind across the deck. This technique was used several times during the war. (*San Diego Air & Space Museum*)

This Army L-4A spotter plane takes flight from the deck of the USS *Ranger* on November 9, 1942. It and two others were flown off to assist American forces ashore in Morocco, but one was shot down and the others badly damaged by friendly fire. Even lacking flaps and with low-power engines, the light planes were easily flown off the deck without assistance. (*United States Navy via The Peter M. Bowers Collection/The Museum of Flight*)

A Marine Corps OY-1 (Stinson L-5) departs the USS *Sargent Bay* (CVE-83) off Iwo Jima in early 1945. With wind over deck, flaps down, and short-field take-off techniques, the light-plane had no difficulty flying unaided off the escort carrier. Although likely a one-way trip (they did not return to the ship), this permitted the aircraft to provide valuable service for the invasion force in an era just proceeding the advent of the helicopter. (*Naval Aviation Archives*)

to just a few because the aircraft had to remain on deck as they did not fit on the elevators. Pipers flying off decks was repeated in the Pacific with L-4s departing an escort carrier during the Leyte landings on October 22–23, 1944. This permitted observation from the first moments of the amphibious assault and the airplanes then landed ashore. The ships would not approach any closer than 50 miles (81 km) and the light-planes had to fly the remaining distance with nothing more than a compass and wristwatch as navigational instruments.

Army from the Sea

For large European ops, the Army did not rely on the U.S. Navy for bringing liaison airplanes near to shore. The air officer to the 3rd Infantry Division, Capt. Breton A. Devol, Jr., conceived a 220-foot (67-m) long decks attached to vessels as small as Landing Ship, Tanks.[5] This 'flight deck' was usually assembled of perforated steel planking and installed about 6 feet (1.8 m) above the deck of the vessel. With the platform just 16 feet (5 m) wide, some of the LST applications had six of the ten L-4s stored nose-down off the sides of the deck, on wheel ramps, with their rudders removed to provide clearance for the airplanes running the deck. For launch, each was pulled up onto the deck, the rudder installed, and then pulled to the far end in preparation for take-off. The tailwheel was placed on a raised platform and the brakes held until the engine was at full power. This reduced the portion of the take-off run required to reach sufficient speed to raise the tail with no wind. Their short take-off, especially with a modest wind over the deck (8–10 kts was the LST's best speed), allowed them to be off in just scores of feet. They were all one-way trips to land ashore following their first mission without an option to return and land aboard.

These measures are known to have been employed in the invasions of Sicily and southern France. LST-906 and -525 were converted for the Sicily landings, though only 525 participated. An LST also supported the Salerno landings on the Italian "boot." LST-386 was ready for the France operation. The Army sought use of an escort carrier for the Normandy landings, but the Navy initially insisted they could not accommodate the request. When they later reversed themselves, the Army had already made other arrangements.

When helicopters were first deployed they also operated off sea vessels in the same manner as the liaison birds. These ships were called USAAF aircraft repair units (floating), modified Liberty supply ships, and several of these were fitted with helicopter platforms. A handful of Sikorsky YR-4B light choppers operated from these ARU "floaters." The helicopters could deliver critical supplies ashore in a short time vice aboard small boats running to shore and then via jeep or hand-carried to the destination. They also collected gear just as quickly for transport to the ship for repair. They are known to have been employed during the Iwo Jima and Okinawa invasions, and supported B-29 bases in the Marianas.

In Gaeta, Italy, LST 906 is being loaded with L-4s from the 3rd Infantry Division on 31 July 1944. Aircraft are being hoisted aboard and then either parked at the forward end of the deck or positioned off the sides on wheel ramps. The short deck with a mere 8 kts sailing into the wind was sufficient to allow the light-planes to get safely airborne. (*National Archives*)

The LST Cub "carrier" is shown in action in the Mediterranean during July 1944, probably just operational testing of the concept. The 3rd Infantry Division's L-4s lie ready to be positioned for the take-off roll or stowed off the side of the narrow deck. Notice the rudders have been removed from those on the wheel ramps to ensure clearance for the aircraft taking off. (*U.S. Army*)

An R-4B (insert) operates off Subic Bay, the Philippines, near the end of the war. Such aircraft flew from USAAF Aircraft Repair Units (Floating) ships offshore to transport spares and equipment for repair back and forth rather than take up sparse space on what may be a small island dominated by an airfield. Thus, the advent of helicopters in modern warfare began. (*National Archives and National Museum of the United States Air Force*)

Floating Solutions

The B-29 raids on Japan were initially unescorted because of the range, with expectations the bombers' defenses and altitude would keep loses to acceptable levels. Nonetheless, means for providing escort were sought. One solution appeared to be placing the fighters aboard carriers along the bombers' route of flight. Navy fighters had respectable range but were not optimized for escort and high-altitude flight as were Army pursuit ships by 1944. The P-51D had been particularly groomed through European operations for such tasks. The long "legs" of Mustangs launched from carrier decks would keep the carriers a safe distance from Japanese islands. However, the fighter was naturally not designed for carrier ops. Even with retrofit of catapult bridle fittings and arrestment tailhooks, the suitability of the flaps for a low-speed approach and ability of the airframe to withstand repeated deck landings was in doubt. Lack of folding wing meant it could not be placed on an elevator and brought below decks on some carriers, but the span would at least clear the island. The corrosive salty environment was another concern, but the typical service life of a fighter and production rate at that point in the war made this a lesser impediment. The potential could only be verified through flight test.

As the war dawned, the USN had been testing the Bell XFL-1, a nasalized spin-off of the P-39 with an inline engine mounted amidships. By that time, it was overweight and unneeded. Unlike the Airacobra, the Airabonita was given a tailwheel as the Navy was not ready for tricycles. However, Bell was encouraged in October 1939 to look at a nasalized XP-39B. By the time the proposal was made in February 1941, interest had waned. In October 1940, Bell had requested a test of a P-39 fitted with a tailhook, likely associated with that program. A single trap was flown by Navy Lt Robert M. Elder, highly experience in carrier suitability trials, ashore at Mustin Field. It ended with the entire tail assembly torn away and the aircraft running off into a chain-link fence.[6] This, no doubt, colored the Navy's impression of adopting Army aircraft to carrier operations.

A shipboard P-51 effort began in 1943, long before the B-29s began Pacific combat operations. On May 17, the USN adopted Mustang IA FD524 (41-37426) and gave it BuNo 57987 (although no Naval designation). During initial assessment ashore, the aircraft was judged unsuitable for carrier ops and the project stalled.[7] This may have been preliminary to the central effort awaiting a P-51D.

What was probably the determined effort to assess the Mustang for carrier basing began in spring 1944 as Project Seahorse. To begin, North American test pilot Bob Chilton flew simulated deck landings in a P-51D, then the premier Mustang.[8] The Navy was sent P-51D (44-14017). The work began with modification of the fighter at NAA's Dallas, Texas, plant or the ship evaluation unit at the Navy yard in Philadelphia.[9] The Mustang was equipped with a hook on the belly centerline, presumably under the wing spar, for the launch bridle. A holdback attach point was installed on the bulkhead at the extreme end of the

The XFL-1 was developed for the USN to explore the potential of inline engines. Though a spin-off of the P-39, a conventional undercarriage was substituted; the Navy felt this was the only acceptable configuration for carrier ops. Ultimately, design issues meant the aircraft never went aboard an aircraft carrier, though there is evidence the XP-39B was subjected to carrier suitability testing ashore that ended with structural failure. (*The Peter M. Bowers Collection/ The Museum of Flight*)

fuselage, no doubt strengthened and possibly with a keel to the next bulkhead forward. The base of the rudder was notched for clearance. A tailhook was fitted to a reinforced bulkhead just aft of the tailwheel. Pneumatic pressure was increased in the oleo struts to reduce bounce on touchdown. Some sources also claim that high-pressure tires were substituted. Directional stability for the low-speed landing approach was enhanced by the addition of an enlarged vertical tail leading edge dorsal extension.

After delivery to the Navy, initial shore-based tests were conducted in September 1944 at Mustin Field with its catapult and arrestment system. Lieutenant Elder was the project pilot. Some 150 launches and recoveries were performed through October. The principal challenge was the 82-mph (132-kph) stall speed, with hard-over rudder required to maintain directional control, and the 90-mph (145-kph) carrier arrestment system limit. However, at 85 mph (137 kph), the speed margin and aircraft controllability were judged safe enough to move on to shipboard landings, judicious throttle control being the key. Landing attitude was also critical. If the aircraft took the cable before the tailwheel was on the deck or with the main gear wheel on the deck first, the landing would be so hard as to damage the aircraft and likely injure the pilot.

On November 14, the aircraft deployed to NAS Norfolk in anticipation of meeting the carrier the next day. Two NAA reps—Mr. Beaupre and Mr. Joe

This P-51D (44-14017) is prepared for carrier suitability trials on the land-based catapult at NAS Mustin Field, Philadelphia. A hook has been added to an aft fuselage and a holdback bar attached to a bulkhead at the extreme rear with the base of the rudder notched. Despite reports that each main undercarriage post was fitted with a hook for the launch bridle, this photo appears to show an attach point under the fuselage. (*NASA*)

Schaffer—went aboard the vessel that sailed that evening. One of the new Essex class carriers, the USS *Shangri-La* (CV-38) hosted the testing during a shakedown cruise off the Virginia Capes. The carrier suitability trials of the Mustang would be her first flight ops (her own aircraft groups still ashore).

Lieutenant Elder flew out to the carrier late morning on the 15th. His landings were made with 35 kts (40 mph/65 kph) wind over deck. On his first two traps, the lieutenant took the 2 wire. Average cable run-out to bring the aircraft to a stop was 82 feet (25 m). Catapult shots had been so benign in Phily that none were thought necessary shipboard and Elder simply flew the aircraft off each time with as little as 250-foot (76-m) roll. He completed five such cycles before flying back to Norfolk (some sources say he did twenty-five cycles.)

The naval officer assessed the visibility as good, especially given the inline engine. It was still an activity with meager margin for error given scant directional control and a small tolerance for landing attitude when taking the wire to avoid airframe overstress. On wave-off, a too-rapid advance of the throttle could produce a disastrous yaw and abrupt roll. Ultimately, Lt Elder had to conclude that the Mustang was simply unsuitable and likely to suffer many accidents during carrier ops. Fortunately, the capture of Okinawa and Iwo Jima, and rapid preparation for B-29 basing, made shipboard escort unnecessary.

Lieutenant Elder flew the P-51D onto the USS *Shangri-La* on 15 November 1944, executing five arrestments and take-offs. The margin on landing attitude and airspeed was narrow but acceptably safe for the experienced pilot. Here, the tailhook added under the aft fuselage snags an arresting cable with the tailwheel on the deck and the mains still airborne. Visibility over the nose for the landings were judged very good. (*Naval Aviation Archives*)

The P-51D catapults ashore had gone so well that none were performed aboard the carrier. Elder begins one of these take-off rolls (and with what seems every off-duty sailor looking on) that were typically 250-foot (76-m) roll with 35-kt wind over the deck. (*Naval Aviation Archives*)

Sea trials showed the Mustang could be flown onto and off the carrier, but the margin for error was exceptionally narrow. With the wrong attitude on landing, the aircraft could be damaged, and too rapid a throttle advance of take-off could produce a loss of directional control. Ultimately, employment of the P-51D off carriers were not required, although it did encourage North American to perform design studies for nasalized Mustangs. (*Naval Aviation Archives*)

North American did not lose interest in a nasalized Mustang and began conceptual work on a redesigned P-51H optimized for carrier ops as the NA-133. As part of this, they sought to have the baseline P-51H evaluated by the Navy. It was August 1945 before the Navy made time for this. The tall-tail P-51H 44-64420 was transferred to the USN unmodified. Lt-Cdr Elder flew the aircraft from Mustin simply to assess its low-speed handling characteristics. Two flights of thirty minutes each on the 31st found the aircraft superior to the "D" for carrier approaches. However, with the end of the war, this project likewise ended.[10]

The inspiration of the Doolittle Raid was not lost on the Navy. The Grumman XTB2F-1 (Model 55) twin-engined, tricycle-gear torpedo bomber was developed in late 1942–early 1943 at Navy encouragement for the large Essex- and Midway-class carriers. However, the 45,700-lb (10,729-kg) maximum weight and 36-foot (10.7-m) span folded was just too much even for these larger ships. Although canceled in June 1944, the mere fact the USN initiated and sustained such a program illustrates changing attitudes towards twins and "trics." A similar

The Grumman XTB2F-1 is seen in mock-up form on June 11, 1944. Developed as a heavy attack aircraft for the new large carriers, it would have replaced the TBF, SBD, and SB2C, but was judged just too big and heavy. Still, a twin-engined and tricycle-gear airplane pursued by the Navy for eighteen months before cancellation reveals an evolution in thinking as to the suitability of these features for shipboard ops. (*Grumman Historical Center*)

effort was conversion of the F7F (a tricycle gear twin) into a torpedo bomber by distending the belly into a weapons bay and enlarging all aero surfaces for the added weight. Initiated in summer 1944 as the XTSF-1 (Model 66), it was canceled in January 1945 for reasons similar to those killing the TB2F.

When the Marine Corps adopted the B-25 in large numbers during 1944 as the PBJ, thoughts of carrier operations naturally floated up. When considering the concept, the Navy asked the very experienced Royal Navy test pilot Capt. Eric Brown his opinion after he had qualified the twin-engined de Havilland Mosquito fighter-bomber (a tail-dragger) for carrier ops—another example that sparked USN interest. Brown had the opportunity to fly the B-25J in simulated carrier approach and landings ashore and was impressed with the power and control for the machine. He endorsed the concept of PBJ carrier suitability trails.[11]

A project to test the Mitchell's return to the carrier came with PBJ-1H 35277 (B-25H 43-4700). It was structurally modified at the NAA Kansas City Modification Center and then passed to the NAMC in Philadelphia for tailhook and catapult launch equipment installation. The evidence is that fittings were installed on both sides of the forward fuselage for attachment of the catapult launch bridle and on the belly for the holdback. Modifications also included new main wheel axles that permitted limited pivoting to support tighter turns during deck positioning. Shore-based tests were then conducted at Mustin.

The heavily armed Marine Corps PBJ-1H was prepared for carrier suitability trials by North American with main landing gear axles that could pivot to a limited degree. This is demonstrated at Mustin Field on October 4, 1944. The nose gear link pin has probably been pulled to allow such a large towing angle. (*National Museum of Naval Aviation*)

Shipboard trials were performed aboard the *Shangri-La* on November 15, 1944, by Lt-Cdr H. S. "Syd" Bottomley.[12] The aircraft arrived late in the day after initially returning to Norfolk to correct an engine problem. On the first arrestment, the aircraft took the 4 wire and was stopped in 120 feet (36 m). The aircraft was promptly moved to the catapult and shot off at a light 27,000 lb (12,247 kg) and 73 mph (118 kph). Another arrestment, this time intentionally off-center, was hard but successful. It caused some minor damage to the hook mechanism and a tire and may have damaged a main gear door because this separated on the next cat shot. The literature contains several variations of the order in which these events occurred, some stating the door separated on the first arrestment. The aircraft then recovered to Norfolk.

Bottomley was encouraged by the test results, though he recommended the hook shank be lengthened to ensure it would not bounce over a cable on the rebound from a hard landing. By this point, the Navy had little hesitation about twin-engined and tricycle-gear aircraft operating from its decks, as evinced by the Tigercat that performed its first shipboard trials the same day as the PBJ. However, welcoming the PBJ onto its decks for anything but urgent combat needs was unlikely. Had the war progressed into 1946 with an invasion of Japan, PBJ operations from carriers might have been pursued.

More curious is evidence of Navy shore catapult tests with a glider. The Taylorcraft XLBT-1 was intended to be towed aloft and self-stabilize on tow until released, carrying a 2,000-lb (907-kg) bomb. It was then to be directed into a target via a television in the nose and a remote operator, or via autonomous guidance. In tests, it was launched behind a fighter that was catapulted. However,

On November 15, 1944, the PBJ takes an arrestment cable near the fantail of the USS *Shangri-La* and stopped in just 120 feet (37 m). The tailhook is installed under the aft fuselage of the bomber. There is no evidence of a fallen gear door some sources report to have occurred on the first landing. (*San Diego Air & Space Museum and National Museum of Naval Aviation*)

The PBJ had less difficulty moving on the deck of the Essex-class carrier, given the vessel's larger size, than the B-25s of the Doolittle Raiders aboard the *Hornet*. Here the bomber taxis under its own power forward to the catapult, passing opposite the island, rather than being towed. The unusual sight is witnessed by many off-duty sailors. (*National Museum of Naval Aviation*)

This angle on the modified PBJ aboard the *Shangri-La* reveals the attachment of the launch bridle and holdback bar. It is positioned on a catapult forward of the island and so clearance is not an issue, the engines having been shutdown to examine damage entailed during the second arrestment before committing to the take-off. (*National Museum of Naval Aviation*)

an XLBT-1 was shot off the shore catapult at Mustin Field by itself. This required modifications to add two attachments under the nose for the shuttlecock bridle and another for the holdback in line with the main gear. More unusual still is at least the design intent that the glider be catapulted simultaneously with its tow-plane.[13] This was almost certainly never demonstrated (or any catapult from a carrier) and, even with a carrier equipped with side-by-side catapults, would require simultaneous launch with disaster ensuing with even a fraction of a second off in timing. Converted from an airplane, the aircraft was also not optimized as a glider.

The Navy was operating outdated aircraft converted to drone before the war as gunnery practice targets. The technology appeared suitable for weaponization, using the aircraft to attack heavily defended vessels, dropping bombs or torpedoes. This ultimately converged on using the aircraft, carrying explosives, to directly strike targets by flying into them. The assault drones would naturally have to fly from carrier decks and so the first concept demonstrator aircraft, the TDN-1 built by the NAF, was operated briefly from the Navy's training carrier in the Great Lakes, the USS *Sable*. This proved the concept (though one aircraft

Why would anyone want to catapult a glider off a carrier when it would likely splash down within a few hundred yards? The author was unable to uncover an answer, but this photograph is evidence of Philadelphia catapult trials with a Taylorcraft XLBT-1 (85266). The open door is for the safety pilot to enter and the fully compressed nose gear strut suggests the holdback and bridle are fully tensioned. (*National Museum of Naval Aviation*)

A Naval Aircraft Factory TDN-1 drone (no pilot in the cockpit) is positioned to fly off from the training carrier USS *Sable* in Lake Michigan on August 10, 1943. The machine was soon at the bottom of the lake as the remote pilot over-rotated, the aircraft stalled, and it rolled off on a wing at low altitude. The drone was a precursor to the production Interstate TDR-1, but that type never operated from carriers. (*National Archives*)

ended in the lake), but the idea did not advance beyond those tests. No sea trials with the follow-on unmanned types were performed. The drone production program floundered, ship captains having no interest in taking on the unfamiliar and disruptive machines with support personnel plus equipment, and operational practicality was marginal. It would be decades following the war before drones appeared again aboard Navy ships.

12
Miscellaneous Projects

Numerous oddball aviation projects were motivated by combat or safety imperatives and required more engineering daring and innovation. The rapid growth of experience and manufacturing means within the American aviation industry during the war years fostered such skills and a "we can and will do anything" attitude.

Further Advanced Trainers

Building two-seat versions of pursuit airplanes was not the practice in the United States at the time the war came home. Consequently, this meant newly minted fighter pilots had to transition based on the strength of skills learned in advanced trainers, ground procedure training aids, and lectures from flight instructors. This did not always prove suitable, especially as flight training was greatly accelerated and condensed to meet enormous total-war demands for aircrew. The number of accidents became quite a concern.

The North American AT-6 (SNJ to the Navy) was built in several models, with a number of variants of the P&W R-1340 engine possessing 600 to 675 hp (447 to 503 kW), as the advanced trainer for both the U.S. Army and Navy. The common specifications were around 5,150-lb (2,336-kg) GW, maximum 210 mph (338 kph), 1,350-fpm (412-mpm) climb rate, and 24,000-feet (7,315-m) service ceiling. As 1944 approached, frontline single-engined American fighters were powered by over 1,300-hp (969-kW) engines, weighing in at around 10,000 lb (4,536 kg), and bettering 350 mph (563 kph), 3,000 fpm (914 mpm), and 35,000 feet (10,668 m). It was a very big step from the Texan trainer to a hot fighter. The same was true for the advanced twin trainer, the Curtiss AT-9 Jeep for transition to twin-engined fighters. Transitioning to twin-engined bombers like the B-26 was too large a step up for many, including the fact it had tricycle undercarriage while the AT-9 was a taildragger. There were, however, trainer versions of the crewed bombers and transports. The desire for more representative trainers for smoother fighter transition was not addressed by the USAAF during the war, and the Navy effort was too late to yields results before the end of hostilities.

A stopgap was a few machines from several fighter types converted with a second seat, either as an official development or a field modification. However, these lash-ups were not taken to any significant production.

Two-seat trainer P-40s appeared throughout the war, all similar in having the fuselage tank and aft decking removed behind the pilot to accommodate a second cockpit under a sliding canopy aft of a fixed bridging segment. These began with two converted P-40Es (40-582 and -633) to become officially P-40ES, though unofficially referred to as TP-40E. Under a requirement issued on January 7, 1943, and granted the highest priority by Gen. Arnold, the conversion was performed by Bristol Aeronautical Corporation of New Haven, Connecticut, at $5,000 each and delivered that summer.[1] These may have served as patterns for others created in airbase shops. Foreign operators may have done the same because at least one Soviets Lend-Lease example has come to light.

When the USAAF next needed Warhawk trainers, they were created by Curtiss. Thirty P-40Ns were converted in Buffalo, looking much like the Bristol design. The last (44-47924) was delivered on November 2, 1944. One innovation was mirrors mounted ahead of the aft cockpit to provide better vision forward or into the front seat occupied by the student. Once again, it is unclear if these were formally designated TP-40Ns, but that is how they were referred to in service. Curtiss also produced 195 kits for additional conversions. This would exceed demand for P-40 training and so pointed to seeking an advanced trainer more capable then the AT-6. This was admirable use of a dated type no longer suited for frontline service. The conversions reached 107 aircraft by June 7, 1945, when the program was shut down.[2]

A particular oddball was a P-40K (42-10181) converted to train maintenance crews to taxi the fighter. After the original airframe had been damaged in a mishap, it was sent to Buffalo where Curtiss fitted it with a second cockpit possessing just a windscreen and the sliding canopy deleted to make both open cockpits. A welded tube frame under the forward fuselage allowed for a "nose wheel" to prevent over-rotation when advancing the throttle too quickly with the brakes locked and the stick not held back, or learning to taxi in the two-point attitude. This *Susie Q* with "training wheels" was operated at the nearby AAF Technical Training School at Camp Curtissair and later taken over by Curtiss.[3] It was effectively rendered unflyable by the modifications.

Prompted by a request from the Fourth Air Force and the Fourth Fighter Command, by whom conversion training was performed on the west coast, Bell created a two-seat trainer from P-39Q-5 42-20024 at their Niagara Falls facility during the latter half of 1943 to serve as an instrument and gunnery trainer.[4] A second cockpit with minimal instruments for the instructor was grafted in place of the nose armament and the transparencies extended over both cockpits. It had a dorsal fin fillet and a ventral strake to restore adequate directional stability, compensating for the enlarge forebody and so represent the unaltered handling

The North American AT-6 advanced trainers were built for the Army, the Navy (as the SNJ), and foreign customers. Many thousands of successful fighter pilots stepped from the Texan into their combat aircraft, but hundreds also came to grief during the transition. The cost in damaged or wrecked equipment, plus injured or dead cadets, prompted at least the Army to seek a means of smoother transition. (*National Museum of the United States Air Force*)

Like the AT-6, the Curtiss AT-9 was a poor transition to high-performance twin-engined combat types, particularly the P-38 fighter. Like other AT twins, the Jeep was a low-powered, light taildragger while also having engines so close to the centerline to reduce yaw in a single engine-out scenario that the non-feathering props crossed in front of the nose. Training mishaps with the poorly-suited trainer were discouragingly high. (*San Diego Air & Space Museum*)

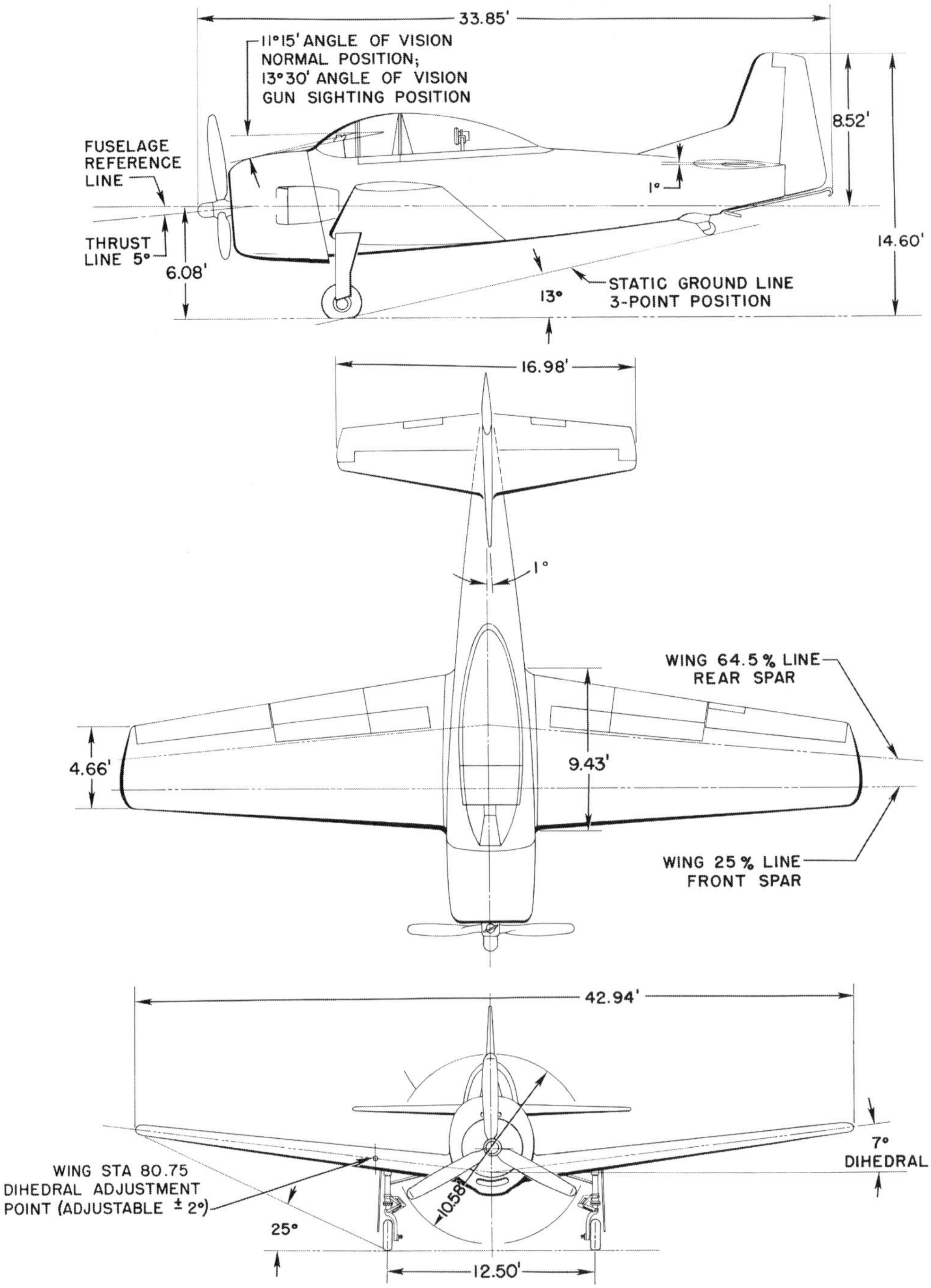

The Navy hesitated to interrupt production of its fighters to create two-seat variants or to seek to fill the performance gap between its trainers and fighters. It was only near the end of the war it gave attention to this subject by seeking a high-performance trainer. It let a contract to North American for the XSN2J-1 shown in this 3-view that only appeared post-war as the T-28 Trojan. (*Author's collection*)

The need for two-seat training versions of fighters drove operators to creating them on their own in capable air base shops or depots. This Soviet example is curious as none of the officially produced "TP-40s" are known to have been supplied to the USSR. The model is unclear but probably an E or K. (*San Diego Air & Space Museum*)

The first official Warhawk conversions were a pair of P-40E fighters to which Bristol Aeronautical added the aft pilot station via their own design (note fixed step for the aft cockpit). The aircraft were used for conversion of pilots coming from advanced training to the type. Designated P-40ES, this example is pictured in 1943 at Luke Field, Arizona, where Chinese pilots were undergoing training. (*Ray Wagner collection*)

This non-flyable P-40K *Susie Q*, shown on May 27, 1943, was modified with two open cockpits and nose 'training wheels' to train maintainers in taxiing the airplane. If the operator revved the engine abruptly with the brakes locked and the stick not held back, the P-40 could go over on its nose to damage the propeller and engine plus cowling. (*National Museum of the United States Air Force* and *San Diego Air & Space Museum*)

One example of the 137 P-40Ns is seen on July 22, 1944. Note the protrusion of the aft sliding canopy and rail extended onto the aft fuselage and relocation of the HF antenna mast farther aft on the spine. Curtiss created some 195 conversion kits but these were not all consumed when the program was halted in summer 1945 with the impending end of the war. (*National Museum of the United States Air Force*)

of the basic P-39. Rolled out on September 16, 1943, the first flight was by Jay Demming and Norman Bethune. The company proposed building kits for service alterations, allowing for ready transition back to standard configuration if needed.

A USAAF evaluation by the 59th Fighter Group at Thomasville AAF, Georgia, found room for improvement. The unofficially designated TP-39 had poor visibility from the front cockpit because of the broad and low-set canopy frame. The rear cockpit was little better. The front was too cramped for suitable control while wearing the standard issue parachutes and the instruments were impossible to read owing to vibration. This station also lacked brake pedals. The aircraft initially possessed a weak interphone between the pilot stations. Most damning was the inability to integrate a suitable gunsight in either cockpit.

Despite the negative evaluation, a dozen P-39Q-20s (Model 39, 44-3879, -3885/7, -3889, -3895, -3897, -3905/6, -3908, -3917/8) were similarly altered, with unclear if any refinements, to become unarmed -22s. These were later designated RP-39Q-22s, the prefix "R" for restricted use. At least two of these odd-appearing machines reached the USSR, who created more on their own with at least variations in canopy construction.

Near the end of 1943, Bell proposed twin-seat Kingcobra conversion kits based on the P-63A-10 as the TP-63A-10 (Model 38), but the Army evinced no interest.

The original P-39 trainer is shown without the wartime censoring that removed the tail number and building in the background from most reproductions of this image. It makes clear this was a P-39Q-5 and not the P-39F long misidentified as the Bell-designated TP-39 (see unique nose marking). The Air Forces evaluation of the aircraft found it unsuitable. (*Jay Miller collection*)

Major William Angus emerges from the forward cockpit of the TP-39 to be greeted by Bell's chief test pilot Robert M. Stanley during flight trials. The USAAF found the front seat too cramped with the seat pack parachute shown, the instruments unreadable, and the lack of brakes unacceptable, not to mention a nearly useless intercom system. Nonetheless, Bell was contacted to build twelve more of the Model 39 with uncertain improvements. (*Jay Miller collection*)

One of the RP-39Q-22 trainers is shown in American markings, though several are known to have been passed to the USSR. It does not show any change to the canopy from the TP-39 despite reports that this was improved with better and higher blending between cockpits. How successful the model was in service is unclear, but the AAF did not go for any TP-63As when Bell offered similar conversion to the Kingcobra. (*Jay Miller collection*)

However, the Soviets converted at least two P-63As (42-69304, 42-70503) and a P-63C (43-11334) as trainers based on the TP-39 design.[5] Bell was preparing two P-63Es (43-11728 and -11735) in 1945 with a second cockpit under a bubble canopy well aft on the fuselage, behind the engine.[6] The cockpit lacked controls and was intended strictly for the observer/photographer during safety chase missions, the XS-1 glide tests being one intended user of the machines. The end of the war left the aircraft as surplus and the conversions were completed on Bell funds.

On the strength of the P-40ES results, two P-47G-15-CUs (42-25266/7) were modified at the Curtiss plant in Evansville, Indiana, where the Thunderbolts were built. A second cockpit displacing some fuselage fuel volume forward of the original cockpit and the canopy extended forward. These TP-47Gs kept their weapons and were employed for advanced instruction in tactics. Curtiss converted a G as the TP-47G-16 for gunnery training. The Eighth Air Force converted a P-47C and two Ds to "Doublebolts" as field modifications for training, liaison, and radar intercept test machines. One such was a war-weary P-47D (42-75276) with the cockpit placed aft of the original, displacing equipment. The canopy over the aft cockpit opened to the right side. Operated by the 63rd Fighter Squadron at RAF Boxted, 56th Fighter Group, CG management was more critical in this configuration.

One of the two TP-47Gs is shown in flight with all wing guns present. Unlike some or all of the few field modifications, the added cockpit went in forward of the original "pit," greatly reducing the capacity of the forward fuselage fuel tank. Note that the forward cockpit (occupied here by a woman) has the mirror above the canopy bow. (*American Aviation Historical Society*)

The desire to carry a second person aloft in the P-38 was driven by an urgent need to demonstrate emergency procedures and other orientation for pilots transitioning to the type. Numerous accidents were claiming aircraft and lives, lending the aircraft an undeserved reputation. Brigadier General Barney Giles, then commanding the 4th Air Service Area Command in Northern California, offered the solution after Army and Lockheed engineers had said it could not be done. He converted three or four "trainers" to be the core of an advanced transition course established at Muroc, though the configuration is unclear.[7]

Further efforts saw "piggyback" measures with the individual squeezing into the equipment space behind the pilot, after moving some gear, with the passenger sitting on the wing spar and hunched over under the canopy. A restraint belt and intercom connection were provided for this "jump seat" that would have been deemed unsafe under peacetime conditions. The first such was a modified Lockheed flight test bird, a P-38E (41-1986) flown in 1942 with altered tail booms for a notional seaplane variant. The flight test engineer in the jump seat greatly relieved the workload of the test pilot. An F (41-7485) piggyback followed for testing and flight demonstrations. A number of similar two-seat P-38s were created via field modifications or factory conversions, some referred to unofficially as TP-38Js and TP-38L-1s.[8] However, other than basic familiarization and incentive flights, little training could be performed as no dual controls were possible as far as is known.

When Lockheed designed and built the P-38M night fighter, a major change to the center pod was necessary to create a proper seat for the radar operator under a taller canopy segment. Again, there were no dual controls and leg room was skoosh. Only a short and slender man found the accommodations comfortable. For the Lockheed *Swordfish* test aircraft described in Chapter 2, the center pod underwent major alterations to fit the full second cockpit, work that was likely beyond the scope of any field organization. Likewise, the radical "Jollie" testbed described in Chapter 8 was not a suitable trainer configuration. The Droop Snoot and Pathfinder modifications that added a bombardier station in an extended nose, sacrificing the guns, was a cramped station not known to have been fitted with dual controls. No other attempts to place a second pilot ahead of the common "pit" are known to have been undertaken. At least one rescue was performed by a downed pilot sitting in the lap of his squadron mate. Transport pods were also developed from under-wing drop tanks to transport personnel, wounded, or vital small cargo.

These men are demonstrating how a second individual could squeeze in behind the pilot of this P-38F. Some modifications could allow for this uncomfortable and unsafe arrangement, to include interphone between the two persons and a restraint harness. Despite the importance of the Lightning, a true two-seat configuration was just not practical given the design layout. (*National Archives*)

Lockheed created a "Piggy-Back" Lightning out of this P-38F to support flight testing and demonstrations, but the observer has only slightly less uncomfortable and at least the pilot did not feel his passenger's breath on his neck. The flight still likely ended with an aching back and knocks on the head if padding was not placed against the overhead canopy. Field piggy-back modifications were likely of this variety. (*National Museum of the United States Air Force*)

Photographed on May 10, 1945, a special modification to at least this one YP-59A is evident. The opening at the top of the nose with a shallow windscreen is for a flight test engineer, although many "demo rides" were undertaken as well. Similar to the Lockheed piggy-back P-38s, this second seat allowed the engineer to collect test data in flight from instruments in the nose volume normally occupied by guns and ammunition. (*Tony Landis collection*)

Following the same pattern, squadrons occasionally modified war-weary P-51Bs (sometimes denoted with a "WW" stenciled on the tail) with a seat aft of the normal pilot station, usually employing the standard canopy parts. Many of these had just a seat in back to serve as a "hacks," ferrying personnel or vital parts and mail, or providing incentive flights for praiseworthy individuals. They were often painted with garish colors and markings for unit esprit or to act as lead aircraft for flights to join up as a formation before breaking away.

Like the P-38, it is believed some "Piggyback" P-51Ds were created as field alterations for familiarization flights, the second individual crouching under the canopy in the small space behind the pilot seat after moving some gear. One field modification was to permit Gen. Eisenhower to inspect the D-Day landing beaches from above Normandy. Ten two-seat TP-51D trainers (44-84610/11 and 45-11443/50) were converted under contract in 1944 from airplanes newly built at the Dallas plant. The fuselage tank was removed and radio gear plus battery relocated. These had complete dual controls and instruments for the instructor who sat low in the rear cockpit under a revised canopy that still left meager headroom. The canopy rail on the spine was extended farther aft and the high-frequency antenna from the vertical tail was attached to the side of the fuselage *versus* through the canopy. The tailwheel was rendered non-retractable by the modification and so the associated wheel doors were removed. Several more TP-51Ds were converted later, some under taller canopies. Wing guns were commonly reduced to four from six, but performance was essentially unchanged. A TP-51M was completed in Dallas on August 14, 1945, but it may have been immediately sent on to the storage depot and scrapped without having been taken up by the USAAF.[9]

Navy fighter training requirements demanded two-seat machines no less urgently than the Army, but the service resisted diverting production assets for such an undertaking. The only example of a two-seat naval fighter trainer to come to light is an F4U-1D Corsair converted by Vought as an unsolicited proposal. The second cockpit was installed ahead of the standard "pit," displacing a fuselage fuel tank. In compensations, fuel was added in the belly and wings, the latter displacing some guns and ammunition, though still with a 26 percent deficit. This V-354 "High Speed Corsair Trainer" almost certainly had the approval of the USN but, coming in 1945 and pitched just after hostilities when resources were shrinking rapidly, it was not approved for production. The single example was ordered restored to its original configuration.

War-weary bombers of every type were used as trainers, enabled by the dual controls common to the type, and sometimes designated with a prefix "T." However, the advent of the very advanced Boeing Superfortress, which was going to be pushed rapidly into combat, demanded other solutions. Training of B-29 crews was especially challenging because of the higher level of technical savvy required compared with earlier bombers. Gunners did not simply have to swing a gun, reload, and clear jams, but instead operated a sophisticated gunsight for remote control of a turret. Training of these men necessarily began before the Superfortress

This P-51D (44-84610) is one of ten Mustangs modified in Dallas with a rear seat under a taller canopy. Equipment was relocated to accommodate the second cockpit with duplicate controls and instruments for the instructor. Similar modifications were created by field organizations. (*NASA*)

This poor but unique image shows the rare two-seat F4U-1D in 1945, and possibly a non-flying mock-up. The modification gave generous canopy space and would probably have had value. However, the Navy never devoted resources for such assets during the war and had little to devote after. (*Vought Historical Archives*)

Training of B-29 gunners, employing new computing gunsights and remote-controlled turrets, begun before the bomber was available in large numbers. This used modified B-24s with two turrets and gunner stations, as shown here by this B-24L. Note the gunsight added in the aft fuselage and nose, and the three turrets without guns (the aircraft at the Kingman, Arizona, storage depot awaiting disposition). (*San Diego Air & Space Museum*)

was available. This employed 160 outmoded B-24Es modified with with engineer stations to serve as the General Electric fire control system, the power turrets, and improvised sighting stations.[10] In 1944, several B-24Ls (initially designated RB-24Ls then TB-24L) had chin, dorsal, ventral, and tail barbettes and modified noses to train B-29 crewmen. Other types had "TB-" trainers and did not resort to surrogates like the B-24Ls for the B-29. So, these modified B-24s may have been intended only to sustain the B-29 fleet until after the initial rush to get it into combat.[11] For example, B-24s were also modified with flight engineer stations to serve as trainers for B-29 flight engineers until Superfortress trainers became available.[12]

Escort Dead End

By summer 1940, the pre-war notion of bomber invulnerability had been demonstrated by the air fighting in Europe as far from unassailable. Although the Americans had yet to experience this first-hand, they felt confident their well-rehearsed approach of daylight precision bombing via mass formations providing mutual defensive fire and accompanied by escorting fighters—at least for a portion if the mission range—would prove at least as effective as the RAF's night-time bombing of area targets. However, although it would be autumn 1942 before the AAF conducted its first bombing missions from the British Isles, they wasted no time in hedging their bet. In June 1941, the Experimental Engineering Section at Wright Field was instructed to explore the possibilities of a "convoy protector aircraft." They hit on the notion of several bombers converted to heavily armed "destroyer escorts" helping defend the formation from enemy interceptors during daylight missions.

The "bombardment escorter airplane" would possess the necessary performance to maintain formation by virtue of being the same type bomber. However, it would have at least two .50-cal guns covering all points in the sphere surrounding the aircraft, with additional armor and leak-proof tanks. Basic requirements were a 1,700-mile (2,736-km) range, no bombs carried, and continuous firing to the rear for four minutes, upper and lower turrets with two minutes of firing, side weapons one minute, and front thirty seconds.[13] This plan was endorsed by senior AAF leadership on September 17, 1941 and a program was kicked off on April 16, 1942. It was to perform experimental conversions to B-17s and B-24s to become B-40s and B-41s, respectively. The 8th Air Force in England provided an August 1942 document detailing requirements for the "convoy escort" and urged completion in six months or February 1943.

As a preliminary effort, Eglin Field modified a B-17F and a B-24D with a Bendix chin turret. The B-17 installation was driven via gunsight in both elevation and azimuth while the B-24 had the sight driving elevation only and azimuth manually controlled. The B-17 design proved superior.[14]

An XB-40 was created under MX-204 by Vega from B-17F 41-24341 on a $161,320 contract. The bomber was delivered to the Cheyenne Modification Center, Wyoming, on August 2, 1942, and was completed in just a month, on September 9. The XB-40 was then delivered to Eglin Field for trials. It had been given additional armor for a total of 2,150 lb (977 kg), a Bendix remote powered chin turret with two .50s and 400 rpg under a more streamlined plex nose, and United Shoe Machinery Corporation (USMC) hydraulically powered twin gun mounts (from a nose turret) at the waist stations (300 rpg), and USMC hydraulic power boost added for the tail guns (550 rpg). All told, the armament totaled fourteen (seven pairs) of .50 cal. A 6,600-lb (2,994-kg) bomb capacity was retained.

The XB-40 was returned to Vega on September 18, 1942, for additional work, flying again on November 10 before delivery on the 17th. A second Martin dorsal turret (two .50s and 400 rpg) had been added in place of the single, ball-mounted radio compartment station gun. After originally appearing with the turret placed in a cut-out of the top fairing from the cockpit enclosure, this was altered to an elegant close-out of the fairing ahead of the second dorsal turret for greater firing coverage. The aircraft typical carried 5,800 ready rounds and 6,500 for reload, but this could be raised to 17,265 (over two tons of ammunition) by trading fuel and by placing some ammunition in the bomb bay.

In the final configuration, the XB-40's empty weight was 2,898 lb (1,315 kg) above the baseline B-17F's. Without bombs, it grossed 3,000 lb (1,361 kg) more than the F, and maximum gross was within 2,205 lb (1,000 kg). Service ceiling was 29,200 feet (8,900 m)—8,300 feet (1,006 m) below the unmodified bomber.

A September 29, 1942, contract supported the creation of the XB-41 by Consolidated in San Diego from B-24D 41-11822 under MX-320. The aircraft,

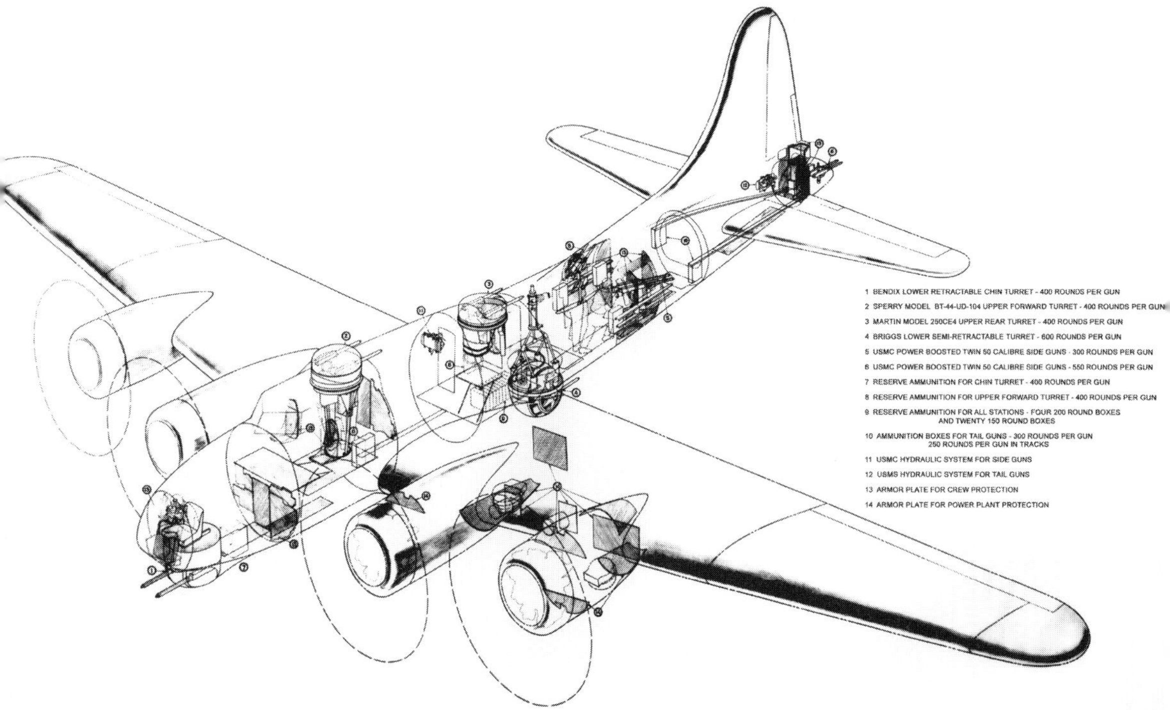

The period XB-40 drawing provides a fine guide to the installed armaments and armor. Special note is made of hydraulic boost for the heavy moving elements and the ammunition feed chutes. The exceptional weight of all these weapons and ammunition can be appreciated by the overview. (*Gerald Balzer collection*)

The XB-40 was developed to explore the potential of the B-17 to serve as the basis for a bomber formation "destroyer escort." This was to help defend against enemy interceptors. The new chin turret, added dorsal turret, and twin-mount waist guns are evident in this image from Burbank in November 1942. (*Gerald Balzer collection*)

as delivered to California on October 25, already with the Bendix chin turret (400 rpg) and so was probably the airframe subject to the Eglin modification and trials. It also already possessed a Motor Products tail turret (800 rpg). The Consolidated work featured a second Martin dorsal turret (400 rpg) added mid-fuselage, 400 rpg for the Bendix chin turret, twin-gun power-assisted mounts at each waist station (250 rpg), and 800 rpg for the Motor Products tail turret. With each a dual-gun installation, this added up to fourteen .50 cal machine guns. The forward dorsal turret with 400 rpg had to be raised, the added structure surrounded by a fairing, to avoid the added unit restricting its field of fire. The Briggs ball turret used 550 rpg. The starboard waist .50s with 250 rpg were in the open gun port while the port pair were inside a protruding, shallow plexiglass fairing that rotated to the sides with the guns within fairings and with an air deflector ahead. Of the 12,420 rounds of ammunition on board, 4,100 was stored in the forward bomb bay.[15] Armor amounted to 1,980 lb (898 kg). The work ran to $26,500.

At least eight test flights of the XB-41 were performed in San Diego before the January 29, 1943, delivery to Eglin. The tests at Eglin ran from February 2 to the 13th. It found this very heavy aircraft had stability problems engendered by an unfavorably aft CG and so was very difficult to maneuver, in addition to poor climb rate and low ceiling. Empty weight was 4,900 lb (2,223 kg) above the baseline "D," and gross weight without bombs was 1,000-lb (454-kg) short of the maximum of 64,000 lb (29,030 kg). Service ceiling was reduced from 32,000 feet (9,754 m) to just 28,500 feet (8,687 m), 14 mph (23 kph) was knocked off the top speed, and fuel consumption was high.

The XB-41 went to Wright Field on February 24 while the Engineering Division considered its options. The immediate reaction was to incorporate the latest improvements from the Liberator production line. Hence, it returned to San Diego to be altered with wide-blade propellers, B-17F Bendix chin turret gunsight, the forward dorsal turret returned to its original height, elimination of some armor, and ammunition was redistributed. The port waist bubble caused visual distortion for the gunner and buffeting, and so was removed. This work added another $50,456 to the program.

Plans to procure thirteen YB-41s was first broached on January 12, 1943, because of delays with the YB-40s. It was suggested 100 was a more practical and cost-effective number, but the January 15 contract change added just the thirteen YB-41s. However, this was then canceled on March 16 and was not to be reconsidered until the XB-41 had proven suitable.

The XB-40 was apparently judged adequate as it became the configuration for thirteen YB-40 service test machines ordered on October 11, 1942. Although Vega had proposed a V-140 production design, the contract went to Douglas. These were B-17Fs flown in November 1942 to the Tulsa Modification Center. They were delivered from February 28 through March 14, 1943, at a cost of $470,000. Some were seen in service with another machine gun projecting from each side transparency in the nose, to be fired by the navigator. The YB-40s were deployed to England in May 1943 for combat trials with the 8th AF, 92nd Bombardment

A B-24D was turned into the XB-41 as another escort bomber experiment. The forward fuselage of the XB-40 gives a view of the raised dorsal turret while showing the added chin turret. The dorsal turret was later returned to normal height. (*San Diego Air & Space Museum*)

The aft fuselage of the XB-41 reveals the added dorsal turret, raised forward turret, twin guns in the starboard waist station, and new tail turret. The aircraft suffered an aft CG condition and so has had blocks placed under the tail skid in the event the aircraft tipped backwards. It was too heavy and unwieldy for practical use. (*American Aviation Historical Society*)

Initially, the port waist guns of the XB-41 were in a rotating plex bubble (insert) instead of an open area also shown. However, the transparency (note air deflector ahead) caused visual distortion for the gunner and generated disturbing buffet. It was subsequently removed. (*Lloyd Jones collection and San Diego Air & Space Museum*)

The twin .50-cal gun mounts at the waist stations of a YB-40 shows the complex and high-quality installation performed by Douglas. Hydraulics assisted the gunner in moving the heavy gun assembly, and overhead ammunition feed chutes ensured a continuous supply. An original feed had the ammunition boxed below the guns. (*Air Force Test Center*)

Group, although one was written off in a crash landing during the journey. By that time, the USAAF bombing offensive was suffering grave losses and there was keen interest in the escort concept.

The YB-40s participated in nine combat missions between May 29 and July 4, 1943, claiming five kills and two probables against one escort felled by AAA. They were not judged successful, as made clear in a June 29, 1943, report from Maj.-Gen. Ira Eaker. The aircraft were near their GW limits, tail-heavy, and draggy. Climb rate and handling were poor. All this made for frustrating formation flying. During the homeward flight, even without bombs, the performance of the still-heavy escort was too different from the bomber formation (relieved of bombs) it was to protect. The formation had to decrease its speed to allow the escorts to keep up, extending the exposure to enemy defenses. The heavily armed escort would become vulnerable if trailing alone. Not dropping bombs at the end of a long and hazardous flight into enemy airspace did little to boost the morale of the escorter crews. Even if performance could be made to match, the aircraft appeared to contribute little that suitably armed bombers in a proper formation could not deliver themselves, and neither was a substitute for true long-range fighter escort. Any combat use was ended in August.[16]

Eglin took the XB-41 again on July 28, 1943. Tests included side-by-side comparisons with a standard Liberator. Reporting on August 5, they concluded that while the CG issue was resolved, maneuverability was still unacceptable. On October 19, they reported the machine would never be suitable for combat and recommended discontinuing the effort. The AAF Board weighed in on November 15 with the same conclusion. By that time, the YB-40s had discredited the convoy

This angle on the YB-40 indicates the concentrated fire the "destroyer" could deliver. However, it also suggests the heavy weight all the armament added to the aircraft at the expense of bombs and speed. These were impediments to its mission and the YB-40 was no substitute for fighters. *(Lloyd Jones collection)*

escort concept and no more work was undertaken. The effort was terminated at the end of 1943, and, in January 1944, the XB-41 was moved to Training Command as a TB-24D.

The B-17 conversion process had continued based on a requirement for two additional aircraft per month for six months beginning in March. Only one of these joined the others in England. After some vacillation, the effort was terminated in September 1943. Just eleven of these added dozen escorts were completed. With program cancellation, the machines were to go to Training Command, so four were configured as trainers. Completed were twenty YB-40s (Vega Model V139-3 from B-17F 42-5732/44, 5871, 5920/21, 5923/25, 5927) and four TB-40s (from B-17F 42-5833/34, 5872, 5926). Some were employed in armament trials and all eventually found a role in Stateside gunnery training. The one benefit was the B-40 chin turret being adopted for the B-17G. The entire bombardment escort undertaking was terminated on June 3, 1944, when Washington made clear there was no requirement for such aircraft. Total cost had been $569,000.

On August 23, 1941, it had been decided that each new bomber would have a variant that could serve as a formation escort, at least until suitable long-range fighters became available. Hence, the fourth YB-29 (41-36957) was modified in 1943 to explore Superfortress potential as an escort with twenty-three weapons. The normal compliment consisted of forward and aft, top and bottom, turrets with dual .50s (the top forward turret later given four .50s), all remotely controlled via three sighting blisters, and a tail turret with two .50s and a 20-mm cannon. Added to the YB-29 was an experimental ERCO nose ball turret with two .50 guns and four side Emerson Model 126 barbettes—two forward of the wing and two replacing the aft gunner blisters, each with two .50-cal weapons. The barbettes were of low profile and remotely controlled. The four centerline turrets were replaced with ones possessing two .50s and a 20-mm cannon, while the tail cannon was replaced with a 30-mm weapon. Although tested, nothing more came of the effort, possibly because the escort concept had been discredited by that time.

The B-26 was also considered in July 1943 for escorting heavy bomber formations after its effectiveness as a bomber was questioned.[17] An H-model was envisioned with a second dorsal turret in the navigator's station, a ventral ball turret with four .50s, revised tail turret, and two 20-mm cannon in the nose. The waist gunner stations would be deleted and armor added. Much would be removed to help compensate for the added weight, including the second pilot. The B-26H was dropped before metal was cut because escort fighters' range was being progressively increased to render the escort bomber unnecessary.

The B-29 was also considered for bomber escort and one of the YB-29s (41-36957) was modified with expanded armament once it became available following baseline testing. This distant side-view shows the numerous machine gun and cannon turrets protruding from the fuselage. The retractable AN/APQ-13 radar bombsight radome is extended between the bomb bays and main landing gear. (*National Museum of the United States Air Force*)

In the nose of the modified YB-29 is the experimental ERCO ball turret. Farther back is the teardrop barbette, a zipper slot supporting azimuth gun traverse. Above is the top forward turret with a 20mm cannon joining the two guns. (*National Museum of the United States Air Force*)

This view shows one of four centerline turrets, each with two .50-cal MGs and a 20-mm cannon (an installation like that in the typical B-29 tail turret). The port side turret replaced the gunner's sighting blister. With all eight turrets remotely controlled and two of four sighting stations eliminated, there seems to have been a paucity of gunner positions given three more turrets above the standard B-29 configuration. (*San Diego Air & Space Museum*)

The idea of increasing the armament on the Marauder (B-26C shown) to serve as a heavy bomber escort included adding another turret over the fore-body, a ball turret (potentially in the bomb bay) with for MGs, and twin 20-mm cannons in the nose. The rounds storage plus feed chutes, placing the machine near its maximum gross weight, would surely have eliminated the bombing capability. (*National Museum of the United States Air Force*)

Atomic Bombers

The Boeing B-29s converted to deliver the first atomic weapons were another example of American aircraft modification prowess, discounting the remarkable story of the A-bomb's development itself. The Manhattan Project was initiated in September 1942 with the goal of producing the "special weapons" by July 1944. This monumental effort was the most secret and costly weapon system program in the country, and likely the world. It was undertaken because of the hope it could bring the war to an early end and save tens of thousands of lives. From the earliest days of the effort, aerial delivery as a bomb was considered the most practical means of application. The bombs were expected to be enormous in dimensions and weight, with long range delivery also anticipated. Only the B-29, then still in development and with a maximum 20,000-lb (9,072-kg) bomb capacity, was likely to be the only suitable bomber for such a mission.

The Project Alberta, or simply Project A, an element of the larger program, worked to adapt the weapons and the aircraft for the atomic strike mission. As the project progressed, the Superfortress entered mass production. Several of the bombers were selected for modification and training of crews while the weapons remained in early design. The aircraft effort was codenamed Silverplate.

The earliest concern was ensuring the bomber delivering the "gadget" would not be caught in the blast effects. A drop from very high altitude gave time during the descent (about forty-five seconds) for the aircraft to turn away and put sufficient distance between it and the explosive shock wave plus radiation flash. The extent of these effects could only be estimated, but all would need to be done to plan for the worse case until data were available. Accurate delivery of the bombs required ballistics data to be collected.

The first test drops of proposed atomic bombs, scaled shapes, occurring on August 13, 1943, at the Dahlgren Naval Proving Ground, Virginia, with a Grumman TBF.[18] Ballistics was also behind a "souped-up" B-17E at Wright Field during summer 1943 to carry a 6,000-lb (2,722-kg) bomb load to 40,000 feet (12,192 m). Dropping weapons from that unusually high release altitude would permit the data to be acquired without waiting for one of the then-rare Superfortresses to become available. The "featherweight" aircraft was stripped of non-essentials. Special performance engines plus superchargers were mounted to permit a climb above the normal service ceiling of 36,600 feet (11,156 m), to which the B-17 seldom ventured. On a July 16 flight, the crew of the *Ready Teddy* made it to a chilly 43,800 feet (13,350 m). In the descent, the No. 1 engine propeller ran away and eventually nearly shook the engine off the wing, and the wing from the fuselage, before the prop departed the aircraft. Eventually, the team worked up to dropping weapons over Chesapeake Bay in front of a special ground-based camera at Aberdeen Proving Ground, Maryland, from which the ballistics data were extracted. Only later did the Wright Field crew understand that their work had contributed to the Manhattan Project.[19]

The earliest conceived bomb shape was codenamed Thin Man, expected to weight 8,000 lb (3,629 kg). This was to be a gun-type plutonium weapon with a charge firing a cone of fissile material at a sphere of the same material into which the cone fit to create a critical mass and initiate the explosive chain reaction release of nuclear energy. To keep the two portions a safe distance apart until triggered meant a bomb of 17.0 feet (5.2 m) length with a 1.9-foot (0.6-m) diameter bulbous head, thin middle of cannon barrel (unrifled naval gun tube), and the initiator rear with aerodynamic fins 3.2 feet (1.0 m) across. Modification of a B-29 to carry this bomb was performed under MX-469, codenamed Pullman.

Aircraft 42-6259, among the very earliest production aircraft from Seattle, Washington, was flown to Wright Field's Engineering Division in early December 1943 for the modifications, completed on February 1, 1944. The dual bomb bays, separated by bulkheads and a retractable bombing radar radome, was modified to a single bay with new twin doors replacing the two pair.[20] Bomb racks and other hardware were removed or altered to support a single weapon in the unitary bay. Two modified glider tow mechanisms were employed to suspend the bomb via its two lugs.

The initial gun-type atomic weapon had a very long and slender shape. Codenamed "Thin Man," this 8,000-lb (3,629-kg) store is shown on a transport trailer positioned within the unitary bomb bay of B-29 42-6259, its thin profile allowing it to fit under the wing box beam seen above. The modification to create the singular bay with long bay doors was performed at Wright Field in December 1943 and January 1944. (*National Atomic Museum Foundation*)

The initial drop tests of dummy Thin Man shapes began at Muroc on March 3, 1944. On the 16th, a dummy fell free with the bay doors closed. Although the bay was then opened and the shape jettisoned, the doors were badly damaged. The aircraft was returned to Dayton for repairs. Newly designed doors were substituted, driven by three electric motors replacing the production pneumatics, along with revised bomb release mechanisms. Further drop tests at Muroc followed in June. However, the Thin Man design was abandoned because insufficient velocity within the gun could be achieved to produce the desired explosive yield due to premature initiation of the chain reaction before the wedge impacted the core. However, new bombs had emerged with outer shapes developed by Caltech.

The new gun-type bomb employed uranium and was named Little Boy. It had a projectile ring that slid over target rings to "assemble" the critical mass. This weapon ultimately weighed in at 8,900 lb (4,037 kg) and was 10.0-feet (3.1-m) long and 2.3-feet (0.7-m) in diameter with a 12.5-kton yield. Just 141 lb (64 kg) of uranium was contained in the casing. Following take-off, crewmen removed protective features that prevented accidental detonation and installed the cordite firing explosive in the gun breech. Another fission bomb under development had a 4.5-foot (1.4-m) diameter sphere of explosives focusing pressure like a lens onto a thick 1.5-foot (0.5-m) diameter aluminum sphere inside which was uranium and at the center, a 3.6-inch (9.1-cm) plutonium core weighing 35.2 lb (16.0 kg). At the very center of the core was a polonium-beryllium initiator which naturally triggered the chain reaction once the core was crushed to a super-critical condition by the focused explosives to yield 22 ktons. This Fat Man bomb weighed 10,300 lb (4,672 kg); it was 10.7 feet (3.3 m) long and 5.0 feet (1.5 m) in diameter. Both weapons were radar-fused for detonation at around 2,000 feet (610 m) altitude. The radar was a tail warning system from a fighter airplane. Fusing was inhibited until fifteen seconds after release from the bomber—preventing premature fusing from radar signals reflecting from the airplane—by timers that were started by wires pulled out as the bomb departed the bay. A barometer was another feature inhibiting arming until low altitude. With all signals positive, powered by batteries, the firing took place followed a tiny fraction of a second later by detonation.

Aircraft 42-6359 was again altered to carry one of these weapons from a single bomb lug. A British bomb shackle and release mechanisms for their 12,000-lb (5,443-kg) deep-penetration bomb, dropped from a Lancaster bomber, replaced the glider tow hardware. An adapter kit permit swap between the Fat Man, considered the standard weapon, and the Little Boy. The newer bombs could fit in a single bay and so the prototype 6259 was modified again to restore the twin bays. Photographs show a Fat Man bomb in the forward bay with unitary doors spanning both bays, so some tests were performed before reversion to the dual bays. These may have been just fit checks. Drop tests of the two new bomb shapes and associated equipment began in September 1944 and continued for several months at a number of locations in Utah and California to include Inyokern and the Salton Sea ranges. During one of these tests, a Little Boy shape prematurely dropped off range and was never recovered.

The Little Boy (top, being prepared at Tinian) and Fat Man (bottom, in loading pit) fusion bombs each weighed approximately five tons and were suspended in the B-29 forward bomb bay by a single lug. A conventional bomb version of the Fat Man, with 6,300 lb (2,858 kg) of high explosives, was dropped in combat as a further means of training the squadron that prepared to deliver the top-secret atomic weapons. (*National Atomic Museum Foundation*)

The Pullman prototype was damaged in a landing mishap in late 1944 and replaced with seventeen similarly modified aircraft under codenames Silverplate and W-47. The Martin-built machines were altered at Omaha, Nebraska, with deliveries beginning in mid-October 1944. The shorter weapons were carried in the forward bay and produced a nose-heavy condition mandating a rearrangement of aircrew and equipment aft to compensate. Operationally, an extended-range fuel tank was carried in the aft bay. A new "weapon officer" or "weaponeer" station was installed beside the radio operator, in the aircraft's forward pressurized compartment, to monitor and prepare the bomb to drop. Centerline gun turrets, gunner sighting stations and side blisters, fire control computer, and associated armor were removed after delivery. The sighting blister openings were covered with plates containing a small scanning window. This left only the tail gunner's armor and weapons. The weight savings and drag reduction improved aircraft performance.

These airplanes were intended for operational employment and so used in training crews of the 393rd Bomb Squadron (Very Heavy) under the 509th Composite Group with all the organizational elements to support and launch the atomic bombing mission. Their principal base became remote Wendover AAF, Utah, where they took up their first Silverplate aircraft in October 1944 and began practicing the bomb delivery techniques. The bombs were to be dropped near the operational ceiling, above 30,000 feet (9,144 m), to permit the bomber time to turn away and escape the blast zone as the weapon fell. A 155-degree diving turn, placing the tail of the aircraft towards the explosion, was judged sufficient for protection provided it stayed above 25,000 feet (7,620 m). The team continued dropping inert shapes of the proposed bombs as part of the ongoing testing and development of the ballistics tables.

Three more groups of Silverplate deliveries continued for a total of twenty-nine during 1945, some of these new rather than machines sent to a modification center. The newest engines, Wright R-3350-41s with fuel injection, were installed along with the reversible-pitch Curtiss Electric propellers. They retained the ability to drop general purpose bombs. Bomb bay doors remained pneumatically actuated for fast motion. Deliveries began in April 1945; these are the B-29s that went to war against Japan, with fifteen deployed. The work was so extensive that each aircraft required 3,469 man-hours and they were the finest Superforts fielded during the conflict. The effort became the highest priority program in the Air Forces as an element of the nation's penultimate secret program.

The size of the A-bombs made it necessary to first lower it beneath ground level, position the aircraft over the 8.0-foot (2.4-m) deep concrete-lined pit, and then raise the bomb into the bay. In some cases, the bomb was lowered via a crane to be placed on a cradle. The bomb and cradle were then raised via a hydraulic lift in the bottom of the pit. The cradle had fine position adjustment to align the bomb lug with the bay shackle. In other cases, the bomb and cradle were on a trailer rolled on tracks over the pit. The lift raised the trailer and bomb so that the tracks could be removed. The lift rotated the trailer 90 degrees before lowering all.

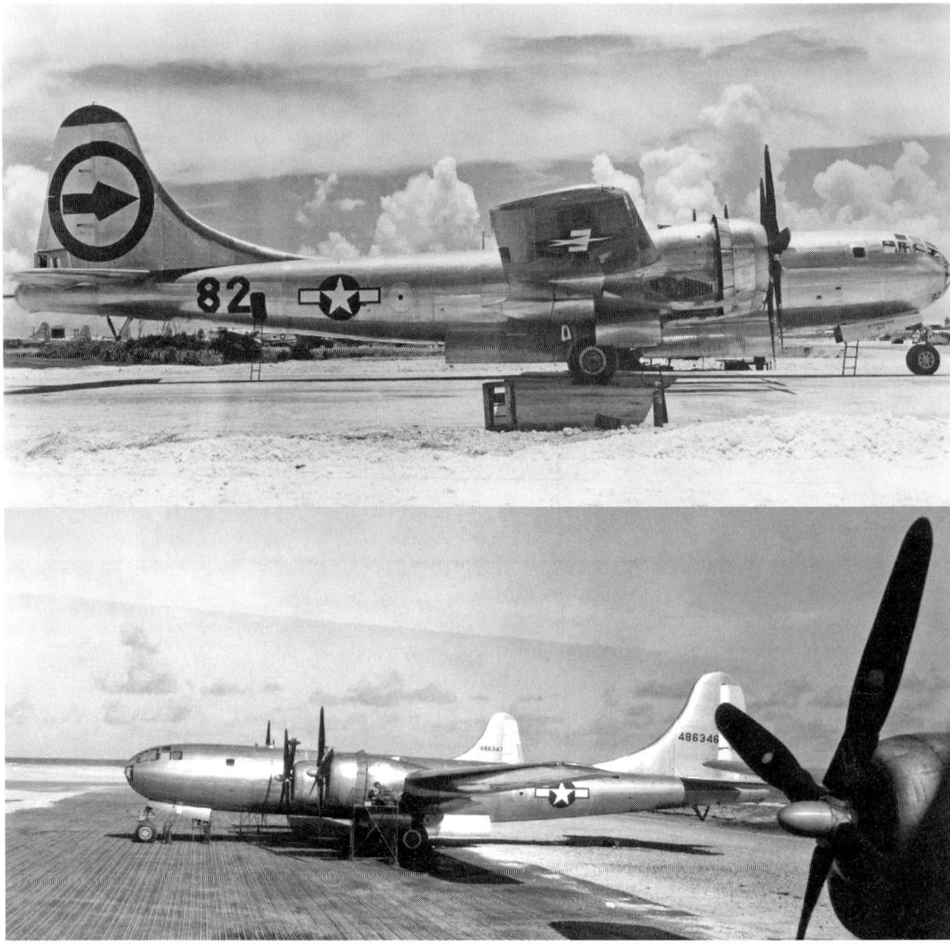

For the mission to deliver the atomic bombs, the latest models and newest B-29s were selected, then specially modified. The most obvious external identification is the removal of the gun turrets and gunner sighting blisters, all openings covered with aluminum plates, leaving only the tail guns. Seen on Tinian is a pair of these Silverplate B-29s including the renowned *Enola Gay*. (*The Peter M. Bowers Collection/The Museum of Flight and National Atomic Museum Foundation*)

The bomber was pushed backward over the pit or positioned itself by reversing props.[21] The bomb cradle was disconnected from the trailer such that it and the weapon could be lifted into the bomb bay. After lifting and attachment, sway braces were installed and fine details of the bomb like radar altimeter antennas were installed and aircraft power connected until ready to drop. With the 5-ton bomb and fuel for a roughly 3,000-mile (4,828-km) round trip, the aircraft was several thousand pounds over gross at take-off.

The first manmade nuclear explosion, the Trinity test with 18.6-kton yield from a plutonium fusion device, was conducted on July 16, 1945, in Alamogordo, New Mexico. Components of the only two operational bombs—a Fat Man and

The Fat Man weapon is seen on the transport trailer positioned over the loading pit, about to be lowered to permit the B-29 to be backed overhead, as the GIs pull away the wheel ramps. The Little Boy bomb was then raised into the forward bomb bay on the cradle that permitted fine adjustment in two axes. After take-off, the final assembly installation of fine details of the weapons were performed. (*National Atomic Museum Foundation*)

a Little Boy—were assembled and transported to the Pacific Theater aboard ship and aircraft. There was considerable work to complete the assembly at Tinian, in the Mariana Islands, with tasks that were among the most exacting and difficult ever performed at a forward combat base. The bombing mission to Japan would be launched from Tinian, then the largest airfield complex in the world after ten months of continuous construction following its capture.

The 393rd had deployed to Tinian in May. While awaiting their mission orders and the special bombs, they performed navigational training flights and participated in actual bombing raids dropping Fat Man shapes. These were filled with 6,300 lb (2,858 kg) of conventional high explosives using contact fuses for a total weight similar to the atomic weapon. The "pumpkins" were initially tested on the range at the Naval Ordnance Test Station at Inyokern. During such a Tinian mission, an inadequately secured pumpkin fell, crashing through bay doors onto the taxiway. Inert shapes of both weapon types were also dropped by the 509th detachment. A Little Boy shape was flown to Iwo Jima to test the pit assembled there.

The atomic bombing missions were flown in daylight and visual conditions to permit good observation of the detonation. These occurred on August 6, 1945, with a Little Boy dropped on Hiroshima and August 9 with a Fat Man delivered onto Nagasaki. The aircraft were hit by a concussion wave from the blast and another reflected off the ground that shock the bomber like flak bursts. Other B-29s went along to make weather reports, photograph the effects, and collect airborne data to include dropping instruments via parachute that would transmit data back to the aircraft. Aircrew donned heavily tinted goggles before the drop.

With two of the frightfully devastating bombs dropped within days of each other by the B-29s that were making almost daily raids, the Japanese had to assume the Americans had many more special weapons. They sued for peace and World War II ended. In reality, it would have been nearly two weeks before an additional weapon was ready to fly and only a few per month thereafter owing to the very slow production of fissile material. The specially modified B-29s were critical in the effort that brought the war to a final end. The total cost of the effort to develop and drop the bombs was approximately $2 billion, and considered money well spent.

Span Change

Some service pilots found occasion to perform pull-outs at or beyond the limit-g of the aircraft, with some structural failures occurring. In the case of the Grumman F6F, some failures occurred in the horizontal stabilizer and elevator, with the outboard portion of one or both surfaces separating from the aircraft. While such breakages probably saved the entire surface from separating (and so aircraft) owing to an inboard shift of the center of lift, reducing the critical root bending load, such failures could preclude safe dive recovery. Addressing this, a peculiar feature of the Grumman F8F-1 Bearcat was that the 3.3 feet (1.0 m) at the tips of the folding outer wing panels (12 percent of the total wing area), including half the aileron span, were designed to breakaway at 8.6 *g* if the pilot exceeded this normal load factor limit. The wing would still possess the 12-*g* ultimate load capability, but the safety wingtip permitted a savings of 230 lb (104 kg) in structural weight for a performance benefit. Since one wingtip might fail during a rolling pull-out owing to asymmetrical wing lift distribution across the span, flight and especially landing with only one tip absent was of great concern.

This concept was initially tested on a "Long Wing" F4F-4 with approximately 3 feet (0.9 m) added to each wingtips that were designed to breakaway. This permitted checking the failure of the weak structural joint on the outboard side of the join in the wing and aileron. These were designed to fail on the bottom and forward end first such that the wingtip would tear away upward and to the rear. The handling qualities could be verified with just one tip removed. Then, a F4F-4 was prepared with wings resembling those of the Bearcat, just 36 feet (11.0

m) span or 2 feet (0.6 m) less than the standard Wildcat wing and reduced to 29 feet (8.8 m) with the tips removed. The outer 4.5 feet (1.4 m) on each side was removed, including half of each aileron, and a 3.5-foot (1.1 m) breakaway section added (14 percent of total area). The tips were to fail under 4.5 *g* of upload at 250 mph (402 kph) as demonstrated in a successful test during April 1944.

Flight tests of the F8F-1 with one Safety Wingtip removed and then both verified the aircraft was well-controlled and could be landed on a carrier since the approach speed was just 19–20 mph (31–32 kph) faster. Finally, an in-flight demonstration of the breakaway feature was performed with good results.

In fleet service, at least one pilot had only one wingtip separate after a pull-out exceeded the *g* limit, and he brought the plane home safely. However, another pilot suffering the same condition apparently could not control the aircraft and was killed. Others may have followed and it became clear the load and vibration spectra of fleet service were stressing the joints in unanticipated ways. Modifications were made and explosive prima chord with electrical micro-switches added to ensure both tips separated almost simultaneously. While this was shown to work, the pyrotechnics were an unwelcome complication on a carrier. Electric shorts during maintenance caused at least one tip to blow off on the hangar deck, killing a sailor. By this point, after the war, the feature was generating such deep suspicion that it was summarily dropped and was not carried far into production.[22]

The Grumman F8F-1 Bearcat originally had breakaway wingtips meant to protect the structure from catastrophic failure in a severe over-*g* condition. This was originally tested on an F4F-4 with extended wingtips grafted on with weak joints. Shown is the test aircraft with these panels compared with a standard Wildcat, and the test aircraft with the Bearcat-like wing after the wingtips had ripped way (note the jagged edge and half aileron span). (*Northrop Grumman History Center*)

Flight tests of the safety wingtip included checks of handling with just a single tip having ripped away. The outer half of the folding panel had a weak joint to permit the separation, along with half the aileron span. These images show two Bearcats that have had a single tip break away, the aircraft in the top view likely a Grumman test aircraft. (*Northrop Grumman History Center*)

Now You See Me ...

Aircraft paint schemes have always been a compromise between camouflage from enemy observation on the ground or airborne, recognition to avoid fratricide, collision avoidance, and unit esprit. It was not long into American involvement in the war when colors and markings were reduced to essentials and concealment alone, plus simplicity for rapid application at the factory, then eliminated almost entirely to save time and materials. Yet some thought was given to additional measures at camouflage. Against a sky background the aircraft usually appeared as a dark silhouette regardless of the under-surface colors. Reducing visual detection range during a torpedo run, for example, would shrink time under gunfire from the target vessel. An unusual experiment in achieving this was undertaken by self-illuminating the aircraft.

The idea originated in 1935 at the Naval Research Laboratory.[23] The initial notion was to illuminate those portions of the aircraft normally in shadow to reduce overall contrast against the bright sky. At first, the lights were to be directed at the aircraft, and a dark aircraft would require more illumination that a lightly colored one. However, it was later decided to aim them away, at the possible observer. This was expected to require less illumination and so lower power consumption. From sufficient distance they would provide a uniform brightness. At that time the power requirement for the lighting at sufficient intensity to eliminate an aircraft silhouette against a bright sky was greater than the state of the art (inadequate generators on the engines or hundreds of pounds of batteries), as shown by a quick flight test at Anacostia employing a Grumman XFF-1. Additionally, a means of measuring the brightness of the sky, to permit adjustment of the lights to an intensity matching that background, was lacking.

The advent of World War II and the Battle of the Atlantic brought the lighting camouflage idea to the fore again. In this case, it was hoped to permit an attack aircraft to make a closer approach to a surfaced submarine before visual detection than without the lighting. If the aircraft could get within thirty seconds of intercepting the boat, they had a much better chance of successfully engaging it before the sub dived. This required illuminating only the forward quarter, or lamps on such surfaces as the nose, leading edges, and cowling lips pointing forward. Thus was born Project Yehudi, named after a magician of the period, under the direction of the NDRC at the request of the AAF. Engaged for the detailed work was the Louis Comfort Tiffany Foundation of Oyster Bay, New York.[24]

A simple ground test with flashlight lamps was promising, their lenses tinted to sky color, mounted on a 2-inch (5-cm) black strip and with a rheostat to adjust intensity. The board was placed atop a roof and disappearing against the sky background when observed 900 feet (274 m) away. Other tests used a simple painted silhouette on a sky-colored panel with holes drilled to permit illumination from behind. By this device, the best position of lamps was determined. This was then extended to a full-size silhouette of a Consolidated B-24 fitted with lamps and suspended between two 100-feet (31-m) towers erected on a hill. There were sixteen lamps across each semi-span and ten in a grid on the nose. For tests in February 1943, the silhouette was observed across the Bay at a 2-mile (3.2-km) range, and it disappeared with the lights properly adjusted.

To put the principle to a practical test, a B-24D (42-40200) was modified at Wright Field in 1943. Lamps were fitted within the wing leading edges inboard of the engine nacelles but under the leading edges of the thinner outboard wing panels. A device was added employing a photoelectric cell exposed to the light background and another exposed to the lights on the aircraft, and output difference indicated on an ammeter. The required level for the light setting was achieved when the rheostat controlling the lamps was adjusted until the ammeter needle was zeroed. The tests in May 1943 found success on an overcast day but less so on a sunny day owing to non-optimal lens filters. It was also concluded that painting the aircraft with highly reflective paint would improve the effectiveness of the self-illumination technique. Obviously, the reflective paint idea would be counter-productive for most other combat scenarios and was not adopted (though ultimately the Liberators were delivered unpainted in reflective bare aluminum).

The B-24 test aircraft was damaged in a landing mishap, but the anti-submarine warfare mission had passed to the Navy. The USN took note of Yehudi progress and asked the NDRC for a system layout for the Martin PBM. A kit was prepared but never installed for test. Instead, the service adapted a TBF-1 for Yehudi trials. In a modification performed at Quonset Point, Rhode Island, four of the lamps were installed on the lip of the cowling, five at the leading edge of each wing, plus one on the leading edge of each horizontal stabilizer. A sensor at the tail provided the background intensity that the pilot matched with a rheostat. The tests in January 1944 had the modified Avenger flying side-by-side with an unmodified example. The standard aircraft was acquired visually at 12 miles (19 km), but the Yehudi closed to 1.7 miles (3 km) before being spotted. It was also concluded that an approach in a crosswind would require flying an arc approach rather than a crab because the latter would render the illumination camouflage ineffective.

With an effective system arrived at, a squadron of Grummans were to be modified for Atlantic operations and a design for production-line installation developed in 1944. A handful of TBM-3Ds were modified for an operational assessment.[25] These changed to six lights around the cowling. The program was apparently suspended. An installation for the Taylorcraft LBT-1, Piper LBP-1, and Pratt, Read and Company LBE-1 glider bombs was also sought, but eventually reduced to just the LBE. This required the automation of the light intensity adjustment in the unmanned glider. The effort stretched to the end of the war at which point it was terminated. The German submarine force was largely beaten by the time of service application and the "little man who wasn't there" (a Yehudi magician joke) went back into hiding.

An experiment that must have caused many a furrowed brow had lights installed on forward edges of this TBM-3D. These reduced the contrast of the aircraft against the sky to reduced visual acquisition by many miles. Several other -3Ds were similarly modified to permit a field demonstration, but this never occurred and Project Yehudi vanished. (*Grumman Historical Center and Jay Miller collection*)

Misleading Deception

The B-17 bomber crews in Europe noticed that the German fighters became more aggressive once the bomb bay doors were opened, the two doors clearly opening to each side. This indicated that the bombers would hold a fixed course for the run into the bomb release point over the target. If it were possible to make the opening of the bay doors less obvious, it might buy the bomber crews a few moments more respite. Through this thought process, a team of mechanics in late 1943 created sliding bay doors for a B-17F. The mechanism unlocked and moved a front door forward and a back door aft along the belly on centerline rails. Although a nice bit of field work, the idea was not carried beyond this point.[26]

Making Noise

While in combat, seeking to conceal an aircraft is a natural tendency, sometimes making more noise is desirable. Following the German example of adding sirens to intensify the terrifying scream of Stuka dive bombers, the USAAF added wind-driven Chrysler sirens to an A-24s (Douglas Dauntless) during combat in the Pacific. It is doubtful this saw use beyond flight trials. Along a different line, the Army field aviation teams would occasionally attach speakers to the exterior their light liaison airplanes. This permitted them to fly low and slow over a combat team on the ground, pull back the power, and deliver a message when radio communication was not possible. This could alert the troops to enemy activity in their area, for example. For a time after the end of the war, the Navy added a huge bank of speakers inside an opening in the aft fuselage of at least one PB4Y to permit aerial public address. This was used to announce the end of hostilities to Japanese soldiers hiding in remote areas.

In another impressive bit of design and fabrication in the field, a USAAF team in the UK created these sliding bomb bay doors for a B-17F during late 1943. The rationale was to make less obvious the preparation to drop the bombs and so delay the reaction of German fighters. The idea probably held more value in drag reduction but was not carried further in any event. (*The Peter M. Bowers Collection/The Museum of Flight*)

This Douglas A-24, a Navy SBD diverted to USAAF dive bombing use, has been fitted with sirens under the wing center-section. This was appropriate for a type of attack the airmen called Banshee, the siren emitting a shriek during a dive intended to sow fear in the enemy. This was not a common installation or mission, on this or other U.S. types. (*National Museum of the United States Air Force*)

The Navy created their own version of the Consolidated B-24 as the PB4Y-2 Privateer for patrol and bombing missions from shore installations. As the war in the Pacific was winding down, several of the machines were turned to a special mission of announcing the end of hostilities to remaining Japanese forces in remote areas. This example (59835) reveals the large speakers installed within an opening in the aft fuselage. (*National Archives*)

13

Foreign Influence

Since the beginning of aerial warfare, opposition aircraft have been of great interest to air elements. Any intelligence on their capabilities is compiled and passed along to operational units for tactical exploitation. Actual examination and flight of the aircraft, especially in mock combat, is a rare bonanza usually providing all necessary information for countering the asset. More is desired for broader intelligence about veiled national resources and aeronautical advances. Consequently, any crashed or forced-landed wrecks, aircraft alighting by mistake inside friendly lines, and those discovered in areas overrun by advancing forces are to be reported, examined, and possibly collected. Combined with pilot debriefings, gun camera film, message intercepts, and interrogations of captives, all the information can be combined to form a clearer picture of enemy order of battle, manufacturing tableaux, and capabilities if not intentions. All this was especially true in World War II. All combatant countries performed these functions and reports were shared with allies.

Evaluations

As with so many other aspects of air warfare, the Americans were behind and late to the game in air intelligence at the beginning of World War II. The interwar years had been fiscally bleak and few resources could be spared for intensive air intelligence activities. Although some collection of information on German aircraft was performed, little effort was expended in collecting intelligence about Japanese resources that were roundly (and incorrectly) considered second-rate. However, as the American's worked with Great Britain before December 1941 and prepared for the possibility of being drawn into the conflict, they observed how the "Brits" collected and evaluated German and Italian aircraft, or French machines put to work by the occupiers. A similar capability had to be assembled at home. The U.S. also watched with interest the application of American air weapons by Allies, reacting as appropriate. A Special Observation Group in the U.K., established in the period before America's formal involvement, included an air officer. After the U.S. joined the conflict, there was an air technical section of the European Theater of Operations, U.S. Army, which monitored British R&D. Membership included at times some of the AAF's best engineers.[1] Hence, American technical exchange with Great Britain was especially bountiful. That with the reclusive and suspicious Soviets was much more constrained, gleaning little of value.

Wright Field's Engineering Division did have a Foreign Equipment Unit. In December 1942, this fell under the Evaluation Branch within the Technical Data Laboratory (TDL). The TDL initially had just twenty-five individuals and little experience evaluating foreign assets. However, they learned quickly from the British example and grew to 750 people during the war years, though overwhelmed and sometimes little-supported with an inadequate distribution of collected information. In general, collected aircraft were evaluated at Wright while armaments went to Eglin. The TDL was moved under the Foreign Equipment Branch in April 1945 and then assumed by T-2 Intelligence beginning in July 1945. The Navy formed a loosely labeled captured enemy aircraft unit (CEAU) at NAS Anacostia in early 1943 with testing performed by the various flight test organizations at the station depending on aircraft type. At that time, the Joint Intelligence Committee, which compiled summaries for the President and other senior personnel, had suggested a joint technical intelligence center. However, the services were not then prepared to work that closely. Consequently, there was a duplication of effort and competition for the assets in-theater and those shipped home. Nonetheless, the CEAU was the model for technical air intelligence units (TAIU) formed in the combat theater with Army, Navy, and Allied personnel.

The first TAIU, or Allied TAIU, was formed in November 1942 in the Southwest Pacific Area (SWPA) based on the earlier army-navy crash investigation, South Pacific Area. This initially included Australian and British elements as the most experienced personnel. The TAIU was established in Melbourne, Australia, and later moved to Eagle Farm, Brisbane. The Allied personnel had performed most of the analysis up to that time.[2] One of the most recognizable products from this TAIU was distinguishing the profusion of Japanese aircraft types via invented names, silhouettes, and photographed scale models.

Other TAIUs were established in 1943 and 1944. The Southeast Asia outfit was based in Calcutta after formation in 1943, and then Singapore. The TAIU-China, under control of the Nationalist government, is not known to have recovered any flight-worthy aircraft. Many Chinese areas were under the control of warlords or otherwise inaccessible. Additionally, locals tended to scavenge a wreck immediately for materials to improve their daily lives. A Pacific Ocean Area team numbered 129 personnel at the end of the war. That outfit was most challenged given the vast region dotted by islands, making the transport of all captured assets to one location very difficult. After summer 1944 more and more intact Japanese aircraft came into their hands, more than was needed of some models. Their coup was aircraft captured at Clarke Field, Manila, on Saipan, and in the Mariana Islands, including some types never before examined intact. The Australia

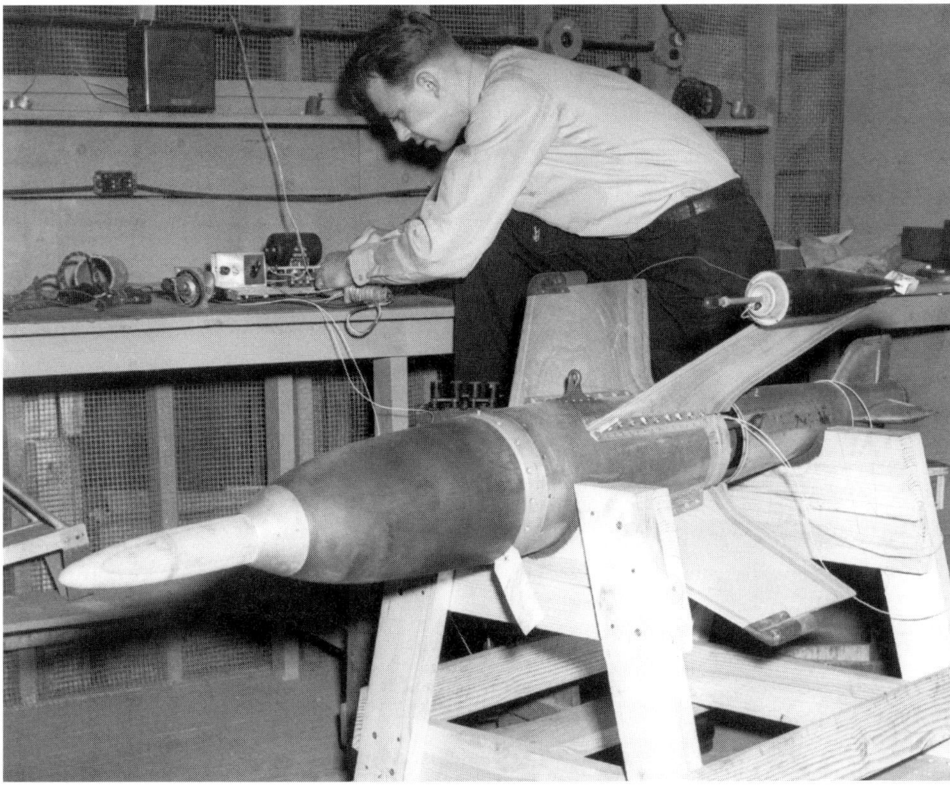

The U.S. air arms were interested in anything associated with aerial combat to included armaments. This German Ruhrstahl X-4 wire-guided air-to-air missile is being dissected and evaluated in an American laboratory. Guidance systems were becoming of particular importance, but the Americans were leading in the field. (*Air Force Test Center*)

operation was folded in July 1944 as the battle lines moved far away. Another SWPA group was set up in the Philippines in October 1944 under the Far East Air Forces and, beginning in February 1945, with aircraft ops at Clarke. Europe did not have a specific TAIU but rather personnel were attached to operational outfits as they moved through areas. They then reported to senior personnel at the RAE where the Americans worked closely with their RAF and Navy counterparts. All captured equipment likewise passed through Farnborough.

The U.K. provided the Americans the opportunity to perform their own evaluation of assets held there or in-theater, and some were shipped to the U.S. The first of the latter was a Messerschmitt Bf 109E that had been initially captured by the French before being passed to the British (as AE479). Arriving in Dayton on May 14, 1942, this machine was subsequently used in the Air Technical Intelligence (ATI) course as a training aid for those preparing to join TAIUs. Organized in 1942 with the assistance of an RAF "intel" officer, Squadron Leader R. A. Colley, thirty-three AAF and ten USN personnel had passed through the course by the end of March 1943.[3]

Apart from captured aircraft, the British permitted American personnel to fly their aircraft and provided some for shipment to the United States for closer examination and testing. Some Soviet types also made it to the U.S., including a Yak-9 and Il-10.[4]

The U.S. Navy and Army finally came to an agreement on a joint air intelligence center to reduce duplication and produce better intel products. All assets of the TAIU in Australia were moved to Anacostia to serve, along with the CEAU, as the nucleus of the Technical Air Intelligence Center. It administratively fell under Naval Intelligence but was to distribute data and equipment of value to both services.

The core of the TAIUs were the ATI officers and Crash Intelligence Officers. The rest of the team included translators (in the Pacific Theater usually Japanese-American soldiers or *Nisei*), photographers, radiomen, ordnance personnel, engine and airframe mechanics, and clerks. The TAIUs examined wrecks, derelicts, and especially potentially operable enemy aircraft, and ordnance. A standardized enemy aircraft report was formulated, requiring close examination, measurement, the collection of sample materials, and photographs or drawings. Small teams of two to six men, usually led by an officer, would respond to reports of an asset worth investigating. Maker's identification plates were vital in determining place and date of manufacture and revealing production capabilities. Analysis of the plates lent vital insight into enemy production assets and capacity. This helped to guide, in part, B-29 bombing targets in Japan.[5] The plates were removed even if nothing else was retrieved. The TAIU SWPA collected some 6,336 plates in their period of operation.

All theater commanders were told the vital importance of air intelligence and asked to do more in assisting efforts. Hence, the TAIU men usually had high-level authority to demand assistance from any friendly unit for lodging, transport, and labor. To gain the help of a combat unit, which was focused on its own mission if not mere survival, in an activity they had never heard of was sometimes a dicey part of the business. The TAIU might have some ground vehicles assigned and perhaps a C-47 or light-planes.

All units were supposed to report enemy aircraft finds to higher HQ and protect the assets from vandalism. The TAIU member was frequently frustrated by finding a potentially fruitful resource stripped of anything useful. Vandalism by souvenir hunters was so prevalent that it was urgent the investigators get to a site as quickly as possible after being reported. Although any such scavenging and dealing of the contraband was against regulations and punishable, it was practiced by all ranks to include the personnel sent to guard the wreck. The vital identity plates were a favorite of GIs, and some were taken out of letters home being reviewed by intelligence personnel.

Some aircraft were delivered intact and flyable by enemy pilots who had lost their way and set down at what they believed to be a friendly airfield. This was rare and most of the evaluated aircraft were laboriously retrieved from remote sites under difficult conditions and carefully restored. In the early war period,

Great Britain and the United States traded examples of their nation's military aircraft for evaluation and design lessons-learned. An example of this is the Spitfire Mk VII (probably EN474) photographed at NACA Langley on September 7, 1944. Other aircraft were evaluated in the host country. (*NASA*)

This Me 262 is how the enemy aircraft investigation teams frequently found assets in the field. Although unit commanders were to secure such equipment, other imperatives and souvenir hunting usually saw useful intelligence resources reduced in value. Especially if the decision was made to restore an aircraft to flyable condition, any vandalism would have to be reversed with great effort. (*Mike Machat collection via Tony Landis*)

the SWPA teams would go after wrecks while dodging Japanese patrols and in exceptionally difficult geography. If the decision was made to move the aircraft to a TAIU location for closer examination or restoration, considerable effort was expended. Some of this required hauling large assemblies across swamps, over mountains, and down rivers, frequently by mobilizing local labor. Many a dangerous adventure lay behind enemy airplanes that later appeared in American airfields.

After some types became well-known and with sufficient flying examples, additional assets were examined for any improvements, substitutions that suggested shortages, degrading workmanship, and omissions. Some parts might be retrieved to restore an aircraft in hand or to keep it operating, the rest left to the souvenir hunters and locals. Aircraft of lesser interest or yet to be assessed were occasionally restored by squadron shops and operated as unit hacks. Even fully intact aircraft would be at least partially disassembled to examine the design, search for manufacturer markings or plates, and ensure there was no hidden damage or sabotage.

If practical, restored aircraft would be assessed in-theater and only later transported to the U.S. mainland. Restoring to flying condition and safely operating a foreign aircraft through flight test to characterize its performance, with little or no information, required skill, care, and determination. American radios, instruments, and other flight gear might be substituted or at least English labels applied. The evaluation pilots might not be test pilots as these were rare at the time, especially in-theater, but rather exceptionally skilled pilots of the airplane class to be flown. The knowledgeable line pilots might be able to make more cogent observations about vulnerabilities and advantages of value to combat units. Consequently, detailed flight test data collection usually awaited movement of the aircraft to the States. This was either aboard an aircraft carrier bound for an American port or the aircraft disassembled and crated for transport aboard a cargo vessel. Some large aircraft were ferried across the vast ocean distances.

In the States, the aircraft were more closely examined by specialists and subjected to more intensive flight testing. Navy trials were initially at Anacostia before this and other testing moved south to NAS Patuxent River. For the USAAF, the assets came to Wright Field for assessment by all the specialists within the laboratories of the Engineering Branch. They might be shown to domestic design teams, particularly at the periodic design conferences where new information was shared to include that collected via intelligence work. Manufacturers could examine a type closely and possibly have it flown by company test pilots. Some examples of very familiar types were provided to manufacturers and many of little remaining value were flown and displayed around the country during war bond drives. Allied nations' aircraft were also evaluated for what might be learned to improve locally produced machines. A Joint Fighter Conference was held at Eglin in 1943 and Pax River in 1944 with representatives from all U.S. services, American industry, NACA, and British plus Canadian air arms. This permitted detailed assessments of what had been learned from years of war and combat aircraft evolution. Captured and Allied fighters were at hand for flight evaluation.

This Bf 109G-2/R2 was shot down on March 1, 1944, by British ground fire in Libya and restored to flight condition by the 87th Fighter Squadron (hence the American markings and British fin flash). It appears to have subsequently suffered an accident as the tip of the rudder is missing. The aircraft was eventually shipped to the U.S. and the airframe ground tested to destruction. (*National Museum of the United States Air Force*)

After undergoing thorough fight test and evaluation, aircraft like this Fw 190 (captured in North Africa and restored to flight by the 79th Fighter Group) would be used as a trainer. Experienced pilots would be permitted to fly the machine for familiarization and the aircraft would be used in mock engagements with units preparing to deploy to a war zone who might face the adversary. (*National Museum of the United States Air Force*)

Sometimes specific information was sought from a foreign aircraft or valuable insights passed along for exploitation. The USAAF sought a Fw 190 canopy to study the use of laminated methyl methacrylate. Other captured German aircraft provided insight into their methods of thermal anti-ice that proved useful in NACA development efforts. Longitudinal trim via electrical pitch incidence change of a "flying" horizontal tail was a feature derived from inspection of captured German equipment and passed along through design conferences. The demand oxygen system placed into service during the war (Chapter 8) was essentially copied from German equipment collected from captured or downed enemy combat aircraft in Europe.[6]

If the article was no longer airworthy or had no further value as a flyable asset, it might be parted out for more detailed and possibly destructive testing. Some machines were taken to Wright Field's structures lab and tested to failure to learn its limits and the benefits of any unique construction techniques.

Sometimes, foreign markings were retained or restored for in-flight photographs to be distributed for recognition purposes, or photos were retouched. Flights were usually escorted by an easily recognized Allied type to discourage over-eager friendlies from shooting down the foreign airplane. Usually the aircraft was stripped to bare metal and fabric and Allied markings applied. The Americans used various coding methods.

Approximately 200 foreign aircraft were shipped back in this manner and the American forces had access to more than 200 captured and domestic aircraft at the RAE and other stations, while hundreds of non-operable aircraft were examined. By spring 1945, the size of the foreign fleet at Wright Field had grown to a point where it occupied six buildings, part of the flight-line hangar, and an outdoor storage area. At that time, they were moved to Freeman Field in Seymour, Indiana, little more than 125 miles (200 km) away or less than an hour when flying. Although called the Foreign Aircraft Evaluation Center, the machines were usually flown to Wright Field for the testing.

Obviously, if the Allies could do it, the Axis could as well. However, the Japanese and Germans went farther and employed some of their operable Allied aircraft to facilitate sneak attacks and lure enemy aircraft into deadly zones. In the case of the Japanese, the aircraft were also used in combat to supplement their own dwindling resources. Aircrew of all countries were told to do their best to render a force-landed aircraft worthless as time permitted, usually by setting it afire. American aircrew were also told to destroy from the air any downed friendly aircraft they observed that appeared to be intact.

The approaching collapse of Nazi German resistance prompted the formation of teams to move quickly to gather materials and aircraft, and interview former enemy air leaders, engineers, mechanics, and aircrew. The Allies and U.S. services formed teams seeking the same objectives and some effort was made to join these. When set in motion the large-scale operations by the USAAF and the Navy saw some heated disputes over rights to discovered materiel. The British were given first choice of new types discovered in this process, though it caused anguish to

An Italian Macchi C.202 Folgore occupies the ramp at Wright Field on August 20, 1943. Probably collected in North Africa, it was restored to flying condition for testing, evaluation, and training. It remains in original colors but with U.S. markings applied over the Italian. (*Jay Miller collection*)

A collection of captured Japanese aircraft are presented to industry representatives at NAS Patuxent River for any potential value they may serve in improving American warplanes. Readily identifiable is a Kawanishi N1K1 Koyo *Rex* floatplane fighter and a Nakajima B6N2 Tenzan *Jill* torpedo bomber to the left. Considerable resources were expended, with great difficulty, getting such aircraft to the States and to the condition for such a presentation. (*Jay Miller collection*)

This Mitsubishi Ki-46-II command-renaissance aircraft was captured at Hollandia in New Guinea, restored by personnel of the 13th Bomb Squadron, and probably photographed at NAS Anacostia during 1945. The growing USAAF portion of the captured aircraft collection had to be moved to Freeman Field, Indiana. By this point, maintaining and evaluating aircraft such as the Dinah was losing importance and, following the war, many such machines were given away or scrapped. (*National Archives*)

some of the American ATI people.[7] However, soon the vast wealth of equipment and documents exceeded any one team's ability to correlate and assess, much less analyze. So, a joint center was established in London for this purpose, with all parties given the indices, summaries, and copies. The same scenario was acted out after the surrender of Japan. A large number of advance aircraft were carefully collected and carried across the oceans in summer and fall 1945.

The collected documents, equipment, plus eventually individuals, all aided American post-war aeronautical progress. In the short term, it helped steer a few decisions in the remaining weeks of the war. For the Americans, they sought to gather the intelligence and equipment for immediate exploitation in the defeat of Japan, including anything the Germans had regarding Japanese equipment and German technology transferred to them. However, this had no immediate influence on combat as the war ended months later.

Legend of the Zero

Before America entered the war, they were hearing about the Mitsubishi A6M "Zero" fighter from Chinese sources or American volunteers operating in-theater. Although accounts of wreck inspections and combat reports outlining the aircraft's capabilities were passed to U.S. military officials, they were largely dismissed as exaggerated.[8] Personnel disbelieved the Japanese could build a world-class combat aircraft and if they did it had to be copied from an American design. Yet, when the U.S. joined the war and began fighting the aircraft directly, their frontline fighter airplanes and tactics did not fare well. The Zero got a reputation as an almost unbeatable killer and many Japanese aircraft encountered in combat were reported as "Zeros." The A6M was later classified as "Zeke" for clarity. The Americans were working on newer fighters but needed insight into the Zero to devise more effective tactics and learn what made the airplane so superior. This was an early focus of the foreign evaluation teams and probably among their most well-known achievements.

The recovered aircraft that truly facilitated detailed evaluation was from one of several flights of naval warplanes that struck the American facility at Dutch Harbor in the Aleutian Islands, Alaska, on June 4, 1942, the second day of attacks. Aircraft 4593, flown by Flight Petty Officer Tadayoshi Koga, was hit by ground fire and began leaking engine oil. The pilot chose to put down on one of the designated recovery sites from which he could then be recovered via submarine. The barren island was 25 miles (40 km) away from Dutch Harbor with what appeared to be a large field of low grass. With gear and flaps down, Koga descended for landing. However, the field was actually a bog and the aircraft immediately flipped over, killing the petty officer. His mates were supposed to destroy any force-landed airplane but, believing Koga might still be alive and trapped, they left the ship unscathed and continued on to their carrier. The submarine searched the shoreline for a while but was driven off by a destroyer.

It was July 10 before the aircrew of a patrolling PBY spotted the aircraft on Akutan Island. A team was sent out the following day and, after burying Koga, assessed the fighter as recoverable. Alerting higher command, the word came back to recover the aircraft if deemed salvageable. It took two expeditions to extract the airplane, placing it on a barge and hauling it to Dutch Harbor on July 15. It was cleaned and thoroughly examined before being put aboard a ship bound for Seattle. There, the airplane was transferred to a transport vessel that sailed south to NAS North Island, San Diego, arriving on August 12. The repairs were extensive and non-trivial, but a skilled team worked around the clock. The Zero was flown on September 20 by Lt-Cdr Eddie R. Sanders, a test pilot from Anacostia. He performed two dozen test flights through October 15 and also flew Navy F4F-4 and F4U fighters against the Zero operated by Cdr Fred Trapnell, director of flight testing at Anacostia. The first flight revealed information of value to pilots fighting the airplane and was promptly radioed to the warzone. The initial test pilot assessment was summarized and distributed to combat units, and Sanders also briefed about 150 pilots at North Island about to deploy to the theater. A more detailed evaluation and additional mock combat with U.S. naval aircraft followed. Some important insights were gleaned that could give pilots an advantage in combat.

While possessing many admirable features in addition to outstanding performance and agility, the aircraft was not an incomparable terror as it had been portrayed. It had significant deficiencies such as poor roll response above 230 mph (370 kph), rolling easier to the left than right, and the engine cutting out under negative *g*. It was built of surprisingly light structure, with no armor or self-sealing tanks, helping give it the excellent performance for a mere 940-hp (701-kW) engine.[9] This also accounted for readily breaking up when hit by .50-cal rounds and cannon shells. The lack of self-sealing tanks meant it 'flamed' easily when fuel tanks were pierced. Close examination should also have settled once and for all the notion that the A6M was closely based on the Vought V-141 that originated as the Northrop 3-A, but this nonsense persisted even following the war despite interviews with the designer and examination of Japanese records.

Additional testing and air combat maneuvering against American types followed. The fighter was moved to Anacostia after the New Year. In preparation for more intensive evaluation, there the aircraft was flown to NACA Langley in early March 1943 for installation of flight test instrumentation. While at Langley the aircraft was also put into the full-scale wind tunnel to quantify some aerodynamic characteristics. Its existence was made known during a May 15, 1943 display at Washington National Airport. It was flown against combat teams heading for the Pacific as a training measure and experienced pilots were permitted to fly the airplane. The Air Forces eventually got their turn with the Zero for the same purpose. The Mitsubishi was damaged in a landing accident on January 5, 1943, but repaired. It went back to North Island in 1944 to serve as a trainer. There, in February 1945, an SB2C pilot accidently taxied into the fighter and chopped the tail and aft fuselage to scrap. The Zero was written off.

Claims that data from Koga's Zero influenced the design of the Grumman F6F Hellcat and Vought F4U are misleading. Both were in early production by the time detailed data were available. While combat experience played a role in designing the Grumman ship, especially the F6F-3 variant, the power, strength, and armament of the Hellcat combined with improved tactics are what permitted that machine and other American fighters to become superior over the Zero and other Japanese aircraft in air-to-air combat. Some Japanese combatants have said that the capture and evaluation of this Zero was the beginning of the end for their military fortunes. This is excessive given the many other factors playing in the outcome of a war. Likewise, the importance of the data collected and summarized for combat units has also been questioned. The reports were concise and widely distributed, helping many squadrons better understand their opponent. Yet, by the time of distribution, most of the lessons had been learned in the field the hard way and earlier reports had guided changes in tactics. Still, in terms of the timing of

This Mitsubishi A6M2 "Zeke" may be the most famous "Zero," seen at Langley on March 8, 1943. Recovered in the Aleutian Islands, transported to San Diego, restored to flying condition, and evaluated with a report issued, all in three months, this aircraft gave vitally important insight into the feared Japanese fighter. This was one of a series of foreign aircraft evaluations that gleaned engineering data and operational information in support of combat forces. (*Jay Miller collection*)

this Zero's capture and the perceived value of the data gleaned, it was possibly the most significant foreign evaluation conducted by America during the war.

Another "Zero" the Americans evaluated was an A6M2 that fell into Chinese hands via a November 26, 1941 force-landed on a beach. This predated the Koga Zero, but that aircraft was flown and evaluated first. The Chinese machine appears to have been examined while still intact. A joint report by the U.S. Navy and Soviet *attachés* prepared before the end of 1941 and passed up channels to the respective headquarters. The secret report was filed without action because there was no formal organization at the time to exploit the intelligence.[10] Months were required to transport the aircraft in pieces inland via beast and manpower. Chinese mechanics put it together at Kunming and members of the American Volunteer Group completed making it airworthy. The restored aircraft flew in October 1942. It was eventually shipped to the U.S. and was among the few aircraft recovered in China. Many other Zekes would come into Allied hands as the war progressed and offered insight into progressive improvements to guide tactics evolution.

This Zeke fell into Chinese hands in 1941 via a forced landing and was then restored to flying condition by Chinese mechanics and members of the American Volunteer Group. In Chinese markings, it was s/n 3372 and the original Japanese code was V-172. It eventually made its way to the U.S. in 1943 to become EB-2 then EB-200, joining a growing collection of foreign types under evaluation. (*National Archives*)

Copycat

Heralded in Germany as the *Vergeltungswaffe Eins* (Revenge Weapon 1) when the V-1s began falling on England on June 12, 1944, this missile marked another step in aerial warfare. While winged missiles had been the subject of R&D for decades, this was the first extensive combat use of such a weapon. The Americans had already expended considerable effort in their guided missile program that included winged systems such as glide bombs, bomb gliders, and bomb drones. The General Motors A-1 "power-driven bomb" was an effort to develop an inexpensive autonomous airplane that could, with dozens of weapons each armed with a few hundred pounds of explosives, saturate a target that would otherwise be unreachable due to defenses or weather. At one point, Arnold had considered purchasing hundreds of the missiles for $700 apiece, but the system proved too balky, range too limited, and the only reliable guidance individual remote radio control with visual targeting via television from a following airplane that essentially eliminated any unique value. So, when the Germans successfully demonstrated an autonomous winged missile (though technically directed and not guided), the AAF took immediate notice.

The German project had begun in mid-1942, though the engine predated this start. The Fieseler Fi 103, or FZG-76, was powered by an Argus-Schmidt 807-lbf (3.6-kN) pulsejet engine. Pulsejets have to be boosted to an operating speed before self-sustained propulsion is possible. The Argus-Schmidt engine, the AS 109-014, had an inlet directing airflow into a face of venturis and one-way spring-loaded flapper valves. These venturis and valves were arranged in rows like venetian blinds. Fuel was atomized with the air in this assembly and flowed into the combustion chamber where it was ignited by spark plug. The high pressure from the fuel–air mixture detonation shut the flapper valves and the flow exited through a discharge pipe. A resulting drop in pressure allowed the inlet flapper valves to open again and the cycle repeated several dozen times per second. Some of the exhaust would flow forward to add to compression and, along with the residual burning and heated components, permitted sustained ignition without further use of the spark plug. The engine created a loud and deep stuttering sound, earning the missile the moniker Buzz Bomb. The engine operated flat out from launch, the aircraft reaching as much as 400 mph (644 kph) while accelerating as fuel was consumed.

The Fi 103 was gyro-stabilized while a barometer directed hold of the pre-set altitude (usually 2,000–3,000 feet, 610–914 m). Guidance was by magnetic compass following a heading determined by orientation of the launcher. These were either fixed concrete and rail structures or mobile steel assemblies, both about 155 feet (47 m) long. The missile rode on a pair of rails while propelled by a gas piston within the launcher that attached to a belly fitting. The piston, which fell away beyond the launcher, was pressurized by a two-component propellant charge to accelerate the missile under 17 *g* to 250 mph (402 kph). Late model Fi 103s had a modest correction function such that the launcher did not have to be aligned with the desired heading. There were only rudder and elevator control surfaces for autopilot use. Pneumatics, via two wire-wound compressed-air spheres, were used to move the surfaces, pressurize the fuel tank for pumping action, and spin some of the gyros. Distance flown was determined by revolutions of the small propeller on the nose turning a counter until a present value was reached. When this occurred, a pair of detonators fired to drive the elevators hard down along with dropping small spoilers at the hinge line while also cutting pneumatic pressure to the rudder servo, all serving to place the missile into a dive. The abrupt pitch usually sloshing fuel away from the drain and starved the engine. This was a deficiency, robbing the impact of kinetic energy. The 1,830-lb (830-kg) warhead had contact fuses.

Hitler was determined to use the missile at the earliest opportunity, along with the V-2 ballistic missile, to terrorize London by saturation bombing. The V-1 was pushed to high rate production while still suffering development problems. Numerous fixed launch sites were erected in the French coastal region to launch the V-1s but subjected to persistent and heavy bombing and then eventually overrun by Allied troops. Mobile launchers had been developed by that time. When pushed beyond the range of London, targeting shifted to Allied transportation centers in Belgium. The summer 1944 missile barrage against London killed thousands of people and destroyed tens of thousands of homes. At the peak, on August 3, 220 V-1s struck the city. Hundreds of thousands of people were evacuated that summer or left of their own volition. Similar results occurred in cities targeted on the continent. The Allied command reacted vigorously with redoubled launch site attacks and improved defenses, going so far as to deploy top secret proximity fuses for AAA shells, previously held in reserve.

With early evidence of the missile's effectiveness and simplicity, the Americans decided on July 4 to reverse-engineer and build "Chinese copies" of the V-1 as rapidly as possible. American missile development to that time made clear a perfected weapon would require perhaps two years and hundreds of test items expended, and this was consistently seen as unreasonable in wartime. So, adopting the V-1 would avoid the lengthy and costly development of a comparable weapon, especially as the missile might yield little advantage over manned aircraft. The V-1 had required just such time and resources in Germany but was pursued for reasons of revenge and not true military value.

Materiel Command was set to the task with $90 million allocated, assigning Maj. Ezra Kotcher as project engineer supported by the Special Weapons Branch of ATSC, Wright Field. The goal of Project MX-544 was ten of these JB-2 (Jet Bomb) missiles, but upped to at least thirteen with two launchers.[11] On July 12, 1944, 2,500 lb (1,134 kg) of V-1 wreckage was flown to Wright Field to begin the work. This was the Fi 103A-1 model and so represented none of the improvements seen on later models of the missile, such as wooden wings and a smaller warhead for extended range.

The Ford Motor Company and Republic Aviation worked with Air Forces personnel to create drawings and solve assembly problems. It was soon decided, in the interest of time and effectiveness, available materials, equipment, and processes would be used instead of replicating the German product exactly. After seventeen days, a copy of the engine had been built and operated on August 1, using some recovered German parts. They managed to squeeze 9 percent more thrust from the design, achieving 900 lbf (4 kN). Ford's Dearborn, Michigan, division, was contracted to build twenty-five power plants. The airframes, consisting mostly of steel, were initially constructed at Wright Field, being delivered in three weeks. Republic assembled the complete missile, the first by September 8, with a run of the integrated systems performed. At some point in July 1944, the contracted number of missiles was increased to fifty.[12] The forces and rates acting on the aircraft had to be known for a suitable stability system to be created from existing American parts. Thus, the first complete airframe was tested in the Wright Field 25-foot (6.2-m) wind tunnel. It was found that the shutter mechanism in the inlet would begin to break up after fifteen to twenty minutes owing to the violence of its operation. The NACA was asked to look into this and proposed coating the grid assembly with neoprene to dampen the shock effect. This extended the service life of the valve to 2.75 hours.[13]

Major Ezra Kotcher (far right), project engineer for the V-1 reverse engineering effort, stands by to answer questions during a tour by Maj.-Gen. Oliver Echols from Materiel Command escorted by a Colonel from Wright Field's Engineering Division. A lieutenant explains the nose and timer spinner of the Fi 103—a portion of the wreckage delivered to Dayton in July 1944. Kotcher's team man drafting tables in a hangar area isolated by dark partitions. (*National Archives*)

The pneumatic servos, gyros, and magnetic compass were tested aboard a C-45 in Cleveland starting on August 25. Hence, guidance and control systems took the most time. The JB-2's dimensions and weights varied just a bit from the Fi 103A-1.

The decision to procure an additional 1,000 units was made in July and contracts were issued on August 2 with an expected $3,000–4,000 per missile. Airframe production was assigned to Republic who built the first seventy-five in Farmingdale, New York, before subcontracting to Willys-Overland of Toledo, Ohio. Ford's contract was extended to provide the PJ-31 power plants on the same schedule but with 10 percent spares added. Air Reduction Sales provided the pressure regulators, Alloy Products the pressure vessels, Jack and Heintz the automatic controls, RCA the remote guidance sets, Northrop Aircraft the launching carts, Monsanto Chemical the launcher rocket motors, and the Army Corps of Engineers would build the launch ramps. Deliveries ran from September to March 31, 1945.

Testing was performed at Eglin with the missiles fired over the Gulf of Mexico. Extensive self-contained facilities were rapidly constructed there to include two

400–500 foot (122–152 m) long concrete and steel launch ramps, some level and some at a 6-degree incline. Without having then examined the German launchers, the Americans had to improvise, choosing to use a cart propelled by four 4,000-lbf (18-kN) solid propellant rocket motors, weighing approximately 220 lb (100 kg) each and burning for about four seconds. Boosting the missile to 220 mph (354 kph), the cart fell away after it and the missile departed the end of the track. Even after examining the German piston launcher in late November 1944, arriving at the suitable charge to propel it at the correct rate without excessive pressure could not be done quickly, and the entire design was considered unsafe. The Americans persisted with the rocket sled.

The first launch was on October 12, 1944, just eighty-nine days from receipt of V-1 wreckage. The launch speed was initially too low, resulting in missile impacts off the end of the ramp or soon after into the water. The number of rockets was increased to five then six and the missile attitude on the cart increased progressively from 6.5 to 8.5 degrees. The higher angles resulted in the elevator of the missile being burned by the forward rockets.[14] All rockets were subsequently moved to the rear of the cart. Only the sixth launch was promising, the missile flying out at 400

The first JB-2 was ready for flight testing in eighty-nine days from arrival of V-1 elements at Wright Field. Test facilities had been built at Eglin Field, Florida, in the interim. Here one of the first missiles is being mounted on the launcher atop the 6-degree incline ramp. (*National Museum of the United States Air Force*)

mph (644 kph) but reaching just 800 feet (244 m) altitude and coming down 8–9 miles (13–15 km) from the ramp. The next launch reached 65 miles (105 km) and was climbing beyond the pre-set 6,000 feet (1,829 m) at 210 mph (338 kph) before being shot down as a precaution. The eighth, on November 11, flew perfectly at the planned 3,500 feet (1,067 m) and greater than 400 mph (644 kph), outpacing the P-63 chase aircraft. It disappearing 60 miles (97 km) beyond the launch point. Regardless, more than half of the two dozen flight attempts through January 20, 1945, resulted in vehicle loss on or soon after leaving the ramp, owing mostly to the assisted take-off method.[15] Cart separation was problematic, delay prompting stall of the vehicle or the cart bouncing back into the missile. The rocket propellant also exploded occasionally and caused the JB-2 to do likewise.

Republic JB-2 characteristics:

span	17.7 feet (5.4 m)	weight, launch	5,025 lb (2,279 kg)
length	27.1 feet (8.3 m)	weight, warhead	2,100 lb (953 kg)
height	4.7 feet (1.4 m)	speed, launch	220 mph (354 kph)
wing area	60.5 feet^2 (1.7 m^2)	speed, maximum	440 mph (708 kph)
fuel	180 gal (681 l)	speed, cruise (optimal)	400 mph (644 kph)
climb rate	1,000 fpm (305 mpm)	range, maximum	150 miles (241 km)
service ceiling	6,000 feet (1,829 m)	duration	25 minutes

In a relatively short time, the Americans made their initial choice of launch method—a rocket-propelled cart riding rails up an incline—effective if not imminently practical. The rocket motors could be hazardous, were costly to produce, and generated an enormous cloud of smoke. After months of work, a mobile ramp of more practical length was devised but still employing smoky rockets. (*National Archives*)

On the basis of the modest success at Eglin, the existence of the program was made public and a second order for 1,000 articles was issued in December, a total cost of $4,464,450 expected for the total 2,050 units.[16] A total of only seventy-four JB-2s had been delivered by December 1, 1944.[17] However, the Air Forces' sights were set much higher. In September, they had proposed production of 1,000 JB-2s and fifty launch sites per month by April 1945, increasing to 5,000 missiles and 250 launch sites per month by September 1945; they were studying the possibility of producing a staggering 1,000 missiles per day.[18] The goal was the ability to fire 100 missiles per day by September, 200 by December, and 500 by January 1946. On January 14, 1945, Gen. Arnold proposed production of 100 launch ramps and 75,000 additional missiles, the latter reaching 100 deliveries per day no later than September 1 and then ramping up to 500 in January 1946. Development of a mobile launcher like the German model was underway, but only tested in spring 1945 and weighing some 40 tons. The General also elevated the program's priority to the highest level and above all other missile projects.

An effort such as Arnold pressed for would cost a staggering $1.4 billion achieved at the expense of other programs owing to funding and a required 60,000 workers plus 5,000,000 feet^2 (464,500 m^2) of manufacturing floor space. Just transporting such quantities to the European Theater would consume a quarter of all shipping assets. This last concern brought the notion of having French workers and factories engage in assembly. Additional stateside airframe manufacturers were expected to be Budd, Firestone, Higgins, Murray, and Nash Kelvinator, plus Continental Aviation and Engineering for engines. It was uncertain if production of the assisted take-off motors could keep pace with the missiles, new chemical plants having to be built that would require a year or more. Many senior leaders opposed such a dramatic shift for a weapon of uncertain value. Getting all the plants equipped and functional for JB-2 production in time to meet the delivery schedule appeared doubtful.

Near the end of January, the War Department denied the USAAF production request until the matter could be studied further. In February, Materiel Command confirmed the cost and national production resource impact of high-rate JB-2 manufacturing, but still recommended production to 1,000 per month by November 1945. While the Army formed its first JB-2 launch unit, orders were placed for a further 10,000 missiles with Willys-Overland the supplier. There may still have been some reluctance to proceed at this quantity because Willys-Overland received a contract for just 5,000 in April 1945 at an expected $26,950,000.[19]

There was intent to incorporate a superior guidance system so that the missiles would not be confined to area targets. The need to acquire 77,000 radio and radar sets plus 100 ground control sets was already identified. Design and testing were underway to devise a less cumbersome launching means that was also less hazardous and wasteful and did not generate such a revealing cloud of smoke. One such was performed in collaboration with NACA to mount ATO rockets such that their thrust passed through the missile's CG and so a "zero-length" launch on a 40-foot (12-m) trailered ramp (less than twice the length of the missile). It was known that the Luftwaffe had fired V-1s from beneath Heinkel He 111 bombers, a single missile carried under one wing just outboard of the fuselage. So, air launch development was directed on December 2, 1944, and design for launching two JB-2s from under the wings of a B-17 got underway. This promised to extend the choice of targets by as much as 1,000 miles (1,609 km) while cutting about 500 miles (805 km) off the bomber's range and free the missile from fixed land launchers. However, heading alignment and point of launch accuracy would be such as to make impact precision three times poorer.

A B-17G (43-39119) was selected and fitted with mounts outboard of the outboard engine nacelles. The aircraft was initially flown with 4,000-lb (1,814-kg) bombs before taking up the JB-2s. The missiles had to be launched within seconds of each other to prevent the heavy lateral CG and asymmetric drag from compromising control. This was initially demonstrated with launches on March 2, 1945. A total of ten air launches were performed that spring at Wendover AAF, but only four were successful.[20] Engine starting was one of the problems. Launches were made from B-29s out of Eglin to explore a potential for use against Japan.

The Americans were working from the basis of incomplete information about the V-1's history. It was fairly clear that the Fi 103 was inexpensive, easy to use in all weather conditions, and difficult to shoot down owing to its speed, low altitude of flight, and small size (though its steady course aided gunnery). Flight was low enough to place it in range of light anti-aircraft guns. The poor fuel efficiency and short range was probably evident. It was initially unknown that the violent engine cycles promoted rapid airframe deterioration from the noise and vibration despite efforts at dampening. The deterioration of the inlet shutter gradually degraded airspeed by about 50 mph (80 kph), helping fighter intercept. Despite a continuous flow of fuel, burning occurred only 50 percent of the time, and so much was wasted and excess weight in fuel was carried. The magnetic compass required very precise alignment inside a non-magnetic building. Of approximately 22,000 missiles fired, roughly 20 percent failed on launch or soon after (some likely due to sabotage or poor workmanship), about 40 percent were downed by Allied defenses, leaving around 40 percent that were "effective."[21] German testing had shown just eighty of 258 missiles fired striking within 9 miles (15 km) of the target at 62 miles (100 km) in range and 19 miles (30 km) at 140 miles (225 km).[22] Those that failed soon after take-off often exploded a short distance away to caused civilian property damage and casualties—something the Germans cared little about when launching from foreign soil. A quarter to half the 1,287 V-1s fired from He 111s failed after launch. They were three time less accurate and fewer than 4 percent reached their targets.[23] Additionally, Hitler's devotion to the V weapons was at great cost to other vital defense programs, including causing a shortage of explosives. It was also evident to U.S. leadership that the V-1 and V-2 had failed to cause any change to Allied decisions regarding progress of the war apart from expending enormous resources in combating the threat both before

Following the German example and seeking a more practical JB-2 launch method, firing from a B-17 was explored. Mounting two 5,000-lb (2,268-kg) weapons on the outer wing panels and firing them in a manner that precluded bomber loss of control was no mean feat. The test aircraft, a B-17G, fired ten missiles at Wendover, Utah, with relatively poor results, reliable missile engine ignition being the principal difficulty. (*National Archives*)

Missile firing from the B-29 was also developed for potential use against Japan where there would initially be no land from which the short-range JB-2 could be flown during the planned invasion. However, the low launch rate and low accuracy of air launch compared poorly with simply using B-29s to bomb targets directly given the fading enemy air defenses. This image, apparently taken near Eglin, shows the missile motor ignited prior to launch. (*National Archives*)

and after they went into action. Heavy bombing of German cities and industries had also not brought that enemy to heel.

Theater air commanders were uniform in saying they saw no role for the JB-2 and did not want to host an experimental weapon. It could be useful to harass the enemy in poor weather grounding manned airplanes, but they wanted missiles only if production did not adversely affect the delivery of all other munitions.

In September 1944, the U.S. Navy, which also had several guided missile programs underway, sought fifty JB-2s. They planned to equip them with radio control and radar beacons for launch from an escort carrier (CVE) and guided by a mother ship airplane to a target. They initiated their program on April 12, 1945, under codename Loon, with the NAMU leading. They studied other launch platforms afloat and from PB4Y-1s. The Army and Navy considered a joint program to fire JB-2s from the decks of LSTs.[24] The Army supplied the first six JB-2s to the USN in February 1945; fifty-one had been handed over by May. The BuAer contracted directly with Republic in June for a further 100 missiles. A launcher was prepared at Point Mugu, California, and a team was training for CVE deployment, but no firings took place before the end of the war.[25]

Development of the ground-launch system eventually yielded reliable hardware, with a 400-foot (122-m) level track and four rocket motors, as shown by ninety-seven consecutive successful flights by May 1945—better than the German record. The ability to have the missile turn to the desired heading after take-off was introduced by the forty-fourth missile.[26] Guidance and control was closing on a radar beacon and remote radio control of the inertial heading with reference to a Plan Position Indicator radar display.[27] A good demonstration of the capability on August 4 had the missile strike within 0.3 miles (0.5 km) of the target at 80 miles (129 km) in range using a C-45 "mother," the best result achieved to that date for such a system.[28] However, comprehensive testing at Wendover Army Test Base, with just a ground-based radar and control station, showed a typical error of 1.5 miles (2.4 km) range long and 0.7 miles (1.1 km) deflection at the 85-mile (137-km) effective range of the missile employing this technique.[29] Additionally, the missiles were coming in at about $8,620 and 500 man-hours each, or roughly twice expectations.[30] Yet, the program was pressed forward while production rate by February 1945 was expected to be just 200 per month.[31]

After VE-Day, the War Department reduced JB-2 production to 7,000 at a rate of 500 per month. During formulation of the plans to assault the Japanese home islands, it became clear the system had little utility given its short range and the paucity of area targets due to the effectiveness of B-29 bombing. Air launch via the B-29 was considered but had no benefit over the use of the aircraft which, by then, was executing virtually unopposed bombing. The firing from ships was also assessed, but poor accuracy would make this a futile exercise. So, even with a proven weapon, the same calculus that caused most American guided missile programs to be slowed or abandoned rendered the JB-2 of little military utility. The capitulation of Japan brought any plans for deployment of the JB-2 Thunderbug to an end and production was truncated to 1,452 on August 14, 1945, then 1,375

The USAAF laid out an enormous production plan to acquire tens of thousands JB-2s. While this was greatly scaled back owing to several factors, the service still acquired more than 1,300 JB-2s—more than any other U.S. guided missile of the war. This photo is unusual in that the motor is apparently not firing and a panel just forward of the forward engine mount appears to be gapping. (*National Archives*)

on September 4, but terminated on September 15 at 1,391 missiles. These were all produced by the original manufacturers (Republic, Ford, *et al*) for $5,575,000.[32] No other American guided and powered missile was produced anywhere near these number during the war.

14

A Step Along

Reichsmarschall Hermann Göring admitted after the war that American aircraft were technically superior to Germany's and that development of the fighter-bomber was particularly telling in his nation's defeat.[1] The Japanese were similarly trounced by an enemy that progressed by leaps and bounds beyond their country's means. This was a remarkable reversal of opinion from 1939, or even 1941, when American airpower was considered second-rate in equipment and level of experience by those then engaged in war. What the United States achieved in a few short years led directly to exceedingly successful and practical post-war aircraft and systems employed worldwide. This account sought to illustrate the human capital, technological means, and expanding experience via aviation research and experimental projects to create this enviable aviation state by the end of hostilities.

Progress

America matched or surpassed ally Britain and enemy Germany in the scope, innovation, and excellence of many aviation designs during the war while lagging in some. Few of these last were due to poor choices or missed opportunities but rather well-considered selections emphasizing the technology America's unique circumstances in the war demanded plus negotiated divisions of labor with the U.K. Most of the more advanced weapons could not reach the field only because the existing arms and the Allied team succeeded in defeating the Axis powers sooner than some feared. Indeed, the American participation in winning the war was done almost exclusively with the weapons at hand or in development before entering the conflict, albeit with continuous maturation and upgrades.

The Americans expended exceptional effort, from the beginning of the war and especially after entering the conflict, to develop new and innovative weapons or enhancements to the same as a national priority. Recognizing the lead of the Axis powers in air weapons, the Americans strove mightily to catch up. Although the military leadership was fairly conservative and worked to restrict resource expenditures to efforts likely to yield combat results in the few years expected for the war, some amount of research and experimentation was still required in support of the push for air dominance. The results stand shoulder-to-shoulder with those achieved in the other combatant nations (only Britain and Germany in the same league), with resounding success in many areas but also shortfalls in other. The capabilities, both material and human that came out at the far end of the crisis, placed the country in a dominant aviation position throughout the world.

The lure of the "next weapon" was not absent in the U.S., and much effort and resources were expended pursuing numerous new developments, some later abandoned. However, they proceeded with more deliberation of what was within technological reach and likely to contribute significantly to the war effort, unlike the Germans. Many of the most advanced German designs, while showing aerodynamic and propulsion innovation, did not proceed much beyond the conceptual or experimental phase and were too far ahead of the state of the art in materials, structures, stability, and control technology to be realized in a wartime environment. Yet, these were pursued to excess with much expenditure of more and more limited resources. The Japanese, on the other hand, resisted changing designs or introducing advanced models in the interest of high production rates and rapid aircrew training while also faced with fewer and fewer resources.

An example of a wartime advance that was most telling only after the conflict was rocket-assisted take-off (Chapter 4). These efforts bore good fruit but was not widely consumed while combat persisted. It simply was not urgently needed and few operational units wished to burden themselves with ATO assets for the few special circumstances it would benefit. The expense and effort of procurement and the supply chain for the devices, modifying aircraft, and training personnel was not justifiable given the state of the war by that time. Routine use with the hundreds or thousands of American sorties launched per day all around the world was never considered. Even the few thousand rocket motors procured by the U.S. Navy, who actually deployed ATO to the fleet, was by necessity limited to a relatively few unique occasions.

Likewise, the more exotic range extension efforts of 1940–1945 supported a few unique missions but were otherwise too immature and cumbersome. External tanks were established as common features (Chapter 7), though wingtip tanks did not see production application on any American airplane until after the war. Aerial refueling was further developed over a post-war period of a decade as AR slowly became common with America seeking a very long-range bomber force to carry the new super-heavy atomic bombs, initially with the B-29 or its direct descendant. This initially built upon the lessons from the trailing lines and hoses methods experimented with during World War II (Chapter 7). The equipment, methodology, and nomenclature of AR established during the war has carried over to the present day.

The modification of B-29s to carry the first atomic bombs into combat (Chapter 12), and the many other examples herein, was revisited many times as aircraft

Rocket jet-assisted take-off devices (called JATO post-war, here on a Navy JM-1 or B-26) was a noteworthy achievement of the war but was little exploited until the post-war era. This was because preparing or repairing runways rapidly by American forces was another remarkable achievement of the war plus the use of water injection into engines boosted airplane performance and made such measures unnecessary. (*National Museum of the United States Air Force*)

were repurposed with add-ons, especially as the new field of electronic warfare dawned.

Cabin pressurization was just too new as war erupted to be adopted in a big way during the conflict. The Germans and British each built a handful of pressurized bombers or high-altitude reconnaissance aircraft, but only America had a large production application in the B-29 (Chapter 8) and was being routinely specified for new designs. Other examples abound. The ditching safety evaluation techniques developed by NACA in 1943 (Chapter 9), using the water tow tanks, were employed for a time with post-war airliners. These and other examples are how weapons and aviation systems normally mature, but it took a devastating war to propel the commitment to undertake the advances that set the course for a new generation of warriors and civilian operators. As a further example, by 1944 the Naval Research Laboratory had devised wing and empennage trailing edge static discharge wicks to reduce radio interference from precipitation static or electrical charge built-up by flight through the atmosphere. These, however, would see application only long after the war.

Despite the comparative caution of the Americans, much effort was expended on marginal projects in an atmosphere (at least through 1944) seeking strenuously to gain combat advantage and close the gap with those nations who had been at war for years. The Brodie System (Chapter 6) is one such example. It was conceived by an individual, funded to demonstration status, and ultimately placed into low-rate production. It had value in permitting aircraft operations in difficult terrain or at sea with comparatively few resources. The system was deployed to land and sea combat zones along with modification kits for L-4 and L-5 airplanes. Ultimately, more than 500 landing and take-off cycles were performed with no fatal accidents. However, it was slow being manufactured and deployed, and so came late to the battlefield. It might have been of great value had the war played out differently, but such are the uncertainties if weapons development, especially in wartime. Both Brodie and Gregory, unaware of how their device had been employed until after the war, would be awarded the Legion of Merit in 1945 for their pioneering efforts.[2] Although its contributions were minuscule, the exercise shows the willingness to move ahead with a unique capability that operational units insisted they needed, despite resistance by AAF leadership. Many similar World War II innovations, where manpower was more plentiful and waste more tolerated, were similarly set aside in a post-war environment seeking greater efficiency.

Criticism of the air force's perceived miserly support of ground troops had been a persistent refrain since a military airplane first took flight. The U.S. Army Air Corps actually worked hard to meet such needs to the point of having more observation airplanes than bombers in 1939 (though there were also Congressional motivations and actions contributing to this state of affairs). Organizational myopia, rapidly shifting tactical requirements, a cumbersome weapon system development process, and the ground arms failing to speak with one voice were principally to blame for the lack of preparedness by 1942. The initial iteration of liaison aircraft was

Seeking a light weight, the B-29 pressurized compartments were classical pressure vessels of circular cross-section tubes and hemispherical end bulkheads using butted joints and the thickest aluminum skins of the period. The nose was also hemispherical to simplify the pressure structure design. The gunner sighting stations were likewise spherical though the turrets, by necessity, had to interrupt the vessel with enforced cut-outs. (*National Museum of the United States Air Force*)

Cockpit pressurization was sought for fighters, but none reached combat during the war. The YP-80A (example shown here) was deployed to Europe in the last weeks before German capitulation. Compared with the heavy canopy framing seen on earlier experimental pressurized fighters, the bubble canopy on the jet is indicative of great strides in design for the feature in a remarkably short time. (*National Museum of the United States Air Force*)

An Army Air Forces Stinson L-5B (44-16835) liaison aircraft is seen on the cable of the Brodie landing and launching system during tests at Wright Field. Many operators were interested in adopting the device and it saw some combat employment, though limited to light-planes. The innovation and willingness to press ahead with a radical idea (though opposed by many) was a noteworthy accomplishment for America in the midst of a momentous war. (*National Archives*)

an example of the Air Corps' Materiel Division formulating specifications to meet their perception of the need expressed by ground forces. This was principally short take-off and landing on unprepared fields with high utility (carrying an observer, light cargo, make radio calls for artillery spotting, etc.). Yet, from the AGF perspective, these were too few, too late, over-thought, and overly complex—more meeting the desires of the airmen than the "ground pounders." It was only the press of war that made it imperative to set aside the overly long aircraft procurement process to buy minimally modified commercial light-planes and not "tinker" with them so that high production rate would not be interrupted (Chapter 2). There was some weight growth and deterioration of short-field performance, but few complaints despite distain by the Air Forces. This shows how the engineering pursuit of a technological solution for a specific performance objective could stand in the way of decisive progress for the achievement of "good enough" in a rapid fashion, fulfilling an urgent combat need. However, the poor result of the Interstate L-6 is an example of the adverse consequences of a rush to production.

The liaison aircraft fulfilled their role with little intervention by the Air Forces (who also adopted them), and a vital lesson was learned. From transporting senior personnel, carrying dispatches and mail, scouting, and artillery fire adjustment, its role expanded to include radio relay, photography, target marking, airdrop, and light attack. This reflected a general willingness to innovate in promptly answering combat needs, and acquiescence by higher authority to permit field innovations—regulations be damned. As in many other elements of the American aircraft development efforts during the war, devoted leadership with eager and talented lower tier personnel combined with a "get it done" attitude in an environment free of corruption allowed sound decisions and rapid progress outfitting the young people sent to war with the best equipment the nation could produce and field. Fortunately, this contributed to victory and a prosperous future.

Air Forces' acceptance of an AGF organic air element operating the L-birds, and then Materiel Division working with them for acquisition of suitable aircraft throughout the war, was an illustration of organizational flexibility. After first resisting, the AAF followed orders and complied without obstruction. This had implications post-war as the Army's organic aviation corps persisted beyond the establishment of the United States Air Force (USAF) in 1947. The liaison aircraft continued to hold value into the 1960s. Yet even before the end of World War II, the helicopter showed the potential for future replacement. Work on airplane STOL technology also rolled ahead.

The development of airdrop capabilities during the war was the beginning of an evolution that continues to the present day. The purpose-built tactical airlifters, with drop-down loading ramps, which appeared at the end of the war, facilitated this evolution. The drop of paracontainers out bottom hatches and bomb bays (Chapter 10) would soon fade from memory. The assault gliders likewise faded after the end of the war as quickly as they emerged at the beginning. Glider and airplane snatch went with them. However, the more radical technique of personnel snatch saw future application in the Vietnam War, as did defoliate spraying from aircraft (Chapter 10).

The tendency for personal opinion and the leaning of individual senior officers to cause sometimes repeated changes in direction of aircraft or model revisions under development had been a matter of some consternation. General Arnold and the Chief of Naval Operations were authorized to supersede competitive procurement rules for the duration of the emergency. This was unprecedented, allowing these individuals to make momentous and generally binding materiel decisions worth millions of dollars in a few sentences, uttered or written in a memo. For Arnold, it was tempered only late in the war by the AAF Board, and he had to answer questions about some decisions before Congress after the war. Although there was a war on and decisions needed to be made promptly, the choices were not carefully studied and the results were not always met with resounding success. The evolution and expanded application of standards and specifications towards the end of the war was one measure to address this problem, ensuring some consistency and a requirement for careful consideration before waiving provisions of these documents. In later years, this would be seen as tying the developers' hands and stifling innovation. The pendulum would swing to and fro well into the future.

Controlled slats and highly articulated full-span flaps, as typified by this Ryan YO-51, were not used on American combat aircraft to achieve short-field performance. Although the technology development by NACA before the war would pay dividends in other applications, basic weight management, simple flaps, and fixed slots were suitable for producing acceptable performance. This lesson in simplicity was carried forward for a time after the war. (*San Diego Air & Space Museum*)

Lessons

The Americans were prone during the first year or two of their involvement in the war to try anything and hang the cost. This was more tempered in later years but all were generally characterized by senior leadership making the decisions to proceed based on their perception of military utility with minimal technological assessment by engineers and scientists, some of those within War Department laboratories. A careful analysis of need by operational units in response to combat experience and enemy weapons was commonly lacking. Of course, such needs evolve rapidly during war as circumstances changed and the enemy reacts. The usually years-long procurement, test, evaluation, and manufacturing process was impractical during total war. Yet, the missed opportunities and examples of excess were food for thought. More care would be required in peacetime as America chose to maintain a military better equipped and with higher readiness, and with forces based around the world. The wartime experience would be revisited in later wars but with more restraint as none represented the same total war commitment and sense of unpreparedness.

After an initial period of putting numerous projects into motion and observing some fail, it was found desirable to standardize on a few types. By late 1944, it also became clear that production qualities were likely excessive. Deliveries ran ahead of need and aircraft were being stored as they emerged from production lines. For example, by mid-1943, it was seen as desirable to reduce the number of transport types to eliminate some maintenance and training burden. Likewise, the number of engine models in production were reduced and some of the more exotic reciprocating projects shelved as turbine equipment looked to dominate the future. The leaders of both services were, by 1945, also positioning themselves for expected post-war cutbacks by pushed ahead with vital developments that were recognized as not bearing fruit before the end of hostilities. The underlying R&D was also re-scoped, though some continued because of the promise for post-war advancement. All this was part of reacting to the enemy and the fortunes of war while adjusting as earlier plans played out and looking to the future. No one had attempted developments and acquisition on this scale, timeline, and pressures of war, and so waste and course changes were inevitable.[3] The Americans managed it as well or better than other combatants.

The feverish reverse engineering and production of the German V-1 Buzz Bomb as the JB-2 (Chapter 13) was remarkable, though the decision to undertake the project is questionable. The politics at the time were that the Air Forces wanted to establish a strong precedent for missile production and deployment to stand above other Army branches and military services when post-war divisions of responsibility for such new weapons were decided. Although the decision was made that the AAF would employ that weapon operationally, many other missiles were on the horizon and the broader subject of roles and responsibilities was still in flux.[4]

The JB-2 was among the first generation of American missiles emerging from the war that was almost hopelessly inefficient, imprecise, and unreliable. Yet they permitted the gathering of experience with such systems.[5] The USAAF and subsequent USAF tested the JB-2 long after the war. The Navy acquired a total 351 Loons from Army production and launched them from shore and short ship-board ramps. They then experimented with firing from submarines using improved rocket boost for a "zero-length" launch. All these trials expended nearly all of the JB-2s for benefit of training and R&D to be applied to other guided missile programs. The American version of the pulsejet and other components from the JB-2 program were applied to new experimental missiles, though ultimately set aside. All this supported the next series of missiles such that the weapons slowly matured over twenty years to practical capabilities.

Other experiences influenced preparations for future conflicts. The struggle to move aircraft like fighters and gliders to distant theaters tied up vital sea transport and placed these resources at risk of attack by an enemy after the rich prize (Chapter 11). Self-deployment capability became a desire and then a requirement in coming decades, generally equating to extended ferry range. Anti-ice and de-ice systems (Chapter 9) developed during the war became standard equipment on

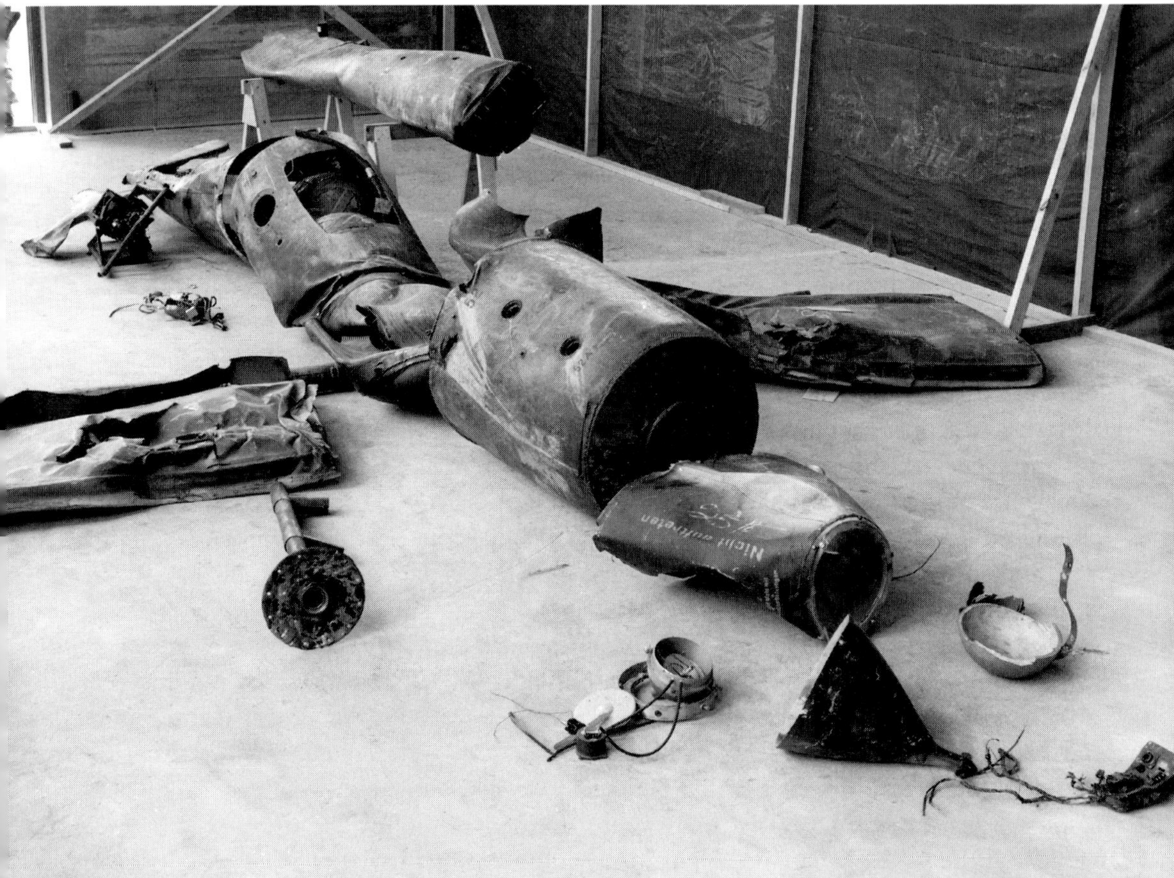

While contributing nothing during the war, the American copy of the V-1 provided the initial ground-launched winged missile that fostered an industry capability during the Cold War that followed. The capabilities and determination that permitted rapid reverse-engineering of the V-1 were emblematic of many endeavors by the U.S. The mobile launcher for the JB-2 shown came at the very end of World War II. (*National Museum of the United States Air Force and National Archives*)

Transport of aircraft to far-flung theaters aboard an aircraft carrier tied-up the vessel and placed all at risk of an enemy torpedo. In the decades that followed, it became a requirement that new designs include a self-deployment capability. This flight deck is crowded with P-47Ns *en route* from Casablanca to Guam on July 16, 1945 in preparation to participate in the final chapter of the conflict with the Empire of Japan. (*U.S. Department of Defense*)

the new aircraft emerging immediately after the conflict to permit all-weather operations and were to become vitally important safety equipment on commercial aircraft. This permitted more regular scheduling of airlines whereas previously flights were canceled based on predicted icing. The long-standing criticality of the work cannot be understated.

Reformulating

Government, academia, and industry accumulated extraordinary experience and capabilities during the war years, orders of magnitude greater than existed before the conflict. This enabled the country to accomplish remarkable aeronautical feats. Yet it was clear such could not be sustained post-war, in the commercial world or the military. As the close of the mammoth conflict appeared on the horizon, plans were formed for the remaining period of hostilities and preparing for post-war R&D. The USAAF began planning for its post-war structure in 1943 and had an Initial Post-war Air Force conceived as early as April 1944.[6] This probably did not begin to affect procurement and R&D funding decisions until

1945. An AAF Materiel Demobilization Plan was approved on September 23, 1944, with priorities defined for ongoing development projects. Continued were those anticipated to be completed within eighteen months of Germany's surrender, those expected to be of value in defeating Japan, and those benefitting long-range military capabilities. Resources were reduced or cut off to those suspended because they met none of these categories.[7]

Even before the end of World War II, Gen. Arnold recognized how greatly technology was affecting the potency of airpower. By autumn 1944, he knew the war was won and did not care if it was technically superior American weapons or sheer numbers that helped decide the outcome. However, to avoid in the future the ill-preparedness the U.S. experienced at the beginning of World War II would require a consistent nurturing of technological advancement toward specific goals through sustained investment and relationships with academia and national laboratories. Ongoing R&D programs would be necessary, both in the services and via funding of outside institutions. Such would need to be financed much more generously than in the pre-war years. Direction and control of these efforts would remain under a military with civilian oversight and guided by advice from boards of civilian experts. In September 1944, Arnold asked Dr von Kármán to head up a group of insightful and experienced engineers and scientists to lay out this course.

Von Kármán's assignment was soon formalized as director of the AAF Consulting Board for Future Research.[8] He chaired the Scientific Advisory Group in which thirty-three principal individuals represented all aspects of science influencing aircraft and aerial weapons development. They were to formulate a vision for the future Air Force guided by technological maturation. They also recommended a standing body, the Scientific Advisory Board under the AAF chief. Their resulting document outlined the reasonable course of aeronautical advancement and probable weapon systems emerging over the next ten years and established a technological forecasting regimen that persisted for decades after.[9]

As the Allies moved into Germany, technical information collection teams were established to comb through sites, interview personnel, and secure documents (thousands of tons) for detailed examination and translation. The investigators included notable researchers and aircraft development personnel. It became clear that with more focused effort, time, better integration of research and military objectives, plus freedom from Allied bombing, the Germans could have extended or even won the war. This was a lesson for the Americans. Although little of the information would affect projects already underway in the United States during the remaining months of the war, it helped focus future efforts along more productive lines.[10] The same process was acted out following Japan's surrender. Immediately after the war, foreign personnel were paid to more clearly document their wartime efforts and also recruited to work in the United States. The Soviet Union did all this as well, though the personnel they rounded up and put to work were treated as prisoners unlike those recruited by the United States.

American aviation progress was moving so fast by the end of the war that many of the collected Axis aircraft and weapons were never fully evaluated as the urgency dissipated and realization there was no longer so much to learn. By 1946, even the most advanced German wartime designs looked dated and impractical, and the Japanese worthless. Much of the captured material was scrapped within a few years. The benefits of personnel and research documentation were more long-lasting. Additionally, organizations researching, collecting, assessing, and evaluating potential adversary systems were sustained beyond the war.

In spring 1945, von Kármán headed a team of personnel surveying the German aeronautical industry and wartime accomplishments after that nation's defeat. The doctor delivered a report to the Air Forces in August 1945 titled *Where We Stand* in which he insisted that sustained air supremacy would rely on such things as manned supersonic aircraft, missiles, and long-range ballistic rockets. These, he stated, were not only possible but must be pursued with enduring funding and encouragement of research, development, and experimentation.[11]

An example of the evolving attitude towards certain technologies is evident in rocket propulsion. As practical rocket motors emerged just before the war, there was the general conviction in the U.S. that rocket propulsion as sole aircraft propulsion was impractical and exceptionally hazardous for all but research aircraft, and so no great efforts should be expended on them. However, the GALCIT researchers were aware of the pre-war work on rocket-boosted and rocket-propelled aircraft undertaken in Germany. Beyond 1940, this insight was cut off by wartime censorship. By mid-1943, the Allies became aware of German rocket-powered aircraft efforts and decided to pursue same, although the imperative that drove the German project (mass Allied bomber formations) had no Allied counterpart. A program was kicked off and Aerojet was funded for more work. It was recognized that rockets were much more challenging to sustain in the field, the propellants usually more hazardous to move than aviation fuels. A close post-war study of the German experience showed the marginal value of their products, though the American solid propellants was a notable contribution to the field of aircraft rocket propulsion. After another decade, rockets were largely set aside as prospective primary propulsion systems and a further decade dropped for ATO as jet engines improved in efficiency. The technology was developed and its practicality assessed, only to be shelved as unneeded. It was this process Gen. Arnold sought to ensure could occur, though hopefully with more enduring results.

A more successful example was also fostered by rocket propulsion; ballistic missiles. All the defense efforts refocusing GALCIT efforts yielded a name change to the Jet Propulsion Laboratory (JPL) on July 1, 1944. Although the Air Forces had cooled toward rockets, the Army's Ordnance Corps had Caltech build short-range artillery rockets during the war and decided to pursue ballistic missiles. It gave the institution a $3 million contract in January 1944 to develop the rocket and ground support equipment with a goal of a 20,000-lbf (89-kN) thrust motor burning for sixty seconds for a 30–40-mile (48–64-km) range. In December 1944, JPL flew the Private A that leveraged off their ATO technology. The 8-foot (2.4-m) missile flew to 11 miles (18 km) in range. They next undertook development of the longer-range Corporal but took a detour to build the two-stage WAC Corporal sounding rocket, again employing American World War II rocket technology. Weighing 665 lb (302 kg) and standing 16 feet (4.9 m), this rocket flew in October 1945 to 235,000 feet (71,629 m) with a 25-lb (11.3-kg) payload, becoming the first manmade object to exit the atmosphere. The space age was dawning, leveraging off the rocket technology brought to fruition during the war.

The growing importance of rockets led Caltech to create a jet propulsion course at the behest of the services. Initially, half the student were military personnel. A new standard for officers to have college degrees was to ensure suitable academic grounding for the technical nature of the airpower forces that had emerged and were foreseen in the near future. An officer cadre supporting R&D would need to possess advanced degrees. The Air Force and Navy would soon establish their own graduate schools for such purposes. The AAF also created a new air engineering development center for aerodynamic and engine testing in Tullahoma, Tennessee, made up of wind tunnels and test cells, eventually named after Gen. Arnold. All this served as underpinnings for the new United States Air Force as a separate armed service co-equal with the Army, Navy, and Marines.

What's Next?

Although more restrained than the Germans in exploring new technologies and starting new development programs, the Americans did much during the war. With some exceptions, most of what the other combatants did the U.S. did as well and also undertook a few unique efforts. At the end of the war, this did not change as the advances by the Germans were examined with the knowledge that the Soviets had collected similar material. There was no let up with the end of hostilities, though paced by smaller budgets.

Americans' perception of their place in the world was greatly altered by the war. They could no longer consider themselves isolated by great oceans. Their ability to affect world events and respond to military emergencies was profoundly expanded by the war. The monumental conflict left the United States with superior weapons, industries, experience, and economy. The capabilities of advancing technology, especially aeronautics and rocketry, supported by a democratic government and commercial or academic institutions, seemed boundless. Looking at the achievements such as presented in this book brought pride, confidence, and resolve. Particularly, the "we can do anything" attitude counted for much in meeting post-war challenges, especially the confrontation with Communism that would soon emerge. These resources and attributes were counted on to ensure the nation's edge against all threats and would generally prove reliable and effective during the decades of Cold War that followed.

The effects of the wartime efforts on post-war developments and the nascent Cold War was monumental. Some neglect was evident in the Korean War waged in 1950–1953 with a considerable number of World War II weapons still employed. Similar experimentation and willingness to consider odd solutions were seen later, such as during the Vietnam War of the 1960s. For two or three decades following World War II, those who had participated shared their creative energies, determination, and sense that America could do anything, especially employing airpower fed by an incredible aviation industry. Such attitudes occasionally led the United States into unfortunate circumstances. While her weapons were seldom inadequate to a task, leadership and a reasonable restraint sometime proved wanting.

Lockheed P-80s were sent to Europe before the end of hostilities, and many additional projects were underway to ensure a U.S. lead in jet aircraft development after the war. This Grumman G-71 design for a naval jet fighter (much like an F8F converted to take the Westinghouse 24C) was in response to a Navy solicitation from September 1944 and, typical of that period, equipped with a straight wing and simple inlet. (*Northrop Grumman History Center*)

Endnotes

Chapter 1

1. Claussen, M. P., *Materiel Research and Development in the Army Air Arm 1914–1945*, AAF Historical Studies No. 50, AAF Historical Office, Headquarters, Army Air Forces, Washington, D.C., November 1946, p. 106.
2. *Ibid.*, pp. 131–132.
3. Gorn, M. H., *The Universal Man, Theodore von Kármán's Life in Aeronautics*, Smithsonian History of Aviation Series (Washington, D.C.: Smithsonian Institute Press, 1992), p. 97.
4. Young, J. O., *Supersonic Symposium: The Men of Mach 1*, An AFSC Special Study (Edwards Air Force Base, California, Air Force Flight Test Center History Office, September 1990), p. 83, Note 53, and Young, J. O., *Meeting the Challenge of Supersonic Flight* (Edwards Air Force Base, California: Air Force Flight Test Center History Office, 1997), p. 63, note 29.
5. The conclusion was drawn by a British Air Marshal and apparently echoed by Lt. Col. George C. Kenney, a rising leader in the USAAC, then in England on an observation mission. AAF Historical Office, *Comparative History of Research and Development Policies Affecting Air Materiel 1915–1944*, U.S. Air Force Historical Study No. 20, Headquarters, Army Air Forces, June 1945, p. 82.
6. Claussen, *op. cit.*, pp. 140–143.
7. von Kármán, T., and Edson, L., *The Wind and Beyond: Theodore von Kármán, Pioneer in Aviation and Pathfinder in Space* (Boston, Massachusetts: Little Brown and Company, 1967), p. 274.
8. Lend-Lease itself brought R&D efforts. The original commercial purchases had specifications from the foreign customer that demanded some measure of research and then development to produce a system suitable for U.K. armed forces. However, when delivering ostensibly American armaments, the substitution of elements (such as radios, machine guns, etc.) within the other's supply system meant some rework and production changes. General Arnold describes how fuel with a higher aromatic content, used in Australia, dissolved the tank self-sealing compound which then clogged fuel lines. This forced an urgent investigation seeking a new tank treatment material. Arnold, H. H., *Global Mission* (New York: Harper & Brothers, Publishers, 1949), p. 303.
9. Dean, F. H. (ed.), *Report of Joint Fighter Conference, NAS Patuxent River, MD, 16–23 October 1944*, (Atglen, Pennsylvania: Schiffer Publishing, 1998), p. 152.
10. Skip bombing was a British innovation that the Americans adopted via trials at Eglin. Likewise, incendiaries were developed based on the European experience but using jellied gasoline to make napalm.

11. Claussen, *op. cit.*, provides these figures, pp. 49, 75, and 120.
12. *Ibid.*, p. 118.
13. Anderton, D. A., *Sixty Years of Aeronautical Research, 1919–1977*, EP145 (Washington, D.C.: National Aeronautics and Space Administration, 1978), p. 23.
14. Arnold's opinion is noted in Dawson, V. P., *Engines and Innovation: Lewis Laboratory and American Propulsion Technology*, The NASA History Series, SP-4306 (Washington, D.C.: National Aeronautics and Space Administration, 1991), p. 19. The observation from the Navy was made by Captain S. B. Spangler of BuAer's Power Plant Design section as recorded in Dean, *op. cit.*, p. 73.
15. Professor von Kármán describes a dispute between NACA and the Army when the latter decided in 1939 to build a new high-speed, large test section, wind tunnel at Wright Field. (This was Arnold's decision following advice from von Kármán.) The services were sometimes frustrated by what they saw as a slow, research-oriented, and excessively conservative approach at NACA. von Kármán, *op. cit.*, p. 226. No doubt such things were the source of debates within congressional committees when it came time to slice-up the federal monetary pie. The professor was the instigator for many test facilities constructed in the run-up to the war to ensure the U.S. remained competitive—well informed as he was on the state of aeronautical research and development around the world. He worked with whomever approached him regardless of federal, corporate, or international 'rice bowl' boundaries.
16. For aircraft production see Craven, W. F., and Cate, J. L., *The Army Air Forces in World War II, Volume Six, Men and Planes* (Washington, D.C.: Office of Air Force History, 1983), p. 350, and Holley, I. B., Jr., *Buying Aircraft: Materiel Procurement for the Army Air Forces*, United States Army in World War II, Special Study (Washington, D.C.: Center for Military History, United States Army, 1989), p. 548. Regarding industrial output, see Kelsey, B. S., *The Dragon's Teeth? Creation of the United States Air Power for World War II* (Washington, D.C.: Smithsonian Institute Press, 1982), pp. 11 and 14.
17. Craven and Cate, p. 423.
18. Grossnick, R. A., *United States Naval Aviation 1910–1995* (Washington, D.C.: Naval Historical Center, 1997), p. 448.
19. Arnold, *op. cit.*, p. 182.
20. *Ibid.*, p. 207. Arnold describes how the Secretary of War's personal aircraft, operated by the Air Corps, lacked an ignition harness suitable for penetrating weather because the low-bidder's offering was deemed unsuitably shielded. Acquiring an acceptable substitute outside the logistics system was verboten. So, Arnold himself obtained harnesses from American Airlines and saw that they were installed.
21. *Ibid.*, p. 412.
22. *Ibid.*, p. 496, and Chilstrom, K. and Leary, P., *Test Flying at Old Wright Field* (Omaha, Nebraska: Westchester House Publishers, 1995), p. 188.
23. Doolittle was an exceptionally experienced aviator as well as an engineer, having received a doctorate in aeronautic engineer from the Massachusetts Institute of Technology (one of the first to do so) and worked as a test pilot. He contributed to the development of instrument flying and 100-octane aviation fuels, both which proved so valuable during the war. Doolittle had left the service as a Major but was returned to active duty, largely due to lobbying by Arnold to change a law that prohibited activating field grade reserve officers. The man had broad technical and managerial acumen as well as fine leadership skills and went on to serve as a combat commander.
24. Lindbergh worked in many capacities within government, the military (including as a member of the Kilner Board), and industry to promote aviation and the build-up of American capabilities. However, he would resign his reserve USAAC commission following high-level criticism of his active advocacy of the U.S. remaining out of the war. This was only after the President, whom Lindbergh held in low regard, offered him the equivalent of a cabinet post for Air (which he declined) that he was considered redeemed. However, even after Pearl Harbor he was not commissioned an officer. He

remained a civilian even later in the war while operating in war zones while testing P-38s.

25. Johnson, C. L., and Smith, M., *Kelly, More Than My Share of it All* (Washington, D.C.: Smithsonian Books, 1985), pp. 100–103, and LeVier, T. and Guenther, J., *Pilot* (New York: Bantam Books, December 1990), pp. 153–171. The turbine wheel failures were due to impurities in the molten metal settling to the bottom of the ingot when cast. The wheels machined from the bottom of the ingot lacked sufficient strength. No one cared to learn and correct such things through hazardous flight trials, but the wartime urgency left few tolerable alternatives.
26. Heinemann, E. H. and Rausa, R., *Ed Heinemann, Combat Aircraft Designer* (Annapolis, Maryland: Naval Institute Press, 1980), pp. 66–67.
27. Air Historical Office, *The Modification of Army Aircraft in the United States 1939–1945*, Army Air Forces Historical Studies: No. 62, Headquarters, Army Air Forces, August 1947, pp. 1–2.
28. *Ibid.*, p. 95, describes demands to convert some elements of the A-24 such as seats, flooring, and fairings, to wood. Douglas resisted and the order was eventually rescinded.
29. In Dean, *op. cit.*, p. 242, Commander P. H. Ramsey, Director of Test at NAS Patuxent River, commented on discovering longitudinal instability in a model of fighter just about to be delivered to Pax for service evaluation. The manufacturer's very experience flight test team admitted they had simply forgotten to undertake the testing. Additionally, Mel Gough of NACA Langley observed (p. 34) that aircraft were progressively evolved through various models without the same thorough testing of the original. The newer models might suffer added weight and drag, and generally degrading handling qualities. Some development deficiencies survived into fleet service and had to be suffered by the operators. An example was substitution of paddle propeller blades on the B-24D that were derided by the aircrew as detracting from performance. Generally, hundreds of planes were built before corrective actions could be taken, if ever.
30. Chilstrom, *op. cit.*, p. 196.
31. *USAF Test Pilot School, 1944–1979* (Edwards Air Force Base, California: USAF Test Pilot School, 1986), pp. 2–3, and *Against the Wind, 90 Years of Flight Test in the Miami Valley*, History Office, Aeronautical Systems Center, Air Force Materiel Command (Wright-Patterson AFB, Ohio, 1994), p. 26.
32. Hansen, J. R., *Engineer in Charge, A History of the Langley Aeronautical Laboratory, 1917–1958*, SP-4305 (Washington, D.C.: National Aeronautics and Space Administration, 1987), p. 219, and Gray, G. W., *Frontiers of Flight, The Story of NACA Research* (New York, Alfred A. Knopf, 1948), p. 17.
33. Anderton, *op. cit.*, p. 22. Gray, *op. cit.*, pp. 122–123, attributes 30 mph (48 kph) recovered for the P-40 and 52 mph (84 kph) for the P-39.
34. Profile drag is a combination of drag from skin friction and from the adverse pressure gradients in the boundary layer owing to the contour of the airfoil. The boundary layer is the thin layer of air adjacent to the wing surface going from zero to the freestream airspeed.
35. Army aircraft serials numbers will be shown as it is done here or in parenthesis following a type or model designation. Navy Bureau numbers, or BuNo, will also be similarly indicated.
36. Heinemann, *op. cit.*, p. 77, describes how the government inspectors at the Douglas A-26 (employing the laminar flow airfoil) plant in Tulsa, Oklahoma, would perform fine tolerance checks, attaching a 1-inch (25-mm) diameter white label where irregularities were discovered. Some aircraft came off the assembly line looking "as if it had been hit by a snow storm." Adherence to the exacting standards proved largely impractical in high-tempo wartime production.
37. von Kármán, Theodore, *Where We Stand* (Washington, D.C.: U.S. Army Air Forces, 1946), p. 46.

38. Chambers, M. A., *Flight Research at NASA Langley Research Center*, Image of Aviation series (Charleston, South Carolina: Arcadia Publishing, 2007), p. 4.
39. Matthews, B., *Cobra!, Bell Aircraft Corporation 1934–1946* (Atglen, Pennsylvania: Schiffer, 1996), pp. 199–203.
40. Nineteen aircraft were systematically tested for the underlying data through 1941, twelve before the war, and sixty were tested by the end of the war. Anderton, *op. cit.*, p. 24, Loftin, L. F., Jr., *Quest for Performance, The Evolution of Modern Aircraft*, SP-468 (Washington, D.C.: National Aeronautics and Space Administration, 1985), pp. 115 and 119, and Hansen, *op. cit.*, p. 183. Phillips, W. H., "Recollections of the Langley Memorial Aero Lab," *AAHS Journal*, Vol. 37 No. 2, Summer 1992, p. 120, recounts that the NACA had an agreement with the War Department to evaluate the third production example of each new type. This was later revised to the fifth article per Chambers, J. R., and Chambers, M. A, *Radical Wings & Wind Tunnels, Advanced Concepts Tested at NASA Langley* (North Branch, Minnesota: Specialty Press, 2008), p. 34. The Army and Navy both developed their own specifications but in cooperation with NACA given their extensive and scientific testing and resulting database.
41. Borchers, P. F., Franklin, J. A., and Fletcher, J. W., *Flight Research at Ames 1940–1997: Fifty-Seven Years of Development and Validation of Aeronautical Technology*, NASA/SP-1998-330 (Ames Research Center, Moffett Field, California: National Aeronautics and Space Administration, 1998), p. 12, Hartman, E. P., *Adventures in Research, A History of Ames Research Center 1940–1965*, NASA Center History Series, SP-4302 (Washington, D.C.: National Aeronautics and Space Administration, 1970), pp. 85–86, Dean, *op. cit.*, p. 122, and Gray, *op. cit.*, pp. 148–149 and 161–162. With flight speeds increasing with all types in every category, the days of fabric-covered surfaces was approaching an end. Maintained for light control surface weight, believed necessary for suitable balance and avoiding flutter, it was also employed during the war to avoid additional use of aluminum. The Douglas C-74, designed in the latter half of the war and first flown on September 5, 1945, still had fabric covered control surfaces. During a limit dive speed test of 372 mph (599 kph) the elevator fabric puckered and the distorted airflow deflected the trailing edge flying tab. This deflection altered the fabric deformation and so the tab rotated back only to produce the fabric pucker again. This instability (flutter) generated such violent oscillations that it tore off the outer wing panels. The crew had to abandon the airplane. Yet, even metal skins of light gauge were distorting under air loads with bulges and wrinkles. Higher gauge material and closer stringer spacing was adopted. Dean, *op. cit.*, p.116. Rippling of the metal skin on the Curtiss SB2C produced turbulent flow separation during dive pull-outs that impinged on the empennage and produced destructive loads until remedied with a stiffened wing structure and reinforced tail. Gray, *op. cit.*, pp. 163–164.
42. Gray, *op. cit.*, pp. 170–171.
43. *Ibid.*, pp. 173–174.
44. Hartman, *op. cit.*, p. 87.
45. Dawson, *op. cit.*, pp. 9 and 228.

Chapter 2

1. Borchers, P. F., Franklin, J. A., and Fletcher, J. W., *Flight Research at Ames 1940–1997: Fifty-Seven Years of Development and Validation of Aeronautical Technology*, NASA/SP-1998-330 (Ames Research Center, Moffett Field, California: National Aeronautics and Space Administration, 1998), pp. 11–12, Hartman, E. P., *Adventures in Research, A History of Ames Research Center 1940–1965*, NASA Center History Series, SP-4302 (Washington, D.C.: National Aeronautics and Space Administration, 1970), p. 82, Gray, G. W., *Frontiers of Flight, The Story of NACA Research* (New York, Alfred A. Knopf, 1948), pp. 59 and 61, and as recalled by Nissen in an interview with the teenaged author.

2. Dean, F. H. (ed.), *Report of Joint Fighter Conference, NAS Patuxent River, MD, 16–23 October 1944*, (Atglen, Pennsylvania: Schiffer Publishing, 1998), p. 116, and Gray, *op. cit.*, pp. 60–62. This aircraft does not appear in the NACA records and so was not in the Committee's possession.
3. Holcomb, M., Raytheon Aircraft Company, *Beech AT-10 Wichita*, SAE Technical Paper Series 2000-01-1679, May 2000, p. 6.
4. Francillon, R. J., *McDonnell Douglas Aircraft Since 1920: Volume I* (Annapolis, Maryland: Naval Institute Press, 1988), p. 201, whereas Williams, N. M., "Globemaster, The Douglas C-74," *AAHS Journal*, Vol. 25 No. 2, Summer 1980, p. 84, states in a caption that the propellers were free-turning.
5. The tufts swirl and even reverse direction in concert with the adjacent airflow.
6. von Kármán, Theodore, *Where We Stand* (Washington, D.C.: U.S. Army Air Forces, 1946), p. 73, gives the lift coefficient of 3.5 figure while Ross, J. C., "On Trial—A Revolutionary Wing," *Popular Mechanics*, January 1949, pp. 144–145, suggests 2.5. The original L-1 wing was very efficient owing to a leading-edge slat, slotted flaps, and drooped ailerons. See also Flatt, J., *The History of Boundary Layer Control in the United States of America* (New York: Pergamon Press, 1961), pp. 123–125.
7. Holcomb, *op. cit.*, p. 6.
8. A servo tab moves opposite the rotation of the primary surface to aid in moving the surface and so reduces pilot effort. Bobweights change stick forces based upon displacement of the stick. The unbalanced tab intentionally increases forces as the surface is moved away from the trim point set by the pilot.
9. Hoover, H. H. and White, M. D., *Lateral-Directional Characteristics of North American XP-51 Aircraft (A.C. No. 41-38) with Beveled Trailing Edge Ailerons in High-speed Flight*, Memorandum Report, NACA, 1942, White, M. D., and Hoover, H. H., *Flight Testing of Modifications to Improve the Aileron Control Effectiveness of a North American XP-51 Airplane (A.C. No. 41-38)*, Memorandum Report, NACA, 1942, and Gray, *op. cit.*, pp. 144 and 146–147. The B-29 rudder more evidently reflected this section.
10. Matthews, B., *Cobra!, Bell Aircraft Corporation 1934–1946* (Atglen, Pennsylvania: Schiffer, 1996), pp. 200 205.
11. Holcomb, *op. cit.*, pp. 6–7.
12. The USAAC and later USAAF designated research projects with the MX-___ numbering scheme
13. See the author's book *American Aircraft Development in WWII: Special Types, 1939-1945*, (Surrey, United Kingdom: Crécy Publishing, 2016) for a full accounting of American wartime rotorcraft development.
14. Pilots commonly dumped brought-back ordnance before landing for this reason.
15. Borchers, *op. cit.*, pp. 20–21.
16. Mr. Custer continued to promote his channel wing concept, building another testbed that was extensively evaluated immediately after the war by the military and NACA. Prototypes of a production design were also built in later years. Decades of tireless work and investment ultimately proved fruitless. An exciting concept and demonstrations could not overcome the fact that the benefits of the channel wing did not outweigh the negatives. See especially Boyne, W., "The Custer Channel Wing Story," *Airpower*, May 1977, pp. 10–12, and Mitchell, K. A., "Mr. Custer and His Channel Wing Airplanes," *AAHS Journal*, Vol. 43 No. 1, Spring 1998, pp. 65–66.
17. Unlike the Germans, the Allies did not arm transport types. For the liaison airplanes, this helped to keep the weight down as accommodating a gun, ammunition, and gunner (usually doubling as observer) would be a severe addition. Especially as most American Liaison and Utility types were developed from commercial products, avoiding the requirement helped ensure a rapid march to production. Lack of the gun was not noted as a significant deficiency during the war. The little airplanes could be flown so low and slow, and turned so tightly, as to confound gunnery of attacking fighters. This is not to say the light-planes were not shot down, but these were relatively few and a gun may have little reduced the losses.

18. Underwood, J. W., *The Stinsons* (Glendale, California: Heritage Press, 1982), p. 65, and Holley, I. B., Jr., Capt., Air Technical Service Command Historical Office, *Evolution of the Liaison-Type Airplane 1917–1944*, Army Air Forces Historical Studies No. 44, Historical Office, AAF Headquarters, Army Air Forces, April 1946, reprinted in *AAHS Journal*, Vol. 51 No.1, Spring 2006, p. 60.
19. Ryan sources provide the first numbers, presented in *Plane Portraits* (Lindbergh Field, San Diego, California: Ryan Aeronautical Company, undated but probably about 1968), p. 6 and repeated by Cassagneres, E., *The Spirit of Ryan* (Blue Ridge Summit, Pennsylvania: Tab Books, 1982), p. 208. The official AAF numbers are reflected in *Army Aircraft Characteristics, Production and Experimental*, Report No. TSEST—A2, ATSC, United States Army, April 1, 1946, p. 52.
20. Cassagneres, *op. cit.*, p. 210.
21. Holley, *op. cit.*, p. 94, and Historical Office, *Case History of the Liaison Aircraft Program*, Air Technical Service Command, Wright Field, Ohio, November 1944, p. 176.
22. Although an alternative to the standard 73-octane unleaded aviation fuel, this 80-octane fuel contained lead, tending to gum-up cylinder valves over time, and did not provide the usual engine performance. The 100-octane fuel used by high-performance aircraft engines was entirely unsuitable, burning-out the engine.
23. Adcock, A., *US Liaison Aircraft in Action* (Carrollton, Texas: Squadron/Signal Publications, 2005), p. 41.
24. Raines, E. F., Jr., *Eyes of the Artillery, The Origins of Modern U.S. Army Aviation in World War II*, Army Historical Series (Washington, D.C.: Center of Military History, United States Army, 2000), p. 298.
25. Holley, *op. cit.*, p. 104.
26. Adcock, *op. cit.*, p. 41, and *Army Aircraft Characteristics*, *op. cit.*, p. 50.
27. Piper Club of France, L-14, piperclubfrance.com/piper-l-14-army-cruiser-ec-aap/, provided a fine summary of this aircraft on this website in 2016. They reported that it was necessary to add 3 feet (0.9 m) at each wingtip, outboard of the slot, to improved handling. This suggests that the original wing was a shorter span than the L-4 because the final span was nearly the same as the Cub. This account is suspicious.
28. Wegg, J., *General Dynamics Aircraft and their Predecessors* (Annapolis, Maryland: Naval Institute Press, 1990), p. 181, and *Army Aircraft Characteristics*, *op. cit.*, p. 51.

Chapter 3

1. *The Pratt & Whitney Aircraft Story* (Pratt & Whitney Aircraft, 1952), pp. 139–140.
2. Dawson, V. P., *Engines and Innovation: Lewis Laboratory and American Propulsion Technology*, The NASA History Series, SP-4306 (Washington, D.C.: National Aeronautics and Space Administration, 1991), p. 19.
3. *Ibid.*, pp. 29–30, and Gray, G. W., *Frontiers of Flight, The Story of NACA Research* (New York, Alfred A. Knopf, 1948), p. 254.
4. Dean, F. H., and Hagedorn, D., *Curtiss Fighter Aircraft, A Photographic History 1919–1948* (Atglen, Pennsylvania: Shiffer Publishing, 2007), p. 276, and Bowers, P. M., *Curtiss Aircraft 1907–1947* (Annapolis, Maryland: Naval Institute Press, 1979), p. 475.
5. Thompson, J., "Vultee Engine-Test Aircraft in World War II," *AAHS Journal*, Vol. 39 No. 4, Winter 1994, p. 278, and Thompson, J., "Air Force for Sale!" *Airpower*, May 1993, p. 40.
6. Thompson, J., *Vultee Aircraft 1932–1947* (Santa Ana, California: Jonathan Thompson, 1992), pp. 20 and 37, and Bradley, R. E., *Convair Advanced Designs II: Secret Fighters, Attack Aircraft and Unique Concepts 1929–1973* (Manchester, United Kingdom: Crécy Publishing, 2013), pp. 177–178.
7. Francillon, R. J., *McDonnell Douglas Aircraft Since 1920: Volume I* (Annapolis, Maryland: Naval Institute Press, 1988), p. 306, and Wolf, W. *Douglas B-18 Bolo, The*

Ultimate Look: From Drawing Board to U-Boat Hunter (Atglen, Pennsylvania: Schiffer Publishing, 2007), p. 191.

8. Johnson, R. E., "Why the B-29 Bomber, and Why the Wright R-3350 Engine?" in *AAHS Journal* Vol. 33 No. 3, Fall 1988, pp. 178–179.
9. Moran, G. P., *Aeroplanes Vought 1917–1977* (Temple City, California: Historical Aviation Album, 1977), p. 80, provides the date for the maiden flight of the V-326A that is reported in many sources to have never flown.
10. *Army Aircraft Characteristics, Production and Experimental*, Report No. TSEST—A2, ATSC, United States Army, April 1, 1946, p. 19, gives maximum airspeed as 327 mph (526 kph) and empty weight as 34,750 lb (15,762 kg) while carrying 2,810 gal (10,637 l) of fuel in the wings for a 3,300-mile (5,311-km) normal range. It is unclear if the numbers in this reference are specification figures or measured flight test values. However, compared with the late-model B-17F (299 mph (369 kph), 34,000 lb (15,422 kg), plus 1,730 gal (6,549 l) and 2,810 miles (4,522 km) with the outboard wing tanks) it does suggest that the boost in range with the "Tokyo Tanks" was a major component of the project.
11. Whitney, D. D., *Vee's for Victory, The Story of the Allison V-1710 Aircraft Engine 1929–1948* (Atglen, Pennsylvania: Schiffer Publishing, 1998), p. 296.
12. *Ibid.* Most accounts give the delivery date as "early 1942."
13. Chambers, J. R., and Chambers, M. A, *Radical Wings & Wind Tunnels, Advanced Concepts Tested at NASA Langley* (North Branch, Minnesota: Specialty Press, 2008), p. 53.
14. Story, R. W., "The GE Schenectady Flight Test Center (Its Origins and Early History)," *AAHS Journal*, Vol. 47 No. 3, Fall 2002, p. 210, and Ordway, F. I., Jr., Maj. Air Corps. Assistant Executive, Materiel Division, "Assignment of B-23 Airplane for Supercharger Test Work," February 9, 1942, and 1st Endorsement, Lewis, R. C. Maj., Air Corps, Acting Assistant Air Adjutant General, February 20, 1942.
15. The examples are found in Dean, F. H. (ed.), *Report of Joint Fighter Conference, NAS Patuxent River, MD, 16–23 October 1944*, (Atglen, Pennsylvania: Schiffer Publishing, 1998), pp. 224–229, and Gray, *op. cit.*, p. 222.
16. Francillon, R. J., *Grumman Aircraft Since 1929* (Annapolis, Maryland: Naval Institute Press, 1989), pp. 70–71 and Andrews, H., "End of the Line ... The Last Curtiss Navy Fighter," *Air Enthusiast Quarterly*, No. 3, no date, p. 98.
17. Stapfer, H., *B-26 Marauder in Action*, Aircraft No. 210 (Carrollton, Texas: Squadron Signal Publications, 2008), p. 58.
18. Johnsen, *op. cit.*, pp. 36–37.

Chapter 4

1. Decker, C. J., Capt., *Memorandum Report on Assisted Take-Off System for Aircraft*, TSEPL-3H-664-359, November 9, 1944, and Stewart, S. R., Col., Chief Equipment Laboratory, Propulsion and Accessories Subdivision, Engineering Division, "Aircraft Assisted Take-Off Device," letter to All American Aviation, Inc., April 27, 1945.
2. Historical Division, Intelligence T-2, *Case History of Assisted Take-Off Devices*, Air Materiel Command, Wright Field, February 1946, p. 1 and summary entry 9, and Bunker, H. G., Capt., Experimental Engineering Section, *Memorandum Report on Assisted Take-Off Methods*, EXP-M-50-395, January 30, 1940.
3. Historical Division, *op. cit.*, entry 9, Chilstrom, K. and Leary, P., *Test Flying at Old Wright Field* (Omaha, Nebraska: Westchester House Publishers, 1995), p. 231, and Keisel, K. M., *Wright Field*, Images of Aviation series (Charleston, South Carolina: Arcadia Publishing, 2016), p. 91.
4. Solid rocket propellants would soon play combat roles from infantry bazookas to artillery barrage rockets and air-to-surface attack aircraft projectiles. These, however,

are ordnance and so outside the scope of this text. Gaseous propellants were seen as impractical from the first for atmospheric flight given the high pressures and likely spherical tanks required that were generally incompatible with contemporary aircraft design. Liquid hydrogen was also impractical given the low density and so large volume storage tankage.

5. Dane, P. H., Capt., Aircraft Laboratory, *Memorandum Report on Conference Regarding D. Goddard's Jet Propulsion Proposal*, EXP-M-51/APR150, September 15, 1941, p. 2.
6. Meyers, E. B., "Air Supremacy, Impulse Reaction Aircraft Engine," undated but approximately May 1942.
7. von Kármán, T., and Edson, L., *The Wind and Beyond: Theodore von Kármán, Pioneer in Aviation and Pathfinder in Space* (Boston, Massachusetts: Little Brown and Company, 1967), pp. 243–244.
8. Gorn, M. H., *The Universal Man, Theodore von Kármán's Life in Aeronautics*, Smithsonian History of Aviation Series (Washington, D.C.: Smithsonian Institute Press, 1992), p. 88.
9. Day, C. L., *Silent Ones, WWII Invasion Gliders Test and Experiment* (Lambertville, Michigan: Charles Day, 2001), p. 43.
10. Grossnick, R. A., *United States Naval Aviation 1910–1995* (Washington, D.C.: Naval Historical Center, 1997), p. 115.
11. Sams, J. H., Lt-Col., Materiel Command Liaison Officer with Bureau of Aeronautics, "Navy Assisted Take-off of Carrier Aircraft," letter to AC/AS, M&S, Chief, Development Branch, August 15, 1944.
12. Carroll, F. O., Brig.-Gen., Chief, Engineering Division, "Status Report on Project MX-121," letter to Commanding General, AAF, May 13, 1944, p. 1, and Smith, H. Y., Lt-Col., Chief Engineering Standards, Service Engineering Section, Engineering Division, "Request for Performance of Functional and Tactical Tests on Jet Propulsion Equipment," letter to President, AAF Board, February 17, 1945, p. 2.
13. Sams, *op. cit.*, p. 3.
14. *Statement of Military Requirements, Assist Take-off Unit*, (Headquarters, Army Air Forces, July 21, 1945).
15. Ober, J. H., Capt., Office, Chief of Administration, Air Technical Services Command, "Report of Progress on B-29 and B-32—Rocket Assisted Take-Off Therefor," letter to Commanding General, Army Air Forces, January 17, 1945.
16. Avery, N., *North American Aircraft 1934–1998, Volume 1* (Santa Ana, California: Narkiewicz/Thompson, 1998), p. 132.
17. Speir, G. B., Lt-Col., Acting Chief, Power Plant/Propulsion Section, "Conference on Assisted Take-off Solid Propellant Rockets," memorandum for record, August 10, 1945.
18. Bornstein, L. M, Capt., Field Artillery, *Report on Observations of Brodie System Demonstration at Coronado, California, 5 and 6 October 1944*, October 10, 1944, pp. 1–2.
19. Encyclopedia Astronautica, astronautix/engines.com, XCALR-2000A-1 entry.
20. Israel, G., "Summary of Investigation of Jet Propelled Fighters," Inter-Office Memorandum, Grumman Aircraft Corp., January 19, 1945, p. 3.

Chapter 5

1. Mach 1.0 is approximately 741 mph (1,193 kph) at sea level on a 32-degree F (0-degree C) day in dry air. In generating lift, the flow velocity increases across the wing and so this is where sonic speeds will occur first. Generating high lift via maneuvering like a dive pull-out can promote shock formation at lower airspeeds. The center of pressure or lift on the wing shifts aft as shocks form because flow velocity decreases across the shock to produce a reduction in lift (so called 'shock-stall') and loss of trailing edge control surface effectiveness. The flow behind the shock is

also turbulent and this impinges on the horizontal stabilizer to cause buffeting. The stabilizer can develop its own shock with effects like that of the wing. The loss of lift on the wing will alter flow from the wing over the tail, changing the flow incidence angle such that the tail down-load influence is greatly reduced. Combined with the aft movement of the center of lift, a pitch-over is experienced. Control forces rise dramatically and effectiveness is minimal. This leads to the pilot feeding in near or full aft stick trying to keep the nose up. As the tail and elevator were sized and placed based upon sub-critical airflow behavior, they produce insufficient rates for recovery unless the speed is reduced below the critical Mach number. Hence, the "tuck under" and dive are difficult to recover from except after entering denser air at low altitude where the speed of sound and critical Mach increases beyond the aircraft airspeed. Even if a pull-out is initiated, the greater lift again promotes shock formation. Some pilots used elevator trim to increase the tail lift and affect dive recovery sooner. However, that risked a dramatic pitch-up and over-g with possible structural failure as the speed reduced past critical Mach. More powerful engines, and heavier airframes to accommodate them, were producing relatively minor increases in airspeed but reduced maneuverability because of the compressibility effects on the propeller and aero surfaces.

2. Bodie, W. M., *The Lockheed P-38 Lightning* (Hayesville, North Carolina: Widewing Publications, 1991), p. 76, Gray, G. W., *Frontiers of Flight, The Story of NACA Research* (New York, Alfred A. Knopf, 1948), p. 153, Hartman, E. P., *Adventures in Research, A History of Ames Research Center 1940–1965*, NASA Center History Series, SP-4302 (Washington, D.C.: National Aeronautics and Space Administration, 1970), p. 98, Johnson, C. L., and Smith, M., *Kelly, More Than My Share of it All* (Washington, D.C.: Smithsonian Books, 1985), pp. 73–74, and von Kármán, T., and Edson, L., *The Wind and Beyond: Theodore von Kármán, Pioneer in Aviation and Pathfinder in Space* (Boston, Massachusetts: Little Brown and Company, 1967), p. 232.
3. Bodie, W. M., "Man-Made Lightning," *Airpower*, November 1973, p. 43.
4. Dean, F. H. (ed.), *Report of Joint Fighter Conference, NAS Patuxent River, MD, 16–23 October 1944*, (Atglen, Pennsylvania: Schiffer Publishing, 1998), pp. 114–115, has Cdr E. W. Conlon of BuAer's Structures Branch providing this explanation.
5. Beck, Peter A., *Manufacturer's Preliminary Brief Model Specification, Airplane, Interceptor Pursuit, Model L-133*, Report No. 2578, Lockheed Aircraft Corporation, Burbank, California, February 27, 1942, pp. 4–5. This maximum speed at altitude is equivalent to Mach 0.91 under standard conditions. This was to be achieved with a straight wing of low-drag airfoil possessing uniform pressure distribution, augmented by boundary layer suction, to increase the critical Mach number, an all-moving canard "trimmer" for very positive longitudinal control, and a high degree of body-blending for reduced drag and potentially less buffet. Two notional L-1000 axial-flow turbojet engines of 5,100 lbf (23 kN) each was to propel the steel airplane. In early 1942, when the proposal was submitted, the challenges such a design faced was understood, yet Lockheed was not best suited to undertake the substantial research program that would proceed detailed design. With the country by then at war, the firm would have many more vital and immediate projects. It was, however, just the sort of project the Germans did undertake with considerable fruitless expenditure of resources.
6. Loftin, L. F., Jr., *Quest for Performance, The Evolution of Modern Aircraft*, SP-468 (Washington, D.C.: National Aeronautics and Space Administration, 1985), p. 115.
7. Hansen, J. R., *Engineer in Charge, A History of the Langley Aeronautical Laboratory, 1917–1958*, SP-4305 (Washington, D.C.: National Aeronautics and Space Administration, 1987), p. 265.
8. Foster, D., *Challenging the Sound Barrier*, X-Planes Profile 9 (Beirut, Lebanon: HPM Publications, 2004), p. 36.
9. Grossnick, R. A., *United States Naval Aviation 1910–1995* (Washington, D.C.: Naval Historical Center, 1997), p. 152.

10. Shortal, J. A., *A New Dimension, Wallops Island Flight Test Range: The First Fifteen Years*, Reference Publication 1028 (Washington, D.C.: National Aeronautics and Space Administration, December 1978), p. 14.
11. *Ibid.*, pp. 9 and 27.
12. Hansen, *op. cit.*, p. 235.
13. The Caproni aircraft had a translating cone in the exhaust nozzle.
14. Hansen, *op. cit.*, p. 240.
15. Young, J. O., *Meeting the Challenge of Supersonic Flight* (Edwards Air Force Base, California: Air Force Flight Test Center History Office, 1997), p. 6.
16. *Ibid.*, p. 8.
17. *Ibid.*, pp. 4–5, and Foster, *op. cit.*, p. 69.
18. Shortal, *op. cit.*, p. 5, Francillon, R. J., *Lockheed Aircraft Since 1913* (Annapolis, Maryland: Naval Institute Press, 1988), p. 240, and Pearcy, A., *Flying the Frontiers, NACA and NASA Experimental Aircraft* (Annapolis, Maryland: Naval Institute Press, 1993), p. 187.
19. Young, *op. cit.*, p. 64, note 43.
20. Miller, J., *The X-Planes: X-1 to X-45* (Hinckley, England: Midland Publishing, 2001), p. 35.
21. The story is told of Bell personnel who obtained small samples of the Rotojet propellants. These they placed in bottles they taped together. Stepping out to an isolated area near the Buffalo plant, they cast the bottles against some rocks and were shocked at the violent eruption that resulted. This settled the matter in their minds. Bilstein, R. E., *Orders of Magnitude, A History of the NACA and NASA, 1915–1990*, SP-4406, The NASA History Series (Washington, D.C.: National Aeronautics and Space Administration, 1989), p. 38.
22. Young, *op. cit.*, p. 4.
23. Hansen, *op. cit.*, pp. 294–295.
24. Hallion, R. P., *The Air Force and the Supersonic Breakthrough*, in Neufeld, J., Watson, G. M., Jr., and Chenoweth, D., (ed.), *Technology and the Air Force, A Retrospective Assessment*, Air Force History and Museums Program, (Washington, D. C: United States Air Force, 1997), p. 55.

Chapter 6

1. Francillon, R. J., *Lockheed Aircraft Since 1913* (Annapolis, Maryland: Naval Institute Press, 1988), p .133, and Grossnick, R. A., *United States Naval Aviation 1910–1995* (Washington, D.C.: Naval Historical Center, 1997), p. 95.
2. Mitchell, K. A., "The Tandem Landing Gear, Martin XB-26H," *AAHS Journal*, Vol. 33 No. 1, Spring 1988, p. 24.
3. Wolf, W., *The Martin B-26 Marauder, The Ultimate Look: From Drawing Board to Widow Maker Vindicated* (Atglen, Pennsylvania: Schiffer Publishing, 2014), p. 173.
4. The reason for the change in airframe for what appeared essentially the same equipment is unclear.
5. Hagedorn, D., *North American's T-6, A Definitive History of the World's Most Famous Trainer*, (North Branch, Minnesota: Specialty Press, 2009), p. 108.
6. Raines, E. F., Jr., *Eyes of the Artillery, The Origins of Modern U.S. Army Aviation in World War II*, Army Historical Series (Washington, D.C.: Center of Military History, United States Army, 2000), p. 201.
7. Pelletier, A. J., *Beech Aircraft and Their Predecessors* (Annapolis, Maryland: Naval Institute Press, 1995), p. 72, and Johnsen, F. A., "Light Twins for the AAF," *Wings*, Vol. 34 No. 4, April 2004, pp. 45 and 52.
8. Stern, D., "Artic Ops Part II: Early Secret Military Cold War Artic Operations," *AAHS Journal*, Vol. 57 No. 2, Summer 2012, p. 100.

9. Raines, *op. cit.*, p. 285.
10. McHugh, M. I., Chief, Procurement and Supply Branch, Officer of Strategic Services, "19 Brodie Arresting Systems," letter to Director, Headquarters, AAF Air Technical Service Command, with contract attached, April 26, 1945; Contract OSS-592', letter to Commanding General, Materiel Command, July 4, 1945, p. 2.
11. Pennel, R. T., Maj.-Gen., Commandant, Field Artillery School, "Brodie Device—Land Rig," letter to Commanding General, AAF Air Technical Service Command,] 4, 1944, p. 1.
12. *Army Ground Forces Light Aviation*, Field Manual FM 20-100, War Department (Washington, D.C.: United States Government Printing Office, September 1947), p. 137.
13. Presentation Branch, *The Brodie System of Landing and Launching Light Airplanes from a Portable Rig* (Washington, D.C.: Office of Strategic Services, July 1944), p. 6.
14. Glines, C. W., *The Legendary Piper Cubs, Their Role in War and Peace* (Atglen, Pennsylvania: Schiffer Publishing, 2005), p. 112.
15. Historical Office, *Case History of The Brodie Launching and Landing Device*, Air Technical Service Command, Wright Field, February–September 1945, pp. 2–3. A substitution of wood was made for the hexagonal steel masts, but these failed compression tests and a redesign was necessary. The braking mechanism had to be optimized to handle both the L-4 and L-5.
16. Historical Office, *op. cit.*, summary entry 78.
17. Strickland, A. C., Brig.-Gen., President, The Army Air Forces Board, *Staff Study of the Brodie System for Launching and Landing Light Aircraft*, Project No. 4100A373.1, May 29, 1945, p. 3.
18. Shepard, B. A., Col., "Brodie System," routing and record sheet, June 8, 1945, and Meisinger, R., M., Production Supervisor, "Conversion of AAF Brodie Systems to Navy Use," Memorandum Report TSMPR4-M-43, June 16, 1945, pp. 1–2.
19. Raines, *op. cit.*, p. 294.
20. Sherrod, R., *History of Marine Corps Aviation in World War II* (Washington, D.C.: Combat Forces Press, 1952), p. 349, and Kriegsman, J. C., "The Piper Cub and the LST Aircraft Carrier (A WWII Poor Man's Carrier)" (unpublished account, undated).
21. These tunnels and tracks were for fast suicide attack boats fitted with explosives for the intent of damaging the propellers and steering gear of the enemy ships. The immobilized vessels would then be more easily attacked by shore artillery and Kamikaze aircraft. The importance of the pilots' observations leading to destruction of this Japanese defensive measure cannot be understated.
22. Raines, *op. cit.*, p. 267.
23. Claims that this vessel was named USS *Brodie* appears false. The LSTs were not officially named. It may perhaps have been a name jokingly applied by the crew. Kriegsman, *op. cit.*, puts the name in quotes when referring to *Brodie* LST 776, suggesting it was an adopted name.

Chapter 7

1. Kelsey, B. S., *The Dragon's Teeth? Creation of the United States Air Power for World War II* (Washington, D.C.: Smithsonian Institute Press, 1982), pp. 67–68.
2. The Flight Refueling Ltd. system is described in multiple sources including Latimer-Needham, C. H., *Refuelling in Flight* (London: Sir Isaac Pitnam & Sons, 1950), and Tanner, R. M., *History of Air-to-Air Refuelling* (Barnsley, United Kingdom: Pen & Sword, 2006). Additionally, the name has been variously given as Flight Refueling or Flight Refuelling. However, the latter was painted on one of the 1939 test aircraft and Tanner, a long-time engineer at the firm, also spelled the name the same.
3. Several proposals for refueled flights to Japan were explored, as outlined in Historical Office, *Case History of Air-to-Air Refueling*, Air Materiel Command, Wright-Patterson

AFB, Ohio, March 1949. One of the earliest plans was B-24s flying a round-trip from Hawaii. This would have seen Navy PBY flying boats refueling B-24Cs. However, the differences in airspeed (172 mph/277 kph cruise and 120 mph/193 kph stall for the heavy bomber and maximum speed of 117 mph/188 kph for the Catalina) made this impractical. The PBYs would have to land to refuel from ships strung along the route, but its open sea capabilities were limited to modest sea states. The expected formation with six AR contacts per bomber, would require ninety-six PBYs plus a reserve and the closest flying boat/sea tanker stationed just 600 miles (966 km) from Japan. The bombers would have to give up payload to carry the refueling gear plus additional engine oil supply. (In the trials during the 1920s it was seen that passing viscous oil via the hose, even if the fluid was heated, was not possible.) Missing one refueling would see the Liberator ditching in the sea. Next considered were B-17Es flying from Midway Island, refueled by B-24D tankers. It was assumed that the AR gear in the Fortress would add 200 lb (91 kg) and the aircraft would be carting two 2,000 lb (907 kg) bombs. One AR was judged sufficient. The B-24 was expected to transfer 1,700 gal (6,435 l) in 30 minutes. The Liberator would be burdened with 1,000 lb (454 kg) of AR equipment and would have been further modified to accommodate additional fuel capacity. The attack on Japan was ultimately flown on April 18, 1942, by B-25s launched from an aircraft carrier (Chapter 11). It would be two years before American bombers next appeared over the Japanese home islands. Although methods of executing such attacks were considered in the interim, including AR, all were judged too risky and yielding too little results for the enormous effort expended.

4. This account is principally drawn from Historical Office, op. cit., as augment by additional research presented by Julian, Thomas A., "The Origins of Air Refueling in the United States Air Force," in Neufeld, J., Watson, G. M., Jr., and Chenoweth, D., (ed.), *Technology and the Air Force, A Retrospective Assessment*, Air Force History and Museums Program, (Washington, D. C: United States Air Force, 1997), and Gardner, B., "Flight Refueling ... The Wartime Story," *Air Enthusiast*, No. 25, August–November 1984.
5. The British had performed trials of the FRL gear in 1940 to include powering the reels, but the kit the Americans were sent apparently lacked this feature. Tanner, *op. cit.*, p. 21.
6. Gardner, *op. cit.*, pp. 42–43 and 80.
7. Stoff, J., *The Thunder Factory, An Illustrated History of The Republic Aviation Corporation* (Osceola, Wisconsin: Motorbooks International, 1990), pp. 38–39, where drawings are shown.
8. For a more complete account of the projects associated with gliders, see the author's *American Military Gliders of World War II*, (North Branch, Minnesota: Schiffer Publishing, 2012).
9. George Cornelius had built and flown a glider and then a light airplane (NX-34212) with the tailless forward-swept wing configuration and associate controls as proof-of-concept testbeds. These featured variable incidence wings. He likely demonstrated the powered aircraft at Wright Field. "The Cornelius Flying Wing," *Aero Digest*, November 1943, pp. 275 and 277.
10. Francillon, R. J., *McDonnell Douglas Aircraft Since 1920: Volume I* (Annapolis, Maryland: Naval Institute Press, 1988), p. 320.
11. Chambers, J. R., and Chambers, M. A, *Radical Wings & Wind Tunnels, Advanced Concepts Tested at NASA Langley* (North Branch, Minnesota: Specialty Press, 2008), pp. 56–57.
12. Dickson, D., "Give us a Tow?" *Aeroplane Monthly*, April 1988, pp. 246–247 and 249.
13. Wegg, J., *General Dynamics Aircraft and their Predecessors* (Annapolis, Maryland: Naval Institute Press, 1990), p. 180.
14. Dean, F. H. (ed.), *Report of Joint Fighter Conference, NAS Patuxent River, MD, 16–23 October 1944*, (Atglen, Pennsylvania: Schiffer Publishing, 1998), p. 109.

15. See the author's *U.S. Experimental & Prototype Aircraft Projects, Fighters 1939–1945* (North Branch, Minnesota: Specialty Press, 2008) for a more complete account of the wartime parasite fighter program.

Chapter 8

1. A supine position was largely dismissed as clearly unworkable. Anti-*g* suits were under development by 1942 and successfully tested in 1943 but remained experimental.
2. Yawing (directional) is produced in this manner by generating drag on one side of the aircraft centerline. This also generates roll via dihedral effect.
3. Donald, D., "Lockheed P-38 Lightning 'Fork-tailed Devil,'" *International Air Power Journal*, No. 14, 2004, p. 131, states that three of the thirteen initial production P-38s were converted with the asymmetric cockpit, but this is not corroborated by other sources.
4. Francillon, R. J., *Lockheed Aircraft Since 1913* (Annapolis, Maryland: Naval Institute Press, 1988), p. 167.
5. One pilot bailed out of a XP-55 but forgot to separate the prop yet still emerged safely.
6. Tuttle, J., *Eject! The Complete History of U.S. Aircraft Escape Systems* (St. Paul, Minnesota: MBI Publishing Company, 2002), p. 27.
7. *Preliminary Handbook of Pilot's Flight Operation Instructions for the Model XP-81 Fighter Airplane*, (Consolidated Vultee Aircraft Corporation, Report No. 204-20, June 20, 1947), p. 23.
8. Johnson, C. L., and Smith, M., *Kelly, More Than My Share of it All* (Washington, D.C.: Smithsonian Books, 1985), p. 51.
9. Bart, H. L., "Development in Cabin Supercharging," *Industrial Aviation*, October 1944, p. 63.
10. Dean, F. H. (ed.), *Report of Joint Fighter Conference, NAS Patuxent River, MD, 16–23 October 1944*, (Atglen, Pennsylvania: Schiffer Publishing, 1998), p. 132, has Bell Aircraft test pilot Jack Woolams mentioning the planned bubble canopy for the P-59.
11. Stern, D. "Dark Horse Running, The Bell and Martin-Bell Cold War Orbital Glide Bomber," *AAHS Journal*, Vol. 61 No. 1, Spring 2017, p. 24.

Chapter 9

1. Engineering Division, *Army Air Forces Materiel Command, Research and Development Projects of the Engineering Division*, Wright Field, Dayton, Ohio, Fourth Edition, January 1, 1944, Section 4 Special Projects, Water Landing Characteristics of Land Type Airplanes, p. 70. See also Gray, G. W., *Frontiers of Flight, The Story of NACA Research* (New York, Alfred A. Knopf, 1948), pp. 76–79.
2. *Fifty Years of Aeronautical Research* (Washington, D.C.: National Aeronautics and Space Administration, 1967), p. 26.
3. Cavallo, S. A., *NASA Headquarters NACA Oral History Project, Oral History Transcript*, interviewed by Johnson, S. (San Jose, California, September 30, 2005), p. 18.
4. von Kármán, T., and Edson, L., *The Wind and Beyond: Theodore von Kármán, Pioneer in Aviation and Pathfinder in Space* (Boston, Massachusetts: Little Brown and Company, 1967), p. 243.
5. Hansen, J. R., *Engineer in Charge, A History of the Langley Aeronautical Laboratory, 1917–1958*, SP-4305 (Washington, D.C.: National Aeronautics and Space Administration, 1987), pp. 110–112.
6. Gray, *op. cit.*, p. 311, and Hartman, E. P., *Adventures in Research, A History of Ames Research Center 1940–1965*, NASA Center History Series, SP-4302 (Washington, D.C.: National Aeronautics and Space Administration, 1970), p. 74. The latter states that

the Catalina could overfly a carrier at 200 feet (61 m) altitude in the dark, with partial power, and go undetected.

7. Hartman, *op. cit.*, p. 74, and Wolf, W., *The Martin B-26 Marauder, The Ultimate Look: From Drawing Board to Widow Maker Vindicated* (Atglen, Pennsylvania: Schiffer Publishing, 2014), p. 59.
8. Much effort was also expended to improve weather forecasting for avoiding icing and provide overall better information to the airmen. The AAF also had such projects as inducing fog dissipation on airfields.
9. Gray, *op. cit.*, p. 315.
10. Borchers, P. F., Franklin, J. A., and Fletcher, J. W., *Flight Research at Ames 1940–1997: Fifty-Seven Years of Development and Validation of Aeronautical Technology*, NASA/SP-1998-330 (Ames Research Center, Moffett Field, California: National Aeronautics and Space Administration, 1998) p. 7.
11. Gray, *op. cit.*, p. 317.

Chapter 10

1. Arnold, H. H., *Global Mission* (New York: Harper & Brothers, Publishers, 1949), p. 348, describes the General taking a particular interest in these kits after hearing gripes from aircrew during a visit to the Pacific Theater. He summoned the responsible procurement individuals to Washington and insisted they use the equipment themselves and then improve same.
2. Aircraft could drop smoke bombs and dye to mark the survivors' location once spotted. "Dinghy packs" could be carried on bomb bay shackles or external store stations, the P-47 being cited as an example, carrying dinghies in underwing containers, in Historical Division, USAF, *Air-Sea Rescue 1941–1952*, U.S. Air Force Historical Study No. 95, Research Studies Institute, Air University, August 1954, p. 36, and Davis, L., ""That others may live," Air Force Search & Rescue, Part One: World War II and Korea," *Wings of Fame*, Vol. 13, 1998, pp. 142–157, p. 143. A radio beacon could also be dropped, deploying an antenna and beginning to transmit upon contact with the water, to mark a survivor location. *Ibid.*, p. 103. In the Caribbean, between January and July 1944, the rescue forces were offering four carrier pigeons to crews with the idea they would release the birds, with their location written on a small note in the birds' leg capsule, to aid in the search. Most crews had little faith in this measure and many refused to take the fowl, or in an emergency paid them no mind. *Ibid.*, p. 102.
3. "Flying Boat Carriers Rescue Platform," *Popular Mechanics*, December 1945, p. 87.
4. Historical Division, *op. cit.*, p. 18.
5. Lloyd, A. T., *B-17 Flying Fortress Part 2 Derivatives*, In Detail & Scale Vol. 11 (Blue Ridge Summit, Pennsylvania: Tab Books, 1983), p. 4.
6. Lloyd, A. T., *B-29 Superfortress, Part 2 Derivatives*, In Detail & Scale Vol. 25 (Blue Ridge Summit, Pennsylvania: Tab Books, 1987), p. 52, reflects the total sixteen machines so-modified but also just three on inventory in 1947–1949. This could reflect some placed in storage after the end of the war as more were brought into service in later years.
7. Historical Division, *op. cit.*, pp. 79, 99, and 134. Wolf, W., *Boeing B-29 Superfortress, The Ultimate Look: From Drawing Board to VJ-Day* (Atglen, Pennsylvania: Schiffer Publishing, 2005), p. 77, makes the uncredited claim that the first Super Dumbo rescue was on 30 May 1945.
8. Davis, *op. cit.*, p. 145.
9. Historical Office, *Case History of the Liaison Aircraft Program*, Air Technical Service Command, Wright Field, Ohio, November 1944, L-5 correspondence summary entry 33 through 36.
10. Piper Club of France, L-14, piperclubfrance.com/piper-l-14-army-cruiser-ec-aap/.

11. Historical Office, *op. cit.*, L-4 correspondence summary entry 36 and 39.
12. Designated FS, this was a solution of sulfur trioxide in chlorosulfuric acid. Reacting with water vapor, FS create tiny droplets of sulfuric and hydrochloric acid. To Those Who Served …, tothosewhoserved.org/usa/ts/usatsc02/chapter09.html#fnr38, pp. 214–215, and Wolf, W., *U.S. Aerial Armament in World War II, The Ultimate Look Vol. 2: Bombs, Bombsights, and Bombing* (Atglen, Pennsylvania: Schiffer Publishing, 2010), p.266.
13. Wolf, W., *U.S. Aerial Armament in World War II, The Ultimate Look Vol. 3: Air Launched Rockets, Mines, Torpedoes, Guided Missiles and Secret Weapons* (Atglen, Pennsylvania: Schiffer Publishing, 2010), pp. 323–324, Wolf, W., *The Douglas A-20 Havoc, The Ultimate Look, V from Drawing Board to Peerless Allied Light Bomber* (Atglen, Pennsylvania: Schiffer Publishing, 2015), p. 407, and "The Immortal DC-3 Part 2," *Take-Off*, Part 53, 1989, p. 1,486.
14. Doolittle, J. H., with Glines, C. V., *I Could Never Be So Lucky Again* (New York, New York: Bantam Books, August 1992), p. 424. In over 1,000 sorties, eight aircraft and seventy-seven crewmen were lost performing this mission.
15. *Army Ground Forces Light Aviation*, Field Manual FM 20-100, War Department (Washington, D.C.: United States Government Printing Office, September 1947), pp. 58–60, and Raines, E. F., Jr., *Eyes of the Artillery, The Origins of Modern U.S. Army Aviation in World War II*, Army Historical Series (Washington, D.C.: Center of Military History, United States Army, 2000), pp. 167, 173, 226, and 257.
16. The first method is described in *Army Ground Forces Light Aviation*, *op. cit.*, pp. 20–21, and the second by Holcomb, M., "'Send Grasshoppers,'" *Wings*, Vol. 13 No. 1, February 1983, p. 48.
17. Day, C. L., *Silent Ones, WWII Invasion Gliders Test and Experiment* (Lambertville, Michigan: Charles Day, 2001), p. 55.
18. Bowers, P. M., *Of Wings & Things, Volume 1: 1972–1979* (Lakewood, Washington: Flyer Media, 2000), p. 166.
19. Lewis, W. D., and Trimble, W. F., *The Airway to Everywhere, A History of All American Aviation, 1937-1953* (Pittsburgh, Pennsylvania: University of Pittsburgh Press, 1988), p. 117.

Chapter 11

1. Lawson, T. W., *Thirty Seconds Over Tokyo* (New York, New York: Pocket Star Books, 2002), p. 71.
2. Schultz, D., *The Doolittle Raid* (New York, New York: St. Martin's Press, 1988), p. 158.
3. Harp, T. R., Maj., NAMC Materiel Command Liaison Officer, "Assisted Take-offs," letter to Commanding General, Material Command, June 20, 1944, and Historical Division, Intelligence T-2, *Case History of Assisted Take-Off Devices*, Air Materiel Command, Wright Field, February 1946, summary entry 94.
4. Marty, J. L., Jr., "The Grasshoppers of Okinawa," *AAHS Journal*, Vol. 55 No. 2, Summer 2010, p. 83.
5. Raines, E. F., Jr., *Eyes of the Artillery, The Origins of Modern U.S. Army Aviation in World War II*, Army Historical Series (Washington, D.C.: Center of Military History, United States Army, 2000), p. 161.
6. Thomason, T., *Bell XFL-1 Airabonita*, Naval Fighters Number Eighty-One (Simi Valley, California: Steve Ginter, 2008), pp. 50–51. A curious aspect to this story is that Elder specified the XP-39B as the mount for this experience. That airplane first flew on 25 November 1939 and was surveyed on 8 June 1940 with just twenty-eight hours logged at the time it was written off in a landing mishap at Wright Field. There is no evidence it was flown to Philadelphia or tested with a tailhook, much less severely damaged in such a test.
7. McLaren, D. R., "The North American Aviation P-51H Mustang, Part I," *AAHS Journal*, Vol. 25 No. 2, Summer 1980, p. 137. See also Van Wyen, A. O., Head, Aviation History

Unit, Op-05D2, November 20, 1968, letter to Capt. R. W. Gruenhagen regarding Navy evaluation of a Mustang, that confuses this aircraft with the later P-51D.

8. "Mustang—The Willing Workhorse—2," *Air International*, October 1983, p. 188.
9. Rusinek, E., "The Sea Trials of the P-51D Mustang 'Seahorse,'" *North American Aviation Retirees Bulletin*, Summer 2002, p. 5, gave the SEU site. It was likely that the structural modifications were made in Dallas and the naval equipment installation done in Philadelphia. Some sources say there were attachment hooks on each main gear strut for the launch bridle, but the photo shown herein disputes that.
10. McLaren, *op. cit.*, p. 100.
11. Brown, E., *Testing for Combat* (Shrewsbury, England: Airlife Publishing, 1994), p. 140.
12. This was the same day the P-51D also performed its testing aboard the *Shangri-La* and the Grumman F7F was going out the first time as well (and landed before the Mitchell to become the first tricycle twin to land aboard an American aircraft carrier.). All three aircraft had flown in formation from Philadelphia to Norfolk on November 14.
13. *Preliminary Pilot's Handbook of Operating Instructions, Navy Model LBP-1 GLOMB*, CO AN 09-50BA-1 (March 15, 1945), p. 1, described that the LBP-1 GLOMB, a Beech counterpart to the LBT-1, was capable of "... snatch or tow take-off from the deck of an aircraft carrier, and is designed for catapulting from a landplane catapult, for snatch take-off or catapulting from land or ship-board catapult with towline attached to a catapulted airplane." The choice of words "designed for" may be suggestive.

Chapter 12

1. Dean, F. H., and Hagedorn, D., *Curtiss Fighter Aircraft, A Photographic History 1919–1948* (Atglen, Pennsylvania: Shiffer Publishing, 2007), pp. 291–292.
2. *Ibid.*, p. 319.
3. *Ibid.*, p. 306.
4. "Conversion of the P-39 into a Trainer," *Aero Digest*, November 1943, p. 228.
5. Gordon, Y., "Bell Cobra Variants, P-39 Airacobra and P-63 Kingcobra," *Wings of Fame*, No. 10, 1998, p. 142, identifies these as all A-models but the third serial number he offers is that of a "C."
6. Carter, H., "Two Thrones for the King," *Warbirds International*, Vol. 37 No. 1, January-February 2018, p. 27. As these were non-military aircraft, they carried no national markings and were referred to as Model 53 with registrations NX41963 and NX41964. *Ibid*, p. 36.
7. Coffey, T. M., *Hap, The Story of the U.S. Air Force and the Man Who Built it, General Henry H. "Hap" Arnold* (New York: The Viking Press, 1982), p. 251, mentions dual controls but such is not known to have been adopted.
8. Francillon, R. J., *Lockheed Aircraft Since 1913* (Annapolis, Maryland: Naval Institute Press, 1988), pp. 170–171.
9. McLaren, D. R., "The North American Aviation P-51H Mustang, Part I," *AAHS Journal*, Vol. 25 No. 2, Summer 1980, p. 127.
10. Wegg, J., *General Dynamics Aircraft and their Predecessors* (Annapolis, Maryland: Naval Institute Press, 1990), pp. 84–85.
11. Wolf, W., *Consolidated B-32 Dominator, The Ultimate Look: From Drawing Board to Scrapyard* (Atglen, Pennsylvania: Schiffer Publishing, 2006), p. 166 and Johnsen, F. A., *Consolidated B-24 Liberator*, WarbirdTech Series Volume 1 (North Branch, Minnesota: Specialty Press, 2001), p. 90, claim B-24Js were modified with B-32 Dominator turrets to support crew training. Research has revealed a single B-24J modified with the Sperry nose and tail ball turrets to support development. Norton, B.,*American Bomber Aircraft Development in World War 2*, (Surrey, United Kingdom: Midland Publishing, 2012), p. 97. Dominator production began with trainer TB-32s before combat machines

were available, unlike most or all bombers, and so surrogate training platforms were unnecessary. *Ibid.*, p. 161.

12. Wolf, W., *Boeing B-29 Superfortress, The Ultimate Look: From Drawing Board to VJ-Day* (Atglen, Pennsylvania: Schiffer Publishing, 2005), p. 225.
13. The coverage to the front appeared suitable until the Japanese and Germans adopted frontal attacks.
14. *Summary of the XB-41 Project*, partial manuscript without author, April 1944, correspondence summary No. 12.
15. The 12,420 figure comes from Watkins, D. W., Col., *Final Report on Test of Armament Installation in XB-41 Airplane*, Proof Department, Army Air Forces Proving Ground Command, Eglin Field, Florida, March 16, 1943, p. 2, though adding up the rounds summary actually yields 12,830. Wagner, R., *American Combat Planes of the 20th Century* (Reno, Nevada: Jack Bacon & Company, 2004), p. 249, delivers an 11,135 number without attribution.
16. Bowers, P. M., *Of Wings & Things, Volume 1: 1972–1979* (Lakewood, Washington: Flyer Media, 2000), p. 36, relates, without citation, that one last use of the B-40 in theater was to eliminate a Luftwaffe decoy that had cost the lives of several B-17 crews. The Germans used captured B-17s to approach an American formation and act as a damaged straggler. This might lure a formation plane to drop back to provide protection for their 'brethren' at which point the guns of the German-manned Fortress would attempt to down the Americans or fighters would be called in. Bowers reports that a B-40, the crew aware of the gambit, dropped back and then shot down the Luftwaffe aircraft.
17. Boyne, W., "Magruder's Marauder," *Airpower*, May 1943, p. 11, and Wolf, W., *The Martin B-26 Marauder, The Ultimate Look: From Drawing Board to Widow Maker Vindicated* (Atglen, Pennsylvania: Schiffer Publishing, 2014), pp. 174–175.
18. Campbell, R. H., *The Silverplate Bomber, A History and Registry of the Enola Gay and Other B-29s Configured to Carry Atomic Bombs* (Jefferson, North Carolina: McFarland & Company, 2005), pp. 42 and 109.
19. Chilstrom, K. and Leary, P., *Test Flying at Old Wright Field* (Omaha, Nebraska: Westchester House Publishers, 1995), pp. 3–8.
20. A similar modification was done to carry the 22,000-lb (9,979-kg) Grand Slam bomb that was loaded from a pit after pushing the bomber overhead. Restricted by the wing box beam, the bomb protruded out the doors cut to accommodate.
21. Campbell, *op. cit.*, pp. 35–37, convincingly describes this with clear photos of the combat operation. Other descriptions of positioning the aircraft beside the pit with the closest main gear truck on a turntable such that the bomber could be swung around and aligned over the pit probably describes a Stateside arrangement, likely post-war. See Rhodes, Richard, *The Making of the Atomic Bomb* (New York: Simon & Schuster, 1986), p. 703. Yet, the pit shown by Thole, L., "Atom Bomber Base, Wendover Army Air Base, Utah," *Air Enthusiast*, No. 108, November/December 2003, p. 32, and Thompson, W., "Unit Heritage, The Atomic Bombers, The 509th Bomb Group in World War II," *Wings of Fame*, Vol. 7, 1997, p. 102, also does not appear to include a pivot plate.
22. Primary sources for the Safety Wingtip are Francillon, R. J., *Grumman Aircraft Since 1929* (Annapolis, Maryland: Naval Institute Press, 1989), pp. 244–245, Dean, F. H. (ed.), *Report of Joint Fighter Conference, NAS Patuxent River, MD, 16–23 October 1944*, (Atglen, Pennsylvania: Schiffer Publishing, 1998), pp. 118–120, 129–130, and 346–351, and Andrews, Hal, *The Grumman F8F Bearcat*, Profile No. 107 (Surrey, England: Profile Publications Ltd, 1966), p. 3. Some details differ between these accounts.
23. Reilly, J. C., Jr., "Project Yehudi, A Study of Camouflage by Illumination," *AAHS Journal*, Vol. 15 No. 4, Winter 1970, p. 256.
24. Johnsen, F. A., *B-24 Liberator*, Warbird History Series (Osceola, Wisconsin: Motorbooks International, 1993), pp. 68–69.

23. Francillon, *op. cit.*, p. 167.
24. Bowers, P. M., *Fortress in the Sky* (Granada Hills, California: Sentry Books, 1976), p. 200.

Chapter 13

1. Claussen, M. P., *Materiel Research and Development in the Army Air Arm 1914–1945*, AAF Historical Studies No. 50, AAF Historical Office, Headquarters, Army Air Forces, Washington, D.C., November 1946, pp. 160–161.
2. Freeman, M. J., "Behind Enemy Lines," *Airpower*, July 1994, p. 11, and Trojan, D., *Technical Air Intelligence, Wreck Chasing in the Pacific During the War*, downloaded from *j-aircraft.com, undated*, p. 9.
3. Kreis, J. F., (ed.), *Piercing the Fog, Intelligence and Army Air Forces Operations in World War II* (Bolling Air Force Base, Washington, D.C.: Air Force History and Museums Program, 1996), p. 122.
4. Chilstrom, K. and Leary, P., *Test Flying at Old Wright Field* (Omaha, Nebraska: Westchester House Publishers, 1995), pp. 202–203.
5. Kreis, *op. cit.*, p. 336, describes the first target being a Nakajima engine factory in Musashino chosen through analysis of plate information.
6. *Ibid.*, p. 124, provides the Fw 190 canopy example while Gray, G. W., *Frontiers of Flight, The Story of NACA Research* (New York, Alfred A. Knopf, 1948), pp. 309–310, is the source of the anti-ice information. The horizontal tail example is derived from Kowalski, B., *Kaiser Fleetwings XBTK-1, Naval Fighters Number 48* (Simi Valley, California, Steve Ginter, 1999), p. 9. Doctor Shelton in Shelton, J. B., Jr., "Altitude Sickness and the Oxygen Mask, The American Experience in Europe During World War Two," *AAHS Journal*, Vol. 44 No. 4, Winter 1999 discusses the oxygen system.
7. Kreis, *op. cit.*, p. 374.
8. Some reports are attributed to Gen. Claire Chennault and the American Volunteer Group in China. *Ibid.*, pp. 30 and 247. Rearden, J., *Koga's Zero, The Fighter That Changed World War II* (Missoula, Montana: Pictorial Histories Publishing, 1995), p. 4, mentions a Fleet Air Tactical Unit bulletin issued in fall 1941 with enough details of the new Japanese fighter to cause one officer to adjust tactics in anticipation of meeting the airplane in combat.
9. One pilot said he believed he could bend the rudder bar if he pressed hard enough, and the wing skin could be seen to buckle in tight turns or high-*g* pull-outs.
10. Mikesh, R., "Made in Japan ... Tested in America! The Full Story of Allied Technical Air Intelligence and the War in the Pacific, 1942–1945 Pt. I," *Wings*, June 1982, pp. 11–12. Confusion surrounds this "Kunming Zero" as most sources attribute its forced landing to February 1941 such that the *attaché* report could be written, transmitted, and stored before the end of 1941. However, Lansdale, James F., "War Prize: The Capture of the First Japanese Zero Fighter in 1941," j-aircraft.com/research/WarPrizes.htm (December 3, 1999), provides a thoroughly researched report that places its landing in November 1941 and availability for foreign examination in summer 1942.
11. Air Materiel Command, *The Development of Guided Missiles*, May 1, 1946, p. 35.
12. *Semi-Monthly Progress Report on JB-1 and JB-2*, February 14, 1945, p. 2, and other documents found among the references, credit the total number of missiles on contract as 2,050 by the end of 1944. However, details of the increase from the initial thirteen, or twenty-five on a 15 July contract per Kay, A. L., *Buzz Bomb*, Monogram Close-Up 4 (Boylston, Massachusetts: Monogram Aviation Publications, 1977), p. 30, to the interim fifty is unclear in available literature.
13. Gray, *op. cit.*, pp. 300–301.
14. Cahill, L. D., *Project MX-544*, Report of Project Engineer, Jack & Heintz, Inc., 16 December 1944, p. 4.

15. Wolf, W., *U.S. Aerial Armament in World War II, The Ultimate Look Vol. 3: Air Launched Rockets, Mines, Torpedoes, Guided Missiles and Secret Weapons* (Atglen, Pennsylvania: Schiffer Publishing, 2010), p. 244.
16. Carney, F. H., Capt., Procurement Division, Air Technical Services Command, teletype regarding guided munitions to Commanding General, Army Air Forces, September 6, 1945, p. 3.
17. Powers, "Progress Report to 1 December 1944 on JB-2 and JB-1 Robot Bombs," Memorandum for Chief of Air Staff, December 7, 1944.
18. Werrell, K. P., *The Evolution of the Cruise Missile* (Maxwell Air Force Base, Alabama: Air University Press, September 1985), p. 63, and Coupland, R. C., Brig.-Gen., Air Ordnance Officer, "Robot Bomb, JB-2," memorandum to Chief of Ordnance, Research & Development Service, September 13, 1944.
19. Carney, *op. cit.*, p. 4. Probably unknown to the Americans at the time, the Germans produced 30,257 missiles in fourteen months (perhaps half of the planned quantity), reaching 3,387 in the peak month. This was partially achieved by employing factories in occupied countries with forced labor. The adverse impact of V-1 and V-2 production on other weapons programs more beneficial to German defense was significant. Zaloga, S. J., *V-1 Flying Bomb 1942–52, Hitler's Infamous "Doodlebug,"* New Vanguard 106 (Oxford, United Kingdom: Osprey Publishing, 2005), pp. 10 and 37–38.
20. Treadwell, T. C., *Strike from Beneath the Sea, A History of Aircraft-Carrying Submarines* (Charleston, South Carolina: Tempus, Publishing, 1999), p. 64 and Werrell, *op. cit.*, p. 77. Wendover had the advantage of crashed missiles generally being recoverable on the range while those that fell into the Gulf off Eglin were seldom recoverable.
21. The literature on this subject varies significantly on the figures and the author has worked to derive rounded numbers from the most authoritative or well-researched sources.
22. Werrell, *op. cit.*, p. 50, and Zaloga, *op. cit.*, p. 8, relates that during development Fieseler had expected 90 percent of the missiles to fall within 6 miles (10 km) of the aim point and half within 4 miles (6 km). The Americans expected half of their missiles to fall within 5 miles (8 km) of a target at the 150 miles (241 km) edge of the missile's range. Pierce, C. H., Jr., Capt., Aircraft Project Section, Engineering Division, *Memorandum Report on JB-2 Pilotless Aircraft*, TSESA-1256, March 1, 1946.
23. Zaloga, *op. cit.*, pp. 22–23, and Werrell, *op. cit.*, p. 58.
24. Fahrney, D. S., Rear Adm., USN (Ret.), *The History of Pilotless Aircraft and Guided Missiles*, unpublished manuscript (prepared for U.S. Navy Bureau of Aeronautics, undated but likely 1958), p. 813.
25. *Ibid.*, p. 545.
26. Echols, O. P., Maj.-Gen., "Progress Report to 3 March 45 on JB-2 and JB-10 Robot Bombs," Memorandum for Chief of Air Staff, March 6, 1945.
27. Powers, E. M., Brig.-Gen., "Report to 19 Apr 45 on JB-10 (Northrop Tail-less) and JB-2 Jet Bombs," Memorandum for Chief of Air Staff, April 27, 1945.
28. Fahrney, *op. cit.*, p. 815.
29. Craven, D. A., 1Lt, Engineering Division, *Memorandum Report Remote Control of JB-2 Pilotless Aircraft with a Modified SCR-584 Radar Set and AN/APM-1 Radio Unit*, TSZSA-7-1253, February 28, 1946. The gear employed at Wendover, with twenty-seven JB-2 firings, were the SCR-584 radar and AN/APM-1 receiver aboard the aircraft. The target was 65 miles (105 km) from the launcher. Only ten missiles functioned suitably for accuracy measurement. There was no apparent assessment of the vulnerability of the system to jamming, but it is believed to have been great and the Germans particularly effective with such countermeasures while Japanese capabilities were not to be dismissed. One of the difficulties was distance to impact after the "dump" command was sent to dive the missile into the target. The Army was then experimenting with a "wing destruction" device to address this issue.
30. Werrell, *op. cit.*, p. 77, and Carney, *op. cit.*, p. 3.

31. *Semi-Monthly Progress Report on JB-1 and JB-2, op. cit.*, p.2.
32. Carney, *op. cit.*, p. 3. Actually, this source gives the total produced as 1,375 while all published sources give the 1,391 quoted here, the difference of sixteen being unclear.

Chapter 14

1. Arnold, H. H., *Global Mission* (New York: Harper & Brothers, Publishers, 1949), p. 579, and Claussen, M. P., *Materiel Research and Development in the Army Air Arm 1914–1945*, AAF Historical Studies No. 50, AAF Historical Office, Headquarters, Army Air Forces, Washington, D.C., November 1946, p. 197.
2. On the basis of this success, Brodie conceived expanding the system to 7,000-lb (3,175-kg) airplanes. He won several patents for the system and sought to interest commercial operators. Suspension of the device between buildings would make intercity air transport easier, he speculated. However, the concept found no buyers. The helicopter soon rendered such cumbersome measures archaic.
3. Dean, F. H. (ed.), *Report of Joint Fighter Conference, NAS Patuxent River, MD, 16–23 October 1944*, (Atglen, Pennsylvania: Schiffer Publishing, 1998), p. 147, mentions an example of a quarter-million noise-cancelling microphones bought with apparently minimal service testing. Worn under the nose like a moustache, it irritated all those who did not have a moustache beneath. When the wearer perspired the moisture released a chemical in the microphone material that irritated the skin. The deficiencies were readily obvious to any fleet user and it was most unpopular. Fortunately, the mics were later used in a boom arrangement from the helmet or headphones to place it in front of the mouth.
4. Wolf, W., *U.S. Aerial Armament in World War II, The Ultimate Look Vol. 3: Air Launched Rockets, Mines, Torpedoes, Guided Missiles and Secret Weapons* (Atglen, Pennsylvania: Schiffer Publishing, 2010), p. 247, reports that the AGF recovered a V-1 in July 1945 and duplicated then tested the engine. They began seeking 25,000 missiles. The bibliographical reference for this information is not cited in the volume and no other official or well-researched source with citations reviewed by this author has a similar report. Fickel, A. A., Col., "Army Guided Missiles Program," Note for Record, November 30, 1944, states that "Army Ground Forces has no "program" except to maintain an active interest in what the ASF (Army Service Forces – *author*) and AAF are doing, and to ensure that as techniques are developed they are applied to Ground Force uses. An outstanding specific example is their following of the AAF "buzz-bomb" development at Eglin Field."
5. The Soviets and French also copied the V-1.
6. Claussen, *op. cit.*, pp. 134 and 174.
7. *Ibid.*, p. 113.
8. Gorn, M. H., *Harnessing the Genie, Science and Technology Forecasting for the Air Force 1944–1986*, Air Staff Historical Study (Washington, D.C.: Office of Air Force History, U.S. Government Printing Office, 1988), p. 18.
9. von Kármán, Theodore, *Toward New Horizons* (Washington, D.C.: U.S. Amy Air Forces, 1946).
10. von Kármán, Theodore, *Where We Stand* (Washington, D.C.: U.S. Army Air Forces, 1946). The swept wing data was most notable, giving renewed emphasis to NACA research and had the immediate result to choosing to develop the Boeing XB-47 bomber with a swept wing to more easily meet the 500-mph (805-kph) airspeed goal.
11. Handleman, P., "Theodore von Karman, the 'Martian' Who Changed the Way We Fly," *AAHS Journal*, Vol. 58 No. 2, Summer 2013, p. 89.

Bibliography

Books

Abel, A., and Abel, D. W., *Bellanca's Golden Age*, The Golden Age of Aviation Series (Brawley, California: Wind Canyon Books, 2004)

Abel, A., Abel, D. W., and Matt, P., *Aeronca's Golden Age*, The Golden Age of Aviation Series (Brawley, California: Wind Canyon Books, 2001); *Piper's Golden Age*, The Golden Age of Aviation Series (Brawley, California: Wind Canyon Books, 2001)

Against the Wind, 90 Years of Flight Test in the Miami Valley, History Office, Aeronautical Systems Center, Air Force Materiel Command (Wright-Patterson AFB, Ohio, 1994)

Anderson, F., *Northrop, An Aeronautical History* (Century City, California: Northrop Corporation, 1976)

Anderton, D. A., *Sixty Years of Aeronautical Research, 1919–1977*, EP145 (Washington, D.C.: National Aeronautics and Space Administration, 1978)

Andrade, J. M., *U.S. Military Aircraft Designations and Serials 1909–1979* (Leicester, United Kingdom: Midland Counties Publications, 1997)

Arnold, H. H., *Global Mission* (New York: Harper & Brothers, Publishers, 1949)

Avery, N., *North American Aircraft 1934–1998, Volume 1* (Santa Ana, California: Narkiewicz/Thompson, 1998)

Becker, J. V., *The High-Speed Frontier, Case Histories of Four NACA Programs, 1920–1950*, SP-445 (Washington, D.C.: National Aeronautics and Space Administration, 1980)

Bergerud, E. M., *Fire in the Sky, The Air War in the South Pacific* (Boulder, Colorado: Westview Press, 2000)

Bilstein, R. E., *Orders of Magnitude, A History of the NACA and NASA, 1915–1990*, SP-4406, The NASA History Series (Washington, D.C.: National Aeronautics and Space Administration, 1989)

Bodie, W. M., *The Lockheed P-38 Lightning* (Hayesville, North Carolina: Widewing Publications, 1991)

Bowers, P. M., *Boeing Aircraft Since 1916* (Annapolis, Maryland: Naval Institute Press, 1989); *Curtiss Aircraft 1907–1947* (Annapolis, Maryland: Naval Institute Press, 1979); *Fortress in the Sky* (Granada Hills, California: Sentry Books, 1976); *Of Wings & Things, Volume 1: 1972–1979* (Lakewood, Washington: Flyer Media, 2000)

Bowman, M. W., *Boeing B-17 Flying Fortress* (Wiltshire, United Kingdom: The Crowood Press, 1998)

Bowman, N. J., *The Handbook of Rockets and Guided Missiles*, Second Edition (Newtown Square, Pennsylvania: Perastadion Press, 1963)

Bradley, R. E., *Convair Advanced Designs II: Secret Fighters, Attack Aircraft and Unique Concepts 1929–1973* (Manchester, United Kingdom: Crécy Publishing, 2013)

Breuer, W. B., *Operation Torch, The Allied Gamble to Invade North Africa* (New York: St. Martin Press, 1985)

Brigman, L. (ed.), *Jane's All the World's Aircraft, 1945/6* (London: Sampson Low, Marston, and Company, Ltd., 1946)

Brown, E., *Testing for Combat* (Shrewsbury, England: Airlife Publishing, 1994)

Bush, V., *Pieces of the Action* (New York: William Morrow and Company, 1970)

Butler, H. K., *Army Air Corps Airplanes and Observation 1935–1941* (Saint Louis, Missouri: Historical Office, United States Army Aviation Systems Command, February 1990)

Butler, P., *War Prizes, An Illustrated Survey of German, Italian and Japanese Aircraft Brought to Allied Countries During and After the Second World War* (Leicester, England: Midland Counties Publications, 1994); *War Prizes, The Album* (Hinckley, England: Midland Counties Publications, 2006)

Byrd, V. B., *Passing Gas, The History of Inflight Refueling* (USA: Byrd Publishing Company, 1994)

Campbell, R. H., *The Silverplate Bomber, A History and Registry of the Enola Gay and Other B-29s Configured to Carry Atomic Bombs* (Jefferson, North Carolina: McFarland & Company, 2005)

Cassagneres, E., *The Spirit of Ryan* (Blue Ridge Summit, Pennsylvania: Tab Books, 1982)

Chambers, J. R., and Chambers, M. A, *Radical Wings & Wind Tunnels, Advanced Concepts Tested at NASA Langley* (North Branch, Minnesota: Specialty Press, 2008)

Chilstrom, K. and Leary, P., *Test Flying at Old Wright Field* (Omaha, Nebraska: Westchester House Publishers, 1995)

Coffey, T. M., *Hap, The Story of the U.S. Air Force and the Man Who Built it, General Henry H. "Hap" Arnold* (New York: The Viking Press, 1982)

Craven, W. F., and Cate, J. L., *The Army Air Forces in World War II, Volume One, Plans and Early Operations, January 1943 and August 1942* (Washington, D.C.: Office of Air Force History, 1983); *The Army Air Forces in World War II, Volume Two, Europe: Torch to Pointblank, August 1942 to December 1943* (Washington, D.C.: Office of Air Force History, 1983); *The Army Air Forces in World War II, Volume Six, Men and Planes* (Washington, D.C.: Office of Air Force History, 1983)

Davis, D. A., *Lightning Strike, The Secret Mission to Kill Admiral Yamamoto and Avenge Pearl Harbor* (New York: St. Martin's Griffin, 2005)

Dawson, V. P., *Engines and Innovation: Lewis Laboratory and American Propulsion Technology*, The NASA History Series, SP-4306 (Washington, D.C.: National Aeronautics and Space Administration, 1991)

Day, C. L., *Silent Ones, WWII Invasion Gliders Test and Experiment* (Lambertville, Michigan: Charles Day, 2001)

Dean, F. H. (ed.), *Report of Joint Fighter Conference, NAS Patuxent River, MD, 16–23 October 1944*, (Atglen, Pennsylvania: Schiffer Publishing, 1998)

Dean, F. H., and Hagedorn, D., *Curtiss Fighter Aircraft, A Photographic History 1919–1948* (Atglen, Pennsylvania: Shiffer Publishing, 2007)

Doolittle, J. H., with Glines, C. V., *I Could Never Be So Lucky Again* (New York, New York: Bantam Books, August 1992)

Engle, E., *Escape from the Air and from the Sea* (New York: The John Day Company, 1963)

Flatt, J., *The History of Boundary Layer Control in the United States of America* (New York: Pergamon Press, 1961)

Francillon, R. J., *Grumman Aircraft Since 1929* (Annapolis, Maryland: Naval Institute Press, 1989); *Lockheed Aircraft Since 1913* (Annapolis, Maryland: Naval Institute Press, 1988); *McDonnell Douglas Aircraft Since 1920: Volume I* (Annapolis, Maryland: Naval Institute Press, 1988)

Friedman, N., *US Naval Weapons* (London: Conway Maritime Press, 1983)

Gelb, N., *Desperate Venture, The Story of Operation Torch, the Allied Invasion of North Africa* (New York: William Morrow and Company, 1992)

Glines, C. W., *The Legendary Piper Cubs, Their Role in War and Peace* (Atglen, Pennsylvania: Schiffer Publishing, 2005)

Gorn, M. H., *Harnessing the Genie, Science and Technology Forecasting for the Air Force 1944–1986*, Air Staff Historical Study (Washington, D.C.: Office of Air Force History, U.S. Government Printing Office, 1988); *The Universal Man, Theodore von Kármán's Life in Aeronautics*, Smithsonian History of Aviation Series (Washington, D.C.: Smithsonian Institute Press, 1992)

Gray, G. W., *Frontiers of Flight, The Story of NACA Research* (New York, Alfred A. Knopf, 1948)

Grossnick, R. A., *United States Naval Aviation 1910–1995* (Washington, D.C.: Naval Historical Center, 1997)

Hagedorn, D., *North American NA-167/AT-6/SNJ*, WarbirdTech Series Volume 11 (North Branch Minnesota: Specialty Press, 1997); *North American's T-6, A Definitive History of the World's Most Famous Trainer*, (North Branch, Minnesota: Specialty Press, 2009)

Hallion, R. P., *The Air Force and the Supersonic Breakthrough*, in Neufeld, J., Watson, G. M., Jr., and Chenoweth, D., (ed.), *Technology and the Air Force, A Retrospective Assessment*, Air Force History and Museums Program, (Washington, D. C: United States Air Force, 1997); *Designers and Test Pilots*, The Epic of Flight series (Alexandria, Virginia: Time-Life Books, 1983)

Hallion, R. P. and Gorn, M. H., *On the Frontier, Experimental Flight at NASA Dryden* (Washington, D.C.: Smithsonian Books, Second Edition, 2002)

Hansen, J. R., *Engineer in Charge, A History of the Langley Aeronautical Laboratory, 1917–1958*, SP-4305 (Washington, D.C.: National Aeronautics and Space Administration, 1987)

Hartman, E. P., *Adventures in Research, A History of Ames Research Center 1940–1965*, NASA Center History Series, SP-4302 (Washington, D.C.: National Aeronautics and Space Administration, 1970)

Heinemann, E. H. and Rausa, R., *Ed Heinemann, Combat Aircraft Designer* (Annapolis, Maryland: Naval Institute Press, 1980)

Herrick, J. W. and Burgess, E., (ed.), *Rocket Encyclopedia Illustrated* (Los Angeles, California: Aero Publishers, 1959)

Holley, I. B., Jr., *Buying Aircraft: Materiel Procurement for the Army Air Forces*, United States Army in World War II, Special Study (Washington, D.C.: Center for Military History, United States Army, 1989)

Hoover R. A., *Forever Flying* (New York, New York: Pocket Books, 1996)

Hunley, J. D. (ed.), *Toward Mach 2: The Douglas D-558 Program*, The NASA History Series, NASA SP-4222 (Washington, D.C.: National Aeronautics and Space Administration, 1999)

Jenkins, D. R. and Landis, T. R., *Experimental & Prototype U.S. Air Force Jet Fighters* (North Branch, Minnesota: Specialty Press, 2008)

Johnsen, F. A., *B-24 Liberator*, Warbird History Series (Osceola, Wisconsin: Motorbooks International, 1993); *Bell P-39/P-63 Airacobra & Kingcobra*, WarbirdTech Series Volume 17 (North Branch, Minnesota: Specialty Press, 1998); *Consolidated B-24 Liberator*, WarbirdTech Series Volume 1 (North Branch, Minnesota: Specialty Press, 2001); *Martin B-26 Marauder*, WarbirdTech Series Volume 29 (North Branch, Minnesota: Specialty Press, 2000); *Testbeds, Motherships & Parasites, Astonishing Aircraft from the Golden Age of Flight Test* (North Branch, Minnesota: Specialty Press, 2018)

Johnson, C. L., and Smith, M., *Kelly, More Than My Share of it All* (Washington, D.C.: Smithsonian Books, 1985)

Jones, L. S., *U.S. Bombers* (Fallbrook, California: Aero Publishing, 1974)

Julian, Thomas A., "The Origins of Air Refueling in the United States Air Force" in Neufeld, J., Watson, G. M., Jr., and Chenoweth, D., (ed.), *Technology and the Air Force, A Retrospective Assessment*, Air Force History and Museums Program, (Washington, D. C: United States Air Force, 1997)

Kelsey, B. S., *The Dragon's Teeth? Creation of the United States Air Power for World War II* (Washington, D.C.: Smithsonian Institute Press, 1982)

Koppes, C. R., *JPL and the American Space Program* (New Haven, Connecticut: Yale University Press, 1982)

Kreis, J. F., (ed.), *Piercing the Fog, Intelligence and Army Air Forces Operations in World War II* (Bolling Air Force Base, Washington, D.C.: Air Force History and Museums Program, 1996)

Latimer-Needham, C. H., *Refuelling in Flight* (London: Sir Isaac Pitnam & Sons, 1950)

Lawson, T. W., *Thirty Seconds Over Tokyo* (New York, New York: Pocket Star Books, 2002)

LeMay, C. and Yenne, B., *Superfortress, The Boeing B-29 and American Airpower in World War II* (Yardley, Pennsylvania: Westholme Publishing, 2006)

LeVier, T. and Guenther, J., *Pilot* (New York: Bantam Books, December 1990)

Lewis, W. D., and Trimble, W. F., *The Airway to Everywhere, A History of All American Aviation, 1937-1953* (Pittsburgh, Pennsylvania: University of Pittsburgh Press, 1988)

Libis, S., *Skystreak, Skyrocket, & Stiletto, Douglas High-Speed X-Planes* (North Branch, Minnesota: Specialty Press, 2005)

Loftin, L. F., Jr., *Quest for Performance, The Evolution of Modern Aircraft*, SP-468 (Washington, D.C.: National Aeronautics and Space Administration, 1985)

Love, T. M., *L-Birds, American Combat Liaison Aircraft of World War II* (New Brighton, Minnesota: Flying Books International, 2001)

Macknight, N., *Tomahawk Cruise Missile*, Mil-Tech Series (Osceola, Wisconsin: Motorbooks International, 1995)

Matthews, B., *Cobra!, Bell Aircraft Corporation 1934–1946* (Atglen, Pennsylvania: Schiffer, 1996)

Miller, J., *The X-Planes: X-1 to X-45* (Hinckley, England: Midland Publishing, 2001)

Mitchell, K. A., *Fairchild Aircraft 1926–1987* (Santa Ana, California: Narkiewicz/Thompson, 1997)

Moran, G. P., *Aeroplanes Vought 1917–1977* (Temple City, California: Historical Aviation Album, 1977)

Myhra, D., *Fieseler Fi 103F*, X-Planes of the Third Reich series (Atglen, Pennsylvania: Schiffer, 2001)

Norton, B., *American Aircraft Development in WWII: Special Types, 1939-1945*, (Surrey, United Kingdom: Crécy Publishing, 2016); *American Bomber Aircraft Development in World War 2*, (Surrey, United Kingdom: Midland Publishing, 2012); *American Military Gliders of World War II*, (North Branch, Minnesota: Schiffer Publishing, 2012); *U.S. Experimental & Prototype Aircraft Projects, Fighters 1939–1945* (North Branch, Minnesota: Specialty Press, 2012)

O'Leary, M., *Boeing B-17 Flying Fortress*, Production Line to Frontline 2 (Oxford, United Kingdom: Osprey Publishing, 1998)

Pace, S., *Boeing B-29 Superfortress* (Wiltshire, United Kingdom: The Crowood Press, 2003)

Pearcy, A., *Flying the Frontiers, NACA and NASA Experimental Aircraft* (Annapolis, Maryland: Naval Institute Press, 1993); *Lend-Lease Aircraft in World War II* (Osceola, Wisconsin: Motorbooks International, 1996)

Pelletier, A. J., *Beech Aircraft and Their Predecessors* (Annapolis, Maryland: Naval Institute Press, 1995); *Bell Aircraft Since 1935* (London: Putnam Aeronautical Books, 1992)

The Pratt & Whitney Aircraft Story (Pratt & Whitney Aircraft, 1952)

Raines, E. F., Jr., *Eyes of the Artillery, The Origins of Modern U.S. Army Aviation in World War II*, Army Historical Series (Washington, D.C.: Center of Military History, United States Army, 2000)

Rearden, J., *Koga's Zero, The Fighter That Changed World War II* (Missoula, Montana: Pictorial Histories Publishing, 1995)

Rhodes, Richard, *The Making of the Atomic Bomb* (New York: Simon & Schuster, 1986)

Ross, F., Jr., *Guided Missiles: Rockets and Torpedoes* (New York: Lothrop, Lee & Shepard, 1951)

Rubenstein, M., and Rubenstein, R. M., *To Join with the Eagles, A Complete Illustrated History of Curtiss-Wright Aircraft from 1903–1965* (Garden City, New York: Doubleday & Company, 1974)

Schultz, D., *The Doolittle Raid* (New York, New York: St. Martin's Press, 1988)

Scutts, J., *Lockheed P-38 Lightning* (Wiltshire, England: The Crowood Press, 2006); *PBJ Mitchell Units of the Pacific War*, Opsrey Combat Aircraft 40 (Oxford, United Kingdom: Osprey Publishing, 2003)

Sherrod, R., *History of Marine Corps Aviation in World War II* (Washington, D.C.: Combat Forces Press, 1952)

Shortal, J. A., *A New Dimension, Wallops Island Flight Test Range: The First Fifteen Years*, Reference Publication 1028 (Washington, D.C.: National Aeronautics and Space Administration, December 1978)

Smith, P. C., *Curtiss SB2C Helldiver* (Wiltshire, United Kingdom: The Crowood Press, 1998); *North American AT-6 SNJ, Harvard and Wirraway* (Wiltshire, United Kingdom: The Crowood Press, 2000); *Vengeance, The Vultee Vengeance Dive Bomber* (Shrewsbury, England: Airlife, 2000)

Stoff, J., *The Thunder Factory, An Illustrated History of The Republic Aviation Corporation* (Osceola, Wisconsin: Motorbooks International, 1990)

Swanborough, G., and Bowers, P. M., *United States Military Aircraft Since 1909* (London: Putnam, 1989); *United States Navy Aircraft Since 1911* (Annapolis, Maryland: Naval Institute Press, 1990)

Tanner, R. M., *History of Air-to-Air Refuelling* (Barnsley, United Kingdom: Pen & Sword, 2006)

Thompson, J., *Vultee Aircraft 1932–1947* (Santa Ana, California: Jonathan Thompson, 1992)

Thompson, S., *Douglas Havoc and Boston, The DB-7/A-20 Series* (Wiltshire, England: The Crowood Press, 2004)

Treadwell, T. C., *Strike from Beneath the Sea, A History of Aircraft-Carrying Submarines* (Charleston, South Carolina: Tempus, Publishing, 1999)

Trimble, W. F., *Wings for the Navy, A History of the Naval Aircraft Factory 1917-1956* (Annapolis, Maryland: Naval Institute Press, 1990)

Tuttle, J., *Eject! The Complete History of U.S. Aircraft Escape Systems* (St. Paul, Minnesota: MBI Publishing Company, 2002)

Underwood, J. W., *The Stinsons* (Glendale, California: Heritage Press, 1982)

USAF Test Pilot School, 1944–1979 (Edwards Air Force Base, California: USAF Test Pilot School, 1986)

von Kármán, T., and Edson, L., *The Wind and Beyond: Theodore von Kármán, Pioneer in Aviation and Pathfinder in Space* (Boston, Massachusetts: Little Brown and Company, 1967)

Wagner, R., *American Combat Planes of the 20th Century* (Reno, Nevada: Jack Bacon & Company, 2004)

Wakefield, K., *The Fighting Grasshoppers, US Liaison Aircraft Operations in Europe 1942–1945* (Leicester, England: Midland Counties Publications, 1990)

Walker, L. E., and Wickman, S. E., *From Huffman Prairie to the Moon, The History of Wright-Patterson Air Force Base* (Wright-Patterson Air Force Base, Ohio: Office of History, 2750th Air Base Wing, Air Force Logistics Command, undated but approximately 1982)

Waters, J. M., Jr., *Rescue at Sea* (Annapolis, Maryland, Naval Institute Press, 1989)

Wegg, J., *General Dynamics Aircraft and their Predecessors* (Annapolis, Maryland: Naval Institute Press, 1990)

Werrell, K. P., *The Evolution of the Cruise Missile* (Maxwell Air Force Base, Alabama: Air University Press, September 1985)

White, G., *Allied Aircraft Piston Engines of World War II* (Warrendale, Pennsylvania: Society of Automotive Engineers, Inc., 1995); *R4360 Pratt & Whitney's Major Miracle* (North Branch, Minnesota: Specialty Press, 2006)

Whitney, D. D., *Vee's for Victory, The Story of the Allison V-1710 Aircraft Engine 1929–1948* (Atglen, Pennsylvania: Schiffer Publishing, 1998)

Wolf, W., *Boeing B-29 Superfortress, The Ultimate Look: From Drawing Board to VJ-Day* (Atglen, Pennsylvania: Schiffer Publishing, 2005); *Consolidated B-32 Dominator, The Ultimate Look: From Drawing Board to Scrapyard* (Atglen, Pennsylvania: Schiffer Publishing, 2006); *The Douglas A-20 Havoc, The Ultimate Look, from Drawing Board to Peerless Allied Light Bomber* (Atglen, Pennsylvania: Schiffer Publishing, 2015); *Douglas B-18 Bolo, The Ultimate Look: From Drawing*

Board to U-Boat Hunter (Atglen, Pennsylvania: Schiffer Publishing, 2007); *Douglas XB-19 Bolo, An Illustrated History of America's Would-Be Intercontinental Bomber* (Atglen, Pennsylvania: Schiffer Publishing, 2017); *The Martin B-26 Marauder, The Ultimate Look: From Drawing Board to Widow Maker Vindicated* (Atglen, Pennsylvania: Schiffer Publishing, 2014); *North American B-25 Mitchell, The Ultimate Look: From Drawing Board to Flying Arsenal* (Atglen, Pennsylvania: Schiffer Publishing, 2008); *U.S. Aerial Armament in World War II, The Ultimate Look Vol. 2: Bombs, Bombsights, and Bombing* (Atglen, Pennsylvania: Schiffer Publishing, 2010); *U.S. Aerial Armament in World War II, The Ultimate Look Vol. 3: Air Launched Rockets, Mines, Torpedoes, Guided Missiles and Secret Weapons* (Atglen, Pennsylvania: Schiffer Publishing, 2010)

Zaloga, S. J., *V-1 Flying Bomb 1942–52, Hitler's Infamous "Doodlebug,"* New Vanguard 106 (Oxford, United Kingdom: Osprey Publishing, 2005)

Monographs

Adcock, A., *US Liaison Aircraft in Action* (Carrollton, Texas: Squadron/Signal Publications, 2005)

Andrews, Hal, *The Grumman F8F Bearcat*, Profile No. 107 (Surrey, England: Profile Publications Ltd, 1966)

Atkins, R., *The North American P-51B & C Mustang*, Profile No. 100 (Surrey, England: Profile Publications Ltd, 1966)

Borchers, P. F., Franklin, J. A., and Fletcher, J. W., *Flight Research at Ames 1940–1997: Fifty-Seven Years of Development and Validation of Aeronautical Technology*, NASA/SP-1998-330 (Ames Research Center, Moffett Field, California: National Aeronautics and Space Administration, 1998)

Chambers, M. A., *Flight Research at NASA Langley Research Center*, Image of Aviation series (Charleston, South Carolina: Arcadia Publishing, 2007); *Naval Air Station Patuxent River*, Images of Aviation series (Charleston, South Carolina: Arcadia Publishing, 2014)

Dann, R. S., *P-40 Warhawk in Action*, Aircraft No. 205 (Carrollton, Texas: Squadron/Signal Publications, 2007)

Davis, L., *B-29 Superfortress in Action*, Aircraft No. 165 (Carrollton, Texas: Squadron/Signal Publications, 1997); *P-38 Lightning in Action*, Aircraft No. 109 (Carrollton, Texas: Squadron/Signal Publications, 1990); *P-47 Thunderbolt in Action*, Aircraft No. 67 (Carrollton, Texas: Squadron/Signal Publications, 1984); *P-47 Thunderbolt in Action*, Aircraft No. 208 (Carrollton, Texas: Squadron/Signal Publications, 2007); *T-6 Texan in Action*, Aircraft No. 94 (Carrollton, Texas: Squadron/Signal Publications, 1989)

Doll, T., *SB2U Vindicator in Action*, Aircraft No. 122 (Carrollton, Texas: Squadron/Signal Publications, 1992)

Doyle, D., *B-17 Flying Fortress in Action* (Carrollton, Texas: Squadron/Signal Publications, undated); *B-29 Superfortress in Action* (Carrollton, Texas: Squadron/Signal Publications, 2011)

Fifty Years of Aeronautical Research (Washington, D.C.: National Aeronautics and Space Administration, 1967)

Foster, D., *Challenging the Sound Barrier*, X-Planes Profile 9 (Beirut, Lebanon: HPM Publications, 2004)

Guenther, B., and Miller, J., *Bell X-1 Variants*, Aerofax Datagraph 3 (Arlington, Texas: Aerofax, 1988)

Kay, A. L., *Buzz Bomb*, Monogram Close-Up 4 (Boylston, Massachusetts: Monogram Aviation Publications, 1977)

Keisel, K. M., *Wright Field*, Images of Aviation series (Charleston, South Carolina: Arcadia Publishing, 2016)

Kempel, R. W., *The Conquest of the Sound Barrier*, X-Planes Profile 7 (Beirut, Lebanon: HPM Publications, 2007)

Kinzey, B., *P-38 Lightning, Part 1*, In Detail & Scale Vol. 57 (Carrollton, Texas: Squadron/Signal Publications, 1998); *P-39 Airacobra*, In Detail & Scale Vol. 63 (Carrollton, Texas: Squadron/Signal Publications, 1999); *P-40 Warhawk*, In Detail & Scale Vol. 62 (Carrollton, Texas: Squadron/Signal Publications, 1999); *P-51 Mustang Part 2*, In Detail & Scale Vol. 51 (Carrollton, Texas: Squadron/Signal Publications, 1997)

Kopenhagen, W., *The V1 and its Soviet Successors* (Atglen, Pennsylvania: Schiffer Publishing, 2000)

Kowalski, B., *Kaiser Fleetwings XBTK-1, Naval Fighters Number 48* (Simi Valley, California, Steve Ginter, 1999)

Libis, S., *Douglas D-558-1 Skystreak*, Naval Fighters Number 56 (Simi Valley, California: Steve Ginter, 2001); *Douglas D-558-2 Skyrocket*, Naval Fighters Number 57 (Simi Valley, California: Steve Ginter, 2002)

Lloyd, A. T., *B-17 Flying Fortress Part 2 Derivatives*, In Detail & Scale Vol. 11 (Blue Ridge Summit, Pennsylvania: Tab Books, 1983); *B-29 Superfortress, Part 2 Derivatives*, In Detail & Scale Vol. 25 (Blue Ridge Summit, Pennsylvania: Tab Books, 1987)

McDowell, E., *P-39 Airacobra in Action*, Aircraft No. 43 (Carrollton, Texas: Squadron/Signal Publications, 1980); *P-40 Warhawk in Action*, Aircraft No. 26 (Carrollton, Texas: Squadron/Signal Publications, 1976)

Mesko, J., *A-20 Havoc in Action*, Aircraft No. 144 (Carrollton, Texas: Squadron/Signal Publications, 1994)

O'Leary, M., *Lockheed P-38 Lightning*, Production Line to Frontline 3 (Oxford, United Kingdom: Osprey Publishing Ltd., 1999)

Plane Portraits (Lindbergh Field, San Diego, California: Ryan Aeronautical Company, undated but probably about 1968)

Report from Aerojet (Azusa, California: Aerojet Engineering Corporation, undated)

Shacklady, E., *The North American P-51D Mustang*, Profile No. 8 (Leatherhead, Surrey, England: Profile Publications Ltd, 1965); *The Republic P-47D*, Profile No. 7 (Leatherhead, Surrey, England: Profile Publications Ltd, 1965)

Smith, R. K., *75 Years of Inflight Refueling Highlights, 1923-1998*, Air Force History and Museums Program (Washington, D.C.: United States Air Force, 1998)

Stapfer, H., *B-26 Marauder in Action*, Aircraft No. 210 (Carrollton, Texas: Squadron Signal Publications, 2008)

Sullivan, J., *F4U Corsair in Action*, Aircraft No. 145 (Carrollton, Texas: Squadron Signal Publications, 1994)

Thomason, T., *Bell XFL-1 Airabonita*, Naval Fighters Number Eighty-One (Simi Valley, California: Steve Ginter, 2008)

Young, J. O., *Meeting the Challenge of Supersonic Flight* (Edwards Air Force Base, California: Air Force Flight Test Center History Office, 1997); (ed.), *Supersonic Symposium: The Men of Mach 1*, An AFSC Special Study (Edwards Air Force Base, California, Air Force Flight Test Center History Office, September 1990)

Weber, L., *The P-38J—M Lockheed Lightning*, Profile No. 106 (Leatherhead, Surrey, England: Profile Publications, Ltd., 1966)

Periodicals

Andrews, H., "End of the Line ... The Last Curtiss Navy Fighter," *Air Enthusiast Quarterly*, No. 3, no date, pp. 98–108

"The Annals of Sugar Baker Two Uncle," *Air Enthusiast*, No. 8, October 1978—January 1979, pp. 1–8, 74–79

"ATSC Reports Successful Launching of Lightplanes from Suspended Cable," *American Aviation*, 15 October 1945, p. 90

Barr, L., "The Lockheed Constellation, A History, Part I," *AAHS Journal*, Vol. 28 No. 3/4, Fall/Winter 1983, pp. 190–205

Bart, H. L., "Development in Cabin Supercharging," *Industrial Aviation*, October 1944, pp. 63–66 and 103–104

Beauchamp, G., "XP-42, Perennial Test-Bed," *AAHS Journal*, Vol. 19 No. 2, Summer 1974, pp. 82–92

Bodie, W. M., "Man-Made Lightning," *Airpower*, November 1973, pp. 20–43; "Thunderbolt," *Wings*, Special Edition No. 1, 1981; "Wine from the Jug, Pt II," *Airpower*, May 1974, pp. 8–31; "Wine from the Jug, Pt V Conclusion," *Wings*, August 1974, pp. 26–43

Bowers, P. M., "Dog of War, Pt. II," *Wings*, February 1996, pp. 8–45; "Streamlining, Pt. II," *Airpower*, November 1991, pp. 10–25 and 34–43; "Super Bomber," *Wings*, October 1973, pp. 10–39; "The Thundering Texan," *Wings*, December 1986, pp. 30–49; "Vengeance!, Part I," *Airpower*, September 1985, pp. 8–23 and 51–53

Boyne, W., ""Cry Havoc!" Pt. II, The A-20 Goes to War!," *Airpower*, July 1976, pp. 50–66; "The Custer Channel Wing Story," *Airpower*, May 1977, pp. 8–19 and 58; "Magruder's Marauder," *Airpower*, May 1943, pp. 8–21

Brulle, R. V., "Don't Panic, It's Just a Compressibility Dive," *Air Power History*, Spring 1996, pp. 41–53

Bullock, W. B., "JATO—The Magic Bottle," *Flying*, February 1953, pp. 25 and 44

Carter, H., "Two Thrones for the King," *Warbirds International*, Vol. 37 No. 1, January-February 2018, pp. 24–27 and 36–43

"Commando, A Dove from Curtiss-Wright," *Air Enthusiast*, No. 34, September–December 1987, pp. 25–42

"Conversion of the P-39 into a Trainer," *Aero Digest*, November 1943, p. 228

"The Cornelius Flying Wing," *Aero Digest*, November 1943, pp. 275 and 277–278

Davis, K., "Clothesline Air Strip," *Flying*, December 1945, pp. 63–64 and 119

Davis, L., ""That others may live," Air Force Search & Rescue, Part One: World War II and Korea," *Wings of Fame*, Vol. 13, 1998, pp. 142–157

Dean, J., "The Falcons of Freeman Field, Testing Japan's Eleventh Hour Entrants," *Airpower*, January 1975, pp. 6–13; "The Forgotten Fortresses," *Airpower*, September 1980, pp. 10–19

Dickson, D., "Give us a Tow?," *Aeroplane Monthly*, April 1988, pp. 246–247 and 249

Donald, D., "Lockheed P-38 Lightning 'Fork-tailed Devil'," *International Air Power Journal*, No. 14, 2004, pp. 124–155

Donner, W. R., "Hightide at High Altitude," *Airpower*, May 1988, pp. 40–55

"Douglas XB-19A," *AAHS Journal*, Vol. 27 No. 3, Fall 1982, p. 160

Dorr, R. E., and Lake, J., "Consolidated B-24 Liberator Part One: Development and Allied Operations, 1939-1943," *International Air Power Journal*, Vol. 4, 2002, pp. 126–163

"Fighter A to Z: Curtiss XP-42," *Air Enthusiast*, November 1976, p. 236

"Fighting Juggernaut, Part Two," *Air International*, Vol. 14 No. 2, February 1978, pp. 81–88 and 96–97

"Flying Boat Carriers Rescue Platform," *Popular Mechanics*, December 1945, p. 87

"Flying Wind Tunnel," *Popular Mechanics*, February 1946, p. 7

Francis, D., "Piper Cub Goes to War," *AAHS Journal*, Vol. 21 No. 1, Spring 1976, pp. 72–79

Freeman, M. J., "Behind Enemy Lines," *Airpower*, July 1994, pp. 10–23 and 44–53

Frost, P., "A Plane Crash in 1944 is Saving Lives Today," *Daily Press*, Newport News, Virginia, 22 February 2009, unknown page number

Gardner, B., "Flight Refueling ... The Wartime Story," *Air Enthusiast*, No. 25, August–November 1984, pp. 34–43 and 80

Gordon, Y., "Bell Cobra Variants, P-39 Airacobra and P-63 Kingcobra," *Wings of Fame*, No. 10, 1998, pp. 115–151

Grant, R. S., "Canada's Thunder Chicken," *Air Enthusiast*, No. 29, November 1985–February 1986, pp. 11–22

Green, W., "The Lockheed XP-49," *Air Pictorial*, Vol. 22 No. 5, May 1960, pp. 176–177

Greene, F., "The 'Wildcat' Story," *AAHS Journal*, Vol. 6 No. 4, Winter 1961, pp. 223–244

Handleman, P., "Theodore von Karman, the 'Martian' Who Changed the Way We Fly," *AAHS Journal*, Vol. 58 No. 2, Summer 2013, pp. 82–92

Hardy, R., "What, No Propeller?," *AAHS Journal*, Vol. 41 No. 1, Spring 1996, pp. 12–16

Hart, E. H., "Curtiss TP-40 is Really P-40ES," *AAHS Journal*, Vol. 12 No. 3, Fall 1967, p. 227

"Have You Seen?," *Flying*, March 1945, pp. 69–71

Hazen, R. M., "Development of the Allison 3420," *Aero Digest*, 1 October 1945, pp. 75–76, 79, and 106.

Holcomb, M., "Crossing the High Frontier," *Airpower*, Vol. 11 No. 5, September 1981, pp. 36–43; "Piper LBP-1 GLOMB," *AAHS Journal*, Vol. 62 No. 1, Spring 2017, pp. 12–18; "'Send Grasshoppers'," *Wings*, Vol. 13 No. 1, February 1983, pp. 40–49

"The Immortal DC-3 Part 2," *Take-Off*, Part 53, 1989, pp. 1,480–1,487

Johnsen, F. A., "Light Twins for the AAF," *Wings*, Vol. 34 No. 4, April 2004, pp. 42–55 and 58–59

Johnson, R. E., "Why the B-29 Bomber, and Why the Wright R-3350 Engine?" in *AAHS Journal* Vol. 33 No. 3, Fall 1988, pp. 174–189

Kempel, R. W., "The World's Fastest Piston-Engine Airplanes," *AAHS Journal*, Vol. 47 No. 2, Summer 2002, pp. 141–150

Kohn, L. J., "The Dawn of the Jet Age," *Armchair Aviator*, Vol. 2 No. 6, July 1973, pp. 32–34; "Vigilant," *Armchair Aviator*, Vol. 1 No. 3, December 1972, pp. 41–45

"Landing on a String," *Flying*, November 1949, p. 70

Larson, G. A., "Douglas B-23 Dragon," *AAHS Journal*, Vol. 49 No. 4, Winter 2004, pp. 255–261

Libis, S., "On Top of Old Smokey, The Amazing Story of 'JATO'," *Wings*, June 2005, pp. 20–27

Love, T. M., "Brodie System," *AAHS Journal*, Vol. 47 No. 2, Summer 2002, pp. 136–140

Lowther, S., "The NACA's First Jet," *Aerospace Projects Review*, Vol. 4 No. 5, September–October 2002, pp. 32–33

Marty, J. L., Jr., "The Grasshoppers of Okinawa," *AAHS Journal*, Vol. 55 No. 2, Summer 2010, pp. 82–92

McLaren, D. R., "The North American Aviation P-51H Mustang, Part I," *AAHS Journal*, Vol. 25 No. 2, Summer 1980, pp. 124–139

Mikesh, R., "Made in Japan ... Tested in America! The Full Story of Allied Technical Air Intelligence and the War in the Pacific, 1942–1945 Pt. I," *Wings*, June 1982, pp. 10–27 and 46–51; "Made in Japan ... Tested in America! The Full Story of Allied Technical Air Intelligence and the War in the Pacific, 1942-1945 Pt. II," *Airpower*, June 1982, pp. 10–25 and 42–51

Mitchell, K. A., "Endless Track Landing Gear," *AAHS Journal*, Vol. 38 No. 1, Spring 1993, pp. 55–57; "Mr. Custer and His Channel Wing Airplanes," *AAHS Journal*, Vol. 43 No. 1, Spring 1998, pp. 62–73; "The Ranger Powered XAT-6E," *AAHS Journal*, Vol. 34 No. 2, Summer 1989, pp. 94–95; "The Tandem Landing Gear, Martin XB-26H," *AAHS Journal*, Vol. 33 No. 1, Spring 1988, pp. 23–25

"Mongrel Testbed," *Air Enthusiast*, Vol. 3 No. 4, October 1972, p. 199

"Mustang—The Willing Workhorse—2," *Air International*, October 1983, pp. 179–189

"Nylon Airport," *Popular Mechanics*, February 1946, p. 38

Pace, S., and Campbell, D., "The Silverplate B-29s, World's First Atomic Bombers," *Wings*, August 2002, pp. 42–55

Peck, J. L. H., "Airstrip in the Air," *Popular Science*, March 1946, pp. 98–99

Pelletier, A. J., "Northrop Connection, The Unsung A-17 Attack Aircraft and its Legacy, Part One," *Air Enthusiast*, No. 75, May/June 1998, pp. 62–67

Phillips, W. H., "Recollections of the Langley Memorial Aero Lab," *AAHS Journal*, Vol. 37 No. 2, Summer 1992, pp. 116–127

Public Relations Office, Air Technical Services Command, "Wright Field Tests Rocket Take-offs," *Army Air Forces Technical Data Digest*, September 1944, p. 67

Regis, E., "Runways of Fire," *Air & Space*, October/November 1995, pp. 68–76

Reilly, J. C., Jr., "Project Yehudi, A Study of Camouflage by Illumination," *AAHS Journal*, Vol. 15 No. 4, Winter 1970, pp. 255–262

Ross, J. C., "On Trial—A Revolutionary Wing," *Popular Mechanics*, January 1949, pp. 144–145

Rusinek, E., "The Sea Trials of the P-51D Mustang 'Seahorse,'" *North American Aviation Retirees Bulletin*, Summer 2002, pp. 5–6

Schoeni, A., "Engine Test Used Seawolf Basic Design," *AAHS Journal*, Vol. 16 No. 2, Summer 1971, p. 154

Scutts, J., "Medium with the Mostest—The B-25 Mitchell (Part 2)," *Air International*, March 1993, pp. 144–151

Shelton, J. B., Jr., "Altitude Sickness and the Oxygen Mask, The American Experience in Europe During World War Two," *AAHS Journal*, Vol. 44 No. 4, Winter 1999, pp. 282–287

Smith, G. G., "More about Jet Propulsion," *Flight*, 19 February 1942, pp. 153–154

Spark, N. T., "The Secret Weapons of World War II," *Wings*, October 2004, pp. 40–56

Stamburger, P., "All American Aviation," *AAHS Journal*, Vol. 7 No. 3, Fall 1964, pp. 198–206

Stern, D., "Artic Ops Part II: Early Secret Military Cold War Artic Operations," *AAHS Journal*, Vol. 57 No. 2, Summer 2012, pp. 98–104; "Dark Horse Running, The Bell and Martin-Bell Cold War Orbital Glide Bomber," *AAHS Journal*, Vol. 61 No. 1, Spring 2017, pp. 21–27

Story, R. W., "The GE Schenectady Flight Test Center (Its Origins and Early History)," *AAHS Journal*, Vol. 47 No. 3, Fall 2002, pp. 208–215

Taylor, C., "Aerial Refueling and the Douglas C-132," *AAHS Journal*, Vol. 56 No. 2, Summer 2011, pp. 82–100

Thole, L., "Atom Bomber Base, Wendover Army Air Base, Utah," *Air Enthusiast*, No. 108, November/December 2003, pp. 28–33

Thompson, J., "Air Force for Sale!" *Airpower*, May 1993, pp. 10–21 and 38–41; "Vultee Engine-Test Aircraft in World War II," *AAHS Journal*, Vol. 39 No. 4, Winter 1994, pp. 276–285

Thompson, W., "Unit Heritage, The Atomic Bombers, The 509th Bomb Group in World War II," *Wings of Fame*, Vol. 7, 1997, pp. 102–113

"Those Versatile Vultees," *Air Enthusiast*, July 1972, pp. 27–32 and 38–42

Williams, N. M., "Bug-Eyed Monster, The Douglas Model 415A the First Globemaster and DC-7," *Air Enthusiast*, No. 60, November/December 1995, pp. 40–53; "Globemaster, The Douglas C-74," *AAHS Journal*, Vol. 25 No. 2, Summer 1980, pp. 82–106

Williams, R. E., and Hamilton, H., "The Douglas XB-19," *AAHS Journal*, Vol. 55 No. 4, Winter 2010, pp. 289–297

Wixey, K., "Magnificent Mustang: Flying Fuel Cans Vought's SB2U Vindicator," *Air Enthusiast*, No. 86, March/April 2000, pp. 62–69; "Magnificent Mustang, A Production History of the North American P-51," *Air Enthusiast*, No. 95, September/October 2001, pp. 45–55

Wolf, W., "The Aero-Engine That Won World War II in the Pacific," *AAHS Journal*, Vol. 54 No. 1, Spring 2009, pp. 27–38

Wright, T., "That Extra Little Lift," *Air & Space*, April/May 2007, pp. 58–61

"XB-38: Fortress with a Difference," *Air Classics Special Edition, Son of Fabulous Flops*, Vol. One, 1990, pp. 58–62

"XP-42: Search for Streamlining," *Air Classics Special*, Vol. 3, 1993, pp. 6–9

Yenne, B., "'Experimental Bomber, Long Range', Boeing XB-15 and Douglas XB-19," *International Air Power Review*, Vol. 5, 2002, pp. 64–171

"Zero-Sen Ancestry," *Air Enthusiast*, Vol. 3 No. 4, October 1972, pp. 199–200
Zichek, J., "'Unknown' North Americans," *Air Enthusiast*, No. 101, September/October 2002, pp. 2–8

Reports and Studies

AAF Historical Office, *Comparative History of Research and Development Policies Affecting Air Materiel 1915-1944*, U.S. Air Force Historical Study No. 20, Headquarters, Army Air Forces, June 1945
Air Force Supersonic Research Airplane XS-1, Report No. 1, U-55038, United States Air Force, January 9, 1948
Air Historical Office, *The Modification of Army Aircraft in the United States 1939–1945*, Army Air Forces Historical Studies: No. 62, Headquarters, Army Air Forces, August 1947
Air Materiel Command, *The Development of Guided Missiles*, May 1, 1946
Army Aircraft Characteristics, Production and Experimental, Report No. TSEST—A2, ATSC, United States Army, April 1, 1946
Beck, Peter A., *Manufacturer's Preliminary Brief Model Specification, Airplane, Interceptor Pursuit, Model L-133*, Report No. 2578, Lockheed Aircraft Corporation, Burbank, California, February 27, 1942
Bornstein, L. M, Capt., Field Artillery, *Report on Observations of Brodie System Demonstration at Coronado, California, 5 and 6 October 1944*, October 10, 1944
Brodie, J., 1Lt, *Report of First Tests of Suspension Landing Apparatus Installed on Ship*, December 22, 1943
Brodie, J., Capt., *Memorandum Report on Trip to Washington, D.C. for Conference Regarding Contracts on Brodie System*, TSEPL-3H-662-16-C2, January 1944
Bunker, H. G., Capt., Experimental Engineering Section, *Memorandum Report on Assisted Take-Off Methods*, EXP-M-50-395, January 30, 1940
Cahill, L. D., *Project MX-544*, Report of Project Engineer, Jack & Heintz, Inc., December 16, 1944
Carroll, F. O., Brig.-Gen., *Details of AAF Guided Missiles Program*, September 2, 1944
Claussen, M. P., Dr, *Materiel Research and Development in the Army Air Arm 1914–1945*, AAF Historical Studies No. 50, AAF Historical Office, Headquarters, Army Air Forces, Washington, D.C., November 1946
Craven, D. A., 1Lt, Engineering Division, *Memorandum Report Remote Control of JB-2 Pilotless Aircraft with a Modified SCR-584 Radar Set and AN/APM-1 Radio Unit*, TSZSA-7-1253, February 28, 1946
Cummings, C. M., Maj., Experimental Engineering Section, *Memorandum Report on Assisted Take-Off Devices*, Air Corps Materiel Division, May 6, 1940
Dane, P. H., Capt., Aircraft Laboratory, *Memorandum Report on Conference Regarding D. Goddard's Jet Propulsion Proposal*, EXP-M-51/APR150, September 15, 1941
Decker, C. J., Capt., *Memorandum Report on Assisted Take-Off System for Aircraft*, TSEPL-3H-664-359, November 9, 1944
Director, ATSC, *Monthly Supplement to Details of Experimental Guided Missiles Program*, date unknown
Engineering Division, *Army Air Forces Materiel Command, Research and Development Projects of the Engineering Division*, Wright Field, Dayton, Ohio, Fourth Edition, January 1, 1944
Experimental Engineering Section, *Memorandum Report on Refueling of Airplanes in Flight*, EXP-M-51/B853, Materiel Division, February 23, 1942
Fisher, L. J., and Steiner, M. F. *Ditching Tests with a 1/16-size Dynamic Model of the Army B-24 Airplane in the Langley Tank No. 2 and an Outdoor Catapult,* Memorandum Report No. L5D07, Langley Memorial Aeronautical Laboratory, Langley Field, Virginia, National Advisory Committee for Aeronautics, April 1945
Guided Missiles Doctrine, Index, Section I Historical Background, June 1946
Hansen, W. J., 1Lt, Engineering Division, *Memorandum Report Launching Device for Pilotless Aircraft*, TSEPL-673-64, 25 May 1945, May 3, 1942
Hawkins, W. M., *Design Features of the Lockheed L-133*, Report No. 2571, Lockheed Aircraft Corporation, February 24, 1942
Historical Office, *Case History of Air-to-Air Refueling*, Air Materiel Command, Wright-Patterson AFB, Ohio, March 1949
Historical Division, USAF, *Air-Sea Rescue 1941-1952*, U.S. Air Force Historical Study No. 95, Research Studies Institute, Air University, August 1954
Historical Division, Intelligence T-2, *Case History of Assisted Take-Off Devices*, Air Materiel Command, Wright Field, February 1946
Historical Office, *Case History of The Brodie Launching and Landing Device*, Air Technical Service Command, Wright Field, February–September 1945; *Case History of the Liaison Aircraft Program*, Air Technical Service Command, Wright Field, Ohio, November 1944

Historical Office, *Case History of XB-41 Project*, Air Materiel Command, Wright-Patterson AFB, Ohio, date unknown

Holcomb, M., Raytheon Aircraft Company, *Beech AT-10 Wichita*, SAE Technical Paper Series 2000-01-1679, May 2000

Holley, I. B., Jr., Capt., Air Technical Service Command Historical Office, *Evolution of the Liaison-Type Airplane 1917–1944*, Army Air Forces Historical Studies No. 44, Historical Office, AAF Headquarters, Army Air Forces, April 1946, reprinted in *AAHS Journal*, Vol. 50 No. 4 Winter 2005, pp. 258–269, and Vol. 51 No.1, Spring 2006, pp. 57–74

Hoover, H. H. and White, M. D., *Lateral-Directional Characteristics of North American XP-51 Aircraft (A.C. No. 41-38) with Beveled Trailing Edge Ailerons in High-speed Flight*, Memorandum Report, NACA, 1942

Jarvis, G. A. and Fisher, L. J., *Correlation Tests of the Ditching Behavior of an Army B-24D Airplane and a 1/16-size Model*, Memorandum Report L6A03, Langley Memorial Aeronautical Laboratory, Langley Field, Virginia, National Advisory Committee for Aeronautics, January 1946

Kotcher, E., Experimental Engineering Section, *Appendix I to Memorandum Report EXP-M-50-681, Plan to Bomb Japan from Midway Island*, Materiel Division, May 3, 1942; *Memorandum Report on Air Refueling of Heavy Bombardment Aircraft*, EXP-M-50-656, Materiel Division, March 26, 1942, with Appendix I 'Plan to Bomb Japan from Midway Island', May 3, 1942

Mahan, T. A., Air Technical Services Command, Memorandum Report TSEPL-3-673-84, *Flywheel Launching Device for Launching Pilotless Aircraft, Type JB-2*, October 8, 1945

Martin-Baker Aircraft Company Limited, *History and Development of Martin-Baker Ejection Systems*, Martin-Baker, Higher-Denham, Near Uxbridge, Middlesex, England, undated

McClashan, D. R., Capt., Kemper, P. M., Col., and Carroll, F. O., Col., Memorandum Report EXP-M-51/Aer180 Addendum 20, *Inspection of Mock-up of a Liquid-Fuel Jet Propulsion Motor*, Experimental Engineering Section, November 2, 1942

Pierce, C. H., Jr., Capt., Aircraft Project Section, Engineering Division, *Memorandum Report on JB-2 Pilotless Aircraft*, TSESA-1256, March 1, 1946

Price, H. C. and Hawkins, W. M., *Summary of Required Research, Model L-133*, Report No. 2580, Lockheed Aircraft Corporation, February 27, 1942

Putt, D. L., Col., Memorandum Report EXP-M-50-708 *Air Refueling of Heavy Bombardment Aircraft*, Materiel Division, June 30, 1942

Russillo, V. D., Lt, and Korchner, R. B., *Status Report in Scale Model of JB-2 Launcher*, March 19, 1945

Seawell, S. D., 1Lt, Flight Test Engineering and Research Branch, *Memorandum Report on B-29A Airplane*, AAF No. 43-93921, TSCEP5ER-1894, May 24, 1945

Semi-Monthly Progress Report on JB-1 and JB-2, February 14, 1945

Sims, T. A., Maj., Assistant Technical Executive, Materiel Division, *Memorandum Report TEX-M-42-5*, January 8, 1942

Stewart, S. R., Col., *Memorandum Report on Special Weapons Development Program*, TSEPL-3-673-37-I, February 28, 1945

Strickland, A. C., Brig.-Gen., President, The Army Air Forces Board, *Staff Study of the Brodie System for Launching and Landing Light Aircraft*, Project No. 4100A373.1, May 29, 1945

Summary of the XB-41 Project, partial manuscript without author, April 1944

Teel, L. L., Capt., *Memorandum Report on Status of Jet Propulsion Projects—Flight Tests and Procurement of Equipment*, ENG-41-4302-12-10, Aircraft Laboratory, Engineering Division, November 1, 1943

Tuttle, D. T., 1Lt, *Memorandum Report on Aerojet Engineering Corporation Conference*, ENG-50-947, Materiel Command, Engineering Division, October 6, 1943

Watkins, D. W., Col., *Final Report on Test of Armament Installation in XB-41 Airplane*, Proof Department, Army Air Forces Proving Ground Command, Eglin Field, Florida, March 16, 1943

White, M. D., and Hoover, H. H., *Flight Testing of Modifications to Improve the Aileron Control Effectiveness of a North American XP-51 Airplane (A.C. No. 41-38)*, Memorandum Report, NACA, 1942

Whitman, W. G., *Report of the Special O.S.R.D. Committee on Jet Propulsion*, Washington, D.C., March 20, 1944

von Kármán, Theodore, *Where We Stand* (Washington, D.C.: U.S. Army Air Forces, 1946); *Toward New Horizons* (Washington, D.C.: U.S. Amy Air Forces, 1946)

Yenser, C. L., Capt., Engineering Division, *Memorandum Report ENG- 51/B853*, Materiel Division, June 25, 1943

Manuals

Army Ground Forces Light Aviation, Field Manual FM 20-100, War Department (Washington, D.C.: United States Government Printing Office, September 1947)

Preliminary Handbook of Pilot's Flight Operation Instructions for the Model XP-81 Fighter Airplane, (Consolidated Vultee Aircraft Corporation, Report No. 204-20, June 20, 1947)

Preliminary Pilot's Handbook of Operating Instructions, Navy Model LBP-1 GLOMB, CO AN 09-50BA-1 (March 15, 1945)

Correspondence

Barnes, G. M., Maj.-Gen., Ordnance Department. Chief, Research and Development Service, "Robot Bomb, JB-2," memorandum to Office Assistant Chief of Air Staff, M & S, Army Air Force, September 30, 1944

Bitting, K. H., Col., Chief of Administration, "Modification of JB-2 Guided Missiles in Storage at the 829th Specialized Depot, Gadsden, Alabama," Technical Instructions to Procurement Division, Maintenance Division, Engineering Division, and Supply Division, July 24, 1945

Burden, J. A., Maj., Production Resources Officer, "Project MX-544," letter to Chief of Engineering and Procurement, Air Technical Services Command, September 23, 1944

Carney, F. H., Capt., Procurement Division, Air Technical Services Command, teletype regarding guided munitions to Commanding General, Army Air Forces, September 6, 1945

Carroll, F. O., Brig.-Gen., Chief, Engineering Division, "Progress Report on Jet Propulsion for Assisted Take-Off," letter to Commanding General, Materiel Command, November 30, 1942; "Status Report on Project MX-121," letter to Commanding General, AAF, May 13, 1944; "Request for Initiation of AAF-NDRC Project," letter to Commanding General, Army Air Forces, January 20, 1945; "USAAF Comment Regarding British Solid Propellant Jet Units," letter to Commanding General, Materiel Command, July 5, 1944

Carroll, F. O., Maj., Chief, Experimental Engineering Section, "Assisted Take-off in Hemisphere Defense," letter to Chief, Materiel Division, September 14, 1940

Chidlaw, B. W., Brig.-Gen., Chief, Materiel Division, "Jet Propulsion Assisted Take-off Program," letter to Commanding General, Materiel Command, December 7, 1943

Clay, L. D., Maj.-Gen., Director of Materiel, "Robot Bomb, JB-2," memorandum to Chief of Ordnance, Research and Development Service, October 16, 1944; "Robot Bomb, JB-2," memorandum to Chief of Ordnance, October 27, 1944

Connor, R., Chief, Division 9, National Defense Research Committee, letter regarding rocket propellants to Commanding General, Army Air Forces, May 21, 1945

Cook, O. H., Brig.-Gen., Chief, Procurement Division, Air Technical Services Command, teletype regarding JB-2 to Commanding General, Army Air Forces, March 30, 1945

Coupland, R. C., Brig.-Gen., Air Ordnance Officer, "Robot Bomb, JB-2," memorandum to Chief of Ordnance, Research & Development Service, September 13, 1944

Craig, H. A., Maj.-Gen., "The Brodie System," memorandum for Commanding General, Army Air Forces, May 29, 1944

Delacroix, R. J., Maj., Assistant Ground Adjutant General, "Suspension Landing Apparatus of Light Planes," letter to Commanding General, Army Service Forces, February 6, 1944

DeLany, W. S., Assistant Chief of Staff, United States Fleet, "'Brodie' System for Launching and Recovering Airplanes—Request for," letter to Commanding General, Army Air Forces, August 19, 1944

Dichman, E. W., Lt-Col., Air Technical Services Command, "Project MX-544, JB-2 Flying Bombs," letter to Commanding General, Army Air Forces, September 27, 1944

Dichman, E. W., Col., Chief, Special Aircraft Branch, Production Section, "Stabilization of Requirements," memorandum to TSEPR, February 21, 1945

Doubleday, D. C., Col., Chief, Engineering Branch, "Extending Range of Control on JB-2," letter to Director, Air Technical Services Command, March 20, 1945

Echols, O. P., Maj.-Gen., Assistant Chief of Air Staff, Material and Services, "Apparatus, Suspended Cable, Launching and Landing Small Aircraft," routing and record sheet to Gen. Giles, 8 July 1944; "Progress Report to 15 November 1944, on JB-2 and JB-1 Robot Bombs," Memorandum for Chief of Air Staff, 18 November 1944; "Progress Report to 3 January 45 on JB-2 and JB-1 Robot Bombs," Memorandum for Chief of Air Staff, January 5, 1945; "Progress Report to 3 March 45 on JB-2 and JB-10 Robot Bombs," Memorandum for Chief of Air Staff, March 6, 1945

Fickel, A. A., Col., "Army Guided Missiles Program," Note for Record, November 30, 1944

Gillespie, J. M., Col., Deputy Chief, Engineering and Procurement, "Status Report on JB-2 Robot Bomb," Inter-Office Memorandum to Deputy Director, Air Technical Services Command, September 7, 1944

Gross, C. P., Maj.-Gen., Chief of Transportation, "Brodie System of Launching and Landing Aircraft," letter to Commanding General AAF, December 31, 1943

Gross, M. E., Brig.-Gen., "Brodie System of Launching and Landing Aircraft," routing and record sheet, June 23, 1944

Gruitch, J. M., Lt-Col., Assistant, Office of the Air Ordnance Officer, "JB-2 Jet Bomb," memorandum to Ordnance Officer, Engineering Division, Air Technical Service Command, January 20, 1945

Hamilton, H., Capt., Assistant Ground Adjutant General, "Ship Type Brodie Device," memorandum for Commanding General, Army Air Forces, December 2, 1944

Hardy, R. E., Brig.-Gen., Assistant Chief of Ordnance, "Robot Bomb, JB-2," memorandum to Headquarters, Army Services Command, November 1, 1944

Harmon, M. F., Maj.-Gen., Chief of Air Staff, "Impulse Reaction Aircraft Engine of Mr. E. B. Myers," memorandum for Maj.-Gen. Edwin M. Watson, May 22, 1942

Harp, T. R., Maj., NAMC Materiel Command Liaison Officer, "Assisted Take-offs," letter to Commanding General, Material Command, June 20, 1944

Holloman, G. V., Col., Chief, Equipment Laboratory, Propulsion and Accessories Section, Engineering Division, "Brodie Device—Land Rig," letter to Commandant, Field Artillery School, December 14, 1944; "Method for Dropping Brodie Gear," routing and record sheet to Capt. Over, TSTEX, January 22, 1945

Holloman, G. V., Col., Chief, Equipment Laboratory, Propulsion and Accessories Section, Engineering Division, "JB-2 Installation on B-17 Airplane," Inter-Office Memorandum to TSEPL-5G, December 2, 1944

Israel, G., "Summary of Investigation of Jet Propelled Fighters," Inter-Office Memorandum, Grumman Aircraft Corp., January 19, 1945

Kemper, P., H., Col., Chief Aircraft Laboratory, "AAFPGC Report Serial No. 4-43-57," letter to Chief, Engineering Division, August 1, 1944; Engineering Division, "Jet Assisted Airplane Take-off," letter to Bell Aircraft Corp., June 24, 1943; "Present Status of Work Sponsored by the Air Forces Under Project MX-121 Concerning Jet Propulsion for Aircraft," letter to Chief, Engineering Division, March 1943; "Status of Jet Propelled Assisted Take-Off Projects," letter to Chief, Engineering Division, 19 July 1943; "Summary of Procurement and Disposition of Solid-Fuel Jet Propulsion Units," letter to Chief, Engineering Division, July 5, 1944

Kershner, R. B., Allegany Ballistic Laboratory, "Meeting on JB-2 Launcher Project," memorandum to Files, August 18, 1945

Kriegsman, J. C. Maj., Air Officer, Headquarters 77th Division Artillery, letter to Col. Wolf with attachment "The Brodie LST," April 16, 1945

Lewis, R. C., Maj., Acting Assistant Air Adjutant General, "Assignment of B-23 Airplane for Supercharger Test Work," letter endorsement, February 29, 1942

Lovett, R. A., Assistant Secretary of War for Air, "Pilotless Aircraft and Guided Missiles," Memorandum for Gen. Arnold, August 2, 1944

Mays, G., Col., "Brodie System of Launching and Landing Aircraft," routing and record sheet to AC/AS Operations, Commitments & Requirements, June 15, 1944

McHugh, M. I., Chief, Procurement and Supply Branch, Officer of Strategic Services, "19 Brodie Arresting Systems," letter to Director, Headquarters, AAF Air Technical Service Command, with contract attached, April 26, 1945; Contract OSS-592', letter to Commanding General, Materiel Command, July 4, 1945

McKee, W. F., Col., Acting, Assistant Chief of Air Staff, Operations, Commitments and Requirements, "Buzz Bomb (JB-2)," Memorandum for the Chief of Air Staff, January 19, 1945

Meisinger, R., M., Production Supervisor, "Conversion of AAF Brodie Systems to Navy Use," Memorandum Report TSMPR4-M-43, June 16, 1945

Meredith, R. A., Lt-Col., Assistant Ground Adjutant General, "Suspended Cable Launching and Landing Apparatus (Brodie Design)," letter to Commanding General, Army Ground Forces, June 24, 1944

Meyers, B. E., Maj.-Gen., Deputy Director, "Procurement of 1000 JB-2 Jet Bombs Per Month," to Commanding General, Army Air Forces, February 7, 1945

Meyers, E. B., "Air Supremacy, Impulse Reaction Aircraft Engine," undated but approximately May 1942

Mills, E. W., Rear Adml, Acting Chief of Bureau of Ships, "316 Landing Ship, Tank, LST-776—'Brodie' Device, Training in Use of," letter to Commanding General, Army Air Forces, September 14, 1944

Ober, J. H., Maj., Office, Chief of Administration, Air Technical Services Command, "Development Program for JB-2," letter to Commanding General, Army Air Forces, September 12, 1945

Ober, J. H., Capt., Office, Chief of Administration, Air Technical Services Command, "Report of Progress on B-29 and B-32—Rocket Assisted Take-Off Therefor," letter to Commanding General, Army Air Forces, January 17, 1945

Ordway, F. I., Jr., Maj. Air Corps. Assistant Executive, Materiel Division, "Assignment of B-23 Airplane for Supercharger Test Work," February 9, 1942, and 1st Endorsement, Lewis, R. C. Maj., Air Corps, Acting Assistant Air Adjutant General, February 20, 1942

Osborne, R. M., Col. Director, Research and Development Division and Irvine, M. M., Col., Deputy Director, Research & Development Division, "Robot Bomb, JB-2," memorandum to The Commanding General, Army Air Forces, October 2, 1944

Patcher, R. O., for Chief or the Bureau of Aeronautics, "Program for the Use of JB-2 Type Flying Bombs from Naval Ships—Establishment of," Letter to CC NAMC, December 26, 1944

Pennel, R. T., Maj.-Gen., Commandant, Field Artillery School, "Brodie Device—Land Rig," letter to Commanding General, AAF Air Technical Service Command, December 4, 1944

Phillips, J. F., Col., Acting Chief, Materiel Division, 'Status of Assisted Take-Off Projects at Materiel Command', memorandum for Maj.-Gen. O. P. Echols, March 20, 1944

Phillips, J. F., Col., Chief, Materiel Division, "Brodie Device for CBI Theater," letter to Commanding General, Army Ground Forces, September 2, 1944; "Suspended Cable Launching and Landing Apparatus (Brodie Design)," letter to Commanding General, Army Ground Forces, October 14, 1944

Pierce, C. H., Jr., Capt., Project Section, Engineering Division, "Report on Trip to Hqs.," AAF, Washington, D.C., April 22, 1945, letter to TSESK-20, April 1945

Powers, E. M., Brig.-Gen., Deputy Assistant Chief of Air Staff, Material and Services, "Launching and Procurement on the JB-2 Bomb," letter to Director, AAF—Air Technical Services Command, January 14, 1945; Memorandum for Col. Phillips regarding Brodie System, July 6, 1944; "Progress Report to 1 December 1944 on JB-2 and JB-1 Robot Bombs," Memorandum for Chief of Air Staff, December 7, 1944; "Progress Report to 3 February 1945 on JB-2 Robot Bombs," Memorandum for Chief of Air Staff, February 5, 1945; "Report to 19 Apr 45 on JB-10 (Northrop Tail-less) and JB-2 Jet Bombs," Memorandum for Chief of Air Staff, April 27, 1945

Quinn, R. S., Lt-Col., Air Officer, Office of Strategic Services, "Air Drop of Brodie Equipment," letter to Director, Air Technical Service Command, December 11, 1944

Roth, M. S., Col., Chief, Aircraft Projects Section, Service Engineering Subdivision, Engineering Division, "Launching Ramp Program," letter to Commanding General, Army Air Forces, March 26, 1945

Sams, J. H., Lt-Col., Materiel Command Liaison Officer with Bureau of Aeronautics, "Navy Assisted Take-off of Carrier Aircraft," letter to AC/AS, M&S, Chief, Development Branch, August 15, 1944

Shepard, B. A., Col., "Brodie System," routing and record sheet, June 8, 1945

Sillin, N. D., Col., "Brodie System of Launching and Landing Aircraft," comment attachment, January 13, 1944

Sims, T. A., Col., Chief of Administration, Air Technical Services Command, "Cancellation of Procurement of 5000 JB-2 Articles," Technical Instructions to Procurement Division, February 17, 1945; "Extending Range of Control on JB-2," Technical Instructions to Engineering Division, March 30, 1945; "Guided Missiles—Procurement of JB-2 Jet Bombs," Technical Instructions to Procurement Division, December 7, 1944; "Guided Missiles—Procurement Program for JB-2 Bombs," Technical Instructions to Procurement Division and Engineering Division, January 18, 1945; "Guided Missiles—Procurement Program for JB-2 Jet Bombs," Technical Instructions to Procurement Division, May 5, 1945; "Procurement of Radio Set AN/APW-1 for JB-2 Buzz Bomb Control', Technical Instructions to Procurement Division, April 10, 1945; "Procurement of Rocket Motors for JB-2 Guided Missiles," memorandum to Procurement Division, November 6, 1944; "Program on Procurement of JB-2," Technical Instructions to Procurement Division, January 31, 1945

Sims, T. A., Col., Deputy Chief of Staff, "Suspended Cable Launching and Landing Apparatus (Brodie System)," letter to Engineering Division, July 27, 1944

Sims, T. A., Lt-Col., Assistant Technical Executive, "Procurement by Bureau of Aeronautics of Sixty (60) 200 Pounds Rocket Motors from California Institute of Technology," letter to Chief, Materiel Division, March 11, 1942

Sims, T. A., Col., Chief of Administration, Air Technical Services Command, "Transfer of Procurement of Rocket Motors for JB-2 to Ordnance," Technical Instructions to Procurement Division, April 25, 1945

Smith, H. Y., Lt-Col., Chief Engineering Standards, Service Engineering Section, Engineering Division, "Request for Performance of Functional and Tactical Tests on Jet Propulsion Equipment," letter to President, AAF Board, February 17, 1945

Speir, G. B., Lt-Col., Acting Chief, Power Plant/Propulsion Section, "Conference on Assisted Take-off Solid Propellant Rockets," memorandum for record, August 10, 1945

Stewart, S. R., Col., Chief Equipment Laboratory, Propulsion and Accessories Subdivision, Engineering Division, "Aircraft Assisted Take-Off Device," letter to All American Aviation, Inc., April 27, 1945

Timberlake, P. W., Brig.-Gen., Deputy Chief of Air Staff, "Brodie System for Launching and Recovering Airplanes," letter to Commander in Chief, United States Fleet, August 30, 1944

Van Wyen, A. O., Head, Aviation History Unit, Op-05D2, November 20, 1968, letter to Capt. R. W. Gruenhagen regarding Navy evaluation of a Mustang.

Vaughan, J. C., Jr., Col., Headquarters of the Army Air Forces, letter to Maj.-Gen. B. E. Meyers, Deputy Director, Air Technical Services Command, subject JB-2 program, January 16, 1945

Webb, C. H., Capt., Chief, Aerial Pick-Up Unit, Miscellaneous Branch, "Disposition of Sets of Brodie System Equipment Procured by Office of Strategic Services," routing and record sheet, August 13, 1945

White, T. D., Brig.-Gen., "The Brodie System," memorandum for Deputy Chief of Air Staff, May 24, 1944

Wilson, R. C., Chief, Development Engineering Branch, "Brodie Suspended Cable Launching and Landing Device," inter-desk memorandum, October 9, 1944; "Suspension Landing Apparatus (Brodie System)," letter to Commanding General, Materiel Command, February 29, 1944; "Suspended Cable Launching and Landing Apparatus," letter to Commanding General, Materiel Command, July 21, 1944; "Refueling of Fighter Aircraft," letter to Commanding General, Materiel Command, January 20, 1944

Wolfe, E. B., Maj.-Gen., Chief of Engineering and Procurement, "JB-2 Large Scale Procurement Program," letter to TSDEP, January 15, 1945

Other

Bruins, B. D., *U.S. Naval Bombardment Missiles, 1940–1958: A Study of the Weapons Innovation Process*, Doctoral Dissertation (Columbia University, 1981)

Cavallo, S. A., *NASA Headquarters NACA Oral History Project, Oral History Transcript*, interviewed by Johnson, S. (San Jose, California, September 30, 2005)

Dupont, R. J., Jr., *Power for Progress, The Story of Reaction Motors, Inc.*, (GodenStateLegacy.com, Issue 12, June 2011)

Fahrney, D. S., Rear Adm., USN (Ret.), *The History of Pilotless Aircraft and Guided Missiles*, unpublished manuscript (prepared for U.S. Navy Bureau of Aeronautics, undated but likely 1958)

Jones, L. J., *Fax Files #3* (Vista, California: Pacific Aero Press, 1989); *Fax Files #4* (Vista, California: Pacific Aero Press, 1989); *Fax Files #11* (Vista, California: Pacific Aero Press, 1993)

Kriegsman, J. C., "The Piper Cub and the LST Aircraft Carrier (A WWII Poor Man's Carrier)" (unpublished account, undated)

Malina, F. J., *Memoir on the GALCIT Rocket Research Project, 1936–1938* (6 June 1967)

McCutcheon, K. D., *OX-5 to Turbo-Compounds: A Brief Overview of Aircraft Engine Development* (undated)

Presentation Branch, *The Brodie System of Landing and Launching Light Airplanes from a Portable Rig* (Washington, D.C.: Office of Strategic Services, July 1944)

Reeder, J. P., *NACA Contributions to the N.A.A. P-51 Airplane*, January 27, 1990

Signor, P. W., *Cruise Missiles for the U.S. Navy: An Exemplar of Innovation in a Military Organization*, (Newport, Rhode Island: Naval War College, June 1994)

Statement of Military Requirements, Assist Take-off Unit, (Headquarters, Army Air Forces, July 21, 1945)

Internet

Aero Files, aerofiles.com

Encyclopedia Astronautica, astronautix/engines.com

Lansdale, James F., 'War Prize: The Capture of the First Japanese Zero Fighter in 1941', j-aircraft.com/research/WarPrizes.htm (December 3, 1999)

Marie, Gaëtan, "The Naval Mustang," mustang.gaetanmarie.com/articles/naval/naval.htm (undated)

Piper Club of France, L-14, www.piperclubfrance.com/piper-l-14-army-cruiser-ec-aap/

"Technical Air Intelligence Unit," en.wikipedia.org/wiki/Technical_Air_Intelligence_Unit

"The New Mitsubishi-Nagoya Zero Fighter," *Tactical and Technical Trends*, No. 5, August 13, 1942, lonesentry.com/articles/ttt08/zero-fighter.html

To Those Who Served ..., tothosewhoserved.org/usa/ts/usatsc02/chapter09.html#fnr38

Trojan, D., *Technical Air Intelligence, Wreck Chasing in the Pacific During the War*, downloaded from *j-aircraft.com, undated*

Index